US Foreign Policy since 1945

Praise for the first edition:
'It is difficult to imagine a better book to recommend to someone who is approaching the subject for the first time' *Political Studies*

US Foreign Policy since 1945 is an essential introduction to post-war US foreign policy. It combines chronologic and thematic chapters to provide an historical account of US policy and to explore key questions about its design, control and effects.

New features of this second edition include expanded coverage of the Cold War, new chapters on the post-Cold War era, a chronology and a new conclusion that draws together key themes and looks to the future. Contents include:

- American foreign policy-making, US power and democratic control
- Containment strategy and Cold War debates
- Economic warfare
- US foreign policy by geographical region
- Power and purpose in US foreign policy
- US interventionism
- Rogue states, WMDs and the war on terrorism
- The neo-conservative foreign policy revolution.

Alan P. Dobson is Professor of Politics and Director of the Institute for Transatlantic, European and American Studies at Dundee University. His books include *Anglo-American Relations in the Twentieth Century* (1995), *Flying in the Face of Competition* (1995) and *US Economic Statecraft for Survival 1933–1991* (2002). **Steve Marsh** is a lecturer in the School of European Studies at Cardiff University. His books include *Anglo-American Relations and Cold War Oil* (2003) and the co-authored *International Relations of the European Union* (2005).

The Making of the Contemporary World
Edited by Eric J. Evans and Ruth Henig

The Making of the Contemporary World series provides challenging interpretations of contemporary issues and debates within strongly defined historical frameworks. The range of the series is global, with each volume drawing together material from a range of disciplines – including economics, politics and sociology. The books in this series present compact, indispensable introductions for students studying the modern world.

US Foreign Policy since 1945

Second edition

Alan P. Dobson and Steve Marsh

Routledge
Taylor & Francis Group

LONDON AND NEW YORK

First published 2001 by Routledge
2 Park Square, Milton Park, Abingdon, Oxon OX14 4RN

Simultaneously published in the USA and Canada
by Routledge
270 Madison Ave, New York, NY 10016

Transferred to Digital Printing 2005

2nd edition 2006

*Routledge is an imprint of the Taylor & Francis Group, an informa
business*

Typeset in Times by RefineCatch Limited, Bungay, Suffolk
Printed and bound in Great Britain by
TJ International Ltd, Padstow, Cornwall

British Library Cataloguing in Publication Data
A catalogue record for this book is available from the British Library

Library of Congress Cataloging in Publication Data
Dobson, Alan P.
   US foreign policy since 1945 / Alan P. Dobson and Steve Marsh. –
2nd ed.
      p. cm. – (The making of the contemporary world)
   Includes bibliographical references.
   ISBN 0–415–38640–3 (hardback) – ISBN 0–415–38641–1
      1. United States – Foreign relations – 1945–1989. 2. United States –
Foreign relations – 1989– I. Title: U.S. foreign policy since 1945. II.
Title: United States foreign policy since 1945. III. Marsh, Steve, 1967–
IV. Title. V. Series.
   E744.D557 2006
   327.73009'045– dc22   2006003267

ISBN10: 0–415–38640–3 (hbk)
ISBN10: 0–415–38641–1 (pbk)
ISBN10: 0–203–13934–8 (ebk)

ISBN13: 978–0–415–38640–1 (hbk)
ISBN13: 978–0–415–38641–8 (pbk)
ISBN13: 978–0–203–13934–9 (ebk)

To my teachers who made the greatest difference – Geoffrey
G. Flitton, David J. Manning and Charles Reynolds.

Alan Dobson

For Clara.

Steve Marsh

Contents

Abbreviations and acronyms

ABM	Anti-ballistic Missile
AGOA	African Growth and Opportunity Act
AIOC	Anglo-Iranian Oil Company
APEC	Asian Pacific Economic Cooperation
ARVN	Army of the Republic of Vietnam (South)
ASEAN	Association of South East Asian Nations
AWAC	Airborne Warning and Control System
BMD	Ballistic Missile Defence
BMDP	Ballistic Missile Defense Program
BTO	Brussels Treaty Organisation
CAFTA–DR	Central American–Dominican Republic Free Trade Agreement
CAP	Common Agricultural Policy
CCP	Chinese Communist Party
CEECs	Central and East European Countries
CENTO	Central Treaty Organisation
CESDP	Common European Security and Defence Policy
CET	Common External Tariff
CFE	Conventional Forces in Europe
CFSP	Common Foreign and Security Policy
CIA	Central Intelligence Agency
CIC	Commander in Chief
CIS	Commonwealth of Independent States
CJTF	Combined Joint Task Forces
COCOM	Co-ordinating Committee
COMECON	Council for Mutual Economic Assistance
CPA	Coalition Provisional Authority
CSCE	Conference on Security and Cooperation in Europe
EC	European Community
ECOWAS	Economic Community of West African States
ECSC	European Coal and Steel Community
EDC	European Defence Community
EEC	European Economic Community
EPC	European Political Cooperation
ESDI	European Security and Defence Identity
EU	European Union
EURRF	European Union Rapid Reaction Force

EXCOM	Executive Committee of the National Security Council
FARC	Revolutionary Armed Forces of Colombia
FDI	Foreign Direct Investment
FMS	Foreign Military Sales
FNLA	National Liberation Front of Angola
FRG	Federal Republic of Germany
FTAA	Free Trade Area for the Americas
FY	Financial Year
G-3	Eurozone, US and Japan
G-7	Group of Seven
G-8	The Seven Top Industrialised Nations Plus Russia
GATT	General Agreement on Tariffs and Trade
GDP	Gross Domestic Product
GNI	Gross National Income
GNP	Gross National Product
ICBM	Intercontinental Ballistic Missile
ICC	International Criminal Court
IFOR	Implementation Force
ILSA	Iran–Libya Sanctions Act
IMF	International Monetary Fund
INF	Intermediate Nuclear Force
IRBM	Intermediate Range Ballistic Missile
ITO	International Trade Organisation
JAP	Joint Action Plan
KAL	Korean Airlines
KEDO	Korean Peninsular Energy Development Organisation
KFOR	Kosovo Peace Implementation Force
KGB	Soviet Committee of State Security
KMT	Kuomintang
MAD	Mutual Assured Destruction
MCA	Millennium Challenge Account
MEPP	Middle East Peace Process
MFN	Most Favoured Nation
MIRV	Multiple Independently Targetable Re-entry Vehicle
MLNF	Multilateral Nuclear Force
MNCs	Multinational Corporations
MPLA	Popular Movement for the Liberation of Angola
MRBM	Medium Range Ballistic Missiles
NAFTA	North American Free Trade Agreement
NATO	North Atlantic Treaty Organisation
NEC	National Economic Council
NGO	Non-Government Organisation
NIEO	New International Economic Order
NORAD	North American Aerospace Defense Command
NPT	Non-Proliferation Treaty
NRF	NATO Response Force
NSA	National Security Adviser
NSC	National Security Council
NSC-68	National Security Council Resolution 68

NTA	New Transatlantic Agenda
OAS	Organisation of American States
OECD	Organisation for Economic Cooperation and Development
OEEC	Organisation for European Economic Cooperation
OPEC	Organisation of Petroleum Exporting Countries
PA	Palestinian Authority
PDD	Presidential Decision Directive
PFP	Partnership for Peace
PJC	Permanent Joint Council
PLO	Palestine Liberation Organisation
PPS	Policy Planning Staff
PRC	People's Republic of China
SAC	Strategic Air Command
SALT	Strategic Arms Limitation Talks
SDF	(Japanese) Strategic Defence Force
SDI	Strategic Defense Initiative ('Star Wars')
SEATO	South East Asia Treaty Organisation
SFOR	Stabilisation Force
SLBM	Submarine Launched Ballistic Missile
SORT	Strategic Offensive Reductions Treaty
START	Strategic Arms Reduction Talks
UFC	United Fruit Company
UN	United Nations
UNITA	National Union for the Total Independence of Angola
UNPROFOR	United Nations Protection Force
US	United States
USACDA	US Arms Control and Disarmament Agency
USAID	US Agency for International Development
USIA	US Information Agency
USSR	Union of Soviet Socialist Republics
USTR	US Trade Representative
VER	Voluntary Export Restraint
VIE	Voluntary Import Expansion
WEU	Western European Union
WMDs	Weapons of Mass Destruction
WTO	World Trade Organisation

Key personnel

NATIONAL SECURITY ADVISERS

Sidney W. Souers	1947–50
James S. Lay Jr	1950–53
Robert Cutler	1953–55
Dillon Anderson	1955–56
William A. Jackson	1956
Robert Cutler	1957–58
Gordon Gray	1958–61
McGeorge Bundy	1961–66
Walt W. Rostow	1966–69
Henry A. Kissinger	1969–75
Brent Scowcroft	1975–77
Zbigniew Brzezinski	1977–81
Richard V. Allen	1981
William P. Clark Jr	1981–83
Robert C. McFarlane	1983–85
John M. Poindexter	1985–86
Frank C. Carlucci	1986–87
Colin L. Powell	1987–89
Brent Scowcroft	1989–93
Anthony Lake	1993–95
Samuel Berger	1995–2001
Condoleezza Rice	2001–05
Stephen J. Hadley	2005–

Timeline

1940s

1945   8 May Germany surrenders; Potsdam Conference; 6 August United States drops atomic bomb on Hiroshima; 9 August atomic bombs dropped on Nagasaki; 15 August Japanese surrender ends Second World War; UN established.

1946   Churchill's Iron Curtain Speech; George Kennan's Long Telegram conceives of containment strategy; inaugural meeting IMF; onset of Greek civil war.

1947   Truman Doctrine offers support against communism in Europe; Marshall Plan announced; National Security Act creates Department of Defence, NSC and the CIA; GATT Round 1, Geneva.

1948   Communist coup in Czechoslovakia; introduction of Deutschmark in West Germany; Berlin Blockade and Western airlift begin; OAS formed; State of Israel declared; GATT enters into force.

1949   NATO formed; Berlin Blockade lifted, GATT Round 2, Annecy; Mao Tse-tung takes control of China; Nationalist Chinese retreat to Taiwan; Soviets explode first atomic bomb; FRG and German Democratic Republic established.

1950s

1950   February Senator Joe McCarthy begins communist witch-hunt at Wheeling, West Virginia; Korean War begins; NSC-68 recommends American rearmament; Japanese Peace Treaty signed; US rearmament begins; nuclear-capable US bombers based in Britain; China enters Korean War; GATT Round 3, Torquay.

1951   President Truman recalls General MacArthur from Korea; ANZUS Pact signed.

1952   ECSC established; Greece and Turkey join NATO; US explodes first hydrogen bomb; Eisenhower elected US President.

1953   Korean War ceasefire; Stalin dies; Krushchev becomes Secretary-General of the Soviet Communist Party; CIA-sponsored coup in Iran reinstates the Shah; USSR explodes first hydrogen bomb.

1954   Geneva Accords on Vietnam; CIA helps overthrow Guatemalan government; first Taiwan Straits crisis starts; SEATO established.

1955   First Cold War summit in Geneva; Warsaw Pact formed; West Germany joins NATO; Baghdad Pact signed.

1956   Suez Crisis; Hungarian Uprising.

1957   EEC created; Sputnik launched into orbit; Eisenhower Doctrine offers US support to Middle Eastern countries.

1958   Second Berlin crisis; second Taiwan Straits crisis starts.

1959   Castro takes power in Cuba; Eisenhower–Krushchev Washington summit; CENTO supersedes Baghdad Pact.

1960s

1960   US U-2 spy plane shot down over Soviet territory; Paris Summit collapses; GATT Round 4, Dillon; UN intervenes in Congo; Kennedy elected US President.

1961   Bay of Pigs invasion of Cuba; Kennedy embarks on rearmament; Berlin Wall built; Alliance for Progress announced; Kennedy–Krushchev Vienna summit.

1962   Cuban Missile Crisis; US–EEC 'chicken war'; US Military Assistance Command established in Vietnam.

1963   Nuclear Test Ban Treaty; Diem regime overthrown in South Vietnam with US acquiescence; Indonesian insurgency in Malaya; President Kennedy assassinated; Johnson becomes US President; GATT Round 5, Kennedy.

1964   Gulf of Tonkin Resolution; China explodes first atomic bomb; Brezhnev succeeds Krushchev.

1965   150,000 US troops to Vietnam; US military intervention in Dominican Republic.

1966   France withdraws from NATO Military Command.

1967   Middle East Six Day War.

1968   Tet Offensive in Vietnam; Soviet troops invade Czechoslovakia; Brezhnev Doctrine asserting Soviet right to intervene in socialist countries; NPT signed; Nixon elected US President.

1969   US Apollo 11 lands on moon; Nixon Doctrine calls for allies to take more responsibility for own defence; West German *Ostpolitik*; SALT begins.

1970s

1970   US expands Vietnam War into Cambodia.

1971   First US trade deficit of twentieth century; Nixon announces New Economic Policy; PRC admitted to the UN.

1972   President Nixon visits PRC; Nixon–Brezhnev Moscow summit; *détente* gathers pace; SALT I/ABM Treaty signed; GATT Round 6, Tokyo; West and East Germany sign Basic Treaty.

1973   Ceasefire in Vietnam; Nixon–Brezhnev Washington summit; US War Powers

Act; Yom Kippur War; military coup in Chile brings Pinochet to power; end of Bretton Woods; OPEC raises oil prices.

1974 Nixon–Brezhnev Moscow summit; Nixon resigns due to Watergate scandal and Ford becomes US President; Ford–Brezhnev Vladivostok summit; UN calls for NIEO.

1975 Ho Chi Minh unites Vietnam under communist rule; SEATO disbanded; Helsinki Accords signed; Angolan civil war.

1976 OPEC splits over oil prices; Carter elected US President.

1977 President Carter emphasises importance of human rights.

1978 President Carter visits Commission in Brussels; Camp David Middle East agreement.

1979 Carter–Brezhnev summit; Islamic fundamentalists overthrow Shah of Iran; American embassy staff held hostage in Teheran; Soviets invade Afghanistan; *détente* collapses; Carter Doctrine proclaims Persian Gulf key strategic area for US; Egyptian–Israeli Peace Treaty; US opens formal diplomatic relations with PRC; Taiwan Relations Act; SALT II signed; Sandinistas seize power in Nicaragua.

1980s

1980 President Carter withdraws SALT II from Congress; Brandt Report; US defence spending increases; Solidarity movement founded in Poland; Reagan elected US President.

1981 Declaration of martial law in Poland; President Reagan cuts taxes and massively increases defence spending; American hostages in Teheran released.

1982 International debt crisis; Spain joins NATO; Caribbean Basin Initiative launched; START begins.

1983 SDI proposed; Reagan's 'evil empire' speech; terrorist truck bomb kills 220 US marines and 21 other US service members in Beirut; US military intervention in Grenada; KAL-007 shot down; West Germany decides to deploy Cruise and Pershing missiles.

1984 Reagan seeks talks with Soviets.

1985 Mikhail Gorbachev comes to power in Soviet Union; Reagan–Gorbachev Geneva summit; Reagan Doctrine pledges support for anti-communist movements.

1986 Reagan–Gorbachev Reykjavik summit; GATT Round 7, Uruguay; Iran–Contra Affair revealed to public; US military strikes against selected Libyan targets.

1987 Reagan–Gorbachev Washington summit; INF signed.

1988 Reagan–Gorbachev Moscow summit; Brezhnev Doctrine abandoned; Bush elected US President.

1989 Soviet troops withdraw from Afghanistan; China massacres dissidents in Tiananman Square; Poland gains independence; Hungary gains independence; Berlin Wall falls; Bush–Gorbachev Malta summit; December communist governments fall in Czechoslovakia, Bulgaria and Romania; Soviet empire ends; US military intervention in Panama.

1990s

1990 Boris Yeltsin elected to presidency of Russia; Germany reunified and admitted to NATO; Iraq invades Kuwait.

1991 Warsaw Pact ends; Soviet Union expires and becomes CIS; START 1 signed; First Gulf War; imposition of no-fly zones over Iraq; Madrid Conference and Arab–Israeli peace process.

1992 US intervention in Somalia; Lisbon Protocol; Clinton elected US President.

1993 European Union created; Oslo Accords signed; START II signed; NEC created.

1994 US withdrawal from Somalia; US intervention in Haiti; NAFTA created; First Summit of the Americas in Miami; Framework Agreement with North Korea to halt nuclear weapons development.

1995 WTO created; US/NATO Operation Deliberate Force in Bosnia; Dayton Accords; Mexican currency crisis; NTA announced.

1996 Helms–Burton Act; Iran–Libya Sanctions Act; bombing of US military barracks at Al-Khobar; SFOR takes over from IFOR in Bosnia and Herzegovina.

1997 NATO–Russia Founding Act; PJC created.

1998 IMF provides largest aid package ever to Russia; Desert Fox – Anglo-American military strikes against Iraq; US Cruise missile strikes against alleged terrorist targets in Afghanistan and Sudan.

1999 Czech Republic, Hungary and Poland join NATO; US/NATO military intervention in Kosovo; Russian troops join KFOR.

2000s

2000 Terrorist attack on the USS *Cole* in Aden; George W. Bush elected US President.

2001 11 September terrorist attacks on Twin Towers, New York, and on the Pentagon; US leads invasion of Afghanistan; Bush–Putin meeting, Slovenia; Bush Doctrine declares no distinction between terrorists and those who harbour them; WTO Doha Talks; US EP-3 reconnaissance plane emergency landing in China.

2002 National Security Strategy of the United States of America proposes pre-emptive/preventative strike doctrine; North Korea admits nuclear weapons programme; US withdraws from ABM Treaty; Russia withdraws from START II; SORT signed; NATO–Russia Council established; Bali bombing.

2003 US launches Second Gulf War against Iraq; 'Rose Revolution' in Georgia.

2004 Bulgaria, Latvia, Lithuania, Estonia, Romania, Slovakia and Slovenia join NATO; 'Orange Revolution' in the Ukraine; presidential election Afghanistan; Madrid train bombings; Bush re-elected US President.

2005 CAFTA–DR signed; Summit of the Americas at Mar del Plata, Argentina; elections to Afghanistan lower house of parliament; elections in Iraq; Egypt's first contested presidential election; Israeli disengagement from Gaza.

Preface

In the first edition we expressed our hope that readers would enjoy the book as much as we enjoyed writing it and that it succeeded in meeting its remit: to impart some understanding of US foreign policy, discomfort cosy preconceptions about the impact of the US upon the world, and encourage our audience to delve deeper into the challenging and sometimes murky realm of post-war American foreign policy. It seems from the feedback that we were largely successful and we were thus delighted to be invited to develop our work further in a second edition.

The aim of this second edition is similar to the first, namely to provide a coherent account of how US foreign policy started out in 1945, how it developed and engaged with a bewildering range of challenges, how it has evolved since the Cold War, and how its formulators have struggled to reconcile American principles with policy practice. To do this we have tried to again strike the delicate balance between providing sufficient information for readers to formulate their independent judgements about US foreign policy issues and providing our own, or renderings of other people's, interpretations and judgements. We have also retained the successful original structure insofar as the book blends chronological, analytic and regional chapters and is written in a way that, after Chapter 1, readers can 'pick and mix' chapters in response to their interests and needs – albeit we strongly recommend reading it from cover to cover!

This book is, however, substantially different to the first. The post-Cold War section has been completely restructured and rewritten to provide more detailed assessment of the end of the Cold War, three new regional chapters and a much fuller conclusion. We have also paid close attention to the comments of reviewers and of readers for the second edition's Cold War chapters, which were encouragingly positive but sometimes reflected our own frustration in having to omit things we felt were important. We have consequently begged, borrowed and stolen extra space to, for instance, provide more coverage of US Cold War policy towards Africa and Europe, new material on nuclear strategy, more analysis of economic statecraft, more detail about *détente* and Carter's human rights policy, greater referencing/guide to reading, and comment on Cold War historiographical debates. Inevitably we still had to edit out some material that we would have preferred to include but hope that what is left goes some way to meeting the advice of our academic colleagues. Finally, and perhaps above all else, we are grateful for the indulgence of Routledge and the series editors. Without their latitude and understanding we would not have been able to produce for students what, in our opinion at least, is an improved, more detailed and more challenging introduction to US foreign policy since 1945.

Alan P. Dobson and Steve Marsh
20 November 2005

1 US foreign policy

Evolution, formulation and execution

I recognize that taking Saddam out was unpopular. But I made the decision because I thought it was in the right interests of our security. . . . People love America. Sometimes they don't like the decisions made by America, but I don't think you want a president who tries to become popular and does the wrong thing.

President George W. Bush, 8 October 2004[1]

President Clinton and I . . . have spoken often about the goals of American foreign policy. Boiled down, these have not changed in more than 200 years. They are to ensure the continued security, prosperity, and freedom of our people.

Secretary of State Madeleine Albright, 1998[2]

Such words provoke more questions than they answer. Not everyone agrees with Bush that it was in US best interests to invade Iraq. In a democracy are presidents supposed to do what they controversially believe is right, even when it is contrary to majority opinion? And Albright's concepts – security, prosperity and freedom – differ in meaning under Cold War, post-Cold War and post 9/11 conditions. So, what exactly is foreign policy and how should it be conducted in democracies? These are not the fatuous questions they may seem. For example, foreign policy has traditionally been seen as the pursuit of the national interest in the external relations of states, but there has never been a precise boundary between the domestic and international spheres and there have always been important non-state actors. Economic well-being, political values and security are always matters of national interest, but these are broad and flexible concepts and strategies for securing them change. As a result, policies have to be constantly recrafted to meet new challenges such as terrorists who do not observe the norms of the state system; intermestic issues in an interdependent global economy, which can often trump the priority of traditional security interests; and organisations such as the United Nations (UN), the European Union (EU) and multinational corporations (MNCs), which play according to international rather than national rules. The change most currently in focus is terrorism and, as Mao Tse-tung observed, terrorists move among the people as a fish swims in the sea. There are often no visible targets for state retaliation and thus the strategy of conventional deterrence – I'll strike you back harder if you strike me – does not apply. How are states to deal effectively with this challenge? Even when the focus falls on the state, analysing how it acts is difficult. Scholars used to simplify things by assuming that states are rational actors. More recently, less rational processes have been emphasised by which political constituencies and bureaucracies mediate perceptions of interests and thus influence and often determine foreign policy outcomes.

Turning to the issue of democracy and foreign policy-making, there may not be time for democratic procedures in a Cuban Missile Crisis and decisions may have to be taken on the basis of incomplete and contested evidence and in the knowledge that there will be unforeseen consequences. At a more purely ethical level, what means are justified to secure the national interest in the face of terrorism, weapons of mass destruction (WMDs) and rogue states?[3] Since June 2002, President Bush has developed a strategy based on unchallengeable US power, its right to intervene preventatively in other states, and its goal of spreading democracy and the free market.[4] These policies directed abroad, and the Patriot Act[5] directed at homeland security, carry dangerous means with them, some of which may threaten to corrupt the democratic state they are supposed to preserve.[6]

Fuller explanations of how policy-makers try to resolve tensions between democratic values and state needs, and how they define the national interest and implement foreign policy in a complex and changing environment, will come later. All that is offered here is a crude template to identify the analytical challenges involved in foreign policy studies.

More specific questions are: who makes US foreign policy, in accordance with what principles, and with what objectives? To answer these questions, we need to develop a picture of both the ancestry and more recent progeny of US foreign policy. John Dos Passos in *Manhattan Transfer* made his characters strive to discover 'the heart of things'. This book aims to do the same with US foreign policy. However, as Dos Passos's characters found, the 'heart' is often elusive or is determined by the eye of the beholder. Let us start by examining some of the arteries, which feed into the heart of US foreign policy.

Idealism and realism

As the US became involved in world affairs, debates developed about how it should conduct its foreign policy. These were often couched in the theoretical terms of realism versus idealism.

Realism is associated with Old World or European diplomacy. It draws on an analysis of human nature and a conception of the logic of geopolitical power relations. In an anarchical world system, where there is no Leviathan to impose order, each state must seek to maximise power to secure its own survival. States may act in concert if it is in their interests to do so, but ultimately the realist vision is of a potential war of all against all where man's life might very probably be 'nasty, brutish and short', as Thomas Hobbes succinctly put it, unless the state has sufficient power to guarantee its own security and stability. Furthermore, states must recognise that human beings have a tendency to conflict as they pursue their own interests and that weapons cannot be defined as intrinsically defensive or offensive: those who wield and face them decide that. Thus, in addition to the danger of predatory human behaviour, a state's defensive measures may be seen as potential for aggression by another, which then responds in kind and sets up the vicious circle of an arms race. This matrix of problems is the traditional geopolitical security dilemma.

Realists explain foreign policy in terms of the state's attempts to maximise security through power. Thus force, diplomacy, duplicity, balancing power, and conduct contrary to democratic principles are all options to be explored in the prudent pursuit of national security. Other states must not be judged in terms of friendship, or their domestic character, or by their stated intentions, but by their power and the maxim that today's friend could become tomorrow's enemy and vice versa. For the realist, the nature of the regime, its disposition and its moral force are all irrelevancies, an attitude caught by Stalin's famous question: how many divisions does the Pope have? Realism thus conflicts with the claim that democracies do not war with each other and with the current US objective to democratise the world as a grand strategy for achieving world peace.[7]

The realist approach has often been derided as amoral, but realists have two responses. In an imperfect world it is absurd to see moral agency as a choice between following or departing from moral principles. Instead, moral agency needs to be seen as a practical dilemma of choice between moral imperatives – to fight in a just cause, or 'thou shalt not kill'. Second, realists want to secure the state because they believe it is imbued with intrinsic moral worth: it creates order, which is the prerequisite for moral action. The crucial problem here arises when foreign policy means conflict with the moral ends of the domestic society to such an extent that they threaten its integrity.

Idealists have optimistic views of humanity and its potential for compromise, accommodation, rational action and cooperation. US idealism stands for self-determination and free elections, open diplomacy, human rights, economic development through the free market, and the avoidance or containment of war, through international organisations, law and collective security. Unlike realism, the over-arching vision is one of multilateral cooperation with other states rather than an ultimate reliance on power that can be wielded by unilateral will, even if it also involves engaging the power of other states through alliances. Underpinning idealism is a conviction that individuals are unique and precious and must not be treated as means to a politically defined end to which they do not subscribe: for example, at the horrendous extreme, the elimination of kulaks or Jews, for the 'greater good of society'. Idealism has been criticised for tending to elevate principles above careful calculation of national interests and achievable results (e.g. in the Vietnam War)[8] and for failing to act prudently in an anarchical and dangerous international system. Seeing when it is necessary to depart from principles, and how far to depart from them in order to preserve them in the longer term, is the dilemma here. In more recent times the realist–idealist debate has been developed further and theories of international relations have proliferated. First, neo-realists, who accept many of the basic assumptions of realism, focus more on the international system, rather than human nature, and identify the character and distribution of power in the anarchical state system as key explanatory variables or logics of the system (see Chapter 9). Second, neo-liberals, who share many of the premises of traditional idealism, believe that there is the possibility of transcending anarchy and the security dilemma as set out in the logics of the neo-realists. They emphasise the importance of multiple actors, confidence-building and the beneficial effects of complex economic inter-dependence, international regimes, law and organisations. Third, Alexander Wendt, a leading exponent of constructivism, cries plague upon both schools of thought and argues that neo-liberal idealism and neo-realism have mis-construed anarchy. For him, anarchy is what states make of it. In itself it is an empty vessel because states and their character change over time: 'anarchies only acquire logics as a function of the structure that we put inside them'. Wendt sees international relations as socially constructed and therefore as holding possibilities for radical change in a way that neither neo-liberalism nor neo-realism could contemplate. However, after asserting such possibilities, he talks of only three kinds of macro-level systemic structures: Hobbesian, Lock-ean and Kantian, characterised successively by unbound violence, violence short of fatalities and non-violence.[9]

This brief foray into the margins of international relations theory by no means exhausts the wide range of possibilities that are now current, but it has at least introduced some of those that have been most influential in practice and more will be considered in Chapter 9.[10]

Exceptionalism and manifest destiny

The US was conceived of by the Founding Fathers as a nation with a mission to propagate a special form of political morality, often captured by the term exceptionalism. Such ideas were abroad in the colonies well before independ-ence: John Winthrop famously envisioned a new moral state as a shining City upon the Hill. Like other spawn of revolution then, Americans brought some-thing different to government. Humanity was conceived of in terms of rights to life, liberty and the pursuit of happiness, and Enlightenment rationalism concluded that a form of government had to be devised to protect those rights. This was done by controlling political power with a written constitution and a bill of rights and by creating a system of checks and balances, between the federal Executive, Legislature and Judiciary, between the Senate and the House of Representatives in the Congress, and between federal and state sov-ereignty. Further safeguards were due process of law and popular elections. The result was perceived as something unique and superior to anything in the Old World, and indeed anywhere else. As the US expanded across the contin-ent in the 1840s, leaders began to speak of America's manifest destiny, which was to bring a shining example of liberty and democracy to other less fortunate peoples. Abraham Lincoln described it as government of the people, by the people, for the people, where people were defined as rights-carrying individuals. This was a society committed in principle to justice and freedom for all. It was an ambitious, moral enterprise and its values were cast in universal language, which referred to all humanity, not just Americans. However, while domestic policy-making was set in a carefully ordered political environment, which enjoyed a working consensus of values (at least for the most part), the field of foreign policy was different. It was not easy to abide by democratic principles in a realm bereft of anything comparable to domestic law and lacking a body capable of enforcing uniform rules of conduct. The international sphere was characterised by anarchy, self-help and power politics, where survival was the overriding priority. This posed problems. In the mid-1970s, President Carter spoke of human rights as absolute principles, but then discovered that overriding needs of national security transformed absolutes into relative moral values. For example, Iran was such an important ally in the cosmic struggle with communism that its appalling human rights record had to be tolerated. Similarly, with regard both to the Soviets' persecution of dissidents like Anatoly Shcharansky and their restrictions on Jewish emigration, Carter had to tone down criticisms for the sake of important advances in national security matters such as the Strategic Arms Limitation Talks II (SALT II). These specific episodes raise important general questions. To what extent can the US conduct a principled and democratic foreign policy? And how far should it go in trying to spread its universal values abroad? These issues have risen to prominence once again in the twenty-first century with President Bush and his neo-conservative advisers. They advocate a foreign policy of power and security for the US, the mantra of traditional realism, but add to that the importance of spreading democracy abroad, the mantra of traditional American idealism. These objectives are to be pursued unilaterally, if others will not follow, and with a doctrine that embraces the radical strategy of preventative strike (see below in this chapter and Chapter 9). To many this smacks of imperialism, but one should not assume that everyone thinks that imperialism is undesirable. Much depends on its character. For example, Deepak Lal believes that empires have brought stability, law and order, and prosperity and that the anarchical state system that has been characteristic in Europe since the Treaty of Westphalia in 1648 is largely an historical aberration. Following the British political philosopher Michael Oakshott, Lal distinguishes between empires of civil association and empires of enterprise. The former in American guise would provide for civil liberties, a legal framework and a global free market – highly desirable in Lal's view. The latter would do the same, but crucially also seek to proselytise the world to American democratic and social values, which would make empire a violently contested vision of the good life and one highly unpalatable to Lal and, in his view, to most other non-westerners.[11]

Isolationism and internationalism: unilateralism and multilateralism

Americans' pride in their society and government, often in the form of exceptionalism, produced two incompatible styles of foreign policy. Both tried to cope with America's universalism in an anarchic state system. The first was isolationism, which aimed to protect the new republic's integrity by avoiding entanglement in European conflicts because European states, until the twentieth century, were more powerful than the US and because they fought according to the rules of amoral power politics, which elevated state interests and survival above everything else. Isolationism also fostered and was often tantamount to unilateralism, a tendency to act alone if one had to play in the international arena. The second style was internationalism, which aimed to spread liberty abroad, to pursue US economic interests, and, from the twentieth century, to seek security through a world reformed in accordance with US principles. During the Cold War the contrast between these principles promulgated abroad, and the failure of US governments to apply them at home to African Americans and the indigenous peoples of North America caused considerable embarrassment, provided fuel for Soviet propaganda, compromised US anti-colonialism, and tended to undermine American efforts to establish good relations with newly independent states. Internationalism often subsumed multilateral policies of cooperation with other states to achieve agreed goals, but this is not always necessarily the case. The policy of George W. Bush is internationalist, in that it engages broadly with the world community, but his administration is characteristically unilateralist in the way it determines and executes policy. Even when one takes the cooperation of allies like Britain into account there is little, if any, give and take involved. Britain either goes along with US policy or it is left out.

In the eighteenth and nineteenth centuries isolationism and internationalism vied with each other strongly. President Washington in his farewell address cautioned that 'it must be unwise in us to implicate ourselves by artificial ties in the ordinary vicissitudes of her [Europe's] politics or the ordinary combinations and collisions of her friendships and enmities'.[12] Extend America's commercial activities by all means, but keep out of Europe's immoral dynastic squabbles. Isolation from Europe's power games was reinforced in 1823 by the Monroe Doctrine, which declared that any European intervention in the Western Hemisphere would be regarded as an unfriendly act. This established the basis upon which the US eventually built what has often been described as western hemispheric hegemony.

Isolationism, however, was a compromised policy. It was reserved for Europe. Elsewhere the US pursued ruthless expansion through hostilities with Indians, Canadians and Mexicans. War with Spain in 1898 brought the US control over the Philippines and Cuba and other islands in the Caribbean and the Pacific. There is little sign of isolationism here. Instead, policy was driven by a greed for both territory and economic gain and a desire to shine the beacon of liberty abroad.

By the end of the century, the US was a major naval power and the spirit and practice of isolationism were challenged. In 1899 and 1900 Secretary of State John Hay issued his famous 'Open Door' notes on China, demanding that the European powers should allow equal and open access there for American commerce. And in 1904 President Theodore Roosevelt proclaimed his Corollary to the Monroe Doctrine, which asserted the right of the US to interfere in civil unrest in Western Hemisphere countries to restore order and protect US economic interests, rather like George W. Bush's preventative doctrine attempts to justify worldwide American interventions. Theodore Roosevelt's internationalism placed isolationism under attack. In 1917 it received further blows when US faith in legalism and neutrality proved to be misplaced: German U-boat warfare and loss of American lives provided the immediate cause for US entry into the First World War (1914–18). However, the sympathies and interests of the Woodrow Wilson administration had lain with the allies well before that and the President was also determined to participate in the peace treaties in order to remould the world according to his liberal principles.

In 1918 Wilson promulgated his famous Fourteen Points. They reconciled isolationism and internationalism by universalising US values. The Old World system was to be replaced by New World internationalism – free trade, self-determination of peoples, freedom of movement on commercial waterways and on the high seas, open diplomacy subject to democratic scrutiny and held accountable to the people, a just and charitable peace without reparations, and a collective security organisation – the League of Nations – to prevent war. Sadly for Wilson, wily Old World leaders compromised his vision and sceptical US politicians undermined collective security by refusing to ratify the Versailles Peace Treaty, thus preventing US participation in the League of Nations. In the twentieth century the US liberal and idealist democratic agenda changed little from Wilson's vision, but how to prosecute it successfully remained elusive. Tension between isolationism and internationalism still continues, though the Japanese attack on Pearl Harbor in December 1941, modern communications, the development of intercontinental ballistic missiles (ICBMs), the need for the global containment of communism, and the re-emergence of an interdependent world economy have pushed isolationism more and more to the fringes of influence. Current US foreign policy-making, however, still shows signs of struggle between unilateralism and multilateralism to determine the character of American internationalism. And unilateralism and multilateralism each have advantages and disadvantages for policy-makers: unilateralism is a more decisive style with little need for compromise and accommodation and is often seen as a viable strategy for the world's only superpower. Many in the George W. Bush administration appear to wish to rely primarily on the unilateral wielding of US hard power in pursuit of American security and the propagation of its values abroad in an ambitious scheme to democratise the world. Yet, no matter how powerful the US might be, it is not omnipotent. It cannot get its way on everything and multilateral cooperation is often needed to consummate American objectives and confer upon them authority and legitimacy – what Joseph S. Nye has referred to as soft power, which he believes to be indispensable for the US.[13] Can the scope of US foreign policy be captured by Manichaean-like divisions between isolationism and internationalism, realism and idealism, unilateralism and multilateralism? The answer has to be no! The fact that there is no clear dividing line between foreign and domestic policy necessarily impairs the isolationist–internationalist dichotomy. Similarly with idealism and realism, there is always a mixture of the two. No American realist has conducted foreign affairs without celebrating the rights, liberties and economic system of the US and allowing such values to influence policy. No idealist has sustained, in pristine form, their principles and moral values when confronted by the need to save the state they value. Bush's invasion of Iraq in March 2003 may be seen by many to epitomise the unilateralism of the current American superpower, but one should not overlook the fact that British and Polish troops went in along with American forces and that there was support elsewhere both inside and outside Europe for the invasion. Even this unilateralism has some multilateral contamination. We thus need to be sensitive to the complexities involved here. Images of idealism and realism, isolationism and internationalism, and unilateralism and multilateralism always need to be nuanced and should be used as analytical starting points rather than definitive explanations. There can be no clear answer to precisely which of these positions is at the heart of American foreign policy because they are all in circulation, albeit carrying different levels of sustenance.

Who makes US foreign policy?

Formal power in foreign policy-making lies largely with the Executive and the Legislature: the Judiciary has only a peripheral role. The Supreme Court has a watching brief, but it has never been assertive and in the Curtis Wright Case in 1936 affirmed the President's use of broad powers. Our main focus must therefore be on the Executive Branch led by the President and on the Congress. At the same time, we must remember that this is a dynamic system, which responds to external factors, technology and domestic changes. Power to formulate foreign policy has thus shifted since 1945 within the bureaucracy, and back and forth between the legislative and executive branches. This has largely been caused by the different characteristics of incumbent presidents, foreign policy setbacks, such as the loss of China to communism in 1949 and the Vietnam War in the 1960s and 1970s, and, more recently, by the transition to a post-Cold War world and the response to terrorism, WMDs proliferation and rogue states. Also, a problem can determine the type of response required and that, in turn, determines who or what does the responding. This is well illustrated by the Cuban Missile Crisis (see Chapter 6).

The President is Commander in Chief (CIC) of the armed forces and chief diplomat, with the power to make nominations for diplomatic appointments and to negotiate treaties. He can also set policy through his State of the Union addresses and announcements such as the Truman Doctrine (1947). However, this list both overstates and understates presidential powers because some formal powers often turn out to be less effective than one might think and informal powers acquired over the years in the practice of the presidency can often be very potent.

The distribution of power: the Congress

The President's power as CIC to commit US military forces overseas is extensive, but limited by both the Congress's constitutional prerogative to declare war and the War Powers Act (1973). The latter allows a president to commit troops to action overseas only for a maximum of 90 days without congressional approval. It was passed as a result of US involvement in Vietnam, where a de facto, but undeclared, war was fought (see Chapter 7). The Act's effectiveness, however, is questionable, not least because of practical difficulties involving the need to respond effectively and swiftly to events such as the Gulf War (1991). There are also legal complications. The Chadha Supreme Court Case (1983) declared congressional vetoes of executive actions illegal. In short, it may be unconstitutional for the Congress to veto an order of the CIC that commits US troops to combat overseas. In the 2003 invasion of Iraq, the Congress actually granted the Executive Branch authority to 'wage war' without making a formal declaration.

It would be wrong, however, to suggest that the War Powers Act is without force, just as it would also be a mistake to overlook the potential effectiveness of constraints that predate it. Their potency depends on congressional willingness to assert and apply them vigorously. Bearing such points in mind, let us examine congressional powers in more detail.

1 Control of the purse strings: this is primarily exercised by the House of Representatives, but, except in extraordinary circumstances (in 1975 Congress refused President Ford's request for funds to help the crumbling South Vietnamese regime), it is an unwieldy device. Presidents can shift resources between areas of policy, or camouflage things through covert operations, and their lieutenants may even divert funds illegally (as in the Iran–Contra Affair 1985–86).

2 A Senate two-thirds majority vote is required to approve both presidential nominees for diplomatic and senior executive appointments and treaties. Refusal to ratify executive nominations for positions such as Secretary of Defense are rare, but the Democrat majority in 1989 rejected President George H. Bush's nominee John Tower, largely on grounds of character flaws, by a vote of 53–47 in the Senate. More surprisingly, the Republican majority in the Senate in 2005 failed to achieve confirmation of President George W. Bush's nominee for US Ambassador to the UN, John Bolton. Unlike Tower, the issues here were mainly to do with Bolton's hard-line views on the UN, though like Tower, he is also an abrasive character. However, as is so often the case, there was another avenue for the Executive to proceed along. In August 2005 President Bush made a recess

appointment (when the Senate went into its autumn recess), which is permitted by the Constitution, arguing that the war on terrorism made the situation too dangerous not to have a US representative at the UN. This allowed Bolton to assume office, at least until January 2007 when a new Congress will take over. Democrats and some Republicans were infuriated by this move and saw it as stretching constitutional powers contrary to their overall spirit in a manner often evident in the heyday of the imperial presidency (see below in this chapter).

Refusal to ratify treaties, as in the case of the Treaty of Versailles (1919), may be rare, but ratification may be so clearly impossible to get that the President abandons the effort, e.g. with the International Trade Organisation (ITO), 1950. Faced with such difficulties, presidents have resorted to executive agreements between heads of state, e.g. security pact with South Korea (1949). In 1954 the Bricker amendment tried to make executive agreements subject to the same kind of approval as treaties, but it fell one vote short in the Senate of the two-thirds majority needed for a constitutional amendment. By the 1970s the post-war average of executive agreements per year was over 2,000 compared with just over 15 treaties, and the contents of many of the former were unknown outside government. Disillusionment with the Executive because of Vietnam made it possible to pass the Case-Zablocki Act in 1972, which requires that the Congress be informed about all executive agreements. But this has not been entirely successful, partly because of nice distinctions between agreements and 'understandings'.

The Senate has constitutionally and traditionally taken the lead in the Congress in foreign policy. Its Foreign Relations Committee is highly regarded and regularly drawn upon by the Executive for advice. In 1995 Chairman Jesse Helms challenged President Clinton's foreign policy establishment with proposed budget cuts and the abolition of the US Agency for International Development (USAID), the US Information Agency (USIA) and the US Arms Control and Disarmament Agency (USACDA). Clinton blocked the more extreme proposals by vetoing the 1996 Foreign Relations Authorization Bill, but $1.7 billion were cut over a five-year period, and only USAID, of the three agencies targeted by Helms, survived as an independent, though diminished, agency.

3   The control of foreign trade and commerce is given by the constitution to the Congress. This has been delegated extensively to the President since the Reciprocal Trade Agreements Act of 1934, but what the Congress can delegate, it can recall. Over the years Congress has insisted: that allies who received aid should embargo trade with communists (the Mutual Defense Assistance Control or Battle Act 1951); on the inclusion of human rights stipulations in trade agreements (the Jackson–Vanik amendment to the 1974 Trade Act, directed against the Soviet Union); on mandating the US Trade Representative (USTR) to retaliate against states using unfair trade practices (clause 301 of the 1988 Omnibus Trade and Competitiveness Act, implemented by the USTR since 1994 by Executive Order of the

President); and it refused to grant President Clinton 'fast track' authority, something invented in 1974 which means that once a trade agreement has been negotiated it has to be accepted or rejected in toto by Congress, rather than being subjected to a series of complicating amendments. In the summer of 2002 Congress renewed trade promotion/fast-track authority for the first time since 1994, something seen as imperative by the Bush administration for progress on bilateral and regional free-trade agreements and the Doha Trade Round established by the World Trade Organisation (WTO) in November 2001.

4   Power of congressional oversight has always existed, but on an ad hoc basis. Thus in 1934–35 the famous Nye Committee investigated US entry into the First World War and blamed bankers and arms manufacturers for US involvement, and in 1987 Senator John Tower led a commission to investigate the Iran–Contra affair. Such committees and commissions come and go, but in 1974 growing concerns about covert activities resulted in the establishment of the Senate Select Committee on Intelligence chaired by Senator Frank Church. It unveiled illegal Central Intelligence Agency (CIA) operations, including plans to assassinate Fidel Castro the leader of Cuba, and led directly to the establishment of a permanent bipartisan Senate Intelligence Oversight Committee (1976) and a House counterpart (1977). Nevertheless, these committees have been rendered somewhat ineffective when confronted by members of the Executive who think their concept of national security trumps constitutional constraints. Thus, the Senate Committee failed to control the shenanigans of the Iran–Contra affair. However, it does have strong powers, including the right to subpoena witnesses and evidence, and an ability to call the Executive to account ex post facto. The ultimate sanction against a President lies with the House of Representatives, which has the power of impeachment. It investigates suspicions of executive high crimes or misdemeanours and can use a special prosecutor to do so. In 1974 this led to the downfall of President Nixon and in 1998–99 to unsuccessful proceedings against Clinton. If there is a case to answer, the President is tried by the Senate.

The distribution of power: the Executive Branch

Although the executive bureaucracy is there to empower, it also checks and controls the President. The State Department is the formal foreign office of the US. In the nineteenth century it was small, amateurish and had little to do. Its influence depended upon the stature of the Secretary of State. In the twentieth century, it became more professional with the reforms of the Rogers Act (1924), but senior diplomatic appointments are still often made on political rather than professional criteria.

The Department's fortunes fluctuated in the post-war period. In the early Cold War, President Truman's inexperience of foreign affairs resulted in his heavy reliance on Secretaries of State George Marshall (1947–49) and Dean

Acheson (1949–53). That enhanced the status of the Department, but the loss of China in 1949 and the communist witch-hunt, initiated by Senator Joseph McCarthy, reversed its fortunes and led to a purge of many of its Asian specialists. Although with Secretary of State John Foster Dulles (1953–59), it seemed that power once again emanated from the Department, and indeed it did, this was more because of Dulles than the Department itself. By the early 1960s a further problem arose: an ever increasing tendency of presidents to use the National Security Council (NSC) and the National Security Adviser (NSA) situated within the Executive Office of the President and established by the National Security Act (1947). During the last 40 years the conflict between the State Department and the NSC for control over foreign policy has often been bitter. This was particularly so during the open feud between Secretary of State Cyrus Vance (1977–80) and NSA Zbigniew Brzezinski (1977–81). At times the State Department has been relegated to conducting everyday affairs and helping to justify and defend policy made elsewhere in the bureaucracy: this was most notably the case with William Rogers during the first Nixon administration. In the mid- and late 1990s there were contradictory developments. Clinton's general preoccupation with domestic matters and attempts to return the NSC to a coordinating role tended to raise the profiles of Secretaries of State Warren Christopher (1993–97) and Madeleine Albright (1997–2001). Yet, at the same time, Congress championed financial cutbacks, staff reductions and some closures of diplomatic missions as part of the post-Cold War peace dividend.

The NSC was set up to coordinate all aspects of national security, and it has grown in stature over the years and drawn power away from the State and Defense Departments. However, some have bucked the trend: George Shultz (1982–89) and Donald Rumsfeld (2001–05 and continuing) were respectively powerful secretaries of State and Defense. President Clinton's first NSA, Anthony Lake (1993–97), tried to move the NSC back to a coordinating role, only to be criticised for failing to articulate clear policy priorities: his successor, Samuel (Sandy) Berger (1997–2001) fared little better. Driven by an overly sensitive concern with public opinion, he was accused of inconsistency and short-termism. Under George W. Bush there have been further shifts of power, especially after 9/11, with much of the policy response coming from Vice-President Cheney and Defense Secretary Rumsfeld at the expense of Secretary of State Colin Powell (2001–05). The NSA during the first administration, Condoleezza Rice (2001–05), who had excellent access to Bush, acted as a rather ineffective power broker, partly because her instincts lay with Cheney and Rumsfeld and not with Powell, whose only ally at times appeared to be British Foreign Secretary Jack Straw. It is too early to say what impact Stephen Hadley (2005–), Bush's new NSA, will have, but with the post-war tendency towards highly personalised presidential power, the rise in importance of the NSA at the expense of unwieldy bureaucracies seems, in retrospect, to have been rather inevitable.

Other departments and agencies – the CIA, the Joint Chiefs of Staff and the Defense, Treasury and Commerce Departments – all have significant, but specialised inputs into foreign policy. In contrast, the President, the NSC, the NSA and the State Department have broad remits, which is why they are so often decisive in policy formulation and execution. However, having identified the central core of the policy-making process, it is important to add that relationships within it fluctuate wildly. How it operates at any one time is determined by the President. Truman depended on the State Department and the NSC. Eisenhower used Dulles and the NSC, but was also unique in making significant use of the Cabinet. Kennedy relied on task forces, ad hoc committees and his NSA, McGeorge Bundy. For President Johnson the famous Tuesday luncheon meetings were vital policy-deciding events. For the following administration it was the Nixon–Kissinger axis that drove things. Ford gave more emphasis to economic constituencies in foreign policy-making, but also depended much on Secretary of State Kissinger. Carter, rather unsuccessfully, tried to marry Secretary of State Vance's liberalism with NSA Brzezinski's hard realism. Reagan allowed a rather fractious NSC to compete with the State Department. George H. Bush ran a tight ship steered through conventional channels, with James Baker and Lawrence Eagleburger as successive Secretaries of State. Under Clinton, the absence of Cold War certainties, which had done so much to determine priorities, meant a more open political scenario with an enlarged intermestic agenda. Clinton clearly acknowledged this with the creation by executive order on 25 January 1993 of the National Economic Council (NEC), to coordinate policy-making processes with respect to domestic and international economic issues. Under Robert E. Rubin, the NEC soon proved itself to be a major force in foreign policy, though under Allan Hubbard it has had to give way to new national security priorities that have come to prominence in the wake of 9/11. Those priorities under the George W. Bush administration have been much influenced by Vice-President Dick Cheney, the most powerful of vice-presidents in recent years and certainly the most influential of any in foreign and security policy.

The changing context and the challenge to democracy

After the Second World War, the changing nature of foreign policy and its own expanded international role challenged the US. How it responded led some to conclude that constitutional restraints had snapped, that there was a growing rift between democratic principles and foreign policy practices, and that power had corrupted both the foreign and domestic domain.

The chief operational changes were in communications, technology and nuclear weaponry, which concentrated power in fewer hands, centred on the president, rather than in the institutional establishment. Rapid communications and ICBMs also emphasised the need for swift and decisive responses to world crises such as the Berlin Blockade in 1948 and Soviet missiles in Cuba in 1962. The need for swift reactions encouraged the creation of the NSC as a parallel bureaucracy more directly under the authority of the president and more responsive to his wishes and commands. Diplomats and foreign policy personnel were increasingly demoted to tasks involving routine affairs and technical matters, and to collecting and disseminating information for high-level talks conducted by their political bosses. Ask yourself: what are the dominant images of foreign policy in the post-war world? Almost without exception, what will come to mind are heads of state meetings such as the one between Bush and Putin in June 2001 when Bush famously said that he would not have invited Putin to his ranch if he did not trust him. This is the age of personal summitry, of diplomacy by presidents and prime ministers. Churchill, Roosevelt and Stalin invented it in wartime and it is radically different from diplomatic experience prior to 1939.

In this new operating environment, policy is conducted under the eye of the journalist and the TV camera. In a very real sense it has gone public. For democracies, this has raised the importance of public opinion in foreign policy-making and, thereby, produced complications. First, expressions of approbation or opprobrium by the public or their elected representatives became more potent – something totalitarian opponents do not generally have to concern themselves with. Second, in sensitive diplomacy such as opening relations with the People's Republic of China (PRC) in 1972 (see Chapter 7) it became difficult to maintain secrecy, and that led to the use of less orthodox means. Ironically, the more intense public gaze has often driven foreign policy into the less accountable and less visible channels of the NSC, the CIA and covert operations. Third, the media can set agendas, or at least encourage and pressure the government to take action – the so-called CNN effect – as over the humanitarian outrages in the Balkans in the 1990s. And fourth, estimations – accurate or otherwise – of what public reaction might be can modify policies, as happened with the Clinton administration's 1993 review of policy for multilateral humanitarian interventions, Presidential Decision Directive 25 (PDD-25). In the aftermath of the death of US Rangers in Mogadishu, Somalia, the document was toned down, for fear of adverse public reaction to a more robust policy, even though subsequent public opinion analysis indicated a continuing willingness to support multilateral interventions for humanitarian and other good reasons.[14]

While enhanced communications and the White House rapid response bureaucracy helped to provide more flexibility, new substantive changes in foreign affairs, ideology and nuclear weapons had a contrary impact. Foreign policy relies upon overwhelming force, lower level coercion, flexible negotiations or a combination of the latter two in order to achieve its goals. In the post-war period, the US enjoyed none of these options in its dealings with the Soviet Union. American power was never sufficient to be able to dictate policy to the Soviets and both its ideology and nuclear deterrent created inflexibility. Things are different in the post-9/11 era, but just as difficult, not least because the perpetrators of international terrorism are little interested in negotiations and are impervious to traditional deterrence strategies.

The ideological rift between American and Soviet values left little room for manoeuvre. At the same time, the danger of nuclear war also meant that there was no leeway for mistakes. The US had to make its nuclear deterrent credible

to the Soviets in clear and forthright terms. American leaders feared appeasement, which had brought the Pearl Harbor disaster and the Second World War
to the US in the 1940s. Peace-loving democracies must not send the wrong
message again. America thus had to be prepared, and be seen as willing, to
fight for freedom. There would be implacable resolve to defend the rights and
interests of the US against communism. Among other things this entailed a
nuclear deterrence strategy that was developed with little if any recourse to
public opinion. There were variations and nuances of strategy along the way,
but the theory of deterrence was never seriously challenged, or the lack of
democratic control over it questioned, except on rare occasions such as in the
famous black comedy film *Dr. Strangelove*.

These conditions arising from ideological, political and economic convictions, and nuclear deterrence strategies produced a sharply divided bipolar
world. This bipolar model appealed to many US decision-makers because,
among other reasons, it made it easier to mobilise public support. It was also
attractive to many scholars as complex events could be slotted into a neat
explanatory paradigm with sharp analytical categories, but it fell far short of
exhausting the complexities of the US–Soviet relationship, never mind what
went on elsewhere.[15] The world was not that simple. Complicating factors
proliferated as time went by. International organisations such as the UN, the
International Monetary Fund (IMF), the North Atlantic Treaty Organisation
(NATO) and the Conference on Security and Cooperation in Europe (CSCE)
emphasised the importance of multilateral diplomacy. Decolonisation created
more states. New factors entered the international agenda such as over-
population, under-development, disease, terrorism, sustainable growth and
environmental degradation. In addition to the ideological rift between East
and West, other doctrines emerged; non-alignment, liberationism and Islamic
fundamentalism, as well as important differentiations within the Western and
Eastern blocs. Finally, there was an awareness of the world's economic interdependence and shrinking size as technology and communications development brought new opportunities and vulnerabilities.

To deal with all of this, the US had a foreign policy capability that was
checked and balanced by the Congress, law and often by competing branches
of the Executive. A 200-year-old isolationist tradition had to be cast off and
public opinion had to be mobilised in favour of a new global and very expensive foreign policy. In addition, policy-makers had to work within constraints
of an inflexible ideology, fear of repeating the appeasement syndrome and the
need to maintain the credibility of America's nuclear deterrent. Successive
presidents got the job done, but the means created a new problem: the imperial
presidency.

The 'imperial' response of the presidents

In attempts to be effective, presidents resorted to various techniques and styles
of policy. Invoking national security has been used to justify much. It is a
trump card empowered by loyalty to the nation. It should carry a warning:

beware! Purging alleged communist sympathisers in the McCarthy witch-hunt, the illegal war in Cambodia (1970), the Iran–Contra affair, the Patriot Act, holding terrorist suspects without trial in a legal limbo world at Guantanamo Bay, and prosecuting the war against Iraq without specific UN authorisation and without a declaration of war, were all justified in the name of national security. It can be a means/end argument run amok.

Nurturing bipartisanship in Congress fostered similar dangers. The Cold War placed foreign policy above adversarial politics and the pointed criticisms that accompany them. The result was swifter and more decisive foreign policy-making by the Executive and a generally complacent and compliant Congress, at least until the Vietnam War. Bipartisanship is appropriate in times of acute crisis when the nation must pull together in order to survive – as in the Second World War – providing that even then it does not go too far. But long-term bipartisanship in peacetime draws the teeth of effective political control.

Presidents have also used the aura of office, the inherent powers of the CIC, the NSC, executive agreements and dramatic announcements such as the Truman, Eisenhower, Carter, Reagan and Bush Doctrines, in order to implement policies. They have used covert operations and other secret channels to avoid the attention of the press and congressional oversight. And they have extracted resolutions from Congress, which delegate vast discretionary powers to the President as CIC. These resolutions included Taiwan/Formosa (1955),[16] the Middle East (1957) and, most notoriously, the Gulf of Tonkin (1964), which enabled President Johnson to escalate the war in Vietnam. Presidents thus developed a highly personalised style. The needs of national security in a world of dangers created by communism and more recently terrorism seemed to justify swift, effective, if at times extreme, measures, and an arrogant use of power. What seemed to have been forgotten was one of the foundational principles of the republic: good causes can be achieved only by good political means.

Arthur Schlesinger delivered a famous diagnosis of the malaise as it manifested itself up to the 1970s in *The Imperial Presidency*.[17] He claimed that the presidency had broken constitutional constraints: it was outside the rule of law. Presidents had snatched war power from the Congress. By the time of Richard Nixon and the Watergate affair, Lord Acton's aphorism of absolute power corrupting absolutely was coming true. Corruption in foreign affairs spilt over into the domestic realm where Nixon attempted to justify his actions by invoking the national interest.

In the aftermath of Watergate, there was a resurgence of congressional assertiveness and a rekindling of the debate about how the US should conduct its foreign policy. The Congress tried to claw back some of its prerogatives through the Case-Zablocki Act and the War Powers Act, and by increasing its powers of congressional oversight. All helped to dethrone the imperial presidency, but the key question was for how long. During the Reagan period, policies in the hands of Colonel North ran out of control, as a small elite tried to divert funds illegally to sustain the anti-communist Contra rebels in Nicaragua. In the minds of North and his co-conspirators, their conception of national security overrode the mistaken democratic will of Congress. The Iran-Contra Affair is a pretty clear-cut case of executive power exceeding its legitimate scope, but the congressional practice of continuing to grant broad powers, albeit legitimately, to the president carries dangers of excessive exploitation – as in the case of the Joint Resolution to Authorize the Use of United States Armed Forces Against Iraq, 2 October 2002, which effectively provided presidential discretion to go to war:

> The President is authorized to use the Armed Forces of the United States as he determines to be necessary and appropriate in order to
> (1) defend the national security of the United States against the continuing threat posed by Iraq; and
> (2) enforce all relevant United Nations Security Council Resolutions regarding Iraq.[18]

Since the Second World War the Executive Branch has developed successive versions of strategic doctrine, largely immune from democratic debate or controls, which raise serious issues concerning the proper use of power by the Executive. Nuclear strategy metamorphosed from a deterrence doctrine premised on the US's unilateral ability to destroy the USSR with virtual impunity, to massive retaliation, to flexible response and to mutual assured destruction (MAD) that was initially based on comparability of nuclear weapons capability, but then later changed to a doctrine of sufficiency, or an ability to inflict unacceptable damage on the opponent after absorbing their first strike. Under Reagan, strategy took a radical turn to try to achieve the goal of invulnerability, first posited by the Strategic Defence Initiative (SDI) or Star Wars, and currently in 2005 modified in the Ballistic Missile Defense Program (BMDP) to protect the US against a limited nuclear missile attack. Security priorities dictated and dictate that the people should defer to the strategic specialists and the politicians. More recently strategic defence doctrine has had to address the threat from terrorism and rogue states, for which the traditional deterrence option is impotent. Albert Wohlstetter, a major influence on leading neo-conservatives, and particularly on a young Richard Perle, has pointed out the significance of smart weapons in this context. They could be used to intervene against rogue states pre-emptively against clear and present dangers or even preventatively against less clear and less present dangers with clinical accuracy and without unacceptable collateral damage (i.e. death of innocent civilians).[19] This introduces a different kind of problem. Deterrence can work passively: pre-emptive/preventative interventions cannot. They necessarily involve strikes against other states, or targets within other states and the loss of lives both foreign and American. This more pro-active strategy, particularly in its preventative mode, highlights both the problem of democratic control of foreign policy and its moral justification.

Some of the above are perennial problems for democracies. Abraham Lincoln struggled to reconcile interests of state with democratic values in the

Civil War when he unconstitutionally suspended habeas corpus, arguing that violation of one law was justified if it meant that the constitution and the Union could be saved. In the end there is no easy solution to this problem. What really count are judgement and the quality of the justification for departing from first principles in order to secure their long-term continuation. In the hands and in the judgement of an Abraham Lincoln we might feel comfortable, but less so in the hands and judgement of a Colonel North. In addition to these perennial problems, however, is the novel and dangerous one introduced by George W. Bush – the strategic doctrine of preventative strike. In examining that strategic doctrine as he revisited the imperial presidency thesis in 2005, Schlesinger expressed fears that George W. Bush had resurrected its dangers once again.[20]

Conclusion

The question of who makes foreign policy cannot be answered without the intellectual context that was outlined in the opening sections of this chapter. That context tells us something about what to look for in terms of the style and some of the presuppositions and beliefs that decision-makers are likely to have: in a way it gives us an angle on who they are. However, even when structured into a coherent ideology, the relationship between beliefs and action is difficult to establish at a general level. Some scholars see ideology and action in a causal relationship. This is generally the case with New Left historians who place much emphasis on the dynamics of capitalism determining US policy (see Chapter 4). Others are less deterministic, seeing ideology as simply a tool for justifying actions ex post facto, or as one among a number of important variables in the explanation of US foreign policy behaviour. Realists believe that systemic structures of the international system explain foreign policy and that these variables override ideological beliefs (see Chapter 9). The new breed of neo-conservatives, in ascendance in George W. Bush's administration, have an unusual combination of idealism and realism with their ideological commitment to the spread of American-style democracy and an emphasis on the unilateral use of American hard power. This could make manifest the dangers identified with what Oakshott and Lal have termed enterprise imperialism.

In later sections of this chapter signposts were erected, which indicate the likely places to look to discover which agency or department, or which office holder, formulates and conducts policy. The direction in which these signposts point will often be determined by both the character and disposition of whoever holds presidential office and the general contours of the international terrain, such as Cold War, post-Cold War and post-9/11 worlds. Although the core, consisting of the President, the State Department, the NSC and the NSA, will always be at the centre of things, other departments and agencies will be influential when matters pertaining to their expertise are at issue. In addition, often having impact on this institutional system are other influences, such as the media, public opinion and lobbyists. Finally, weaving in and out of the interstices of policy-making runs the work of the Congress, consulting, advising, overseeing, empowering and restraining.

Although the traumas of the 1970s sensitised the Congress and the public to important problems to do with the evolution, formulation and execution of foreign policy, and particularly to the problem of democratic control, they provided no easy or automatic answers. The Cold War superpower confrontation continued to provide national security grounds for an assertive and energetic foreign policy run by the Executive. With the end of the Cold War and the demise of the immediate security threat to the US, greater potential for constraining and democratically controlling the formulation and execution of policy seemed to emerge. The post-Cold War world challenged long-held convictions that the US must play a major international role, that the main priority of that role was and still is containment of potential challengers, and that national security demands a bipartisan consensus to empower the President to act vigorously and with a great deal of discretion in foreign policy. The Clinton administration emphasised assertive multilateralism to deal with international problems and sponsored a policy of engagement and democratic and free-market enlargement to replace containment. But, these attempts to redefine US foreign policy had only limited success (see Chapters 9 to 12). The death of US troops in Somalia in 1993 led to disillusionment. There soon emerged a lack of consensus, a more partisan approach to foreign policy, and more concentration on economic issues, exports and jobs. That drew traditional domestic constituencies into the foreign policy arena, made direction of foreign policy more difficult, and injected democratic powers of control forcibly into the foreign policy-making field. For better or worse, what has been termed the constitutional invitation to struggle for power was reintroduced into foreign affairs, but then came 9/11 and once again immediate priorities of national security took centre stage and were used to trump other priorities that for a short while had emerged in the 1990s. Once again debate arose about the proper use of power, its democratic and constitutional control and the answerability of the Executive to the Congress and the public. For many, the spectre of the Imperial Presidency seemed immanent once again in the atmosphere that now pervaded Washington.

2 The US and the Cold War
Explanation and containment

The Cold War was born in the mid-1940s: terminal illness took hold in 1989 and it expired in December 1991 along with the Soviet Union. But, what caused it: historical enmity, economic rivalry, an ideological crusade, a geopolitical power struggle, or a complex mixture of all four? And once it arrived, how was it to be dealt with? The US answer of containment strategy was as simplistic as it was amorphous and confronted American policy-makers throughout the Cold War with fundamental questions and terrible dilemmas. Did the best guarantee of international security lie in the threat of mass nuclear genocide? What were the limits of American power? What tools should be used to pursue containment? What, even, was the primary objective of containment: victory or managed coexistence?

Cold War: origins and debate

US–Soviet relations before 1945 were mixed but antagonisms generally predominated. The US supported, with other capitalist powers, the Whites in the Russian Civil War and refused to recognise the Soviet Union until 1933. After recognition relations improved, but then deteriorated badly because of Stalin's purges and show trials of the 1930s, the Nazi–Soviet pact of 1939 and the subsequent partitioning of parts of Europe. From 1941 until 1945 there was a Faustean pact against Nazi Germany. America acknowledged the huge Soviet physical, material and human cost incurred in defeating the Germans and the Soviets were grateful for US Lend–Lease aid. Nevertheless, relations were still punctuated with disputes and suspicions. The Soviets feared a separate Anglo-American peace with Hitler that would allow Germany to continue the war on the eastern front (a sort of Nazi–Soviet pact in reverse). When that did not happen they suspected that the West deliberately delayed D-Day to leave the Red Army to do most of the fighting against the Wehrmacht. For their part, the Americans were suspicious about the Katyn massacre, which slaughtered much of the Polish officer class (we now know that it was a Soviet and not a Nazi war crime), and about the pause of the Red Army before entering Warsaw, which allowed the Nazis to level the Ghetto and eliminate the pro-Western Polish Home Army. There were also recurrent mutual suspicions about post-war intentions.

Three clusters of economic facts were of great significance. First, the Soviets were bitterly disappointed when the US abruptly stopped much needed Lend–Lease aid after victory in Europe. This was required by American law, but they perceived it as an unfriendly prelude to US demands for political concessions in return for aid: a tactic that President Truman did indeed pursue. Second, the US had become the world's economic colossus in the war. How to sustain that concerned US planners deeply. It was particularly important to avoid a return to the inter-war division of the world economy that had seen the US turn inwards, Britain retreat behind reinforced barriers of its empire, Germany attempt informal economic predominance in Central and South-eastern Europe, Japan dominate a co-prosperity zone in East Asia and the USSR attempt socialism in one country. Their answer was to internationalise New Deal reforms to make the face of capitalism acceptable and its performance more stable and accountable by exercising US management through the IMF and the General Agreement on Tariffs and Trade (GATT). The Soviets, though, did not share this economic vision and by 1946 had rejected participation in the US grand capitalist design. Third, Europe needed economic reconstruction to promote self-help and this meant that Germany's economy, as the potential economic powerhouse of Europe, had to be revived. The Soviets would perceive that as a threat because most of Germany was under Western control but the alternative of the US pouring in endless resources to feed, house and clothe people was unacceptable. The dollar and humanitarian cost would be too high, America would lose important markets and there was a risk that a post-war recession would deliver again the kind of social and political unrest that had fostered totalitarianism in the 1930s.

Defeat of Germany and Japan allowed the incompatibility of Western capitalism and Soviet communism, derived from different economic systems and clashing views on individual and collective rights, to regain prominence. Ideological differences surfaced over economic issues and the treatment of Soviet-liberated Europe. Controversy arose about democracy and freedom. The West resented Soviet sway over Poland especially when Britain and France had, at least nominally, gone to war to safeguard it from Nazi totalitarianism. The Soviets stipulated that the Polish government had to be 'friendly'. This was understandable given that the USSR had been invaded three times in 30 years via Poland and had lost over 20 million people in the most recent attack. However, Soviet-style democracy for Poland was hard for Americans to accept and contrary to what they thought had been agreed at the Yalta Conference in early 1945. Furthermore, potential American and Soviet leadership of liberal democratic and communist movements respectively imbued domestic politics worldwide with a Cold War strategic quality. The West feared that post-war conditions encouraged both the popularity of socialism or communism and Soviet 'subversion' of non-communist regimes. The CIA concluded in 1947 that the principal threat to American national security was economic collapse in Western Europe and the consequent accession to power of communist elements.[1] This was made more likely by burgeoning communist party memberships – respectively 1 million and 1.7 million in France and Italy,

1945–47 – and by the weakened condition of traditional European politics and interest groups following the depression and a second world war just 30 years after the Versailles Peace Treaty concluded the 'war to end all wars'. Farther afield Europe's colonial powers struggled to retain their imperial possessions as instruments for recovering their own economic power and status, and in the process they strengthened the association made by nationalist movements between the West and colonial repression.

Geopolitical concerns were prominent for both Stalin and Truman. Postwar America enjoyed a power position that was unprecedented, but it was also very aware of how technology had rendered the homeland vulnerable, of its interdependence with Western Europe especially, and of its dual interest in an open trading system and avoidance of a return to the geostrategic competition that had led to the Second World War. Stalin's rapid consolidation of Central and Eastern Europe as a Soviet sphere of influence has often been criticised as unnecessary and provocative. Yet, from the Soviet perspective history, ideology and security demands arising from the USSR's particular geostrategic position justified stripping German assets and creating an extensive buffer zone in Europe. The future of Germany was uncertain and the traditional problems of its *Mittellage* were yet to be overcome – other than through quadripartite Allied occupation. Also, the USSR's position vis-à-vis the US was unenviable. It had a greatly inferior industrial base, an economy less than one quarter that of the US, no atomic weapons, very limited naval and power projection capabilities, and lengthy borders with potentially multiple enemies. For example, after the split with China in the 1960s, it had to deploy approximately 25% of its conventional forces along the Sino-Soviet border. It was thus logical to complement a 'friendly' Poland with reincorporation of the Baltic States, which protected maritime access to the central Russian plain and land access to Leningrad, and the securing of communist control over Romania, Bulgaria and Hungary – all of which had been willing German wartime accomplices.[2] It was reasonable, too, to resent the exclusion of Soviet forces from the occupation of Japan, Western demands for national self-determination within Soviet-controlled Europe and, particularly, the apparent reneging on commitments made at Potsdam when in September 1946 US Secretary of State Byrnes aired plans for German rehabilitation and self-government, at least within Anglo-American zones of occupation.

Which of these factors was paramount in triggering the Cold War has been the source of heated debate. Traditional American interpretations emphasised a defensive US response to a Soviet threat whereby the Kremlin's quest for world domination thwarted Roosevelt's plans for peaceful accommodation and collaboration through the UN. The subsequent revisionist school emphasised instead factors such as US economic greed and America's own expansionist tradition, especially its uncompromising drive for a capitalist world economy that structurally empowered itself and was so clearly contrary to Soviet interests. In turn, both interpretative schools have been criticised for their essentially bipolar attribution of causes of the Cold War. Many historians advanced a more complex picture whereby the superpowers were the central players but were also used and influenced by third parties for purposes often little to do directly with the Cold War.[3] This spawned from the 1970s a host of other explanations that have been broadly characterised as post-revisionist, corporatist, neo-realist or world systems. Still further revisions are currently underway as a consequence of new material becoming available, especially from former Soviet archives. Knowledge of the onset of the Cold War has increased, but the possibility of a consensus about its causes has all but disappeared.[4]

The road to containment

President Roosevelt pondered the dilemmas of providing for international security and prosperity for much of the war and concluded that regardless of ideological differences it was imperative to co-opt the Soviets into post-war security arrangements. Those arrangements were an artful mixture of idealistic collective security apparatus and realist power politics. The UN looked like a collective security organisation where all would be responsible for each other's security, but effective policing depended upon great power unanimity. Derived from this realist view of power was the provision of the right of veto for the USSR, the US, Britain, France and China – the permanent members of the Security Council. In addition, Roosevelt and Truman expected that each great power would have primary responsibility, working with the UN, for its own area. Implicit was recognition of Western and Soviet rights to zones of influence and that, although internationalism had gained the ascendancy over isolationism in the US, there was no American desire to remain in the heart of Europe.

The problem with all this was how to maintain great power consensus. The Second World War redistributed world power dramatically and left France temporarily out of the power equation, China in the throes of civil war, Germany prostrate, and Japan occupied and devastated by the atomic trauma of Hiroshima and Nagasaki. Britain was severely weakened militarily and economically and faced huge problems as a result of its unusual dependence on overseas trade, which had been severely disrupted, and of nationalist challenges to its imperial possessions. The key considerations were consequently Soviet power, US power and the danger of a revival of German power. Once the Soviets and Americans began to fear each other's intentions, neither side could allow Germany to move fully within the other's camp. This was why the German problem was such a sensitive issue and why partition became semi-permanent.

Matters were made worse because the allied working relationship between Stalin, Roosevelt and Churchill was broken in 1945, first by Roosevelt's death and then by Churchill's electoral defeat. In April 1945, evidence of strained relations surfaced in a notorious meeting between President Truman and Vyacheslav Molotov, the Soviet Foreign Minister, whom the President scolded for Soviet failure to keep agreements on Poland. Truman still resisted the hardline approach favoured by the British and sent Roosevelt's old trusted stalwart

Harry Hopkins as a personal envoy to Moscow to try to sort out problems: the gesture was to little avail. Confusion about the Potsdam Conference (1945) agreement about reparations and Soviet dominance of Poland, unilateral actions in Eastern Europe, non-participation in the IMF, demands on Turkey, and refusal in early 1946 to honour a wartime agreement to withdraw from northern Iran, all alarmed the US. After strong American demands, and suffering adverse publicity in the UN, the Soviets eventually withdrew from Iran, but Truman was now worried about their intentions. With the UN rendered largely ineffective by the veto and an ideological divide, it became clear that the US would have to look after its own security affairs. In Washington, hardline anti-communists in the State Department were making their voices heard, especially after Stalin's belligerent call for Soviet rearmament in February 1946. George Kennan, a long-standing Soviet expert, responded with the most famous diplomatic message of modern times – the Long Telegram – from the US Moscow Embassy on 22 February. He warned of the USSR's tendency to expansion and of the need for the US to oppose it resolutely. This articulated many of the inchoate fears and concerns in the minds of Washington officials. British Prime Minister Winston Churchill then added to the anti-Soviet momentum in his famous speech at Fulton Missouri on 5 March 1946. Conjuring up apocalyptic dangers with his powerful rhetoric, he dramatically called for Anglo-American cooperation to resist Soviet communism and spoke of an iron curtain having descended from Stettin in the Baltic to Trieste in the Adriatic.

The US began to act with less regard for Soviet sensitivities in prudent moves to safeguard Western interests. In May 1946 General Lucius Clay suspended German reparation shipments from the American zone of occupation. In December 1946, British and American zones of occupation in Germany were merged to create Bizonia. On 24 February 1947, Britain formally informed the US that it could no longer give military assistance to Greece and Turkey: two key countries where the Soviets were thought to have ambitions. President Truman responded with one of the most dramatic diplomatic announcements of all time and demonstrated clearly internationalism's triumph over isolationism in the US. The Truman Doctrine pledged help to countries to resist aggression from internal or external sources and more specifically provided assistance to replace Britain's in Greece and Turkey.

In May 1947, William Clayton, Under-Secretary of State for Economic Affairs, reported that economic distress in Europe was far worse than anticipated and forecasted political and social disaster unless action was taken. A month later, the new Secretary of State, General George Marshall, who was less conciliatory than his predecessor James Byrnes, proposed a European Recovery Programme in his famous Harvard Speech. This became the Marshall Plan and ultimately provided Europe with over $13 billion of economic aid spread over five years subject to participating countries devising a common recovery programme as a prelude to European unity.[5] Technically, it was open to Soviet participation, but neither the US nor its closest ally, Britain, had any intentions of allowing them to take part. In fact, they correctly anticipated that the USSR would regard the plan as an attempt to lure Soviet satellites into the Western camp and, consequently, find unacceptable its conditions and its inherent potential to spread capitalist contagion to command economies. With the implementation of Marshall Aid came the economic division of Europe and, most important of all, of East from West Germany. This was highly provocative to the Soviets with the danger of capitalist infection spreading via a newly created Deutschmark into Eastern Europe. They reacted by closing ground access to the Western redoubt in Berlin, thus precipitating the first major Cold War crisis. The West countered with a prolonged airlift from June 1948 to May 1949.[6] The USSR moved to consolidate its hold over Eastern Europe, establishing the Council for Mutual Economic Assistance (COMECON) in 1949 and shifting from coalition tactics to a process of Stalinisation, removing, most notably in Prague, the last vestiges of pro-Western elements from government. Meantime Western European countries began to organise for defence against both the USSR and a potential *revanchist* Germany. In March 1948 Britain, France and the Benelux countries concluded a mutual defence agreement through the Brussels Treaty Organisation (BTO). However, this lacked the capacity to counter the 2.9 million men that the USSR still had under arms and so, under great pressure, the Truman administration finally provided a security guarantee to Western Europe. In April 1949 the US agreed the North Atlantic Treaty Organisation (NATO), an intergovernmental military alliance that provided for mutual defence. It subsequently dominated West Europe's hard security arrangements throughout the Cold War and became the principal vehicle of American influence in Europe (see Chapter 5).

NATO's first Secretary-General, Lord Ismay, famously described the organisation's function as being to 'keep the Americans in, the Russians out and the Germans down'. Ineluctably, lines were being drawn. A sequence of actions and reactions, security concerns and clashing ideologies, economic incompatibilities, difficult personalities, and the historical baggage of mutual suspicions were snatching defeat from the jaws of victory. War was to be succeeded by Cold War, not by peace.

Containment and its conduct

In July 1947, Kennan anonymously published in *Foreign Affairs* an elaboration on his Long Telegram entitled 'The Sources of Soviet Conduct'. He wrote: 'Soviet pressure against the free institutions of the Western world is something that can be contained by the adroit and vigilant application of counter-force at a series of constantly shifting geographical and political points.'[7] This became known as containment and became official policy under Kennan's stewardship as Director of the newly established State Department Policy Planning Staff (PPS). He believed that there were five key industrial centres in the world: the US, Britain, Germany and central Europe, Japan and the Soviet Union. Four were in the West and one was in the East and this was the way things should remain. Elsewhere, the West could be flexible, because points on the periphery were expendable. Over the next 42 years, containment went through various permutations along a continuum that stretched from selective flexible power responses to meet whatever threats were mounted by the enemy, to a commitment to massive retaliation against whatever breach of the containment line was made. Where the US should stand on this continuum preoccupied its strategists throughout the Cold War.

The particular stances of successive US administrations are examined in Chapter 3, but it is important to acknowledge at the onset that resolving upon a strategy of containment immediately posed US policy-makers with enduring questions and problems. Foremost of these was: what was the ultimate object-ive of containment? Was it the defeat of the USSR or the managed coexistence of the two superpowers? American emphases ebbed and flowed herein and it is fascinating to find upon the end of the Cold War the George H. Bush adminis-tration working hard to support a weakened Soviet Union and its leader Mikhail Gorbachev as a partner in stability.

Containment also continually asked of what means the US should use and develop in its prosecution. Calculating Soviet actual military capability required assessment of numbers and types of strategic and theatre nuclear forces; conventional air, ground and naval forces; power projection capability; civil defence; and active defences. To this was added potential forces vested in a state's technological base, research and development activities, number and expertise of skilled technicians, availability of critical resources, economic strengths and vulnerabilities, and the quantity and quality of reserve forces.[8] It quickly became apparent that nuclear weapons would be a centrepiece of the US–USSR relationship and that strategists would face major challenges in managing the nuclear balance. These weapons were not so much about waging but deterring war and were also sources of political influence, coercion and military advantage. Moreover they begged terrible questions. What constituted an unacceptable loss? The McNamara criterion set this at 400 megaton-class nuclear warheads delivered to the designated targets of a pos-sible adversary on its territory. The objective was to ensure that the US could kill one-quarter to one-third of the Soviet population and destroy two-thirds of Soviet industrial capacity in a retaliatory strike. These criteria underwent a number of subsequent revisions but exactly what the Soviets thought consti-tuted an unacceptable loss nobody knew with certainty. Also, how did the Soviets regard nuclear weapons – as instruments for defence, political leverage or military superiority? How did they see US nuclear capabilities and strategy – superior or inferior, in relative ascendancy or decline, as aggressive or defen-sive? Furthermore, immense destructive power was vested in highly fallible human hands and control systems. But MAD assumed perfect rationality and perfect detection. This meant that all nuclear states would behave by the rules of MAD, that no leader would risk launching a first strike in the hope of disabling their adversary's second-strike capabilities and that complete secur-ity was guaranteed of the launch decision process. Nor could there be false positives, possibility of camouflaging a launch or imperfect attribution. In retrospect it is known that these assumptions did not prevail. In the Cuban

Missile Crisis, Soviet troops in Cuba had battlefield nuclear weapons and ultimate control over these weapons depended on the local commander and his loyalty to the Kremlin (see Chapter 6). On 6 December 1950, US officials initially confused flights of geese with a Soviet launch and in 1979 alone 78 missile display conferences were called to evaluate detections potentially threatening the US.

Strategists had also to respond to relative changes in nuclear capability and to technological advance. American atomic strikes against Japan during the Second World War initially conferred upon the US arsenal enormous power, for it demonstrated willingness to use that destructive capability. However, this willingness was at a time of no conceivable retaliatory response and thus became increasingly uncertain as the USSR developed its own nuclear arsenal and delivery systems. In fact, the Soviets tested with unexpected speed their first atomic bomb at Semipalatinsk on 29 August 1949, something greatly assisted by significant espionage within the Los Alamos project. The US had clear strategic supremacy during the 1950s and the Eisenhower administration adopted a policy of massive retaliation in 1954, which focused on mass destruction of enemy civilian populations. That was increasingly challenged from the late 1950s because it lacked strategic flexibility and the development of submarine launched ballistic missiles (SLBMs) made a survivable nuclear force possible and a second-strike capability credible. In addition, the risks associated with massive retaliation increased exponentially as the Soviet nuclear arsenal grew and they successfully tested an ICBM. Incautious rhetoric by Soviet leader Krushchev contributed to consequent US fears of a 'missile gap'. This subsequently proved fictitious but demonstrated nevertheless the importance and potential dangers of the perception factor in managing the nuclear relationship.

US nuclear strategy consequently shifted again in the early 1960s, especially under Secretary of Defense Robert McNamara, towards MAD. Strategic stability would be provided for by the US and USSR each having either a first-strike or second-strike capability. This fuelled an arms race and put the emphasis on second strike as a defensive option, particularly as both sides developed multiple independently targetable re-entry vehicles (MIRVs) that rendered effective anti-ballistic missile (ABM) systems greatly more difficult and expensive. For instance, the US LG-118A Peacekeeper missile could hold ten warheads with an explosive yield in excess of 230 Hiroshima-type bombs. To calm this arms race the US looked in the late 1960s and 1970s to finesse MAD with notions of political sufficiency or 'essential equivalence'. Under this formulation US nuclear capabilities had to be sufficient to ensure both nuclear stability and that Soviet nuclear forces were not able to become instruments of political leverage, coercion or military advantage. The Carter administration complemented nuclear weapons sufficiency with a countervailing strategy. Endorsed in PD-59 on 25 July 1980, this determined that US nuclear forces had to be sufficiently flexible to enable a graduated response to Soviet attacks. This theoretically enhanced the US deterrent by obviating the dilemma of massive retaliation in the face of Soviet aggression that was serious but which fell short of total war. The objective was to convince Moscow that any level of aggression would incur an unacceptably high price. It did not reject MAD based on targeting urban and industrial targets but did seemingly accept the plausibility of fighting a limited nuclear war that, by prioritising the destruction of the Soviet leadership and military targets, emphasised counter-force rather than counter-city strikes.

The concept of limited nuclear war was fraught with dangers, not least uncertainty about Soviet reciprocity and about how to ensure 'management' in an inevitable crisis situation that would prevent escalation to total war. Some critics also saw the possibility of limited nuclear war as destabilising because it theoretically reduced relative risks and in reality required that the US obtain superiority in limited war capabilities.[9] These criticisms became particularly vocal once the Reagan administration added an aggressive nuclear build-up and announcement of SDI to rhetoric about limited nuclear war.

SDI met well the idea that 'in order to extract maximum benefits from the deployment of military forces, their structure and modes of operation must be deliberately aimed at projecting images of power in ways that are readily absorbed by the world-wide "audience" of political actors and opinion-makers'.[10] Yet missile defence theoretically contributed to strategic destabilisation by promising the US relatively greater defence against nuclear attack. In the case of threshold states, or those having recently acquired nuclear weapons, SDI potentially neutralised their first-strike option and made them more susceptible to coercive American diplomacy. In the case of the USSR it encouraged ideas of a 'survivable' nuclear war and, in Soviet eyes at least, the likelihood of an American first strike in the expectation that the US could absorb at acceptable cost those retaliatory Soviet missiles that penetrated its missile defence shield.

These different permutations of US nuclear strategy were all in one way or another flawed. According to Lawrence Freedman, stability ultimately came to depend 'more on the antithesis of strategy rather than its apotheosis – on threats that things will get out of hand, that we might act irrationally, that possibly through inadvertence we could set in motion a process that in its development and conclusion would be beyond human control and comprehension'.[11] The nuclear age also threw up sharp ironies and apparent contradictions. A US that promulgated liberalism, democracy and human rights embraced the possibility of mass nuclear genocide as its premier defence. The US also invested far less in shelters to ensure the survivability of its civilian population in the event of a Soviet nuclear attack than in ensuring sufficient survivability of its triad of ICBMs, SLBMs and strategic bombers to guarantee that annihilation would be mutual in the event of full-scale war and that the consequent nuclear winter would destroy much of what life was left on earth. Indeed, Arnold Toynbee prophesised in 1948 that the nation-state and the split atom could not coexist on this planet.[12] Furthermore, fear of Armageddon effectively made the Clausewitzian idea of war as an instrument of policy redundant and, especially after the Cuban Missile Crisis, both sides abandoned military victory in favour of regulating nuclear arms competition.

In the 1960s agreement was struck to ban nuclear and other weapons from Antarctica and nuclear weapons tests in the atmosphere, outer space and under water. The May 1972 Interim Agreement on the Limitation of Strategic Offensive Arms froze deployment of ICBMs, limited the growth of SLBMs and provided for the ABM Treaty, which was generally regarded as codifying nuclear deterrence based on mutual vulnerability and became seen as the cornerstone of strategic stability. Even the Reagan administration became known as much for the Strategic Arms Reduction Talks (START) and Reagan's abhorrence of nuclear weapons as for SDI and its initial reinvigoration of the Cold War.

This combination of containment and the nuclear core of the Cold War had profound consequences for how and where the Cold War was fought, and for the US itself. While direct US–USSR nuclear war became countered by mutual vulnerability, the peaceful division of Europe as the Cold War front-line was maintained foremost through a tacit quid pro quo. US nuclear guarantees to NATO effectively offset perceived Soviet conventional superiority while the USSR countered NATO's integration of conventional and battlefield nuclear weapons – essentially a first-strike doctrine – by stressing that even limited nuclear attack on its forces would be regarded as global nuclear war. This in turn progressively shifted the focus of the Cold War to the periphery and to limited superpower conflict by proxy, which often led US policy-makers to overlay complex regional problems with simplistic and frequently inappropriate containment prescriptions. As will be seen in subsequent chapters, the policies of the USSR were often lesser obstacles to US objectives than were power vacuums, economic dislocation, revolutionary nationalism and internecine dispute. In many cases US economic largess and supply of arms, military training and logistical support to proxy forces exacerbated indigenous problems, even if at the Cold War level US and Soviet initiatives were held in balance. Also, US policy-makers frequently faced difficult choices between American principles of democracy, anti-colonialism and national self-determination and the demands of maintaining beneficial short-term stability, which might best be served by cooperation with colonial powers and dictators, subverting democratic processes, or even armed intervention – especially in the Western Hemisphere in defence of the Monroe Doctrine.

Containment also necessitated that the US develop an extensive network of allies and alliances throughout the Free World. These were sources of security contributions, political influence, strategic raw materials and offensive and defensive military bases – especially important before the development of ICBMs in ensuring Soviet nuclear vulnerability. At the same time these allies were often a significant drain on American resources, uncooperative in elements of American strategy and, especially in the Third World, less interested in the Cold War than in development and local antagonisms. As will be seen later, the Truman administration invested billions of dollars in European post-war economic and military recovery but Western Europe later posed significant economic challenges to the US and its member states often pursued policies not favoured by Washington – such as *Ostpolitik*, France's *force de frappe* and resistance to the possible use of the atomic bomb in Korea and the deployment of Pershing II and Cruise missiles in Europe in the 1980s. Third World countries absorbed US resources but frequently failed to deliver the political and economic reforms favoured by American policy-makers and demanded a New International Economic Order (NIEO) in the 1970s. US client states exploited their strategic significance to secure economic, political and military advantage, and occasionally the US completely lost its investment as unpopular regimes it supported were overthrown – such as the Shah's Iran. In short, containment led the US to face the classic dilemma of a hegemon: how much of the burden of maintaining the system could it sustain, and for how long, without over-extending itself and entering relative decline?

Then there was the problem of deciding what, in a policy of containment, constituted the national interest. Could the US tolerate non-alignment? How credible was domino theory and what national interest criterion justified the Vietnam War? Were there regions of the world in which the US did not have a vital national interest? Did the US national interest differ from collective Western interests and, if so, to what effect? Should the US wage nuclear war for limited objectives and/or in defence of physically distant allies? If so, when and why? Was it right to dedicate so much of America's resources to containment at the expense of neglected domestic issues, especially when allies consumed American security and contributed proportionately less? Answers to these and still more questions differed depending on where on the containment continuum an administration stood, international circumstances at the time and the temper of domestic politics.

Finally there was the question of appropriate tools for fighting the Cold War. Nuclear calculations meant that strategic deterrence consumed massive amounts of American economic, technical and material resources. One estimate put the cost of maintaining US offensive strategic forces during the Cold War at almost \$2 trillion.[13] Yet this massive investment was made principally to maintain superpower stalemate, albeit that there were significant political spin-offs and, especially during the Reagan administration, there were ideas that accelerated nuclear build-up might economically cripple the USSR and cause its weakening if not collapse. This shifted the military calculation to ensuring sufficient conventional forces to thwart a Soviet attack on a scale that was not deemed to exceed the threshold of cause for nuclear war – itself undefined – and to supporting client states, allies and proxy fighters. Beyond this military means had declining utility, certainly in influencing the overall Cold War balance. It consequently became important to marshal other instruments to fight for the hearts and minds of the world's peoples, attack the principles of the Soviet system and combat communism's potential allure, especially in the case of Third World nationalist movements that were often preoccupied with fighting Western colonialism. It also became important to deny the Soviets technology and resources, to send signals of intent and resolve short of military action to allies and enemies alike, and even to socialise the Soviets into the Western system through selected East–West trade. All of this put increasing emphasis on diplomacy, psychological warfare, holding together US allies and economic statecraft (see Chapter 4).

Conclusion

The precise causes and origins of the Cold War remain debated and interpretations will continue to be refined as theories of international relations evolve and particularly as former Soviet documents become available for public scrutiny. That said, simplistic interpretations blaming either the US or USSR have been discounted and replaced with much more nuanced accounts. These acknowledge variously the impact of technological change, Great Power rivalry, particular state security concerns, interplay between the domestic and international realms, international political economy, ideological rivalry, national liberation movements and the role of non-state actors. Furthermore, the variety of accounts owes much both to the availability of material, which has become more voluminous over the years, and sometimes to the political inclination and preconceptions of the writers of history.

US policy-makers also interpreted world events through their own values and the prescriptions of containment strategy. The transition from winning the war to losing the peace was remarkably quick and technology dictated significantly where and how the Cold War would be fought. Yet policy-makers at the time had no sure knowledge of this and wrestled continuously with the contradictions within containment and tried to react judiciously to uncertain threats on the basis of incomplete information. It is this human factor that made nuclear Armageddon frighteningly possible and resistible. It is also, as will be seen in the next chapter, what helped position successive US administrations differently along the containment continuum.

3 Superpower collaboration and confrontation

US containment policy, 1950–91

Containment gave policy-makers a sense of purpose and an interpretative framework. It reduced complex local and regional problems to 'simple' calculations of East–West balance and competition. It was also a strategy readily communicable to domestic and international constituencies. As such it was a galvaniser of support for US policy and a great legitimising weapon, making 'acceptable' all variety of practices by invoking national security to justify dubious means for righteous ends. Ordinarily such practices would be seen as highly contentious and compromising of American leadership and moral authority.

Containment also encouraged overly prescriptive interpretations that were often inappropriate to local or regional problems. As a concept it was nebulous and underwent many incarnations in response both to different US administrations' interpretations of it and to evolving economic, technological, political, military, geostrategic and psychological conditions. Was it right to calculate East–West exchanges in zero-sum terms or, as Kennan suggested, was there scope for more flexibility? Was negotiation acceptable from any position other than one of overwhelming strength? How could allies best be held together, how much dissension could be tolerated, and how much control over them did Washington actually have? How much scope was there for adventurism and 'roll-back' in the nuclear era?

Truman and NSC-68

The first important twist to US containment policy was effected in 1950, largely by Paul Nitze, Kennan's successor as Director of the State Department PPS. The inspiration for this major review was multifaceted. First, the international system had evolved into a rigid bipolar configuration that challenged Kennan's flexible version of containment. Second, the Truman administration needed a bold policy in order to overcome American isolationist sentiment and to deflect charges of being 'soft' on communism, accusations which were emboldened by spy scandals and later by the onset of McCarthyism. Third, international events had deteriorated badly. While the Democrats had 'lost' China to Mao Tse-tung's communists in 1949, the Soviets had consolidated their power in Eastern Europe, challenged the West with the Berlin blockade and broken the American monopoly on the atomic bomb. Finally, a series of fears reflected a lack of confidence: fear of appeasement in the face of a new totalitarian challenge to democracy, fear that the economic crises of the 1930s might recur and lend weight to communism as a viable alternative to capitalism, and fear that decolonisation would weaken Britain and France especially and provide new opportunities for communism in the Third World.

The response to all these factors was National Security Council Resolution 68 (NSC-68), one of the most important, most debated and arguably the most seriously flawed documents in modern American history. Its general thrust was not new. Many of its objectives and assumptions had been set out previously in NSC-20/4 in November 1948: namely that the Soviets were intent upon expansionist strategies, the communist design meant that the Free World was in peril, and that it fell to the US to lead the resistance against the 'red menace'. The novelty of NSC-68 lay in its global reach, its military emphasis and its harsh tone. This had three serious and dangerous implications for US containment policy. First, the flexibility of Kennan's original version was lost because, in transforming containment from a selective to a perimeter fence strategy, the traditional hierarchy of interests became so blurred that national and global security became indistinguishable. Thereafter, policy-makers persistently failed to distinguish between geopolitical and ideological containment. Second, militarisation had profound implications for the means by which the US would combat communism. To rely on nuclear weapons threatened to lead the US into an appeasement trap because, unless it was prepared to start nuclear war as an indiscriminate response to every challenge, irrespective of the importance of the interests at stake, it would be forced to yield to Soviet pressure. Each time that happened, it would lose credibility and invite the Kremlin to push harder, particularly as the Soviet nuclear arsenal began to offset the strategic advantage of the American. Consequently, contrary to Kennan's ideas, the US and its allies had to develop conventional force capabilities to supplement the nuclear deterrent and be prepared and able to act wherever communism threatened. This militarised version of containment dominated both the rest of the Cold War and American society as a vast military–industrial complex developed to service the demands of NSC-68. Third, the 'tone' of NSC-68 was couched in apocalyptic terms: 'The issues that face us are momentous, involving the fulfilment or destruction not only of the Republic but of civilisation itself.'[1] Perforce America needed to take the initiative against communism and to change the nature of the Soviet system through a range of activities, including psychological and economic warfare, political pressure and covert operations. Moreover, NSC-68 formulated a Cold War calculus based on a 'zero-sum game', whereby any gain for communism would be a loss to the West. It was thus important that any negotiations with the Soviets should be from a position of overwhelming strength so as not to lose any ground, either literally or psychologically. The image and credibility of the US were more significant than ever before because policy-makers were convinced that perceptions of change in the balance of power were just as damaging as quantifiable ones. In other words, the US had constantly to send the right signals and warnings to allies and enemies alike in order to give the appearance and/or reality of either maintaining the status quo or improving the West's position.

Had it not been for the outbreak of the Korean War in June 1950, it is extremely unlikely that NSC-68 would have secured the backing of Congress because of the vast expense involved. Once approved, though, its effects were profound and obvious. In the short term, defence expenditure mushroomed to over $50 billion, or 18.5% of US gross national product (GNP). To maintain the American strategic supremacy, Truman approved the development of the hydrogen bomb and US commitments overseas were increased, most notably by the decision to fight a land war in Asia to repel communism from South Korea (see Chapter 7). Also, to enhance the capabilities of the Free World, new alliances were sought and existing ones strengthened. In September 1950, America bolstered its commitment to conventional defence in Europe, in part to give heart to allies there and in part to persuade them to accept West German remilitarisation. Furthermore, to counter criticism of the loss of China, the Truman administration took a hard, even provocative, line against Mao. In June 1950, the US Seventh Fleet was ordered to patrol the Taiwan Strait. This reversed Truman's gradual disengagement during the late 1940s and recommitted American support to Chiang Kai-shek's nationalists, whom Mao had driven from the Chinese mainland on to Taiwan.

In the longer term, NSC-68 both secured a bipartisan consensus in foreign policy, which would endure for two decades, except for a brief partisan skirmish over General MacArthur's conduct of the Korean War, and set the contours of American strategy for the remainder of the Cold War. It also successively secured the primacy of security above all other aspects of the budget, the militarisation of containment, and America's coming of age as a global police officer. However, the internal inconsistencies and oversimplifications in NSC-68 meant that it also bequeathed a series of problems to subsequent administrations. Significantly, Kennan did not endorse NSC-68.

NSC-68's vision of Kremlin-dominated world communism caused the US to misinterpret international affairs and to neglect initial opportunities to exploit fragmentation within the communist camp. The blurring of national with global security interests meant that instead of enhancing US security through an arms build-up, NSC-68 disproportionately increased US commitments and provided a dangerous recipe for overextension. The prescription that the US should only negotiate from a position of overwhelming strength provoked legitimate Soviet security fears and ran counter to the hopes of some Americans of socialising them into the existing international system. Furthermore, NSC-68 exposed the US to charges of hypocrisy and perversion of its own values. The authors of NSC-68 claimed that the US was disadvantaged significantly vis-à-vis the Soviet Union because the Kremlin had no moral standards other than those which served the communist revolution. Yet, at the same time, they declared that 'The integrity of our system will not be jeopardized by any measures, covert or overt, violent or non-violent, which serve the purpose of frustrating the Kremlin design'.[2] Most dangerously of all, NSC-68 failed to distinguish between geopolitical and ideological threats and thus, in the brutal frankness of J.L. Gaddis, made 'all interests vital, all means affordable, all methods justifiable'.[3] Just how a constitutional democracy could subscribe to this and still hold true both to itself and to its self-proclaimed moral superiority was a question that troubled successive administrations throughout the Cold War.

Eisenhower and the New Look

Eisenhower largely endorsed NSC-68. He accepted its view of international communism and the dangers it identified of communist subversion. He became extremely fond of the imagery of nations toppling successively to communism like a row of upended dominoes. But this was not as simplistic as it might first seem: Hitler had successively toppled types of dominoes in the 1930s period of appeasement when he rearmed, remilitarised the Rhineland, and annexed Austria, then the Sudetenland, and then the rest of Czechoslovakia. Eisenhower also believed that a communist victory anywhere was a triple defeat for the West: a potential ally was lost, an implacable enemy gained a new recruit, and US credibility was damaged. Furthermore, his Secretary of State, John Foster Dulles, epitomised a missionary vision whereby the world aspired to be like America and America had to champion the rights of both the voiceless and, at times, unenlightened. In fact, the battle between 'right' and 'wrong' was so clear that Dulles had little time for either non-alignment or neutrality, concepts he regarded as short-sighted and immoral.

Eisenhower's New Look strategy, which emerged in 1953 from a government review called Operation Solarium, differed significantly from its predecessor in several respects. It rejected the profligacy of NSC-68 with its assumption that 20% of GNP could be devoted to defence. The Republicans were committed to balanced budgets and tax cuts and Eisenhower was personally convinced that the US people would not sanction an indefinite sacrifice for an unwinnable war, which is what defensive containment seemed to entail. Whereas Truman had justified massive expenditure on the grounds that it was the threat of communism, rather than bankruptcy, which challenged America, Eisenhower warned that care had to be taken that waging containment did not impose so many demands upon the American economy that it destroyed the very system it was trying to defend. This was all too possible if the budget got out of hand, or if rigid regimentation were necessary to harness productive capacity, or if the US got sucked into costly conflicts. Indeed, Eisenhower's first major contribution to this approach was to end the expensive and futile fighting in Korea. Thereafter, he cut back on military personnel and reined in military expenditure so successfully that throughout his administrations the defence budget remained significantly lower than Truman's, ranging between $35 and 42 billion.

The crux of the New Look was thus to accept the principles of NSC-68 but to prosecute them in ways that did not overburden American society. The resulting containment strategy had three key themes: renewed focus on nuclear weapons, burden-sharing with allies, and covert, economic and psychological warfare. Eisenhower took the US back to a reliance on its superiority in air power and nuclear weapons, so much so that he and Dulles conceived of small nuclear bombs as tactical weapons to be deployed in the event of a European conflict. The deterrent of massive atomic and thermonuclear retaliation had the double advantage of being cheaper than conventional forces and reducing reliance on overseas bases. Eisenhower authorised the B41, equivalent to 400 Hiroshima-type bombs, doubled the size of the US nuclear stockpile between 1953 and 1955, and deployed low-kiloton nuclear warheads in Europe that could be used as tactical weapons in a limited war. Dulles, in an aphorism for which he became infamous, proclaimed that the art of Cold War statecraft had become brinkmanship: 'The ability to get to the verge without getting into war is the necessary art.'[4]

The corollary to massive retaliation was to devise ways to retain some semblance of flexibility at minimum cost, particularly in the battle for the Third World. This came in three forms. First, the US looked increasingly to alliances and regional cooperation. The burden of global containment had to be shared, particularly in the Middle East where the US struggled to project unilateral power. It was important, too, to develop and display a sense of shared purpose in order to encourage resistance to communist subversion, to deter Soviet encroachment, and to subdue regional internecine disputes for the sake of a common front against communism. The ultimate aim was to encircle the Soviet Union and China with states aligned with the US. This would erect a perimeter fence and allow other states to guard it with their, rather than US, conventional forces. With this objective in mind, the US secured the integration of West German forces into NATO to bolster the European theatre. In the Middle East, it sponsored the Northern Tier and the Baghdad Pact (later CENTO). For Asia, it agreed on 8 September 1954 to the South East Asia Treaty Organisation (SEATO), comprised of itself, Britain, Australia, New Zealand, Pakistan, France, the Philippines and Thailand, and continued the ANZUS Pact concluded by Truman with New Zealand and Australia in 1951. These arrangements were supplemented by bilateral defence arrangements with countries such as Japan, South Korea and Nationalist China.

The second way to retain flexibility was to seize the Cold War initiative. The Republicans had criticised containment as 'negative, futile and immoral' because it did nothing for those enslaved by communism. In contrast, Dulles laced his public declarations with aggressive rhetoric about 'liberation' and 'rolling back' the frontiers of communism. This was predominately psychological warfare with the triple hope that, by striking various poses and sending messages, it would be possible to galvanise the American public, reassure American allies and discomfort the Soviet regime. However, Dulles's aspirations were also underpinned by what became a hallmark of Eisenhower's presidency: covert operations. The CIA helped to overthrow governments in Iran in 1953 and Guatemala in 1954 and tried unsuccessfully to do the same in Indonesia in 1958. It undertook, with the British, provocative intelligence-gathering over-flights of Soviet territory, and was also involved in guerrilla activities in North Vietnam, promoted disorder in Eastern Europe and monitored sections of both American and allied societies.

The final means to avoid dangerous rigidity were efforts to reduce tensions with the Soviets and to regulate the conduct of the Cold War. Eisenhower was concerned about an unsustainable arms race and the influence within America of the industrial–military complex, the latter featuring in his Farewell Address in January 1961. Key European allies were also interested in negotiating with the Soviets, especially British Prime Minister Winston Churchill, who was deeply troubled by Britain's vulnerability in the event of a nuclear exchange and desired at least to reduce East–West tension and at best to fashion some sort of grand Cold War settlement.[5] As Churchill observed at Bermuda in 1953, 'There should not be a question of finding a reason for suspicion for giving evil meaning to every move of the Soviets.'[6] Moreover, opportunity for dialogue seemingly improved as a result of auspicious changes in the international system, notably the winding down of the war in Korea, Stalin's death and allied arrangements which allowed West Germany to enter NATO and rearm.

During his presidency, Eisenhower held three summits with Soviet leaders, there were five foreign ministers' meetings, and a series of lower level talks ranging from arms control to culture. Cynics have interpreted Eisenhower's willingness to parley with the Soviets, in his later years in office, as just another form of psychological warfare. For example, they claim that his Open Skies initiative at the first Cold War summit in Geneva in July 1955, which proposed aerial surveillance of military installations to minimise the threat of a surprise attack, was an attempt to embarrass the Soviets, who were unlikely to accept. Others have seen a limited form of *détente* in Eisenhower's policy, especially towards the end of his second administration after McCarthyism was discredited and Krushchev had become the clear leader of the USSR. Eisenhower did abandon Truman's insistence on negotiating only from a position of overwhelming strength but his actual commitment to *détente* is questionable given the cavalier use of U-2 reconnaissance planes over the USSR in the run-up to the Paris Four Power Summit in May 1960. When the Soviets brought down a U-2 on 1 May, only two weeks before the summit, it created such a diplomatic furore that the conference was aborted.

All things considered, the New Look attempted 'containment on the cheap'. Truman's policy had been an assured response calculated to meet, but not exceed, the initial provocation wherever it might take place. Eisenhower's policy maintained certainty of response, but introduced uncertainty as to place and nature. The gamble was that uncertainty would breed Soviet caution and gain the US the initiative. Eisenhower was relatively successful. The defence budget was controlled, the US did not become embroiled in another foreign war, and relations with the Soviets were relatively peaceful – despite the US brandishing nuclear weapons over Korea and Taiwan, and the Soviets doing likewise over the Suez Crisis in 1956. Meantime US diplomacy, psychological warfare and economic statecraft sought to consolidate US allies and to prise Soviet satellites away from Moscow, especially Yugoslavia. However, this relative success may well owe as much to good luck as to good judgement because Eisenhower failed to resolve many of the contradictions bequeathed him by NSC-68. The Republicans contracted US means to prosecute containment short of nuclear retaliation, but actually increased US commitments through their alliance policy. Their rhetoric about 'roll-back' alarmed allies and raised false hopes, sometimes with disastrous effects, such as in the 1956 Hungarian uprising, which the Soviets mercilessly crushed. Although prepared to exploit differences between Moscow and its European satellite states especially, the administration failed to capitalise on Sino-Soviet differences, and a combination of Dulles's hostility to non-alignment and the difficulty of distinguishing between national liberation and communist movements jeopardised US integrity in the Third World. Indeed, this often swept the US into a posture pitted against both change and its traditional anti-colonial values. Furthermore, brinkmanship, relying predominantly on nuclear weapons, was dangerously rigid, held potentially disastrous consequences, and was morally repugnant for many. It embraced the potential for mass nuclear genocide as America's principal defence and forced consideration of a first-strike strategy and the treatment of nuclear weapons as conventional weapons, despite the fact that NATO war games revealed that even a limited nuclear conflict would destroy most of Central Europe. Moreover, retrospective analysis has indicated that in the Taiwan crisis in 1955 Eisenhower took the US far closer than previously thought to the 'nuclear brink'.[7]

Kennedy, Johnson and flexible response

By the 1960s, the Cold War was changing in terms of focus and required strategy. The Soviets and the Chinese were busy supporting Third World liberation movements and on 4 October 1957 the USSR launched Sputnik 1. This demonstration of Soviet technical ability to develop ICBMs suggested that they were rapidly closing the technological gap and that the nuclear relationship was headed towards stalemate. The Cold War confrontation now focused on the problem of dealing with nuclear power that could inflict unacceptable damage on each side if war were to come, and with winning the battle for the allegiance of Third World countries.

The Kennedy administration effectively oversaw a qualitative change in the nature of the Cold War and a turning point in containment policy. Kennedy's approach, encompassed by the slogan the 'New Frontier', focused on two things: MAD and the battle for the hearts, minds and capabilities of the Third World. In both of these aspects Kennedy wanted the capacity for flexible response, and it was clear in the run-up to the 1960 presidential election that his differences with Eisenhower were rooted in means rather than ends. Kennedy subscribed willingly to containment strategy, the domino theory and the zero-sum calculus. He recognised the importance of alliances and advanced little in the way of a more nuanced understanding of varieties of communism, regardless of increasingly obvious Sino-Soviet tension. He also accepted, particularly after the 1962 Cuban Missile Crisis, the need to negotiate ground rules with the Soviets for the conduct of the Cold War. After the crisis, both sides recognised that they had to avoid head-to-head confrontation at all costs and stabilise nuclear relations, something epitomised by the Limited Nuclear Test Ban Treaty of 1963. What Kennedy took issue with was Republican unwillingness to fund the resources necessary to maintain not just the American nuclear deterrent at appropriate levels, but also to invest in conventional forces and the battle for the Third World. He accused Eisenhower successively of allowing a missile gap to develop with the USSR, of adopting a passive or reactive containment policy, and of so starving conventional American forces that the US was helpless in the face of 'brushfire challenges'. So great had the gap between means, perceived interests and commitments allegedly become, that Kennedy was convinced that US credibility was in the balance. He came to office consequently promising to 'pay any price, bear any burden, meet any hardship, support any friend, oppose any foe to assure the survival and the success of liberty'.[8]

Kennedy and his highly influential Defense Secretary, Robert McNamara, felt that Eisenhower had taken the US back to the 1940s with a choice between humiliation and nuclear war. Their approach, rather like Truman's, was to develop the means for flexible response. Eisenhower's balanced budgets and low inflation were meaningless when the communist threat remained undiminished and American workers were repeatedly laid off through no less than three economic recessions. Instead, Keynesian economic policies could fulfil Kennedy's commitment to full employment and economic expansion while also empowering the hands of US policy-makers to protect America's global interests. Fortuitously, the Berlin and Cuban crises justified Kennedy's spiralling defence expenditure in the same way that the Korean War had Truman's.

Foremost among Kennedy's concerns was the missile gap, a perception of Soviet technological prowess encouraged by the launch of Sputnik into earth orbit, the US Gaither Report in 1957 and injudicious Soviet rhetoric. Kennedy moved quickly to counter this perceived 'window of vulnerability'. He approved an accelerated strategic missile build-up sufficient to guarantee the US an indisputable second-strike capacity: the US would be able to absorb a Soviet first strike and still be able to mount a devastating response. The theory was that nuclear relations with the Soviets could be stabilised by MAD, whereby deterrence was based on mutual vulnerability rather than the US supremacy of the Truman years. In 1961, the defence budget increased by 15% and, by 1964, the Polaris submarine fleet and the number of Minuteman missiles had almost doubled. Also, in 1964, McNamara revealed plans for a long-range missile force of over 1,700 delivery vehicles – 1,000 Minuteman I and II ICBMs, 54 land-based Titan IIs and 656 Polaris SLBMs.

All of this was on the back of a fiction. There was a missile gap but it was massively in America's favour. Rather than the estimated 400–500 Soviet ICBMs the USSR actually had just four. The Kennedy administration almost certainly knew this from information provided by U-2 flights and reconnaissance satellites, operational since November 1960. Nevertheless it used rather than disabused the misperception to push through its massive increase in military spending. Meantime nuclear build-up was complemented by a major commitment to fighting communism in the Third World, where the battle was characterised by subversion, guerrilla warfare and clientelism. Whereas Dulles had simply opposed communism when it arose, Kennedy's idealism committed him to treating the cause as well as the effects. To deal with the effects, he increasingly emphasised non-military and non-conventional elements of containment, particularly the expansion of counter-insurgency techniques that were epitomised by the Green Berets and Jungle Warfare Schools in the Panama Canal Zone and at Fort Bragg. For treating the cause, Kennedy prescribed economic aid and educational activities. These included the Peace Corps, which by 1963 had dispatched 9,000 volunteers to over 40 countries, and the Food for Peace project which used American agricultural surpluses to aid the Third World, albeit netting the US $1.5 billion annually in return. Most ambitiously of all, Kennedy wanted to nation-build around progressive movements so that the US could champion rightful claims to independence rather than support the conservative regimes used predominantly by Eisenhower. For this programme Kennedy drew intellectually on the work of Walt Rostow and his book *Stages of Economic Growth*[9] and targeted Latin America for special attention. There he launched his most enterprising project: the Alliance for Progress (see Chapter 6).

Flexible response became the hallmark of the Kennedy and Johnson administrations but, for all the former's idealism and the latter's political savvy, their brand of containment was no less flawed than their predecessors'. Some mistakes were inherited. For example, they both had over-simplistic views of communism and of the international system and failed to distinguish between geopolitical and ideological threats. This had tragic implications for Johnson in Vietnam and caused Kennedy major problems in Latin America where his liberal idealism ran into America's vested interest in the status quo. Diversity could be tolerated only if it were either controlled by America or followed economic and political principles broadly in line with the American model.

Kennedy's and Johnson's versions of containment also brought new problems. Insistence on an indisputable 'second-strike' capacity embraced MAD and necessitated massive expenditure. Also, the failure to establish a hierarchy of interests had enormous consequences. First, it caused Kennedy and Johnson to mortgage US credibility with ever increasing instalments to buy victory in Vietnam. Second, it put intolerable strains on the economy and American people, which Eisenhower had warned against doing. In the 1960s, the US could bear the costs of Kennedy's flexible response even less than it could the cost of Truman's NSC-68 in 1950. The US balance of payments problem deteriorated because of swollen military budgets and confidence declined in both the dollar and American leadership. Allies became harder to control and domestic opposition to the Vietnam carnage jeopardised bipartisan support for containment. Indeed, Johnson's decision not to seek re-election in 1968, and the plethora of anti-war incidents, signalled that containment was in crisis.[10]

Nixon, Ford, Carter and *détente*

The Nixon, Ford and Carter years marked the second major and long overdue shift in containment strategy. Whereas the Eisenhower, Kennedy and Johnson administrations were all variations on a theme set out in NSC-68, under Nixon new interpretations as well as tactics emerged. The most important of these was an effort to address the problem caused by NSC-68's failure to distinguish between geopolitical and ideological threats. This timely overhaul of defective US assumptions was due to a symbiotic relationship between world and domestic events. Abroad, the American position was in jeopardy. The Soviets were about to achieve nuclear parity. Vietnam was unwinnable and Nixon had the thankless task of securing 'peace with honour'. Furthermore, American weakness and a seemingly less aggressive Soviet posture tempted the alliance system to unravel. On the one hand, militarily weak organisations such as SEATO and CENTO were a constant drain on America's depleted resources. On the other, economic boom in Western Europe and Japan and their serious opposition to American policy in Vietnam and the Middle East meant an increasing challenge to US leadership. As for the home front, the backlash against the Vietnam experience ushered in a new era of popular neo-isolationism. The American people would not tolerate the overseas commitments necessary to maintain a global perimeter fence. Moreover, Congress moved to reassert its control over the presidency through measures such as the War Powers Act and exercised renewed vigour in its role of executive oversight.

In short, relative economic decline and the end of the bipartisan foreign policy consensus meant that, when waging containment, Nixon, Ford and Carter operated under far greater constraints than any of their predecessors. This prompted a long overdue review of national interests, variations of communism, and the nature of the international system. The Nixon Doctrine, promulgated in July 1969, tried to reduce the damaging expectation–capability gap created by American overextension. The US would provide the nuclear deterrent for the West and honour its treaty commitments in the event of non-nuclear confrontation, but it would not necessarily provide manpower to stave off communist aggression. Nixon's declaration also demonstrated a marked shift away from the zero-sum calculations of previous administrations. In an era of reduced US capability and confidence, Kennan's ideas were resurrected: it was no longer accepted that every battle had to be won, or even fought, to maintain the East–West balance.

New assessments of power and the international system closely accompanied this attempt to rediscover the hierarchy of US interests so carelessly sacrificed by NSC-68. In 1972, Nixon recognised that bipolarity was breaking down and that American ability to sustain post-Second World War structures was under tremendous strain. This was indicated by the collapse of the

Bretton Woods system, Third World demands for a NIEO and the challenge from the Organisation of Petroleum Exporting Countries (OPEC). He also deduced rightly from American impotence in Vietnam, from MAD's effect on the use of nuclear weapons, and from the shockwaves of the energy crisis in 1973, that a multidimensional calculation of power was necessary. Moreover, communist China was now too powerful to be ignored and should be engaged with in order to help balance Soviet power. Together, recognition of these realities offered new hope of containing communism without bankrupting the US. In many ways, the US had gone full circle and returned to Kennan's original hypothesis: five centres of power – now the US, Western Europe, Japan, China and the Soviet Union – balancing each other and with flexibility around the periphery. This provided more opportunity for trade-offs to mitigate tension and an opportunity to shape a New World Order that would recognise the legitimate security concerns of all states, including the Soviet Union.

Perhaps the most radical rethink concerned the role of ideology in defining threats and interests: Nixon and Ford 'down-graded' it. Carter tried to redefine its role. At one stage, Carter was concerned less with notions of East–West conflict than with human rights and idealistic notions of a global community based upon economic welfare cooperation in an interdependent world. It has been claimed that the Nixon–Ford move away from justifying US foreign policy in terms of an ideological crusade marked the 'socialization of American foreign policy by the state system'.[11] In fact, it was a pragmatic adjustment to a peculiar combination of faltering American power, international systemic change and a period of neo-isolationism in which anti-communism was no longer a galvanising 'clarion call'. The most important outcome of this was that the US re-established a hierarchy of interests based on calculations of geopolitical power rather than the confusion of NSC-68.

The resulting policy, known as *détente*, was defined by NSA Henry Kissinger as the evolution of 'habits of mutual restraint, coexistence, and, ultimately, co-operation'.[12] Again, the ultimate goal was containment, but this time it was conducted in a long series of US–Soviet summits. A combination of American resolve and inducements aimed to integrate the USSR into the very international system that US policy-makers had long been convinced the Soviets were determined to overthrow. The most prominent characteristic of US policy was Kissinger's use of linkage, a negotiating strategy rooted in the American reversion to a more flexible version of containment. Relieved of zero-sum calculations, Kissinger was able to engage the Soviets in a series of talks, each conditional on the other, so that trade-offs could be secured and increased cooperation established through a complex 'carrot and stick' style diplomacy.

In terms of inducements, *détente* was designed to supplant bipolar conflict with new agreements and rules that enhanced each country's stake in cooperation with the other. For example, food and technology were to be used as non-military weapons to socialise the Soviet Union into the existing order, perhaps in the long term even to make it partially reliant on Western markets.

Even more prominent, though, were direct negotiations to reduce East–West tension, particularly in the field of nuclear weapons. The Soviets were approaching parity and the US feared the cost of a renewed arms race. Nixon and Kissinger thus accepted nuclear sufficiency and negotiated with the Soviets to sustain MAD – hence moves to control nuclear proliferation and limit ABM systems. Indeed, the symbol of *détente* became Strategic Arms Limitation, and in May 1972 Nixon and Brezhnev duly signed SALT I, which consisted of 16 articles designed to limit ABMs and establish interim agreements to limit offensive strategic missiles.

The counterpart to the 'carrot' was the 'stick' – American resolve – and this was demonstrated in several ways. First, there was a great show of fulfilling commitments, such as aiding Israel in the 1973 Yom Kippur War and escalating the Vietnam conflict in order to negotiate for peace from a position of strength. Second, and much more audacious, were Kissinger's policy of linkage and attempts to play communist states off against one another. The most dramatic move in this strategy was the opening of relations with communist China. Trade-offs and cooperation with the Soviets were underwritten by using the threat of a Sino-American alliance to apply pressure on Moscow to abide by the rules. This threat was made particularly plausible as China squared up with the Soviet Union on the Manchurian border and laid claims to the leadership of world communism. Nixon's trip to Peking in 1972 marked a revolution in containment strategy and ended one of the most absurd charades of post-war US foreign policy: that Taiwan was China and that the world's most populated country did not officially exist.[13]

Overdue enlightenment was thrust upon the Nixon and Ford administrations by international and domestic circumstances, but *détente* nevertheless marked a logical adjustment of containment strategy. Ends and means were better aligned. The escape from ideology increased flexibility in dealing with different communist regimes and in exploiting differences between them. Focus on the Kremlin as the only power capable of destabilising the international order, as conceived of by Nixon and Kissinger, enabled a rationalisation of US commitments and alliance obligations. And, by combining 'carrot and stick' measures, a credible attempt was made to fulfil the containment aim of socialising the Soviets into the international system. Moreover, the timing of *détente* was propitious, for the Soviets were in a potentially responsive mode. Deepening problems with China required approximately 25% of Soviet manpower to be deployed along the Sino-Soviet border and they were nervous of weakening control over the Eastern bloc and about the impact of Western European policies such as *Ostpolitik*. In addition, they had an agenda to pursue that looked like *détente*, specifically to bring the Second World War formally to a close (there had never been a peace treaty) by concluding an agreement to recognise existing frontiers in Europe.

Washington perceived this agenda as potentially dangerous, for it might divide Western allies and, were it successful, undermine the justification for the large US troop presence in Europe and provide Moscow with more room to manoeuvre to try to draw West Germany into the Soviet orbit. After much discussion and agonising, the CSCE was convened in Helsinki in November 1972 and went through tortuous negotiations there and in Geneva until 1975 when the Helsinki Accords were finally signed. President Ford and Kissinger came under a hail of criticism at the time for signing away Eastern Europe to the Soviet empire. However, things were a little more complex than that. Kissinger, while dismissive and derisive of the multilateral diplomacy that went on at the CSCE, nevertheless took interest at crucial stages of the negotiations and ensured that despite recognition of the territorial status quo, there was also a provision for the peaceful change of boundaries – something that became of great importance in 1990 with the reunification of Germany. Furthermore, the West Europeans wove into the Helsinki Accords what turned out to be important human rights provisions. All European countries were to be measured by their human rights record and an ongoing review process was established: each time the CSCE met it was required to set the date of the next meeting before it recessed.

The Soviets do not seem to have recognised the potency of these provisions, which soon encouraged dissidents in the Eastern bloc, as did Carter's human rights policy. Carter wanted to restore America's moral leadership and to conduct foreign policy in a way that rejected Kissinger's *realpolitik* in favour of international law, open diplomacy, promoting self-determination and universal human rights, avoiding the use of force, pursuing nuclear non-proliferation and further relaxing Cold War tensions through economic and arms control agreements. This was a worthy ambition, and was pursued with determination and delivered some success. Carter quickly signed three human rights accords that had been overlooked by previous administrations – the hemispheric American Convention on Human Rights and two UN Covenants, one on economic and cultural rights and the other on civil and political rights. His administration protested the human rights practices of enemies and allies alike. Chile, El Salvador, Ethiopia, Nicaragua, Uganda and Uruguay all had either economic or military aid suspended. Carter also capitalised upon the CSCE agreements to praise the human rights performance of Romania, Yugoslavia and Poland and had the State Department express sympathy for the Charter 77 dissident group in Czechoslovakia, all in the hope of encouraging wider discontent in the Eastern bloc.

Carter also pursued his interest in reducing Cold War tensions, promoting international peace and practising a more flexible version of containment. In 1978 he sponsored the Camp David peace treaty between Israel and Egypt and in the face of great opposition concluded the Panama Treaties that provided for the end of US occupation of the Canal Zone and for the gradual reversion of the Zone and the Canal to Panama. His administration also engaged in negotiations designed to restore diplomatic relations with Cuba and Vietnam, and on 1 January 1979 recognised the PRC and withdrew formal recognition of Taiwan and of the 1955 Mutual Defense Treaty. The latter substantially eased tensions in the Far East, even though quasi-diplomatic US–Taiwan ties continued after passage of the Taiwan Relations Act. Furthermore, Carter pushed aggressively within SALT II for deeper cuts in US–Soviet nuclear arsenals than those agreed by the Ford administration. This caused some friction but agreement was eventually struck to limit US and Soviet nuclear forces to 2,250 strategic nuclear delivery vehicles, restrict the number of warheads to be placed on each missile and provide for verification. It also placed a limit of 1,200 launchers of MIRVed ballistic missiles, no more than 820 of which were launchers of MIRVed ICBMs.

However, while *détente* as an approach to containment suffered less from the inconsistencies that characterised NSC-68 it still faced formidable obstacles. It was uncertain whether the Soviets would, or could, implement *détente* fully[14] because while the nuclear relationship and severe economic problems gave them a vested interest in cooperation they rightly feared that *détente* would make it increasingly difficult to hold the Eastern bloc together. Neither was *détente* universally popular at home. It had the misfortune to be associated with the Watergate scandal and ran up against a series of conservative and vested interests, including the conservative right, the powerful Zionist lobby, the US military and the still-influential Cold War warriors, epitomised by Paul Nitze's Committee on the Present Danger, which in 1979 campaigned against Carter's defence and arms control policies. It also ran into a Congress anxious to reassert itself in the wake of Vietnam. For instance, the hopes of Presidents Ford and Carter of using economic incentives to socialise the USSR were undermined by the Senate's insistence on the Jackson–Vanik amendment. This made a trade agreement and extending most favoured nation (MFN) treatment conditional upon the Soviet Union allowing more Jewish emigration and was obviously unacceptable to the Soviets because it was tantamount to interference in their internal affairs.

It also proved difficult to reconcile *realpolitik*, moral principles and aspirations for *détente*. Uncertainty about the extent to which Moscow controlled communist-leaning liberation movements helped persuade Nixon to continue the Vietnam War for four years and to unleash the CIA to destabilise the freely elected Chilean government of Salvador Allende. The contradictions were even worse within Carter's foreign policy as he struggled to reconcile pushing human rights, reaching diplomatic settlements with the Soviets, and guaranteeing sufficient military power to protect national security.[15] Carter spoke the language of morality and humanitarian concern, but too often, for his credibility eventually compromised principle to geostrategic realities. He was no more able than any other post-war US president to avoid collaborating with dictatorships such as the Shah's Iran, which formed a key part of US Middle Eastern strategy, and other regimes that afforded strategic bases, such as the Markos dictatorship in the Philippines that provided military bases at Clark Field and Subic Bay. He also backed down over his welcoming of Soviet dissidents and former political prisoners to the White House when Moscow retaliated by cracking down harder on internal dissent and threatening repercussions for arms reduction talks. Furthermore, Carter's moral certitude and attempted break with Kissinger's *realpolitik*-style *détente* actually threatened to be more rather than less confrontational because it created an impression that the US had moved from tacit coexistence to being satisfied only with a fundamental change in the Soviet system.[16] Carter's ability to stay true to his principles and especially *détente* progressively weakened in the face of a series of reverses abroad and sustained domestic criticism, led by the American right, of his allegedly weak handling of defence and foreign affairs. He was castigated for the conduct of the Iranian hostage disaster, which began in 1979 in the wake of the Islamic fundamentalist revolution against the Shah's Iran when extremists held US officials in Teheran. His critics likewise seized upon the so-called Soviet offensive in the Third World as evidence of Kremlin duplicity and the dangerous naivety of trying to move the basis of foreign policy from 'power to principle'. From the mid-1970s onwards, the US suffered setback after setback on the periphery, from the fall of Saigon in 1975 to a series of communist advances in Africa and the Sandinista revolution in Nicaragua.

By the time the Soviets sent 85,000 troops into Afghanistan, Carter was an incumbent under siege and desperately anxious to signal resolve to the Soviets and to the American people in the lead-up to the presidential election. Concern for human rights had become his Achilles' heel and the President was in full retreat from *détente* and swinging violently to a new hard line. Human rights criticisms of regimes such as the Argentinean Junta were muted. Ties with pro-Western dictatorships were buttressed – such as a $500 million deal for the Markos regime in 1979 that provided it with modern weapons in return for five further years of base access. Plans for troop withdrawals from South Korea were reversed. And the Carter Doctrine asserted that any attempt by an outside power to gain control of the Persian Gulf region would be regarded as an attack on vital American interests. As for direct US–USSR relations, high-technology sales were halted, feed grain shipments were embargoed, and America boycotted the 1980 Moscow Olympics. Carter also withdrew SALT II from Senate consideration in the full expectation that it would be rejected anyway as a consequence of cooling East–West relations. At the same time he endorsed PD-59. Once critical of advocates of limited nuclear war, Carter shifted position to endorse a countervailing strategy that enabled him to tell the US people, and the Soviets, that his administration had enhanced American ability to wage nuclear war.[17]

Reagan and the Second Cold War

When Reagan came to office the Second Cold War was already underway. Among other things this was due to Soviet use of the respite provided by *détente* to regather their strength and to a serious flaw in Nixon's and Kissinger's linkage strategy devised to pressurise them into good behaviour. While the US had cut back on trade with the Soviets, the pain that this inflicted was dulled to insignificance because the flow from Western Europe and Japan generally continued. However, accusations that the 1970s, the 'decade of neglect', had left America defenceless were false: Carter had reversed the post-Vietnam slump in the defence budget and in 1980 expanded it to $127 billion.

Nevertheless, Reagan tapped successfully into US needs to be purged of Vietnam, to see an end to 'weak' post-Watergate leadership, and to shake off the paralysing self-doubt imbued by an America in decline. The Reagan Doctrine and the revolutionary SDI captured the imagination of a disillusioned American public. Reagan promised 'dynamic self-renewal' and his prescription was simple: recovery of military supremacy, renewal of messianic purpose and a return to free enterprise. Containment was central in all of these things. Rearmament needed a purpose to convince Congress to fund it. Scaremongering about the Soviet threat did just that. The need to contain a rejuvenated threat to American values promised to recover the sense of common purpose and pride in the American way of life that had pervaded the early Cold War years. Finally, containment provided justification for using free markets rather than aid to foster development in the Third World; as Reagan liked to argue, governments did not solve problems, they subsidised them.

However, while Reagan's strategy for containment is clear, his tactics are not. Analysis is handicapped by lack of primary sources and plagued by the 'Reagan paradox': the contradictions between his warmongering rhetoric and practical 'peace-making', his New Right creed and operational pragmatism[18] and his invocation of the 'evil empire' and a generally well-managed, if not always friendly, relationship between the superpowers during his administrations. In addition, Reagan was one of the most ineffective presidents of all time when it came to dealing with disputes within his administration: 'No Reaganite "grand plan" shines through this fog' of policy muddle, bureaucratic disorder and his spectacular but disingenuous gestures.[19] For containment this meant contradictory policies as hardliners such as Defense Secretary Caspar Weinberger pushed remorselessly for aggressive confrontation whilst influential moderates, such as Secretary of State George Shultz and ultimately Reagan himself, pushed for selective containment and a resurrection of linkage.

Nonetheless, broad themes can be discerned. Reagan re-emphasised ideology and placed moral crusade at the forefront of containment policy. At his first White House press conference, he accused the Soviets of using *détente* to promote world revolution and claimed that 'they reserve the right unto themselves to commit any crime, to lie, [and] to cheat'. Later, in 1981, he attributed all the unrest in the world to the Soviet Union and in 1983 delivered his infamous 'evil empire' speech. This potent combination of paranoia and moralism was particularly evident in his attitudes towards Central America. Alarmist assessments of Soviet intentions were 'emotional and so lacking in factual support that it invited accusations of disingenuousness',[20] yet falling dominoes were nevertheless revisited and the communist advance portrayed as a challenge to Manifest Destiny.

Beyond this, Reagan's containment policy was an awkward and inconsistent 'pick and mix' of previous strategies as he attempted to reconcile a renewed messianic globalism with the debilitating 'Vietnam Syndrome' and the pragmatic constraints of the 1980s, such as alliance attitudes and the relative decline of US power. His militarisation of containment smacked heavily of

NSC-68; but it was ironic that an otherwise fiscally conservative Republican administration was prepared to fund rearmament through massive deficit spending. While US foreign aid was slashed, Reagan embarked upon the most rapid increase in defence spending in US peacetime history. He launched a five-year $180 billion programme to modernise US strategic forces. He reversed Carter's cancellation of the B-1 bomber, approved a 600-ship navy and stepped up preparations to deploy Pershing II and Cruise missiles in Western Europe. In his first three years, Reagan increased defence expenditure by 40% in real terms and by 1985 the US was spending $300 billion per annum on defence. Reagan also alarmed the Soviets and US allies alike by his apparent disregard for nuclear stability. Announcement of SDI undermined the ABM Treaty that had for two decades been the cornerstone of strategic stability. Moreover, coming hard on the heels of Carter's leaked countervailing strategy the package of SDI and accelerated nuclear deployment could not be interpreted by Moscow as anything other than highly provocative and dangerous. It is perhaps no coincidence that in November 1983 Kremlin leaders temporarily interpreted NATO exercise Able Archer as a real US nuclear first strike.

Reagan's general perspective on containment, however, was reminiscent of Eisenhower's. He returned to Dulles's themes of 'liberation' and 'roll-back', but was even more ambitious. The Soviet system was in economic crisis and, by taking the initiative, the US could add to its distress. Some hoped to cripple it via a new arms race. Others looked to 'roll-back' communism in the Third World and in this they had some success because, while their view of containment was global, they were generally careful about the extent and nature of their commitment, despite their expansive rhetoric.

In light of the Vietnam legacy, US troops were used sparingly, especially after the slaughter of US marines in the Lebanon in 1983. Thereafter, they were restricted to actions such as the overthrow in October 1983 of the Marxist government on Grenada. Much more use was made of the counter-insurgency operations popularised by Kennedy, of the proxies favoured by Nixon, and of the covert operations that had been the penchant of Eisenhower. The CIA budget soared and the administration frequently shielded its funds and activities from congressional scrutiny. For example, it controlled much of the $2 billion given to El Salvador between 1980 and 1985, was integrally involved in organising the Nicaraguan Contras, and had extensive dealings with General Noriega in Panama. The US also funded its proxies generously. In 1985, $250–300 million went to Afghan rebels and $15 million to the anti-communist force, UNITA, in Angola. By 1987, the Nicaraguan Contras had received $100 million, non-communist resistance groups in Kampuchea $20 million, and anti-Marxist groups in Ethiopia over $0.5 million.

Paradoxically, at the same time that Reagan rearmed, pursued roll-back in the Third World and postured aggressively vis-à-vis the Soviets, he moved towards *détente*. Whereas the NSC-68 elite interpreted negotiation from strength as entailing Soviet capitulation, Reagan was more flexible. Some have suggested that the vitriol of his first years in office was designed to construct the domestic political base necessary to enable lasting *détente*.[21] This attributes to Reagan both a questionable prescience and a dubious long termism, but there is little doubt that he was more liberal than many of his advisers and found nuclear defences distasteful. He encouraged trade with the Soviet Union, notably in September 1983 when he concluded the biggest grain deal ever, but it was nuclear weaponry that became the centrepiece of his quest for East–West political accommodation. Early efforts focused on an Intermediate Nuclear Force (INF) treaty and the so-called 'zero option' – no deployments of Cruise and Pershing missiles in Europe in return for USSR withdrawal of its SS-20s. This would have so disadvantaged the Soviets that it has often been seen as a tactic simultaneously to rearm and score 'peace points' with nervous allies and against the Kremlin. Nevertheless in 1983, after Soviet–American relations reached their lowest ebb since the Cuban missile crisis, Reagan transformed arms limitation to arms reduction talks and relaunched *détente* with an announcement in late 1984 of new talks linking INF, START and weapons in space.

Ultimately Reagan's version of *détente*, due to a combination of mutual interest and personal diplomacy, produced greater results than did US initiatives in the 1970s. In Mikhail Gorbachev, who became General Secretary of the Soviet Union in March 1985, Reagan found a partner in leadership. On a personal level the two shared a penchant for personal summitry and established a rapport, particularly at their meeting in October 1986 in Reykjavik, which mellowed the Cold War atmosphere. Even more importantly, they had a coincidence of interest in relaxing East–West tensions. Reagan was resigned to the 'long haul' but keen nevertheless to be seen as proactive, rather than simply responding to Soviet policies. Gorbachev needed a period of respite during which to restructure the Soviet economy in a way that allowed sustainable development, particularly in terms of tackling inefficiency and balancing military expenditure against consumer demand. As a result, Reagan and Gorbachev held four crucial summits between 1985 and 1988 that helped change the course of the Cold War. A new sense of optimism permeated superpower exchanges and was reflected in groundbreaking agreements, such as an INF treaty in December 1987 that provided for the destruction of an entire category of nuclear missiles.[22]

Bush and the end of the Cold War

In 1989, George Bush succeeded Reagan. An unenviable task awaited him. President Bush lacked Reagan's charisma and ability to disguise the deep contradictions within US foreign policy. He also inherited problems that ranged from economic recession to significant discontent among NATO allies, despite the close relationship that had existed between Reagan and Britain's Margaret Thatcher. Furthermore, Bush faced a Cold War that differed markedly from that of the hostile, yet relatively easily managed, situation of the early 1980s. In January 1987, Gorbachev launched *perestroika* and in late 1988 proposed to disband and withdraw six tank divisions from Central and

Eastern Europe and to cut unilaterally 500,000 troops from the Soviet armed forces over the next two years. Also, throughout the first half of 1989, the Bush administration was regaled with reports of Soviet economic weakness and discontent among their satellites. This highlighted a critical question that had arisen during the later Reagan years: was the Soviet Union undergoing lasting change or was Gorbachev restructuring with a view to resurgent power and renewed superpower confrontation? As reforms seemed to spiral out of control, a fascinating new factor was also added to the equation. As Secretary of State James Baker put it, 'What happens if Gorbachev loses, if things go to hell in a handbasket over there?'[23] In other words, would the end of the Cold War really be a victory for the US or the precursor to something much worse?

Standing at the confluence between Cold War and 'New World Order', Bush had a plethora of options. He could pursue roll-back in the Third World with far greater expectations of success than those harboured by Eisenhower and even Reagan. He could capitalise on the Reagan–Gorbachev dynamic and take *détente* to heights unimagined by Nixon and Kissinger. Or he could meaningfully challenge Soviet power in Eastern Europe. At the same time, though, he was under great competing pressures. The break-throughs of the Reagan era raised public expectation that the Cold War was ending and that the US would provide imaginative leadership to win the peace. Within the administration there were those such as Baker and the Chairman of the Joint Chiefs of Staff Colin Powell who tended to believe that Gorbachev was sincere in both his reforms and his declaration on 4 June 1990 during a visit to the US that 'The Cold War is now behind us. Let us not wrangle over who won it.'[24] On the other hand, Bush, NSA Scowcroft, Secretary of Defense Cheney and Deputy NSA (later CIA Director) Gates were more sceptical. This was hardly surprising given that 40 years of American foreign policy had been dedicated to combating the USSR and that despite all that had been happening, a policy paper on national security strategy in January 1988 had still emphasised that the USSR remained the greatest threat to US interests and that it was essential to 'judge Soviets by actions, rather than words'.[25]

Bush's approach reflected these different pressures and his inherent conservatism. On 12 May 1989, he talked of moving beyond containment to a policy of integration, whereby the USSR would be brought into the community of nations. However, this was largely rhetoric to appease public opinion because Bush had privately resolved in April 1989 upon a less inspiring policy of 'status quo plus'. This consisted of broadening the superpower dialogue while slowing the momentum created by the Reagan–Gorbachev dynamic until the latter's commitment to, and intentions of, reform could be tested. In 1990, Bush was pushed into a slightly more expansive policy by massive domestic and international pressure. The unimaginative 'status quo plus' was replaced by a slightly more optimistic approach based upon five objectives: to encourage Gorbachev's reforms; to maintain the territorial integrity of the USSR; to conclude arms controls favourable to the US lest

Gorbachev be replaced by hardliners; to ensure that a reunified Germany obtain NATO and EC membership; and to achieve a stable and democratic Eastern Europe.[26] Still, though, Bush's foreign policy remained largely reactive to events rather than proactive in pursuing these objectives.

Bush's approach to containment had merits. It is all too easy to use hindsight to criticise a pragmatic, cautious policy that was evolved in turbulent times. Bush needed to demonstrate American leadership and was prepared to capitalise on Soviet weakness to take vigorous unilateral action against Panama in December 1989 and to lead the 1990–91 military intervention in the Gulf against Iraq. Yet he also needed to check what might transpire to be unwarranted expectation of the Cold War ending for reasons of strategic conservatism, domestic political calculations, to buy time to revise 40 years of American policy focus and to hold the Western Alliance together. Indeed, just prior to Bush's inauguration, Brent Scowcroft publicly speculated whether Gorbachev's real aim was to drive a wedge between the US and its allies.[27] It thus made sense to require Gorbachev to pass various tests of commitment to *perestroika*, including liberalisation of Central and Eastern Europe and renunciation of the Brezhnev Doctrine (promulgated in 1968 and claiming Soviet rights to intervene in the affairs of socialist states).

Gorbachev offered this and more, including announcing withdrawal from Afghanistan, ceasing arms transfers to Nicaragua and agreement to dismantle the Krasnoyarsk large-phased early warning radar system, which could be used for missile defence. This being the case Bush sensibly embraced the USSR cautiously as a partner in stability and developed policies and a personal relationship with Gorbachev designed to encourage further Soviet reforms. The two met for the first time in December 1989 in Malta, where Bush offered cautious promises of negotiations on a trade treaty, efforts to lift the Jackson–Vanik amendment and possible Export–Import Bank credits. Thereafter he moved to bolster the USSR and underwrite the reform process. Tied aid was used to push the Soviet Union into further reforms. MFN trading status was eventually granted, packages were developed to help with market reform, and promises made about developments in arms control verification.

This cautious diplomacy delivered significant rewards, albeit that deepening Soviet crisis and European allies provided much of the actual momentum. The future of Germany was one of the biggest and most difficult issues to resolve. France and Britain were reluctant to see a reunified Germany once more at the heart of Europe, as were the Soviets given legitimate concern for the future security of homeland borders. Bush invested significant political capital in overcoming these obstacles and eventually steered the way to the historic signature on 12 September 1990 of the 'Two plus Four' agreement that paved the way for German reunification on 3 October 1990. Britain, France, the USSR and the US all renounced rights formerly claimed in Germany, including Berlin; Soviet troops were to be withdrawn by 1994; and a reunified Germany was to enter NATO on condition that NATO troops were not stationed in East Germany. Germany also made a series of concessions to assuage other states' security concerns. It reaffirmed the Basic Law pledge not to develop nuclear weapons; accepted limits of 370,000 personnel on its armed forces; and formally accepted the territorial losses imposed after 1945 by renouncing claims east of the Oder–Neisse line.

Substantial progress was also made in securing disproportionate Soviet military reductions and for settling post-Cold War conditions in Europe. On 19 November 1990 NATO and Warsaw Pact leaders concluded the Conventional Forces in Europe Treaty (CFE), which provided for equal levels of East–West conventional armaments. This was essential for precluding surprise attacks and large-scale offensive operations in Europe beyond Russian borders. It also provided further mutual reassurance by establishing both central zonal limits to prevent destabilising force concentrations in Europe and regional limits. This clearly favoured the West given long-standing Soviet conventional superiority in Europe, and by the end of the reduction period in 1995 over 52,000 battle tanks, armoured combat vehicles, artillery pieces, combat aircraft and attack helicopters had been verifiably dismantled or converted.[28] Contemporaneously the Bush administration pushed on with the START negotiations inherited from the Reagan administration and, in July 1991, START I was finally signed. This provided for a verifiable reduction in US–Soviet arsenals of 30–40% and established a series of ceilings, including one of 6,000 warheads. The objective was to secure equal aggregate levels in strategic offensive arms at significantly lower levels of mutual destructive capacity. However, it was ultimately thought that START I favoured the US because removal of MIRVed ICBMs, especially SS-18s, seemingly strengthened in relative terms American second-strike capability and therefore provided added reassurance against a potential Soviet first strike.[29]

Bush pragmatism, though, exacted a high moral, practical and political price. Bush effectively took containment to the opposite end of the spectrum from whence it had started and in the process revealed more painful contradictions of US foreign policy. Whereas Truman had looked to contain Soviet strength and achieve outright victory, Bush decided that US interests lay in preventing outright victory and containing Soviet weakness. The US had to prop up the 'evil empire' in the dual hope of maintaining stability and that the USSR would reform itself in a way acceptable to the West. Unsurprisingly, this threw up all sorts of other unpalatable contradictions too. For example, Lithuania declared independence in March 1990 and Bush seemingly gave it political support when, on a tour to Europe in June 1990, he declared that he wanted 'to see Lithuania have its freedom. We are committed to self-determination for the Baltic States.'[30] However, Bush also feared that if he capitalised upon Gorbachev's weakness and challenged communist power in Eastern Europe, especially given a large Russian population in Lithuania, he might bolster Soviet hardliners or generate systemic weakness with unpredictable consequences, or possibly do both. As a result he tolerated Soviet intimidation of the breakaway republic and stood by as Gorbachev deployed troops and tanks on to the streets of Vilnius. The contrast between this and Bush's promises of freedom and 'integration' was stark, and it was bitterly ironic that Bush felt it necessary to abandon the freedom of others in order to support the very regime that denied them their freedom and which 40 years previously the US had vowed to destroy. Furthermore, there is some truth in claims that Bush's wait-and-see approach surrendered the Cold War initiative taken by Reagan and that insofar as his belated engagement of Gorbachev saved neither him nor system stability, the Cold War ended despite American policy. Certainly Bush's disparagement of the 'vision thing' and pursuit of 'status quo plus' helped create an impression of an event-driven rather than pro-active administration and played so poorly publicly that it ultimately contributed to his electoral defeat by Clinton in 1992, irrespective of his considerable foreign policy achievements.

Since that time, debate has raged as to how much credit to give to Reagan and his policies for bringing about the end of the Cold War. Did his hardline rhetoric and massive rearmament force the Soviets into an unsustainable and ultimately disastrous arms race? Was his meaningful negotiation from strength the key to unlocking superpower antagonism? Did Western Europe's own form of *détente* with the East, grave strains within NATO, and the burgeoning anti-nuclear movement force moderation upon his second term? Or was American policy a relatively minor factor in Soviet collapse compared to structural economic problems, onerous commitments such as Afghanistan – the Soviet Union's Vietnam – and an overextension in the Third World that eventually saw it, as well as the US, challenged as imperialist? History is, after all, littered with the rise and decline of empires.

This debate is explored further in Chapter 9 but what is certain is that neither Reagan nor Bush was any more able than their predecessors to make containment work coherently. First, key enabling factors were missing. Reagan never instilled into the Second Cold War the American commitment and leadership that characterised the first. Key allies, notably in Western Europe, came to see the US, rather than the USSR, as the more likely cause of conflict and disagreed sharply with Reagan's policies in the Middle East, Central America and with the bombing raid on 'terrorist' Libya in 1986. The American people and Congress, too, were sufficiently divided that Reagan could neither exorcise the ghosts of Vietnam nor re-establish the imperial presidency, as the Iran–Contra scandal demonstrated in 1986–87. Second, American means palpably could not meet the return to global containment. 'Reaganomics' transformed the US from the world's major creditor in 1981 to its largest debtor and, with the Wall Street crash of October 1987, ushered in a new recession. Third, Reagan's moralism vis-à-vis the Soviets and their interference in other states contrasted sharply with his own extensive use of covert operations, gunboat diplomacy in Grenada, and support for undemocratic and brutal regimes, such as in El Salvador. Public attempts to square this long-standing and damaging circle simply heaped ridicule upon the administration. In March 1981, Secretary of State Alexander Haig labelled as terrorists all revolutionaries except those fighting communism, and the US Ambassador to the UN, Jeanne Kirkpatrick, famously distinguished between authoritarian dictatorships which were friendly to the US and capable of evolving into democracies, and left-wing totalitarian dictatorships which were not. Finally Bush, as he dealt with the twilight of Cold War, revealed two of the great ironies of post-war US foreign policy. First, like other self-proclaimed champions of the Free World who preceded him, he sacrificed the rights of the peoples of Central and Eastern Europe to Cold War priorities, albeit perversely this time to support rather than undermine the USSR. Second, Bush's caution demonstrated that 40 years of containment had socialised the US to such an extent that it had greater interests in the status quo than in actively seeking an end to the Cold War.[31]

Conclusion

At considerable cost of lives and US constitutional and political virtue, containment helped to maintain the integrity of the Free World against the communist challenge. That containment endured throughout the Cold War as the guiding principle of US foreign policy is, in one sense, surprising because, however it was formulated, it was replete with contradictions, blinding oversimplifications and sometimes frighteningly rigid prescriptions. Yet, it was not one strategy but many strategies that evolved in accordance with the interplay between perceptions of policy-makers, variables in the international system, domestic politics and, perhaps especially, the nuclear relationship. Its different incarnations progressed from Kennan's original flexible model through NSC-68's rigid prescriptions, massive retaliation, flexible response, *détente*, the 'Second Cold War' and finally to 'status quo plus'. The purpose also seemingly changed in line with perceptions of American homeland vulnerability and the unacceptable levels of brinksmanship demonstrated in the Cuban Missile Crisis. The drive for victory through military preponderance was abandoned and from Kennedy onwards, although it was never explicitly explained to the American people, containment policy became less about winning, and more about not losing the Cold War. Successive administrations thereafter accepted the need for system stability and perpetuated East–West stand-off and struggled to maintain allied and American public support for a seemingly unwinnable war against communism, especially once Vietnam tore American society apart.

Some even argue that containment was not a strategy at all but rather a general statement of intent, a clarion call to action, or a convenient catchphrase which justified the expansion of American interests in a post-colonial world by whatever means policy-makers thought necessary. Secretary of State Dean Acheson testified long after the event that NSC-68 was designed to 'bludgeon' the mass mind of top government into allowing Truman to make a decision and be able to carry it through. What is certain, though, is that for two principal reasons the debate about containment will continue. First, its importance and effectiveness as a means of regulating and then, ultimately, ending the Cold War will be tested by historians as more archival material becomes available from both East and West. Second, containment was as nebulous as it was simplistic. It could be, and was, used as justification for almost any American action or non-action, often with seemingly little relevance to Cold War issues. Consequently, writers of different genres and political persuasion have great scope for interpretation.

4   Economic statecraft, 1945–89

US economic statecraft has always prompted fierce debate. Liberals see US capitalism as flawed, but benign and progressive, while New Left historians and world systems theorists see it as an aggressive force, which ruthlessly exploits other countries. Paul Kennedy discerns a pattern of US relative economic decline since 1945: Joseph Nye does not. Stephen Gill sees supranational capitalism emerging with hegemonic control of the world emanating primarily from US corporations and the capitalist ethos that permeates Washington. Others, like Susan Strange, assert that an international political economy exists, which challenges both traditional distinctions between security and economic concerns and state-centric analyses of international relations. Strange sees states functioning in an interpenetrated and economically interdependent world, where one not only needs to concentrate on military security, but also on production, financial and knowledge structures. The US has controversially wielded sanctions extraterritorially against friends, for example, in the wake of the declaration of martial law in Poland in 1981, and used sanctions equally controversially against Iraq between the First and Second Gulf Wars. Contemporary globalisation, driven largely by forces emanating from the US, poses challenges to long-held conceptualisations of identity, has emphasised the world's prosperity divide, and raises issues of governance, particularly over MNCs and finance capital, which now circulates with unprecedented velocity. Currently there is much talk about the US exporting democracy and spreading the free market, which some see as part of the evolutionary pattern of globalisation while others see it as crude Americanisation. If even part of these claims is accepted, then our present concern with economic statecraft is justified.[1]

Facts, figures and motives

If one were to compile seven wonders of the twentieth century, US economic performance in the Second World War would be one of them. The figures are staggering. Gross Domestic Product (GDP) rose from $88.6 billion in 1939 to $135 billion in 1945. At the war's end, the US held $20 billion of the world's $33 billion of gold reserves. It made half of the world's goods, had over half of the world's shipping, provided one-third of the world's exports and carried over 73% of the world's combined domestic and international airline passengers. The US was an economic colossus, but an important factor needs to be borne in mind here: the vast proportion of all this was produced and consumed domestically. More than any other major economy, the US had enormous self-sufficiency, and this did not change significantly until the 1960s. Exports and imports together in 1960 still constituted only approximately 10% of GDP, but that figure gradually rose over the years so that by 2004 it stood at over 30%. On the basis of this late development, it could be argued that the large cost of US foreign economic policy must have been justified by security rather than economic considerations. This sounds persuasive, but it misses important points.

The US participated in the international economy in a massive way after the Second World War because of an inextricable mixture of concerns about security and prosperity. In the 1930s US liberals changed the architecture of capitalism by making its face more humane, by introducing regulatory governance, and by making it more accountable to the people. This was the New Deal: a mixture of pragmatism and the economic prescriptions of the great British economist John Maynard Keynes. During the war, President Roosevelt and his advisers decided that the New Deal needed to be internationalised, with the dollar as the key currency and the US at the centre of management. Six key ideas underpinned this: economic discrimination had to end because it caused friction and war; a free market would bring global prosperity; America needed new markets abroad to absorb its productive capacity otherwise there would be renewed depression; the US needed access to key strategic goods such as oil, bauxite, rubber, tungsten and uranium, which it could not source adequately at home; profits beckoned for US capitalism; and managing the system would facilitate the exercise of overall US power. For these reasons, rather than because of a uni-causal capitalist dynamic often invoked by New Left historians, the US moulded and managed a new economic world order. Spero and Hart note three facilitating conditions: concentration of power; shared interests; and the presence of a dominant power willing to take on a leadership role.[2] The outcome has often been branded US hegemony.

Hegemonic stability theory

Charles Kindleberger in analysing the Great Depression articulated hegemonic stability theory.[3] Arguing that lack of governance had caused the Depression, he claimed that a hegemonic leader was needed to shoulder the costs of creating and sustaining stable economic systems for the international public good. Some of the hegemon's public good costs are not directly related to the economic system, but are part of its overall power base. Such costs for the US have been the defence umbrella for Western Europe and Japan, and the underwriting of European integration through the Marshall Plan. The problem that arises for the system from this is that secondary states acquire the same technology as the hegemon through the free market, but they do not have to shoulder the costs of leadership and may become unconscionable free-riders. They thus benefit relatively more from the system and this creates the hegemon's dilemma: 'To maximise one's own returns requires a commitment to openness regardless of what others do. To maximise one's relative position, on the other hand, calls for a policy of continued closure irrespective of others' policies.'[4] The hegemon must decide whether to continue and watch itself decline relative to others, though still gaining in absolute terms, or abandon its leadership role and watch the system disintegrate with all losing in absolute terms, but others relatively more than itself. In the light of this dilemma, there has been much reflection about how to maintain an orderly and prosperous system.

A hegemon emerges at a time of international crisis when the previous system is collapsing. By definition it has the greatest power derived from a combination of hard economic and military power and soft economic, normative and cultural power. It is the latter that enables it to socialise others into its way of doing things and this is often seen as its most potent characteristic, though its power to coerce is also ever present. The hegemon, depending on whether it is benevolent or exploitative/coercive, will either carry the costs of providing public goods and tolerate free-riders, or seek to tax and exploit others. An example of the latter is the way the US has exploited the unique position of the dollar to sustain high levels of domestic US consumption while suffering an enormous balance of payments deficit. In 1960 the US had a balance of payments surplus on goods and services of $3,508 million. In 2004 it had a deficit of $617,075 million, with an accumulated deficit of well over $4,000,000 million since 1975, the last time the account was in surplus.[5] In sustaining the system, the hegemon will be forced to compromise with others as it suffers relative decline. This is the most difficult variable to assess. When is the hegemon exercising power and when is it bowing to pressures from others? When does it cease to be hegemonic?[6]

Management of the world economy, 1945–73

Government policy that came forward with this hegemonic vision at the end of the Second World War was not popular everywhere in the US. Distinguished traditions of US protectionism and unilateralism were potent enough to prevent the ITO being ratified by Congress and so the world had to make do with the GATT from 1948 until the inception of the WTO in January 1995. US protectionism has waxed and waned since the war and should not be dismissed as a spent force.

Multilateralism, the key concept in the IMF and the GATT, facilitated the operation of international capitalism. The IMF, through the Bretton Woods system, made all currencies convertible at exchange rates pegged to the dollar whose value was fixed at $35 per fine ounce of gold. And the GATT reduced tariffs through the principles of reciprocity and MFN. For example, Britain would reduce the tariff on US planes in return for a US reduction on British jewellery (reciprocity) and then these new rates would be extended to all other members of the GATT (MFN). However, the GATT, while a facilitator of tariff reductions on manufactured goods, was not effective in the agricultural realm, exempted service industries and regional economic groupings from its brief, and had ineffective enforcement powers. Nevertheless, through the operation of the GATT and the IMF, the US hoped for freer trade and for the US dollar to become supreme in the monetary system.

American multilateralism was never pure. It was shot through with self-serving exceptions in the agriculture sector, in the airline and maritime industries, and even in GATT procedures, where the Americans rejected the idea of across-the-board tariff reductions in favour of reciprocity and MFN. With these procedures they could use their economic strength more effectively. The US had privileged management positions in all the institutions set up to manage the new economic world order. No organisation, until the creation of the WTO, could really stand against the US, among other reasons because of its veto power. Throughout, the Americans ensured that their idealistic principles also conformed to realist calculations of self-interest.

The US hoped that their new universal economic order could be implemented speedily after the war. That hope was dashed because the Soviets refused to participate, the economies of Western Europe were not fit enough to play the game, and the Cold War imposed new priorities. Economic disorder in Western Europe and the imperative of fostering a speedy recovery, in order to inoculate it against the spread of communism, led the Americans to adopt regionalism, and that compromised their multilateralism further because regionalism discriminates against outsiders. They pumped $13 billion of Marshall Aid into Western Europe, encouraged integration and tolerated European preferential tariffs and currency controls, which discriminated against US exporters. Bretton Woods was partially suspended and the GATT, after substantial cuts in tariffs in 1947, lay largely dormant until the 1960s. The US accepted these public good costs for the sake of immediate security priorities and the hope that regionalism would be an effective midwife for multilateralism.

In 1958 general currency convertibility was finally delivered: the Bretton Woods system came into full operation and there was renewed momentum for tariff reductions. The Dillon GATT round, 1960–62, reduced the rate on manufactured goods by an average of 10%. However, the rebirth of multilateralism coincided with the emergence of serious economic difficulties in the US. Its long period of vast expenditures overseas on defence, economic assistance and aid, and the rise of efficient competitor economies in West Germany and Japan, all began to tell. Also, the creation of the European Economic Community (EEC) in 1957[7] and, more specifically, its intention to create a Common Agricultural Policy (CAP), which threatened the continuation of vast US agricultural sales in Europe, worried the Americans. Throughout the 1950s the US had a balance of payments deficit, though its trade balance was always in healthy, if steadily declining, surplus. However, by 1960 foreign-held dollars exceeded US gold reserves and this led to a loss of confidence and heavy selling, which developed into a run on the dollar.

These economic developments deeply worried President Kennedy and he sought to restructure relations with Western Europe and to renew the drive for freer trade (see Chapter 5). He had little success with restructuring and even the success of the Kennedy GATT round of 1963–67, which cut tariffs on manufactured goods by 35%, was not enough to avert the looming crisis. The US continued to overstretch its commitments beyond its resources. President Johnson's escalation of the Vietnam War and his costly Great Society domestic reforms exacerbated the structural problems already evident at the start of the decade. In 1971 the US ran a trade deficit for the first time in the twentieth century, inflation and unemployment were high, and the US could no longer sustain the Bretton Woods system because of pressure on the dollar. Things had changed since 1945 and President Nixon dramatically tried to adjust US policies to the new realities. On 15 August 1971, he announced the New Economic Policy. He imposed a 10% import surcharge and devalued and disengaged the dollar from gold. Later it was floated on the foreign exchanges to find its market value. The US, instead of shouldering public good costs for the sake of the system, tipped them on to the rest of the industrialised world. The Americans argued that it was up to them to solve the problem of the weak dollar and the US trade deficit by reinflating their economies and by reducing their exports to, and increasing their imports from, the US. By 1973 the US was no longer in charge of its own economic destiny, and, in fact, Nixon's new economics meant the death of Bretton Woods and danger for multilateralism. The stark realities which US economic problems impressed upon its leaders also had an important impact on the way Nixon and Henry Kissinger recrafted US Cold War strategies (see Chapter 3).

Second World challenges: cold economic warfare

Well before developments challenged post-war multilateralism, the Soviet Union posed serious problems that prompted Americans to deny it trade and forgo potential profits for US industry. Nikita Krushchev, in a characteristically angry outburst in 1963, captured the paradox of this when he screamed: 'Who the hell do these capitalists think they are, to believe that they can go around and not act like capitalists?'[8]

The use of strategic embargoes and sanctions is as old as history, but the nuclear age ushered in new priorities. The immediacy of nuclear destruction and the onset of Cold War persuaded US policy-makers that they should embargo the export of strategic items to communist states in the hope of maintaining American technological dominance. As policy formed between 1947 and 1951, however, problems arose to do with objectives and scope and how to make the embargo effective.

Washington wanted a strategic embargo to restrict the development of Soviet weapon systems and exacerbate inefficiencies in the Soviet command economy, which might eventually cause its collapse. But, to do this, the concept of strategic had to be stretched even beyond what are known as dual-purpose items, i.e. those that have both civilian and military uses. Accepting this policy objective made drawing the line between goods that should and should not be embargoed extremely difficult. Definitions of strategic are flexible or fungible in any case. For example, it might be more effective to embargo the export of buttons rather than guns if your opponent is less efficient at producing them. As wits have observed, soldiers cannot fight and hold their trousers up at the same time. More significantly, if an opponent has to shift limited resources to the production of buttons, which it can produce only at high comparative costs, then that diminishes overall output. Some in the Truman administration wanted a total Western ban on trade with the Soviet Union to maximise such effects, but four factors prevented that. The first was that the volume of US exports was so tiny that a total ban on them would have negligible effect. Second, a total ban would be provocative, could lead to Soviet retaliation against American allies, and it would also jar with the much vaunted US principle of non-discriminatory trade. Third, the countries of Western Europe already received massive amounts of dollar aid, but if their trade with the Soviet Bloc were curtailed savagely then they would lose materials important for their reconstruction, which the US would then have to replace with more dollar aid. And fourth, to be effective, the US needed a multilateral embargo, which meant cooperation with European allies, but they were not prepared to impose draconian trade measures against the Soviets.

The outcome of these considerations was the establishment of the Co-ordinating Committee or COCOM and a Consultative Group at the end of 1949 consisting of all NATO members except Iceland (Japan later joined in 1952). The COCOM, a highly secretive and officially unacknowledged committee, drew up multilateral embargo lists for the duration of the Cold War. However, they were never totally satisfactory for the US, which always maintained its own longer national embargo lists. The US exerted pressures on its allies to bring the COCOM into line with its national lists through Marshall Aid and, most notoriously, through the Mutual Defense Assistance Control (Battle Act) 1951, which threatened to terminate US aid to those countries that traded items forbidden by the US national lists. It is difficult to assess just how coercive these pressures were. Battle Act retribution was only ever invoked once. On all other occasions when violations occurred the president waived its provisions on the grounds of US national security interests. It is also important to remember that America's European allies did not need much persuading to embargo sensitive military technology, but they were reluctant to include other categories. They believed that trade would undermine communist regimes and seduce them into Western ways. During the Korean War there was widespread agreement on tightening the embargo, but, once the war wound down, the Europeans with the British in the vanguard, pressed for and achieved a major liberalisation of the lists in 1954 and an abandonment of the harsher embargo against the PRC, known as the China differential, in 1957. Americans accepted these changes with great reluctance, but realised that rigid opposition might provoke a total collapse of the multilateral system and that an American embargo alone would be ineffective. There were few signs of hegemonic dominance here.

In 1957 the Soviets launched Sputnik and demonstrated their technological prowess. By the 1960s the Soviet economy was flourishing and was able to offer trade and economic incentives to Third World countries. This worried the US and began to shift the focus of the Cold War away from head-to-head confrontation to a battle for the hearts and minds of the Third World. The Kennedy administration thus made a major reassessment of its embargo policy. It concluded that it was largely ineffective. Soviet technology had not been noticeably hampered in its development, the Soviet economy had grown strongly in the 1950s, and the regime looked in no danger of collapse. At the same time, US firms were being denied markets by the US national embargo lists that were open to their West European and Japanese competitors, and the periodic squabbles over the length of the COCOM lists were causing disruption in the Western Alliance. Why then should the embargo continue?

Walt Rostow, Chairman of the State Department PPS, 1961–66, provided an answer. While acknowledging that the original goals set for the embargo had not been achieved, he argued that it would be highly dangerous to abandon it without concessions from the Soviets. The embargo had become an important symbol of US Cold War strategy and there was danger of a wrong message – declining US resolve – being sent to friend and foe alike, if the US were to abandon it unilaterally. Instead, America should use the embargo to extract agreements from the Soviets to restrain their actions, and to behave in the international economy so as not to gain political advantage in Third World countries or to cause distortions in the free market.[9] For the remainder of the Cold War, with the possible exception of the Second Cold War 1979–83, US policy pursued this type of policy pragmatism. It was unable to make much progress during the Vietnam War, but an important component of Nixon's and Kissinger's *détente* and linkage policies was the offer of more trade with the West (see Chapter 3). The strategic embargo, except for non-negotiable areas such as weapons and high-technology dual-purpose systems, now became a flexible tool of diplomacy used for trading concessions with the Soviets or making symbolic statements of disapproval, such as Carter's grain embargo imposed in the wake of the Soviet invasion of Afghanistan. There were few who thought in the 1970s that it could significantly restrict Soviet technology or cause an economic implosion in the Soviet Union. However, in the first Reagan administration such ideas re-emerged.

Some of the Reagan administration's hard-line ideologues such as Defense Secretary Caspar Weinberger, William Brady in the Commerce Department, William Clark, NSA, and advisers such as Richard Perle and Richard Pipes, saw the situation in the early 1980s 'as a historic opportunity to exhaust the Soviet system'.[10] This was to be achieved by a two-pronged strategy: to squeeze exports in order to deny the Soviets new technology; and to stretch their economy to snapping point by forcing them to respond to a massive US arms build-up. Reagan appears to have had a rather different agenda and the bare facts tell a pragmatic rather than a consistent doctrinaire story. The US imposed sanctions on Poland and the USSR in December 1981 after the Polish declaration of martial law and the crackdown on the Solidarity trade union reform movement. Equipment for the Soviet oil industry was one of the key targets. Sanctions were later imposed extraterritorially against US allies in the summer of 1982 if their firms, or US subsidiaries based abroad, exported Western technology contrary to the new embargo. However, exemptions were made and the extraterritorial sanctions were lifted in November 1982 in the wake of defiance and protest from allies. In August 1983 the US lifted the embargo on oil pipeline-layers, and when Brady, Clark and Weinberger sought to introduce another round of sanctions in response to the Soviet shooting down of the Korean civilian airliner KAL-007 which had strayed into its airspace, it caused a real furore with William Root of the State Department resigning in protest. Secretary of State Shultz successfully headed off this new drive for more intensive cold economic warfare.[11] Successively in January and August 1984, Washington lifted most of the sanctions on Poland, and at the beginning of 1985 the first US trade mission since 1978 went to Moscow.[12] Needless to say, by this time most of the ideological hardliners had left the administration.

Despite all the violent criticisms of *détente*, in the end, Reagan practised something similar himself. Reagan was a great communicator and he used economic sanctions and the COCOM embargo primarily as forms of communication to bring the Soviets to the negotiating table. Even during 1981–83, when US rhetoric resonated with the clamour of strategic and economic aggression, and the ideological hardliners were at their most potent and presented with rich opportunities, a state of all-out cold economic warfare was never achieved nor even prevailed as a policy objective within the Reagan administration. Four main reasons may be offered for this. The volume of US trade conducted with the Soviet Union was still too small for its suspension to inflict damage. Differences with allies pre-empted the possibility of an effective tighter multilateral embargo. Bureaucratic differences and conflict within the administration provided the opportunity for the ideological hardliners to achieve tactical advantages, but they did not have the strength within the administration to sustain them beyond the short term. And the final and decisive reason was that Reagan intended to negotiate with the Soviets from a position of strength. He expected his overall strategy, including the array of economic tactics deployed, to bring the Soviets to constructive agreements rather than to vanquish them and their system.[13]

Third World challenges: justice versus efficiency

The 1970s not only challenged the US, but the whole ethos of Western capitalism. Capitalism might be the most efficient way of producing wealth but it fell far short of the ideal in distributing it. Assaults upon the entrenched position of the West came from writers at home such as Harry Magdoff,[14] who highlighted American economic imperialism and the fact that US 'aid' extracted handsome profits from poor countries (see Chapter 6). From abroad, criticism came from writers such as Frantz Fanon who attacked racism and the unjust legacy of colonialism.[15] Groups such as OPEC became more assertive and the economically underdeveloped non-aligned 'Group of 77' started to call for a

NIEO which would distribute resources and wealth more equitably. Specific demands were made for exemption from some of the GATT rules and to emulate OPEC's success by forming other cartels to raise commodity prices. They also demanded more credit, aid and management power in institutions such as the IMF. At the same time, there were linked and growing criticisms of the operation of Western MNCs for exploiting underdeveloped countries, for distorting their economic growth, and for creating an alienated clientele class often comprised of ex-patriots and supportive of corrupt, authoritarian local regimes. These demands and criticisms came at a bad time for Washington. Already troubled by recession, President Gerald Ford saw the NIEO as unacceptable socialist demands for a redistribution of the world's wealth. Counter-claims asserted that the free-market model was the most efficient and would eventually bring prosperity to all. In 1975 Secretary of State Kissinger made the most robust of US responses when he warned OPEC that the US would not tolerate oil prices rising to such an extent that they fundamentally threatened Western economies. Successive administrations also rejected criticisms of MNCs and defended them for bringing employment, investment and development and as a means for the international dissemination of technology and efficient production techniques. Such apologias sounded hollow in Guatemala and Chile where coups in 1954 and 1973 respectively against progressive regimes had been, at least partially, organised with the help of US companies.

While the demands of the NIEO were either not met or only partially achieved, it should not be overlooked that there were some successes. In 1977 Robert McNamara, President of the World Bank, called upon ex-German Chancellor, Willy Brandt, to assume the chairmanship of the Independent Commission for International Developmental Issues. On 12 February 1980 the Brandt Report was presented to the UN. It was sympathetic to the aspirations of the Third World, but it coincided with further world economic turmoil and only modest achievements were secured. For example, more resources were channelled into the Third World, often from private sources, and their proportion of world capital investment rose from 16.5 to 23.3% during the 1970s, but investment and growth were uneven. One effect of this was that the unity of the non-aligned countries was undermined. Countries like Brazil and the Asian Tiger Economies such as Singapore, Hong Kong, South Korea and Taiwan, developed interests more compatible with the advanced Western countries as they emerged from underdevelopment. Also OPEC became less effective as the West developed alternative power and oil sources. These developments further compromised the unity and effectiveness of the Group of 77. In retrospect, it was all a bit like trying to square the circle, expecting the weak to prevail against the strong.

The empire strikes back, 1973–89

As the economic turmoil of the 1970s continued, President Carter and Secretary of State Vance tried to resurrect some order through a series of economic summits, which aimed to coordinate national policies in a mutually helpful way. In particular, they strove to persuade West Germany and Japan to stimulate recovery by reinflating their economies, but with little success. In 1979 the overthrow of the Shah of Iran by revolutionary Islamic fundamentalists sparked off a new oil crisis, which reignited inflation in the West and led to further economic disarray and recession.

Entering office in 1981, President Reagan epitomised the type of inconsistency that has loomed so large in US foreign economic policy since 1971. He adopted aggressive unilateral policies to deal with trade issues and developed domestic economic policy in contradictory ways, which had negative effects on the world economy. Reagan intellectually rejected Keynesianism, cut taxes, raised interest rates to squeeze out inflation, but increased government spending massively on rearmament (a practical form of Keynesianism in recession), as a key strategy in the Second Cold War. These policies fostered a consumer-led recovery, fed largely by foreign imports. The impact on the international economy was substantial. High interest rates for the dollar, which remained the dominant international currency despite US economic problems, sucked in massive amounts of foreign investment, which in turn helped to offset the impact of the enormous US trade deficit. According to scholars like David Calleo, this was characteristic of an exploitative hegemon in decline.[16] These developments made the international economy more volatile and created a tendency for damagingly high interest rates elsewhere. The hardest hit were Third World countries, which accumulated massive service payments on dollar debts. This precipitated a crisis throughout the international economy. In 1982 Mexico announced that it could not service its debts of $80 billion and by 1990 total debts of the Third World stood at $1.3 trillion. Catastrophe was averted by rescheduling, writing down and cancelling debts, and by offering new aid.

This economic volatility brought forth some new initiatives. Hoping to build on the success of the Tokyo GATT talks, 1973–79, the US pushed for what became the Uruguay round 1986–93. In international monetary matters, the Europeans took an initiative in 1978 and produced the European Monetary System in their quest for stability. At the Plaza Hotel in New York in 1985, the US followed their example and agreed with Japan, Britain, France and Germany to seek more coordinated efforts in international economic policy, especially in monetary exchange matters. In the following year, Canada and Italy joined to form the Group of Seven (G-7).

Clearly, the US had not abandoned multilateralism, but this was not its only line of policy. Unilateralism, aggressive deregulation in industries where the US could benefit (such as the airline industry),[17] and moves towards protectionism were all part and parcel of policy during the 1980s. Successive USTRs under Reagan, William Brock III and Clayton Yeutter aggressively attacked reprobate trade partners and a particularly assertive policy was adopted to try to diminish the trade deficit with Japan. The US negotiated a large number of 'voluntary' agreements to limit the flood of imports. These agreements were voluntary in name alone: they were backed by aggressive diplomacy and threats of retaliation if they were not accepted and complied with. The limit on imports of Japanese cars was and remains the harshest post-war bilateral control that the US has negotiated. US trade relations with Japan reached their nadir in 1987 when, for the only time, the US followed through threats with actual sanctions in the case of Japanese exports of strategically important semiconductors. The US was also unhappy with barriers to service industries not covered by the GATT. By 1985 it was clear that non-tariff barriers were key issues in world trade and these applied in service, banking and financial sectors where the US felt it would have competitive advantages in a freer market. To many, these contradictory strategies seemed to be symptomatic of hegemonic decline. Now the US felt obliged to pursue its own national economic interests in the best way it could. Sometimes this would mean multilateral liberalism, at others protectionism or coercive bilateral arrangements, and by the end of the decade a free trade regional pact for North America was also under consideration.

Conclusion

Notwithstanding the negative responses to the demands for more justice in the world economy in the 1970s, there were many manifestations of US good intention and generosity throughout the Cold War: the Marshall Plan, the Alliance for Progress (see Chapter 6), public good costs shouldered by the US and overseas aid generally. Unfortunately, all too often such cases were compromised by Cold War priorities, or local conditions of corruption and authoritarianism, or unrealistic expectations about what the free market could achieve. The uneasy relationship that emerged between Western capitalism and the needs and aspirations of the Third World was something that would persist over time and pose ever more challenging problems for US foreign policy.

While America's strategic embargo did not achieve what its authors originally intended, it continued to contribute to foreign policy objectives. It did not significantly impair Soviet weapons technology, nor limit its economic growth, nor was it a significant cause of the eventual collapse of the Soviet Union (see Chapter 9). However, it did provide an important means of sending psychological and symbolic messages to foes, allies and America's domestic constituency about the resolve of the US to wage the Cold War vigorously. It provided a means of making manifest US moral condemnation of the Soviets, for example, when they invaded Afghanistan. It provided a means to communicate deterrent threats. And it provided a means of negotiating *détente*. In short, this type of economic statecraft carries nuances with it that are often overlooked or discounted when the question is asked: do sanctions and embargoes work?

The problems confronting the US in the 1970s and 1980s were different to those of 1945. Power was now more widely distributed among a larger number of nations, interests and values varied more between states, and the US was neither willing nor able to shoulder the burdens of leadership. Furthermore, while capitalism was immensely successful, it had created disparities in development, which both impacted harshly on the Third World and destabilised the international economy. Finally, there was no clear vision of what was needed as there had been in 1945.

Nixon had begun to confront America's economic shortcomings, but his remedies fell far short of solving them. The fall of Bretton Woods heralded a turbulence that spread beyond monetary problems. The US was confronted by new challenges posed by its relative economic decline. It was entwined in economic interdependence and troubled by severe recessions triggered by massive fuel price increases in 1973 and 1979. It was no longer able to absorb economic costs for political pay-offs, as it had done for the sake of the defence of the West and the development of the EEC, nor was it powerful enough to play a dominant economic managerial role. For many, this spelt the end of US economic hegemony. There was now a process of adjustment to influencing rather than dominating the world economy, which was also paralleled by more caution in the making of US foreign commitments and insistence that allies take more responsibility for their own security. The harsh fact was that in 1971 the international economic policy of the US had embarked upon a most turbulent sea of troubles with inadequate navigational equipment. Initially the voyage was under the constraints of Cold War imperatives, which largely subordinated economic to strategic priorities, but even so these constraints do not fully explain the contradictory directions that US economic policy pursued. One needs to appreciate also that the US after 1971 had to pursue its own economic interests in a system that was far less stable and far less dominated by American priorities and influence than had been the case since 1945.

5 The US and Europe, 1950–89

Was containment in Europe a success, a failure or a misreading of key European dynamics? Is it accurate to talk of US hegemony or even empire in Europe, be it the constructs of neo-Marxist economic determinism or voluntaristic forms, such as Geir Lundestad's 'empire by integration/invitation' and Charles S. Maier's 'analog of empire'?[1] Whatever the answers, it is clear that after 1950 Western Europe was a difficult theatre for US policy-makers because of interdependencies and the importance of alliance multilateralism. 'Inconvenient' leaders could not be toppled, nor client states built, nor economic aid be used to determine outcomes decisively. Western Europe's long-established states were America's key allies and disturbingly prone to regard the Cold War as an important but secondary issue next to defending their established interests, adjusting to a post-colonial world and contending with economic globalisation. They came to bite the hand that fed them, for their recovered stability owed much to US security guarantees, economic largess and consistent support for West European integration.

The nature of the problem

By 1950 Europe was, at least theoretically, probably the easiest place to wage containment. With the notable exceptions of Franco's Spain and Salazar's Portugal, the US could deal with countries where liberal democracy, capitalism and 'suitable' religions were well established. There were no difficult decisions required about political shades of revolutionary nationalist movements, and the clarity of the line drawn between East and West contrasted sharply with the jungles of Asia and the conflict-strewn Middle East. This line was established by Marshall Aid and COMECON, institutionalised in the aftermath of the Berlin Blockade in 1948 and consolidated beyond realistic challenge by the creation of NATO in 1949 and the Warsaw Pact in 1955. The only exceptions to Moscow's total control in the East were Tito's Yugoslavia and (from 1960) Albania. US policy towards Europe became focused on maintaining an East–West military stand-off, primarily through nuclear deterrence, and on using psychological warfare and economic statecraft to increase Soviet difficulties in keeping its satellites in close orbit. Despite periodic lofty American rhetoric about 'roll-back', nobody seriously believed that anything could, or should, be done when the Soviets brutally suppressed uprisings in Hungary in 1956 and in Czechoslovakia in 1968. To do otherwise would have risked drawing superior Soviet conventional forces across Europe and precipitating a nuclear conflict.

As far as any contested geographic region could be regarded as strategically stable during the Cold War, then Europe was it. Moreover, West European governments positively wanted continued American involvement in European affairs. They recognised their political, economic and military weaknesses and their vulnerability to the Red Army and communism. Even Western Europe's most powerful nation, Britain, while triumphant in the defeat of the Axis powers, was economically dependent on another country – the US – for the first time in its history. External support as well as intra-European cooperation was needed to enable West Europe to revert successfully to peacetime production and pre-war trade patterns. European states also needed to import security for fear of possible German revanchism and/or Soviet territorial expansionism. They did look to self-help. In March 1947 the Anglo-French Dunkirk Treaty was signed and in 1948 BTO was created. However, these initiatives were also designed to secure a US security guarantee for Europe, without which European defence was palpably deficient.

These European calculations provided powerful *realpolitik* arguments in favour of securing American political, economic and especially military commitments to Europe, even if a price had to be paid in return. Indeed, the Europeans were particularly receptive to American policy concerns because of their weak bargaining position and their fears of another American retreat to isolationism – concerns about which were sharpened by the abrupt termination of Lend–Lease aid and by rapid US demobilisation.

Yet, despite transatlantic cooperation in the Second World War and their shared political and social cultures, Western Europe still posed US policymakers with some of their most difficult problems. Why was this so? The beginnings of an answer lie in the enormity of the challenge to craft, from the wreckage and animosities within Europe, structures that would be friendly to the US, strong enough to resist communist subversion, cooperative enough to work together for political reconstruction and far-sighted enough to allow the rehabilitation of West Germany and Italy. Western Europe had also to be persuaded to dedicate scarce resources to rearmament and remobilisation at a time of severe domestic economic dislocation and shortages of manpower and basic consumer needs. Furthermore, US–European interdependence was already such that American political and economic fortunes rested on both the economic rejuvenation of Western European states and on deterring them from introspection that would damage American exports and leave the US with intolerable security burdens.

The states of Western Europe were nearly all democracies, but they were also very different in their political, economic, social, cultural and historical experiences, which soon complicated America's task greatly. France and Britain were colonial powers with a global outlook. West Germany was first occupied and then a semi-sovereign state that sought reacceptance into the international arena, but it also harboured desires for reunification. Spain was under Franco's fascist dictatorship and countries such as Finland, Sweden and Austria took refuge in Cold War neutrality. Nor were historical enmities and wartime experiences simply forgotten. Franco-German rivalry had been the focal point of two world wars and it became a cornerstone of French policy to exploit German weakness for economic and security advantages. Similarly, Greece and Turkey continued their long-running battle over Cyprus even after the US brought them within NATO in February 1952.

Another potential problem was that the Soviets would lure Western states into Cold War neutrality, a fear underscored by Austria accepting this status after Krushchev's withdrawal of the Red Army in May 1955. The principal concern after the Berlin Blockade was that West Germany might accept neutrality in return for reunification. This would be disastrous. West Germany was the linchpin of American policy in Europe because its geostrategic position, manpower and economy were vital to containing communism, and NATO's Forward Defence Strategy was based on the River Elbe. In 1957 the Soviets implicitly offered Bonn this trade through the Rapacki Plan, and followed up with an ultimatum in November 1958: either the West entered talks within six months over Germany or Krushchev would conclude a separate peace treaty and transfer East Berlin to East German control. Eighteen months of intermittent parleying between Eisenhower and Krushchev only soured their relationship, particularly when an American U-2 spy plane was brought down deep over Soviet territory in May 1960 and caused the Paris Four Power summit to be aborted. Eventually, Krushchev settled the issue of Berlin de facto by building the Wall, and in September 1971 the USSR and the West formally acknowledged the division of Berlin, with the Western sector linked to, but constitutionally separate from, West Germany.[2] Nevertheless, US policy-makers still feared the potential consequences of *Ostpolitik* and worried about weakening West German support for the Cold War.

More general problems stemmed from European *realpolitik* and from US interdependence with Western Europe. Deep tensions existed within US policies between anti-colonialism and reliance on Europe's colonial powers for Cold War defence in the Third World, which often resulted in US officials antagonising colonial and Third World allies alike. US policy-makers wanted Britain and France especially to maintain their international commitments and to furnish resources and overseas bases from their colonial possessions. At the same time they wanted to ally the US with the forces of Third World nationalism and criticised their colonial allies if they failed or refused to guide benevolently their colonies through to stable independence. These problems were exacerbated in two ways. First, there were creeping commitments. The US felt it necessary to help colonial powers fight against communist insurgents, but then found that it inherited ongoing obligations when the European powers withdrew. The most infamous example of this was Vietnam. Second, US policy-makers could not deal with the European powers in isolation from the rest of the world. Sometimes this gave them additional leverage over European allies, but on occasion they were forced to make concessions to them, even against their better judgement. For example, the US gave assistance in the early 1950s to France in Indochina in part to secure French support for West German rearmament through the European Defence Community (EDC). Likewise, it had to balance the Anglo-American special relationship against its initial preference that Britain lead European integration. How much pressure Washington could apply on London to overcome the latter's resistance to pooling sovereignty with European neighbours was limited by Britain being America's foremost partner in global containment and in managing the Bretton Woods system.[3]

Furthermore, it was not without good reason that the Founding Fathers had sought to remove America from the vicissitudes of Old World politics. American policy-makers soon found their European counterparts anxious to entangle them in European affairs and to push competitive agendas distinct from anti-communist containment. France recognised its need of American economic and military support but disagreed initially with US ideas for rehabilitating West Germany and disliked the prospect of an American-dominated Europe. Resistance to the latter hardened once Marshall Aid ended, and Washington later became concerned about Charles de Gaulle's aspirations for a French-led Western Europe to become a 'third force' between the superpowers. Even Britain could not be relied upon to agree with American policies or to prioritise anti-communism in the way that successive US administrations did. Its policy-makers resented British economic dependency on the US – symbolised by the contentious 1946 loan agreement – and many thought this situation to be but temporary. Their principal objective became to transmute '[American] power into useful forms',[4] these forms stretching far beyond containing communism to include the defence and promotion of British interests.

American policy-makers thus frequently found that their calculations were much different from those of their European counterparts. This was demonstrated by US–West European differences over whether to confront or negotiate with the Soviets. In November 1951 American policy-makers, preparing for a summit meeting between Truman and Churchill, detected 'a basic difference in our points of view' vis-à-vis the Soviets. The British, they felt, were taking a short-term perspective that inclined them to relax tensions with the Soviets somehow. US objectives were 'farther forward and longer run in character'. Rather than to freeze an unsatisfactory situation the Americans wanted the West to develop a position of overwhelming strength before negotiating with the Soviets so that it could force a retraction of their power.[5]

US–West European tactical differences became especially pronounced in the context of nuclear weapons. In West Germany particularly there was great ambivalence. While welcoming the security provided by hosting the greatest concentration of nuclear weapons in Western Europe, it also greatly feared nuclear war. Green, pacifist and left-wing groups led protests against nuclear weapons being deployed in West Germany, particularly during the Reagan era. Nor were fears of nuclear war and anti-nuclear protests confined to West Germany. Britain quickly perceived the particular vulnerabilities of a small, densely populated country in the nuclear age, which encouraged it to develop an independent nuclear deterrent and to favour minimising Cold War tensions. Furthermore, Western European countries had reservations about US deployment in Europe of tactical and intermediate range nuclear weapons and about its willingness to wage all-out nuclear war in the event of a conflict in Europe. These reservations were not unfounded. NATO exercise Carte Blanche, which simulated the use of tactical nuclear weapons, indicated that limited nuclear warfare would be total for Europe and less effective as a deterrent than total war. Moreover, US handling of the Cuban Missile Crisis (see Chapter 6) heightened fears that reckless American policies might drag Western Europe into a devastating nuclear exchange without any of its states having a say.

Integration: the panacea for Western Europe?

How could Western Europe overcome its historic divisions and contribute to the prosecution of global containment? A starting point had to be military security. The Truman administration was reluctant to cast aside George Washington's caution against America becoming entangled in alliances. However, it became increasingly obvious that West European capabilities were insufficient to counter the USSR, especially once the Soviets detonated their first atomic bomb in 1949. Under great pressure from Britain especially, the Truman administration eventually guaranteed Western Europe's security through NATO, which became the principal hard security organisation and forum for transatlantic security dialogue. NATO drew in countries from beyond the BTO that were of strategic significance in their own right, such as Norway, and/or had control over strategically important territories, such as Portugal with its control of the Azores, and Denmark with its connection with Greenland. NATO also became far more than a military alliance. It developed an extensive committee system that dealt with subjects as diverse as collective defence, foreign policy consultation, settlement of intra-alliance disputes and cooperation on cultural, scientific, economic, technical and even social issues.

Initial US atomic supremacy made offsetting West Europe's immediate military vulnerability relatively straightforward. More problematic were its vulnerability to communist subversion, potential long-term dependence upon the US and possible fragmentation before Soviet pressure, economic incentives and invitations to neutrality. The Truman and Eisenhower administrations' principal answer to these problems was to 'remake Europe in an American mode'[6] by encouraging European integration. Transplanting the American model of interstate trade and a single market to Europe would stimulate economic recovery and in the medium term provide the US with a strong trading partner. GATT, the World Bank and the IMF would help ensure that the 'price' paid by America for sacrificing its original post-war commitment to international free trade to the sponsorship of regional integration would be temporary. Toleration of discriminatory trade arrangements in Western Europe and of its preferential overseas linkages even promised to ease both the dollar shortage and America's resource transfer to Europe. The faster the European economies regenerated then the quicker the US would be freed of onerous aid commitments. Also, colonies provided European powers with non-dollar raw materials and, as commodity producers, access to dollars. Without them the US would have had to find other ways to obviate further material and currency shortages. These reasons help explain why the Truman and Eisenhower administrations accepted, for example, both the inherent dollar discrimination of the Sterling Area – irrespective of the rules of GATT, the IMF and provisions of the Anglo-American loan agreement – and a limited obligation to indemnify Britain for any loss of gold or dollars arising from European transactions with the overseas Sterling Area.[7]

Changing the very fabric of European politics through pooling sovereignty was also thought to offer numerous advantages. A United States of Europe based on the American federal model offered opportunity to export US democratic and free market values as well as political structures to Western Europe. As Kelleher has argued: 'The existence of a Europe "like us" was a precondition to the establishment of an international order conducive to American political and economic interests.'[8] A federal system might also tame volatile nationalisms without destroying Europe's cultural, political and historical diversity. As such, integration promised to be a vehicle for political reconstruction and psychological reconciliation. Nowhere was this more important than in offering an 'answer' to the German question. When the Cold War began to intensify in the late 1940s and early 1950s it was far too soon to grant West Germany full sovereignty, not least because of justifiable French opposition. Yet, West German economic, political and, even, military power had to be harnessed to Western Cold War defence and reconstruction. It was vital, too, to the consolidation of West Germany's fragile democracy that Chancellor Adenauer could demonstrate his country's economic development and reacceptance by the Western Alliance, including France. Cooperation, deepening interdependence and, in particular, supranational controls offered a compromise position between German independence and the restoration of full national sovereignty.[9]

US policy-makers generally believed that a united Western Europe was best placed economically and militarily to resist communist subversion and to contribute more effectively to its own security. This was reflected in their sponsorship of the European Payments Union, which by providing credit on a monthly basis was designed to speed the recovery of European trade previously restricted by bilateral payments arrangements. It was also reflected in the ambition, from the Eisenhower administration onward, that a united and prosperous Western Europe should serve as a force of attraction to Soviet Eastern European satellites and contribute thereby to Soviet difficulties in controlling the Eastern Bloc. Most controversial, though, were American ideas for rearming West Germany. On 12 September 1950, Secretary of State Acheson dropped 'the bomb at the Waldorf': West Germany had to be rearmed within NATO to the tune of ten divisions because of the increased military demands created by the globalisation of containment and the outbreak of the Korean War. France objected for fear of losing control over West Germany and lest remilitarisation resurrected German nationalism and weakened democratic control in the Federal Republic of Germany (FRG). However, it was unable to resist US pressure to rearm West Germany, not least because of its need of American economic aid and support in Indochina. It consequently advanced the Pleven Plan whereby all German military units, but only a percentage of French units, would be integrated into a supranational army. This would protect French security interests and limit any German sense of military identity. The Eisenhower administration disliked the obvious inequity of these ideas but did see political and military advantages in a supranational European army. Dulles famously spoke of an 'agonising reappraisal' that warned of possible US withdrawal from Europe if the EDC failed. Ultimately he accepted a British-sponsored alternative. The 1948 Brussels Treaty was extended to Italy and West Germany to form the Western European Union (WEU), and Britain made additional military commitments to continental Europe, which, among other things, were designed to reassure the French. Nevertheless, Dulles still bemoaned the loss of supranationalism in this arrangement: 'This was always to me the most important aspect of the EDC.'[10]

America's most direct sponsorship of integration came in the formative years of the late 1940s and early 1950s. The distribution of Marshall Aid was made conditional upon a collective European response and an integrated plan for European recovery. That spawned the Organisation for European Economic Cooperation (OEEC), which the Americans hoped would evolve into some sort of binding customs union and stimulate positive integration. They also supported the 1948 Hague Conference and encouraged European federalists. Between 1949 and 1960 the US channelled $3–4 million to various federalist activities in Europe, and in 1950 helped steer the leadership of the European Movement away from British influence towards the more ambitious approach of Belgian Foreign Minister Paul-Henri Spaak.[11]

The Truman administration enthusiastically endorsed the proposal of Jean Monnet, head of the French economic modernisation programme, for a European Coal and Steel Community (ECSC). Concerns about its cartel implications paled next to the prospect of putting essential ingredients for war-making under supranational control, binding the FRG tighter to the West, and fostering Franco-German reconciliation. In April 1951, the Treaty of Paris duly established the ECSC with a membership of West Germany, France, Italy and the Benelux. The Eisenhower administration likewise welcomed agreement in 1957 of the European Economic Community and Euratom. It was hoped that the former would encourage modernisation of weaker economies, promote intra-European trade and spur the Community to accept greater external trade liberalisation. This latter objective was complemented by work within GATT and by encouraging British EEC candidature in the belief that Britain would make the Community more outward looking and counterbalance French protectionism. As for Euratom, this offered a potential way to channel continental nuclear ambitions into a supranational framework, which promised to be more effective and easier for the US to influence than multiple national programmes.

Successive American administrations routinely endorsed the widening and deepening of European integration as being in the interests of America, Europe and the Free World. This did not mean, however, that there were no tensions within their support for European integration. American policy-makers quickly recognised that promoting regionalism risked strengthening discrimination against US economic interests and storing up difficulties for the future exercise of American influence over their erstwhile protégé. There was indecision about how far they wanted Britain integrated into Europe, not least because its reluctance to cede sovereignty might derail the progress made by the six signatories of the ECSC and EEC. And there was concern that an EEC caucus within NATO might weaken American leadership there. Nevertheless, Washington initially assumed that transatlantic interests were sufficiently complementary to ensure that integration developed in tandem with an atlanticist security framework. Doubts about this complementarity developed from the mid-1950s, but American policy-makers continued to believe that the benefits of European integration outweighed its costs. It made conflict within Western Europe unthinkable and so successfully overcame Franco-German antipathy that their relationship became the axis of European integration throughout the Cold War and beyond. Integration also delivered economic prosperity and security to Western Europe: the EEC far out-performed the rival British-sponsored European Free Trade Association, and between 1958 and 1967 intra-EEC trade doubled as a percentage of member states' total trade.[12] Most important of all, European integration helped both to secure the dual containment of Germany and the USSR and to restrain French ambitions, unpalatable to the Americans, for developing Europe as an independent third force.

Beware your allies?

Although the US and Western Europe were locked together by fear of the USSR, economic interdependence and shared values, there were episodes of severe transatlantic friction. Examples include Truman's intimation that he might use the atomic bomb in Korea, Eisenhower's stance during the Suez Crisis, US unilateralism in its handling of the Cuban Missile Crisis, US policy towards Vietnam and the wisdom of Reagan's reinvigoration of the Cold War and his subsequent bilateral strategic arms reduction negotiations with the Soviets. There were also regular differences arising from Western Europe's reluctance to adopt such hard-line anti-communist stances as America's. For instance, key allies in Western Europe, including Britain, recognised the People's Republic of China long before the US did. Similarly there were recurrent tensions within strategic embargo policy, over the West European abandonment of the China differential and about their preference for less extensive COCOM control lists than those proposed by Washington (see Chapter 4). Even within NATO there were running sores that long survived the controversy over West Germany's eventual integration into the Alliance in May 1955. US administrations repeatedly berated their NATO allies for failing to dedicate more resources to the collective defence effort; despite the fact that they consistently provided 80–90% of the land forces in Europe. Disputes continued about control over armaments levels, the development of interoperability and competition over the production of technologically advanced weaponry. And, above all else, there was competition for influence within NATO and recurring West European fears about whether US security guarantees would hold good should the Cold War become 'hot'. Indeed, US Secretary of State Acheson noted in retrospect the irony of the marine band playing at the NATO ceremony in April 1949 'I've got plenty of nothin' and 'It ain't necessarily so'.[13]

By the mid-1950s American policy-makers had to revisit assumptions about complementarity between US and Western European interests. Four key problems confronted them: US relative economic decline, the implications of the nuclearisation of NATO strategy, fears of a West German *rapprochement* with the USSR, and General de Gaulle's vision of a French-led Europe as an independent 'third force'. Although the challenge from the East, which centred on Berlin, was settled by the building of the Berlin Wall, this actually fed American fears about the interlinked challenges of Western Europe's growing economic strength and de Gaulle's ability to hijack the integration process for French ends. In particular, would German dissatisfaction with the West's response to Krushchev and the construction of the Berlin Wall drive Bonn further into the arms of de Gaulle and to favour greater accommodation with the Soviets?

American influence over Europe was in relative decline by the mid-1950s. Marshall Aid was over and the Mutual Defense Assistance Program, which took over from it during the Korean War, was being run down. Economic recovery and NATO guarantees made West European countries relatively less concerned about communist subversion and the Soviet military threat. And, most especially, the US economy had begun to falter under the burden of containment and in the face of the rise of competing centres of economic power. In 1958–59 the US payments deficit increased markedly, 1960 witnessed the novelty of a run on the dollar, and foreign holdings of dollars exceeded the US gold reserve for the first time. Between 1957 and 1963 the US lost $7.4 billion from its gold reserves and a pattern similar to that which had afflicted Britain since at least the Second World War appeared to be emerging: imbalance of payments, sluggish growth, inadequate export income to fund overseas commitments, faltering international confidence in the currency and complications for its domestic role arising from that.[14] Moreover, matters seemed set to worsen. First, Kennedy rejected Eisenhower's commitment to balanced budgets and low inflation in favour of Keynesian economic policies that were designed, at least partially, to finance a massive increase in defence and overseas spending. Second, Japan and Western Europe were both experiencing rapid growth and becoming serious economic competitors to the US, a development that America helped to underwrite through its initial commitment to their economic reconstruction and then by subsidising their security. Third, European integration was beginning to exact some of the economic costs that American policy-makers had foreseen. Creation of the EEC brought with it new discriminatory policies, such as a Customs Union with a Common External Tariff (CET) and a Common Agricultural Policy (CAP). These policies would damage US exports to Europe and elsewhere, particularly if Britain were to join the EEC with preferential deals for its Commonwealth and dependencies and without a simultaneous liberalisation of the CET.

The nuclearisation of NATO strategy developed in the 1950s due primarily to perceived conventional inferiority vis-à-vis the Soviet Union. This perception was widely shared within NATO, though its accuracy was later questioned.[15] However, continental European NATO allies suspected that Britain and America also favoured nuclearisation so that they could reduce the economic costs of their conventional commitments to Europe and redeploy troops elsewhere. This aggravated tensions within NATO about control over the nuclear arsenal and how to mesh the conventional 'shield' and the atomic 'sword'. NATO's official strategy called for Forward Defence, which meant repelling Soviet aggression as far east as possible. Continental European NATO members feared nevertheless that in the event of conflict, Britain and the US would adopt a peripheral strategy that would allow continental Europe to absorb the brunt of a Soviet attack before trying to reconquer what was left after a month of conventional armoured operations accompanied by tactical nuclear strikes.[16] In addition, the prospect of reduced conventional American commitment to Europe increased Western Europe's fear of an American nuclear betrayal. Would Washington wage total nuclear war for the sake of Europe or might the US and USSR manage a limited nuclear war that destroyed Europe but left their homelands relatively unscathed? Even the British indirectly broached this question, no doubt remembering the American 'nuclear betrayal' in the aftermath of the Second World War that was symbolised by the McMahon Act. The 1964 British Statement on Defence argued that 'if there were no power in Europe capable of inflicting unacceptable damage on a potential enemy he might be tempted . . . to attack in the mistaken belief that the United States would not act unless America herself were attacked'.[17]

One consequence of this was that much of nuclear policy within NATO became more concerned with mutual reassurance than warning the Soviet Union.[18] This reassurance included America maintaining a substantial troop presence in Europe as a 'trip wire' or 'plate glass' between Western Europe's conventional defence and America's nuclear guarantee. Just as importantly, the nuclearisation debate provoked divergent European responses. For Britain it re-emphasised the importance of maintaining its own nuclear deterrent as a tool of influence and insurance. However, it was happy that this be kept within the existing Atlantic framework and after aborting its Blue Streak missile programme and agreeing at Nassau to purchase Polaris as a replacement, Britain increasingly relied on America for its 'independent' deterrent. France reacted differently, especially once de Gaulle returned to power in June 1958.

Nuclear dependency on an uncertain American guarantee created vulnerability and political dependency on the US. These fears were underscored by Eisenhower's failure to support France in the Suez Crisis, the Soviet launch of Sputnik in 1957, and by Kennedy's failure to consult allies when responding to the Cuban Missile Crisis. France exploded its first atomic bomb in 1960 and de Gaulle developed the *force de frappe* as a central instrument in his challenge to American leadership in Europe. The logic of liberating Europe of strategic dependence drove French interest in Euratom and in the possible development of a European deterrent, which potentially included atomic weapons cooperation with West Germany.

Bonn had promised not to develop atomic weapons, but as the front-line of any East–West conflict in Europe was anxious that NATO guarantees remained as automatic as possible. However, it did play on Western fears of a nuclear Germany and indicated its desire for greater control over nuclear decisions that affected it. Recent scholarship has also presented archival evidence that suggests West German Chancellor Adenauer especially was interested in using Euratom 'as the quickest way to gain the option to produce nuclear weapons'.[19] Washington saw grave danger in the combination of German concern about control of nuclear weapons, exclusion from nuclear technology and disillusion with US handling of Berlin's future. Bonn might seek conciliation with the East and/or be drawn into de Gaulle's vision for a united Europe from the Atlantic to the Urals. The Americans were so sensitive to this threat of Franco-German desertion that, when Paris and Bonn signed a Treaty of Friendship in 1963, President Kennedy called it 'an unfriendly act'.[20]

The Kennedy administration responded to these problems with a utopian dream. Britain should enter the EEC to improve the latter's atlanticist perspective. A multilateral nuclear force (MLNF) should be developed to give the semblance of nuclear equality among NATO's key members but establishing overall US control. And, in Kennedy's Grand Design of 4 July 1962, Congress would approve the Trade Expansion Act and thus enable the US to use the next GATT talks to develop some sort of transatlantic free trade area. These ideas betrayed a gross misreading of the political environment in Europe and of the extent of American power. Neither France nor Britain would give up its independent nuclear deterrents and the MLNF was finally compromised when Kennedy, still trying to rebuild Anglo-American relations after the 1956 Suez Crisis, felt compelled to offer Prime Minister Macmillan Polaris missiles in December 1962. This deal at Nassau also provided de Gaulle with the perfect excuse to veto British membership of the EEC in 1963: Britain would be a 'Trojan Horse' for American interests in Europe and undermine integration. As for US ideas of a transatlantic free trade area, these too failed to materialise. Instead, the Dillon Round demonstrated that the EEC's growing economic power meant that the US could no longer dominate GATT and relations between the two degenerated into the first serious trade dispute in 1962, the so-called 'Chicken War'.[21]

De Gaulle's radical assault upon American leadership stalled in the face of West German loyalty to NATO, lack of Soviet interest in his vision for Europe and insufficient French resources to then develop much more than a regional nuclear capability, which, when combined with problems of warning times, made a European deterrent independent of the Atlantic Alliance difficult to present as a credible reality. Nevertheless, the remainder of the 1960s still saw American leadership under increasing pressure. Washington became preoccupied with Vietnam and its prosecution of the war there provoked increasingly fierce criticism from within and without NATO. Even Britain declined to meet President Johnson's request in July 1966 for just token forces – not even a platoon of bagpipers.[22] Moreover, there was widespread scepticism in Europe that South-east Asia had become the new front-line of the Cold War and fear that the diversion of American resources to the periphery compromised the strategic centre. Interestingly, the father of containment, George Kennan, shared this view. In February 1966 he told the US Senate that involvement in Vietnam was diverting attention from 'great and potentially more important questions of world affairs' and that 'in some instances assets we already enjoy and hopefully possibilities we should be developing are being sacrificed to this unpromising involvement in a remote and secondary theatre'.[23]

Charles de Gaulle certainly took advantage of US preoccupations in Vietnam to promote French influence and undermine America's position in Western Europe. The importance of the American nuclear guarantee prevented West Germany from sacrificing Washington for Paris, but the US could not dissuade either de Gaulle or West German Chancellor Brandt from establishing economic and cultural ties with the Eastern Bloc. Nor could de Gaulle be prevented from undermining the political and economic position of the US. In 1966, he damaged NATO by withdrawing France from its Military Command structure and in doing so forced the removal from French soil of the organisation's headquarters and of 26,000 US troops. In 1967, he again thwarted US hopes to use Britain to open up the EEC by vetoing its entry for a second time. He also successfully attacked the Bretton Woods system, which was seen as the hallmark of US economic hegemony. De Gaulle speculated against sterling and in the mid-1960s demanded that the US Treasury redeem in gold several hundred million dollars. This helped force British devaluation in November 1967, set off another wave of speculation against the dollar, and ensured that by 1970 US ambitions for the Bretton Woods system and multilateralism were in free-fall.

From 1970 to 1989, the US tried intermittently to improve transatlantic relations, particularly once de Gaulle left office. Some of these efforts were singularly unsuccessful, such as when the Nixon administration, without consulting its European allies, declared 1973 the 'Year of Europe'. President Carter made a better impression in 1978 with what was the first presidential visit to the European Commission in Brussels. GATT continued to be useful in mitigating transatlantic economic friction, and offset agreements with West Germany helped to ease the financial burden of keeping US troops in Europe and undermined support for Senator Mike Mansfield's repeated calls in the 1970s for US troop withdrawals. NATO, despite French spoiling actions in the mid-1960s, remained the cornerstone of transatlantic security cooperation. For instance, in 1977 the Carter administration secured a pledge from NATO member states to increase defence spending by 3% per year from 1976 until 1986, and in May 1978 a Long Term Defence Programme was agreed that included improvement across a range of capabilities and an upgrade of theatre nuclear defence. The latter was propelled by Soviet deployment of SS-20 missiles and the Backfire bomber, and culminated in agreement in December 1979 to base Pershing II and ground-launched Cruise missiles in several European countries from December 1983.

Overall, though, the post-de Gaulle era brought little success for American hopes that Europe would either accept greater economic sacrifices to underwrite the American economy, or defer to Washington's political leadership, or become more outward looking. Instead, it became clear both that the economic balance of power had shifted markedly and that the US was increasingly out of step with Western Europe.[24] Nixon reacted to the problems of the 1960s by trying to develop as many bilateral links as possible between Washington and West European capitals in the hope that this would give the US more leverage than dealing through the European institutions. Nevertheless, the US received increasingly selective support on both Cold War and economic issues because Western Europe was conscious of its growing economic power and felt relatively little threat from the East. In the early 1970s, West Germany refused to help the dollar and, despite Nixon's attempts to prevent it, the Bretton Woods system duly collapsed. Moreover, this important source of American power was soon supplanted in Europe by the EC's creation in 1978 of the European Monetary System, which 'in a sense, represented a German-led declaration of monetary independence from the dollar'.[25]

Nor could America take European political support for granted. Most NATO members refused to support the US during the Yom Kippur War in 1973 and EC member states began to coordinate their foreign policies through European Political Cooperation (EPC), which, although often fragile, nevertheless demonstrated growing European willingness to disagree with Washington. In June 1980, the EC declared against US policy and in favour of a Palestinian homeland and participation in Arab–Israeli peace talks. In 1986 EPC refused to support US measures against Libya in retaliation for its alleged terrorist links and, while Britain provided facilities, France and Spain notably denied their airspace to American aircraft involved in launching military strikes against selected Libyan targets. The EC even seemed willing to challenge American policy in the Western Hemisphere. The two agreed in wanting reform of Fidel Castro's regime in Cuba but, whereas the US imposed a punitive total economic embargo, the EC preferred engagement and socialisation of Havana, including humanitarian aid and developing trade links. There were differences also over the civil war in El Salvador and the conflict in Nicaragua between Contras and Sandinistas following the 1979 revolution. The US backed the Contras in Nicaragua and successive repressive governments in El Salvador. The EC, however, provided Nicaragua with considerable food aid and, at the 1983 Stuttgart European Council, called for a peaceful resolution to conflicts in Central America based on principles of respect for human rights and, poignantly for America, non-intervention. In September 1984 it also took part in what became known as the San José Process; the US was noticeably absent from this first meeting, which was designed to explore avenues for peaceful settlement of regional conflict.[26]

Transatlantic friction became particularly acute during Reagan's first term.[27] His resurrection of the Anglo-American special relationship with Margaret Thatcher revived the long-debated issue of Britain's commitment to integration, even though it had finally joined the EC in 1973. More importantly, the majority of Western Europe did not subscribe to his reinvigoration of the Cold War, feared the repercussions of his bilateral negotiations with Gorbachev over nuclear weapons, and considered SDI to be a grave threat to strategic stability (see Chapter 2). Major popular opposition developed to the deployment of US Cruise and Pershing II missiles in Europe. European governments resented Washington's simultaneous insistence on bilateral American–Soviet talks and demands that they should make greater commitments to containment. They also refused to abandon growing economic links with the East. For instance, in the early 1980s there was a major transatlantic disagreement over sales of oil and gas industry equipment to the USSR and the construction of a pipeline that would deliver Siberian gas supplies to Western Europe. In June 1982, the Reagan administration, believing that the transfer of technology and equipment to the USSR would indirectly aid its military effort and its national security, imposed sanctions on American subsidiaries and licence holders in Western Europe involved in the pipeline project. The EC denounced the action as illegal and took measures to compel national companies to fulfil their legally binding contracts. Even Margaret Thatcher 'continuously harangued the President and his advisers about the extraterritorial application of US sanctions'.[28]

These increasing differences reflected the changing balance of power within US–EC relations and the latter's greater freedom of manoeuvre as the Cold War wound down. They also resulted in a much more defensive American posture towards European integration, which was apparent in Reagan's extreme sensitivity about US leadership. As the EC enlarged its membership and its economic strength grew, so too did the tension between European political integration and American leadership in Europe through NATO. When France proposed reactivating the WEU in 1984, the Reagan administration feared that it was an implicit challenge to NATO supremacy. When the EC agreed the 1986 Single European Act, which aimed to create a single European market by 1992, Reagan responded with protectionist measures and alarmist images of a 'Fortress Europe'. And when it came to international trade, Washington and Brussels were frequently locked in conflict. The European Commission studiously avoided liberalising European policies lest it damage either European competitiveness or the fragile political consensus upon which further integration depended. This, coupled with European introversion as economic depression hit in the early 1980s, meant that the CAP continued to be a major transatlantic sore, as did issues relating to banking, insurance, public procurement and the airline industry.

Conclusion

Despite the irritant of Berlin, the Cold War condition of Europe was quickly stabilised and American policy-makers became preoccupied as much with preserving American influence and holding their allies in check as with the Soviet Union. Successive administrations stressed the pre-eminence of US-dominated NATO and encouraged European integration as a way of reconstructing Europe while also securing the dual containment of the USSR and Germany and resisting de Gaulle's leadership challenge. The results were at best mixed. Nixon once warned the Europeans that they could not have US cooperation and participation on security issues and at the same time engage in confrontation, or even hostility, on the political and economic fronts. He was wrong. The European nation-states knew that they were geostrategically, politically and economically invaluable to Washington, and once NATO was established they were freer to reassert themselves. US commitment to containment policy ironically allowed the Europeans to see the Cold War often as an issue secondary to their post-war adjustment to the more powerful and enduring force of economic globalisation.

Did America 'win' the battle in Europe? If the battle really was simply to contain communism, then the US succeeded. However, if policy-makers misread the dominant dynamic in European capitals, then that success needs major qualification because the Europeans used the US ruthlessly for their own ends. In particular, in relative terms, they freewheeled in the security domain and exploited the competitive advantage that this gave them in the economic and political spheres. When the Cold War ended, US–West European interdependence was as immutable as it had been in the immediate post-war years. However, the balance of power had so shifted that Washington, if ever it had been, could no longer be sure of being able to block West European actions, let alone determine them. The EC had enlarged to 12 countries and further admissions were certain to follow the collapse of the Berlin Wall. Its economic power within GATT and policies such as CAP and the Single Market threatened to undermine US interests. And the future of NATO and American influence in Europe were brought into question by the loss of a common enemy and by French-led European interest in security arrangements that were less dependent on the US.

Finally, what does all of this reveal of American power and influence in post-Second World War Europe? Western Europe was undoubtedly a supplicant to the US for security throughout the Cold War, especially for the nuclear guarantee. The US was also able to exercise considerable political and economic influence and created structures that institutionalised its power, including GATT, IMF, World Bank and NATO command. Concomitantly, relative US power waned over time as it laboured under the burdens of maintaining the Western economic and security systems. This is the stuff of classic overstretch and hegemonic decline. Yet, even at the peak of its power in the immediate post-war years, America struggled to impress its will upon its major European allies. France scuttled the EDC; Britain refused to lead European integration; the Scandinavian countries declined to participate in supranational integration; Norway and Denmark disassociated themselves from NATO nuclear strategy; and France pulled out of the Military Command. Even Marshall Aid eroded only the edges of national sovereignty.[29] These contradictory indicators ensure that debate about American influence over Western Europe will continue to produce different positions along the spectrum of opinion from J.L. Gaddis's voluntaristic empire, R.T. Griffiths's view of American hegemony theory being outdated, K. Schwabe's argument of American decline after the EDC debacle, and A.P. Dobson's rejection of the whole idea that 'hegemony' can accurately capture the nature of the US relationship with Europe.[30]

6 Hegemony and the Western Hemisphere

Debate about US power is endless, but there is a consensus that it has been preponderant since 1945. Following on from this come the now familiar claims about US hegemony and this nowhere seems more apt than in the Western Hemisphere where there have been regular interventions by the US into the affairs of other states and continuous attempts to socialise them into free market ways, liberal politics and anti-communism.[1] For a while, after Franklin Roosevelt proclaimed the Good Neighbour Policy in 1933, the US specifically rejected the idea of interventionism in Latin America. However, Cold War priorities soon mandated intervention once again on national security grounds, sometimes through threats of economic reprisal, sometimes through covert activities, and sometimes by a bald reversion to old ways that had been publicly formulated and justified by Franklin's cousin Theodore Roosevelt in his famous 1904 Corollary to the Monroe Doctrine. This went beyond trying to keep Europe out of hemispheric affairs and sought to justify US intervention in them as and when necessary:

> Chronic wrongdoing, or an impotence which results in a general loosening of the ties of civilized society, may in America, as elsewhere, ultimately require intervention by some civilized nation, and in the Western Hemisphere the adherence of the United States to the Monroe Doctrine may force the United States, however reluctantly, in flagrant cases of such wrongdoing or impotence, to the exercise of an international police power.[2]

Self-interest, arrogance and idealism were deeply embedded in this doctrine and they flowed naturally from traditional conceptions of manifest destiny and American exceptionalism. These were thus not new characteristics of US foreign policy and nearly a century later were to be reformulated by the administration of George W. Bush to justify America's right to intervene preventatively across the globe to deal with terrorism and WMDs and to spread democracy and the free market. Immediately after the Second World War, US strategy in the Americas was more defensive – to contain communism – but this gradually developed into a more pro-active policy of interventionism in its backyard.

After the Second World War, the US had important security interests to protect in the region, most notably the Panama Canal Zone, which the US had obtained in 1905 and which provided a short route for the US navy between the Atlantic and the Pacific. The US also had important investments, markets and sources of supply in Latin America. To post-war US leaders, all these interests were threatened by communism. As in Europe, the fear was not of a red army, but of red ideas subverting countries from within and thus threatening US security and vested economic interests. With the global challenge from communism it seemed essential to ensure that the rules of the system – market economies, liberal political values and anti-communism – should at least be enforced in the backyard. With these containment ideas in mind, the US signed the Rio Military Pact in 1947, which promulgated the principle that an attack on any American country would be taken as an attack on them all. A year later, a further hemispheric management structure was created at Bogota, the Organisation of American States (OAS). Contrary to US wishes, however, article 15 of the OAS charter outlawed intervention in the internal or external affairs of any other state. This principle was soon flouted.

Guatemala, 1954

The first challenge to the hegemonic prerogatives of the US arose in Central America, and its response set a pattern for the future. In 1944, General Jorge Ubico's dictatorship over Guatemala came to an end. He had compared his brand of justice with God's and Hitler's. There followed a period of mild reform to deal with land distribution – the most serious economic problem of Latin America. In Guatemala 50% of the population held 3% of the land and the elite 2% held 60%. In 1951 a more robust reformer came to power, Jacobo Arbenz Guzman, but he had the problem of the Boston-based United Fruit Company (UFC), which owned over 60% of the arable land, paid low wages, cheated the government out of legitimate revenue and under-utilised the land it owned.

In March 1953, Arbenz appropriated a quarter of a million acres from the UFC and offered to compensate the company at the level it had valued the land for tax purposes, $600,000. The UFC responded by demanding $15.8 million: a sum that Secretary of State John Foster Dulles pronounced as no less than required by international law. Unfortunately for Arbenz, both John Foster and his brother Allen Dulles, Director of the CIA, had close connections with the UFC through their family law firm.

Over the following months there followed a murky story of intrigue and propaganda. Guatemala received a shipment of small arms from the Eastern Bloc and was falsely denounced as communist. John Foster Dulles conjured up the spectre of a communist assault on the Panama Canal Zone, of reds swarming up (over 1,000 miles from Guatemala) to, and then no doubt beyond, the Central American isthmus into Mexico and on to the US itself. As opposition to Arbenz was stirred up, the CIA laid its plans. It found a willing collaborator in Colonel Castillo Armas.

The CIA colluded with the long-established Somoza dictatorship in Nicaragua and trained troops there under Armas. The propaganda war was stepped up and then, on 8 June 1954, Armas led a small army into Guatemala. Its success was not immediate and so American-flown planes dropped charges of dynamite on Guatemala City, after which the government and its army parted company: Arbenz was isolated. Armas took over, returned the land to the UFC, and shot most of the supporters of the previous regime. His government was corrupt and it brutalised and held back the development of the country. This was a classic case of neo-imperialism: control without the trappings of formal empire. There were all the components identified by New Left writers such as William Appleman Williams: the economic forces of capitalism, the power of government enlisted for their defence, propaganda and subversion of the democratic process, the use of secretive and largely unaccountable power of the state in the form of the CIA, and the demonisation of the enemy as communist.[3] This pattern, with minor variations, was to occur time and again in the Western Hemisphere once the Guatemala coup had set the precedent. But, it was not just Americans who learnt from this. Fidel Castro would not make the same mistake as Arbenz and allow a feeble military attack to cut away his military support. In Cuba he created a people's army that would require more than a minor surgical operation to sever it from its political leaders. As a result Cuba became the key Cold War issue in the Western Hemisphere and for a while in October 1962 it held the entire world stage all to itself.

Cuba and problems in the Western Hemisphere

On New Year's Day 1959, Fidel Castro and his guerrilla army marched into Havana and ended the much hated, violent, oppressive and deeply corrupt regime of Fulgencio Batista. Four months later he visited the US: it was not a success. Dispute still continues as to whether he was pushed away by the Americans, or voluntarily chose communism. It was probably a mixture of both. By February 1960, already colliding with US interests as he tried to assert Cuban control over the economy, Castro turned to the Soviets for help and signed a trade agreement with them. Soviet Premier Nikita Krushchev then pronounced provocatively that the Monroe Doctrine was dead and welcomed Cuba as a new liberating force in Latin America. The US retaliated. It renounced the Cuban sugar quota, severed diplomatic relations in early 1961, and instigated an economic embargo. Eisenhower also made plans to remove Castro by force through CIA-trained expatriate Cuban dissidents. Thus President John Kennedy, on entering the White House in 1961, came face to face with one of the most volatile issues of his presidency: Cuba and how to deal with it. Much to his later regret, he took the advice of the CIA and accepted the invasion plan laid by his predecessor. It went ahead at the Bay of Pigs on 17 April 1961 in the expectation that it would prompt a popular uprising. Instead, disaster struck. The invaders never got off the beach and there was no uprising.

The Cuban problem remained: its significance was as much symbolic as anything else. The way that the US conceived of its own position in the Western Hemisphere, and trumpeted it abroad, meant that any loss to communism would necessarily be seen as a major defeat. So, the US could not give up after the Bay of Pigs. Kennedy unleashed CIA Operation Mongoose to try to unseat Castro. Or perhaps one should say debeard him as one plot involved a poison that removed facial hair! These tactics failed, but angered Castro and provoked fear of another invasion, and thus led him deeper into the Soviet embrace.

The Cuban Missile Crisis

The CIA told Kennedy on 15 October 1962 that the Soviets were building medium (MRBM) and intermediate range ballistic missile (IRBM) sites on Cuba.

The context of the crisis not only demonstrates how intermingled US domestic and Cold War issues had become, it also explains much about how events unfolded. Kennedy had come to power with a flamboyant commitment to get America moving again, retake the initiative in the Cold War, and pay any price and bear any burden for the sake of liberty. The world, however, proved to be more intractable than his optimistic can-do rhetoric suggested. Kennedy suffered a series of setbacks. They started with the Bay of Pigs and continued with a difficult summit meeting with Krushchev in Vienna, the Berlin Crisis and the building of the Wall, difficulties in Laos and a deteriorating situation in Vietnam. In none of these did Kennedy perform well. So, when the missiles were discovered on Cuba, there were a number of background considerations that informed his actions. He was politically vulnerable. His performance had not matched his election rhetoric and October 1962 was the eve of the mid-term congressional elections. Kennedy was also aware that he was the first Democrat president since Truman, and Truman had left office under a hail of criticisms about being weak on communism, failing to end the war in Korea, and for losing China. Kennedy's concerns about these things should not be seen solely as selfish political considerations that pushed him into a hardline response. The radical right in the US was strong and, in his view, dangerous. Two years later, the Republican opponent of Lyndon Johnson, Barry Goldwater, reputedly suggested 'lobbing one into the men's room at the Kremlin', 'one' being a nuclear bomb. The survival of Democrat leadership was seen as important for the continuation of moderate and rational policies as well as for Kennedy's career. In addition, there were other influential factors. Kennedy was part of that generation that had a horror of appeasement because of its consequences in the Second World War. Kennedy felt that the US had to be resolute, send the right messages to Krushchev and get the missiles out of Cuba. Among other things, this would prevent the Soviets from using them as a bargaining ploy to make gains elsewhere, such as in the Western redoubt in Berlin, or regarding US missile deployments in Turkey. The Americans felt that if they gave way to blackmail, then the

Soviets, like all blackmailers, would be back for a second, third and fourth tranche. The great danger with this was that eventually the US would have to say no, but then it would have lost credibility. The Soviets would not believe American protestations. The supposed bluff would be called and nuclear war would probably follow. These important considerations were much written about soon after the crisis. More recently, however, evidence has come to light that Kennedy's commitment to flexible response held an option in reserve that would have gone down, if not an appeasement-like, at least an accommodating route that actually involved a trade of Soviet missiles on Cuba for US missiles in Turkey.[4]

The Soviet role in the crisis also had complications, some of which have only recently been revealed. Although Kennedy felt under pressure from Soviet foreign policy and Soviet-inspired liberation movements, Krushchev also felt threatened. Kennedy's rhetoric was combative and contrary to many views expressed in the 1960s and 1970s, Krushchev did not perceive of him as inexperienced and lacking resolution. An invasion force had assaulted Cuba and the US had embarked upon a massive rearmament programme. Moreover, although the launch of Sputnik indicated that the Soviets had stolen a technological lead, which promised improved nuclear weapon delivery systems, things had in fact gone disastrously wrong. They had only a handful of operational ICBMs and Krushchev knew that the USSR was vulnerable to a US first strike. He therefore boasted misleadingly that the Soviet Union had no need to station missiles outside Soviet boundaries while secretly moving to close its temporary window of vulnerability by placing IRBMs and MRBMs on Cuba. Coupled with his public commitment to supporting liberation movements, this redoubled Krushchev's determination to secure Castro against a possible second American invasion.

After the Americans discovered their presence, Strategic Air Command (SAC) was placed on DEFCON II, which, among other things, was a deliberate attempt to try to intimidate the Soviets: the next state of alert was tantamount to being at war. There was never any argument about the fact that the missiles had to go. They could not stay for three reasons. First, they would have had a psychological impact, which would have been very damaging politically and could have provoked a dangerous and possibly uncontrollable right-wing backlash. It was bad enough having a communist state in the Western Hemisphere; to have a nuclear-capable one was just not acceptable. It would have altered the perceptions of the relative standing of the US and the Soviet Union in the Cold War and, as Kennedy commented, perceptions contribute to reality. Second, the missiles on Cuba would have strengthened the Soviet Union's strike capability and cut down on the warning time. Third, if the Soviets had been allowed to succeed in developing a nuclear base on Cuba, it might have encouraged them to other acts of adventurism and a blundering into unintentional nuclear war.

However, consensus on the need to remove the missiles did not translate into consensus on what to do. Before telling the world about the missiles Kennedy established the Executive Committee of the NSC (EXCOM) to consider policy options. It was comprised of key personnel from the NSC, Soviet specialists, the foreign policy establishment and people close to the President, most notably his brother, Attorney-General Robert Kennedy. The EXCOM's initial enthusiasm for an air strike soon receded when it became clear that it would involve Soviet casualties, that the military could not guarantee 100% success (thus posing the possibility of a retaliatory nuclear strike from Cuba), and that a follow-up invasion would very probably be needed. The EXCOM eventually produced six options: do nothing; apply diplomatic pressure; ease Castro away from the Soviets; impose a naval blockade; mount an air strike; invade. This range of options was whittled down to the idea of using limited force in the form of a blockade, or quarantine as it was less provocatively called, with the military options held in reserve. From being hawkish at the outset, the EXCOM pulled back under pressure, particularly from the Kennedys and Defense Secretary Robert McNamara. The most dove-like official was Adlai Stevenson, US Ambassador to the UN, who wanted to make concessions and stick to diplomacy. For years people thought that this had been entirely rejected by Kennedy, but recent evidence indicates otherwise.

On Monday, 22 October, the President publicly announced the discovery of the missiles and went on to make seven main points: the US would impose a naval quarantine to prevent further shipments of aggressive weapons; there would be increased surveillance and US forces would stand ready to meet all eventualities; any nuclear strike from Cuba anywhere in the Western Hemisphere would be deemed to be a direct Soviet attack upon the US; US forces at Guantanamo Bay would be strengthened; the US would coordinate with the OAS and NATO; a meeting of the UN Security Council would discuss the situation; and Kennedy called upon Krushchev to end this threat to peace.

Krushchev's initial response was truculent, but on Wednesday, when the quarantine came into operation, Soviet ships turned back. On Friday the Americans showed their resolve without being over-provocative by stopping and boarding a US-built, Greek-crewed, Lebanese-registered ship chartered by the Soviets. The same day they received an offer from Krushchev: he would remove the missiles in return for a guarantee of Cuba's sovereignty. But then, on the following day, the Soviets also demanded that the US remove its nuclear missiles from Turkey.

Kennedy went along with the view of the majority in EXCOM that there could be no public trade of missiles because it would look as if the US were sacrificing Turkish for American interests and that would have generally undermined allied faith in the US. Nevertheless, Kennedy mused at one point that it would not look good in the history books if there were a nuclear war because he had refused to withdraw obsolete missiles from Turkey. The Americans decided to accept the first offer from Krushchev and ignore the second. At the same time, Robert Kennedy met with Soviet Ambassador Dobrynin and explained the political difficulties for the US that a public connection between the removal of Cuban and Turkish missiles would cause, but he undertook to remove the latter unilaterally within a short period of time. This decision was not taken in the EXCOM. Neither was another important decision made by John Kennedy. He instructed Secretary of State Dean Rusk to prime an ex-American UN official, Andrew Cordier. In the event of the quarantine not working and the situation deteriorating, Cordier should stand by to approach UN General Secretary U-Thant and ask him, as an independent third party, to propose a trade of the Turkish for the Cuban missiles. Whether Kennedy would have taken this more accommodating route, or whether he would have resorted to military action, we shall never know, but circumstantial evidence suggests he would have opted for the UN initiative. On 28 October Krushchev agreed to remove the missiles in return for a US guarantee to respect Cuban sovereignty.

The crisis was at an end, but it had been a close-run thing. Many came to see it as a model for successful crisis management, but not everything was under such tight control as one might have wished. A US U-2 high-altitude reconnaissance plane strayed perilously into Soviet air space during the crisis and one was shot down by Cuban and Soviet gunfire on Saturday, 27 October. The Americans badly miscalculated the size of the Soviet force on Cuba and, unknown to them, if they had invaded they would have been confronted by Soviet troops equipped with battlefield atomic weapons. Orders issued by the President and his immediate lieutenants were not always carried out and control over the Soviet nuclear arsenal on Cuba depended upon the loyalty of the local commander.[5] Instead of a model for crisis management more recent scholarship, for example, Richard Ned Lebow's, has emphasised both Kennedy's and Krushchev's willingness to learn and adapt as the crisis proceeded. Fortunately there was time for this to occur and it was helped by information each received during the crisis and by their mutual correspondence.

What did the US learn from the crisis and what came after? Both the US and the Soviet Union were deeply disturbed by the crisis. Both sides had seriously miscalculated the other's intentions and as a result had stared into the nuclear abyss. The Americans had wrongly assumed that the Soviets would not deploy missiles in Cuba, largely because they had underestimated Krushchev's commitment to defending Cuba and to shoring up the Soviet Union's strategic vulnerability. The Soviet leader for his part proceeded to deploy without seriously assessing either the likelihood of discovery prior to the missiles becoming operational or how robust the US response might be.[6] But in the end both sides realised that the overriding imperative had to be the avoidance of nuclear war: an imperative that was made palpable and vivid by the crisis. Several developments followed rapidly in its wake. A hot-line between the White House and the Kremlin was installed. Emphasis was placed on stabilising the superpower nuclear relationship and avoiding head-to-head confrontation. Soon progress was forthcoming from arms talks. In 1963 the Partial Test Ban Treaty was signed and, despite Vietnam, the two superpowers moved gradually towards *détente* and SALT.

US relations with Cuba remained hostile. The economic embargo still continued and was given added bite by the Helms-Burton Act in 1995.

Periodically problems flared up over refugees and Soviet military activities during both the Nixon and Carter years. In 1979 the 'discovery' of a Soviet brigade on Cuba was made much of in the media and caused a veritable political storm until the Soviet invasion of Afghanistan stole the limelight. The issue finally faded away once it was revealed that the Kennedy administration had in fact sanctioned such troop levels on Cuba. For America, Cuba continued to be symbolically important as an outpost of communism and as a breeding ground for subversion in the Western Hemisphere. Its allies thought that this was much exaggerated while the Cold War was still being waged: why, after its end, America should continue with such hostility, they found even more difficult to understand.

Kennedy's Alliance for Progress and Reagan's Caribbean Basin Initiative

Presidents Kennedy and Reagan came from different political parties – Democrat and Republican respectively – but they were both fiercely and pro-actively anti-communist and saw advantages in developing economic initiatives in Latin America and the Caribbean to strengthen containment. In each case much was made of economic development, but if evaluated on this criterion both programmes were failures. However, from the perspectives of containment and the promotion of American corporate interests they were qualified successes, albeit at the cost of many lives and much misery in those countries that the US purported to be helping.

The years 1958, 1959 and 1961 were symbolically important for the US. In 1958, US Vice-President Richard Nixon was spat upon in Caracas. In 1959 Castro took over in Cuba. And in January 1961 Nikita Krushchev, buoyed up with recent communist technological and economic successes and the upsurge of radical activity in the Third World, announced belligerently that the Soviet Union would support the rising tide of liberation movements. A gauntlet had been thrown down, this time not for a direct duel between the First and Second Worlds, but for one fought indirectly for the hearts and minds of the Third World. If this duel were to be won by the US, it had to be won first and foremost in the backyard where instability threatened to provide opportunities for communist progress and where the containment line had already been breached by Castro's success on Cuba. The new strategy for the Western Hemisphere called for more subtlety than the overt interventionism in Guatemala and at the Bay of Pigs. Hearts and minds in Latin America would hardly be won over by such arrogant use of power. Such subtlety was embodied in the Alliance for Progress. President Kennedy proposed this scheme on 13 March 1961 and Latin America signed up for it later that year on 17 August at Punta del Este. The plan was for the US government to provide half of a projected total of $20 billion of foreign aid over ten years with private capital also coming from US corporations and a further $80 billion of investment being generated by Latin American states themselves. The stated goals were prosperity, an annual growth of 2.5% in per capita income, land reform and more stable and more democratic government: the unstated and paramount goal however remained security through containment.

Presidents Kennedy and Johnson both ideally wanted peaceful democratic reform and economic prosperity in Latin America, but they had only marginal success. The problem was that US government and corporate interests in the end always sided with the status quo in preference to even mildly reformist movements, which they feared might consort with the communists, or be irresolute in containing them. The US was caught on the horns of a dilemma: it disapproved of oppressive right-wing regimes in the region, but preferred them to communism and so for the sake of a 'greater good' supported them in the vain hope that one day they would reform themselves. After Castro's victory, the Americans had living vindication of their fears: Marxism had broken through the hemispheric perimeter. However, much of this was a self-fulfilling prophesy: in supporting oppressive regimes for fear of communism, the US perpetuated conditions that were not conducive to economic reform or attractive for new US and foreign investment and all this made it more difficult for indigenous reform movements to progress. Non-communist opposition groups saw US aid come in and no reforms take place, so they looked elsewhere for outside help and found it in the Soviet Bloc. The disaffected thus came to hate the US and to associate with communism. This action–reaction syndrome nurtured conditions for the spread of the very thing that the US was trying to eliminate. And US corporations complicated all of this because they feared that radical changes in Latin America might reduce the value of their vested interests.

The Alliance for Progress failed in its stated aims of achieving social, economic and political reform. It gave some impetus to Latin American economic growth, but wealth accumulated among the elite, not the people. Land reform remained a major problem and, despite repeated American calls for reform, in practice US policy often aided and abetted the status quo. Thus in 1962, when Honduras attempted land reform, it fell foul of the Hickenlooper Amendment to the 1962 US Foreign Assistance Act, which stipulated that US assistance would be suspended to any state that nationalised American property without appropriate compensation, or taxed US property excessively. As in Guatemala in 1954, the UFC was the problem. Honduras had nationalised some of its land and in the view of both the company and the US government the compensation provisions were inadequate. Threatened by the prospect of the Hickenlooper Amendment being invoked, Honduras backed away from reform. On other occasions, even when nationalisation went ahead, US corporations often benefited more than their host state. For example, when the Brazilian government nationalised a subsidiary of ITT Industries Inc., the company was awarded inflated compensation, for which the Brazilian government was later reimbursed by the US with Alliance for Progress funds. Some saw this as a type of US government subsidy for US corporations.

The Alliance for Progress was well meaning towards Latin America, but primarily it strengthened and enriched the forces of oppression and US corporations, promoted US exports and opened some new avenues for

US investors. As the decade advanced, according to Harry Magdoff's classic study *The Age of Imperialism*, more money left Latin America in debt repayments and repatriated profits than entered. To people like Raul Prebisch, the founder of dependency theory, this came as no surprise. Since the late 1950s he had identified the conditions that perpetuated poverty – exporting cheap food and materials and importing expensive manufactured goods – and advocated import substitution with development of indigenous manufacturing industries as a route to prosperity. Unfortunately, achieving this was easier said than done. Capital accumulation for investment was difficult when profits from exports often went into the pockets of foreign corporations such as the UFC in Guatemala and Exxon in Venezuela, and foreign sources of capital were either expensive and led to the debt and repayment flow problems identified by Magdoff, or else were geared to promoting US manufactured goods, which inhibited the growth of domestic industrial production. The lack of political stability and a notion of distributive justice, which would foster large consumer markets, were other major obstacles. The Alliance for Progress made little impact on these problems, did not achieve its stated aims, and Washington's interest in them gradually dwindled as the 1960s progressed and foreign policy energy was increasingly monopolised by Vietnam. Aid through the Alliance for Progress had also taken on a more military aspect as time went by and by 1970 there were more military regimes in Latin America than in 1960. In 1973 the OAS disbanded the permanent committee that it had set up to implement the Alliance for Progress and the initiative was at an end.

Nearly a decade was to go by before the US would turn once again to a major economic initiative to strengthen containment. In the early 1980s in Central America and the Caribbean, no less than elsewhere, the Reagan administration vigorously committed itself to opposing communism and left-wing subversion. The result was a complex strategy that involved direct intervention as in Grenada, covert intervention as in Nicaragua, and economic and military assistance to a broad swathe of right-wing and reactionary regimes. In the forefront of economic assistance was the Caribbean Basin Initiative, announced by President Reagan in 1982. It was formulated in the 1983 Caribbean Basin Economic Recovery Act and came into effect on 1 January 1984. Like the Alliance for Progress it was prompted by a desire to strengthen containment and respond to the challenges posed by leftist movements, this time in countries such as Nicaragua, El Salvador and Grenada, as well as Cuba. Also like the Alliance for Progress, while the initiative offered preferential economic treatment and promised more aid, the concessions were hedged with qualifications and the aid for economic as opposed to military purposes made little impact. The US would not extend help to states it deemed to be communist or to those that had expropriated US property. Furthermore, key commodities were excluded from the agreement and others were added to the exclusion list later on the insistence of US economic interests and their spokespeople in the Congress. From a purely economic point of view the initiative had little impact on relieving poverty and promoting economic development, though US corporations and consumers again tended to reap benefits. The attention of the US government once again switched back to more traditional ways of dealing with communists and subversives, and it was not until the 1990s that the US reconsidered the implications of Central American and Caribbean poverty and instability. Even then it was not until the administration of George W. Bush that anything really concrete was achieved.

While the stated goals of both the Alliance for Progress and the Caribbean Basin Initiative remained unconsummated, the unstated goal of security through containment and the promotion of US interests (including those of corporate America) had been nurtured. But this was not enough to satisfy American ambitions. Cuba remained under Castro's control, despite the abortive Bay of Pigs invasion and the Missile Crisis. Meanwhile, the romantic features and revolutionary adventures in Latin America of his lieutenant, Che Guevara, created an icon for disaffected youth throughout the world. If the Soviets could get one client state, they could still get more and that had to be prevented for economic, strategic (especially after the Missile Crisis) and political reasons. Aid continued under both Kennedy's successor Lyndon Johnson through the Alliance for Progress and during Reagan's second term of office under the auspices of the Caribbean Basin Initiative, but such strategies were demoted in importance. The implacable resolve to oppose communism wherever and in whatever guise it might take in the Western Hemisphere would have to be implemented by other more robust means, and once again that came to mean intervention as and when necessary for both Johnson and Reagan.

As and when necessary

The American invasions of the Dominican Republic in 1965 and of Grenada in 1983 have similarities that resonate with echoes from Guatemala in 1954. In the Dominican Republic, repression by the military government of Donald Reid Cabral, who was backed by the US, caused instability. Part of the opposition was branded as communist, though it was not a particularly strong faction. In Grenada, the situation became unstable as the pro-Cuba radical Michael Bishop was assassinated in 1983 and replaced by the even more radical Bernard Coard. There were ties between Grenada, Cuba and the Soviet Union, and Cubans were busy building a large runway that the CIA alleged could be used for refuelling Soviet planes. The US had justifiable fears about threats to the Panama Canal and the strategic sea-lanes in the Gulf of Mexico. In both the Dominican Republic and Grenada cases, the US made much of the danger of communism and the threat to the lives of US citizens. It was this latter point that was used as the pretext for the respective invasions. A semblance of peace was created in the Dominican Republic, though political repression continued. In Grenada there were elections and a new, less radical, government took over.

The stories of Chile in 1970–73 and Nicaragua in 1985–86 also have much in common, but this time covert operations by the CIA and the staff of the NSC provide the common thread. In Chile, the US used money to encourage political opposition and its influence to undermine the economy. The aim was to sabotage the government of the freely elected, pro-Marxist President Allende. These policies went on for three years. Then, in 1973, independently of the CIA, but clearly taking advantage of the instability engineered by it, General Augusto Pinochet mounted a successful military coup that brought a reign of oppression and terror to what had previously been one of the most peaceful and progressive of Latin American countries.

The Nicaraguan problem was more visible and more difficult. Nicaragua had a bleak history of dictatorship and impoverishment at the hands of the US-supported Somoza dynasty. A famous, but probably apocryphal, quote attributed to President Franklin Roosevelt referred to President Anastasio Somoza as 'a son-of-bitch, but he's our son-of-a-bitch'. In 1979 the Sandinista rebels overthrew the dynasty and a junta was set up to rule by decree with Daniel Ortega always playing an important role and eventually becoming President in 1985. The new government did take money and arms from the Soviets, had connections with Cuba, supported the left-wing guerrillas in El Salvador and suppressed human rights at home, but it also tried to address the problems of poverty and land ownership and was generally a less brutal and autocratic regime than that of Somoza. Nevertheless, in Washington everything was viewed through an anti-communist lens and Reagan swiftly suspended US aid to the country and National Security Decision Directive 17 (23 November 1981) authorised the CIA to spend $19 million on military aid to support the Contra Rebels, right-wing opponents of the Sandinistas. Curiously, Reagan, who had a natural ability to empathise with and move with the pulse of the American public on so many things, stubbornly remained wedded to his policy of destabilising the Nicaraguan government even after public opinion came out strongly against it, and after Congress prohibited further aid to the Contras in the Boland Amendments of 1982 and 1984. Despite all this, the campaign continued. The CIA and members of the NSC made arms sales to Iran both to help free hostages held by Middle East terrorists and to provide money for the Contras. This was contrary to the explicit wishes of the US Congress. The mission to keep the Western Hemisphere clean of communism had taken on the appearance of a holy war that went beyond formal policy-making and which broke the bounds of constitutional constraints. Intervention as and when necessary was construed so broadly that it got out of proportion to the threat and became a corruptive force within the US that many saw as a greater danger than the cancer of communism in the Western Hemisphere it was designed to eradicate. In 1986, before the Iran–Contra scandal broke, the administration managed to push another military aid package worth $100 million for the Contras through the Congress and so the proxy war continued. Later estimates suggested that well over 25,000 Nicaraguans lost their lives. In El Salvador where the support was given to an ever increasingly right-wing series of governments in their fight against left-wing guerrillas, the death toll was nearly three times that figure.

American pursuit of containment in the Western Hemisphere began to be discredited, not only by liberals in the US, but by conservatives as well. When it was revealed that Colonel North and others had deliberately flouted the strictures of the Congress and continued to funnel aid to the Contras anxiety and dismay grew even more, At home the government was seen to have corrupted constitutional checks and balances in order to pursue a policy the American people and the Congress did not support. Abroad in Nicaragua and El Salvador, America supported insurgents in one and government oppressors in the other and appeared to be oblivious to the ethical and political nuances involved. There was no quarter given. There was no willingness to see the shades between black and white. Moderates in Nicaragua and El Salvador went unheard and unsupported. Ironically in 1990, Daniel Ortega and the Sandidnistas, who the Americans had demonised as communists, antidemocratic extremists and authoritarian destroyers of human rights, stood down peacefully after losing the 25 February elections.

Conclusion

The US has not just been motivated by a drive for hegemonic dominance in the Western Hemisphere by socialising it into liberal democratic politics and the free market and cleansing it of communism by following the pattern of interventionism established by the successful coup in Guatemala, or by exercising more covert forms of power. During the early Carter administration promoting human rights, even at a temporary cost to US influence, was an important feature of policy. In 1978, despite fearsome opposition, the President pushed the Panama Treaties through the Senate: they gradually ceded the Canal and the Zone back to Panama. From one perspective this was a highly moral self-denying ordinance, from another a realistic adjustment to changing political and strategic realities: both seem somewhat at odds with the idea of hegemonic leadership. In 1982, the Reagan administration was unable to bring Argentina to heel and provoked considerable opposition in Latin America by siding with Britain and against the anti-communist military junta in Buenos Aires in the Falklands War.

Even when the US pursued policies designed specifically to maintain its hemispheric leadership, it did not always prevail. Economic influence and socialisation into US norms failed in Guatemala, Cuba, the Dominican Republic, Chile, Grenada and Nicaragua. Instead, the US had to resort to covert or outright military intervention. Ironically, the support of authoritarian right-wing dictators because of the overriding priority of security and the containment of communism encouraged the continuation of conditions that were uncongenial to the development of the economic model the US wished to cultivate in the Western Hemisphere. Hegemonic success again seems highly qualified. Moreover, even when force was deployed, it was not always successful, as Cuba still amply demonstrates. Thus, hegemony is a notion that needs to be used carefully. In US experience in the Western Hemisphere, it would appear that in the pursuit of hegemonic control, the means came to undermine the very values and institutions that hegemonic leadership was intended to preserve for the system. Those means pushed indigenous reform movements

7   The US and Asia, 1945–89

Asia, where the arrogance of power began and, at least temporarily, ended. In August 1945 President Truman authorised a form of indiscriminate bombing which slaughtered 400,000 Japanese civilians in Hiroshima and Nagasaki. The world awakened to the new atomic order and at its head was the US, economic powerhouse and sole possessor of the atom bomb. Thirty years later President Nixon oversaw the conclusion of the most humbling defeat in modern American history as a Third World state forced the self-proclaimed champion of the Free World to sue for peace. The lives of 55,000 service personnel, $150 billion and 10 million tons of bombs had been squandered in a futile attempt to win a limited war in Vietnam that, for the North Vietnamese, could have no limits. Massive US military strength was insufficient to win this type of conflict, and the impact of the war on America, commonly referred to as the Vietnam Syndrome, was of greater significance for its foreign and domestic policy than any other Cold War experience. An anti-war movement swept through American society and sparked a period of congressional reassertion that challenged the Imperial Presidency and hampered American leadership of the Western Alliance until the Reagan revival in the 1980s.

Close behind Vietnam in significance were the questions asked of US policy-makers by China, Korea and Japan. The loss of China in 1949 revolutionised the geostrategic topography of the Cold War and sent shockwaves that undermined the Truman administration and reverberated around American society in the form of the McCarthy witch-hunts. It also prompted one of the most bizarre episodes in US history as successive administrations refused to recognise the PRC and insisted instead that nationalists, driven on to the island of Taiwan, represented the true and only China. Then there was the Korean War.[1] This gave the stamp of legitimacy to NSC-68's globalisation of containment and defined the contours of American foreign policy for the next 20 years. Finally, there was Japan, perhaps the bitterest American enemy during the Second World War. Here, US fear of communism overcame sentiment and policy-makers helped reconstruct Japan into their foremost Cold War ally in Asia and, ironically, their fiercest economic rival.

The 'loss' of China

In April 1947 a paper by the US Joint Chiefs of Staff ranked Japan, China and Korea as 13th, 14th and 15th respectively in a hierarchy of strategically significant states. The top seven were all in Europe and it was these that were the focus of American attention. However, while the US struggled with the Soviets in Eastern Europe and over Berlin, the Asian position developed in a way that would plague US policy-makers for most of the 1950s and 1960s.

The first major development came in China. Americans have a long history of interest in China, stemming back through early Christian missions, Hay's Open Door Notes and the 1844 Treaty of Wangxia that accorded the US trade and extraterritorial rights. However, for much of the early twentieth century China was torn by civil war, particularly after the death of Sun Yat Sen. On one side were the dominant nationalists, known as the Kuomintang (KMT), who were headed by Chiang Kai-shek. On the other were the communists (CCP), led by Mao Tse-tung. The Americans favoured Chiang for reasons of ideology and because he led China's fight against Japan in the 1930s. As the Second World War approached, the US thus looked to Chiang as both an ally in the Far East against Japan and as the man to bring China, its market and its raw materials into the capitalist community. Indeed, Roosevelt's post-war vision saw China as one of four world policemen, along with the USSR, Britain and the US (later expanded to five with the inclusion of France).

With these things in mind the Americans spent vast amounts of money propping up Chiang, who repaid them by using his best forces against Mao rather than the Japanese. Mao's forces, though, fought both Chiang and the Japanese. Consequently, they captured the nationalist petard and combined it with communist ideology to make sweeping gains throughout the Chinese countryside. As the war ended, General Marshall was charged with the impossible task of brokering a ceasefire between the KMT and CCP. He failed, not least because the US continued to aid Chiang, and China collapsed into bitter civil war.

When Mao forced the KMT to flee to the offshore island of Taiwan in 1949, the Americans had lost China. For some time there had been a certain inevitability about the communist triumph and, without making an unthinkably large military commitment, there was little the US could have done to salvage Chiang's position on the mainland. A lengthy apologetic in the guise of Truman's 1949 China White Paper sought in vain to explain this to an enraged American public. Mao's victory had enormous implications for American domestic and foreign policy. Coming as it did in the same year as the Soviet atomic bomb and revelations about espionage in the wartime Manhattan nuclear research project, the loss of China led to an orgy of American recriminations. These were nowhere more vitriolic and influential than in the McCarthy communist witch-hunts, which sought to explain US setbacks as the work of spies and traitors. It was a grandiose conspiracy theory which never stood up to critical analysis, but which appealed, nevertheless, with such force that it wreaked havoc upon both the Truman administration and, ironically, American civil liberties. The State Department was wastefully purged of its China specialists, and government officials, military personnel and defence contractors all had to take loyalty oaths. After these were extended to their families, over 20 million American citizens had been subjected to investigative procedures.[2]

In foreign affairs, McCarthyism helped to tie the hands of American policy-makers. Containment became an intolerant and blinkered strategy which, in the name of democracy and freedom, imprisoned American society for two decades and helped to divide the world with an unforgiving simplicity. It also fathered ill-considered policies. For example, the Americans knew that throughout the Second World War, Stalin had been unsympathetic to Mao and had actually sent aid to the Kuomintang, knowing full well that Chiang would use it against the communists. They knew, too, that after the war the Soviets had looted Manchuria and created enormous resentment among the Chinese. Furthermore, US allies, notably Britain, told the Truman adminis-tration not to regard China and the USSR as inevitable partners. Yet, Ameri-can policy-makers either remained blind to, or were precluded by American public opinion from exploiting, the differences between Stalin and Mao. Instead, General Marshall and Secretary of State Dean Acheson testified before the Senate that they would never recognise the existence of Red China. This led to a bizarre situation in which the US continued to regard Chiang's corrupt and vanquished regime on Taiwan as the Government of China and to deny the PRC a seat in the UN. Moreover, there can be no doubt that when Mao concluded a treaty of mutual assistance with Stalin in February 1950, America's short-sighted and doctrinaire policy had helped to push him closer to the Soviets.

The US further antagonised Mao in 1954, when it locked itself to the Nationalist regime by blocking the PRC's attempts to liberate Taiwan and its tiny offshore islands of Quemoy and Matsu. Eisenhower reaffirmed US com-mitment to Chiang and in January 1955 he secured the Taiwan Straits Reso-lution from Congress, which was effectively a blank cheque to use military force against the PRC, including tactical nuclear weapons. It took over 20 years for the Americans to realise the error of this approach. In the meantime, they unloaded upon the rest of Asia their collective anguish at the loss of China.

Korea and growing problems in Indochina

Hard on the heels of the loss of both China and the US atomic monopoly came Korea and Indochina. The Korean War, among other things, enabled the Truman administration to get NSC-68 passed by a Congress hitherto unenthusiastic about increasing US commitments overseas. It was also a conflict that had been waiting to happen. During the Second World War America and the Soviet Union decided that, after Korea had been liberated from the Japanese, it should be temporarily divided between them during a transition phase to full independence. However, with the Soviets north and the

Americans south of the 38th parallel, the onset of the Cold War portended grave possibilities. Both sides withdrew their troops but began to build up their clients. The Soviets sent military aid and advisers to develop North Korean forces, led by Kim Il Sung. The Americans, with some reservations, propped up Syngman Rhee in South Korea. He was an unpopular, petty dictator, who made only minimal genuflection to democratic principles and was an embarrassment to the US. Nevertheless, when North Korea launched a surprise attack on 25 June 1950 the US rushed to his aid, despite the fact that in January 1950, Acheson had explicitly excluded Taiwan and Korea from the US defence perimeter in Asia.

Opinion has divided about the reasons for Kim Il Sung's action. Was he Stalin's puppet or an ardent Korean nationalist? Did Rhee provoke him in the hope that war would bring Western salvation for his crumbling regime? Or was, as recent evidence suggests, Kim Il Sung given the green light by Stalin?[3] Even more important, why did the US react with such speed and force? It has been suggested that the Americans feared that a communist-controlled South Korea might incline Japan to neutralism, which would deprive them of their strongest position in Asia and their closest air bases to eastern USSR. Also, if Japan were to be developed as a counterweight to China, it needed markets and raw materials in Asia.

US troops had occupied Japan since September 1945. General MacArthur, the Supreme Allied Commander, had overseen an Americanisation of the Japanese political system which included a strong emphasis on the free market, representative government, civil liberties and decentralised power. Once the Cold War began, the US looked to a liberated Japan as a key partner and, from the 1948 Dodge mission onwards, it encouraged Japan's economic recovery. When the Korean War broke out, Truman expedited a peace treaty with Japan. Signed in September 1951, the San Francisco agreement saw the Americans successfully exclude Soviet participation. They also traded reparation claims against Japan from a host of countries in return for the Japanese alliance against communism and the grant of American military bases in Japanese territory, most notably on Okinawa. Rather like the German solution in Europe, the Americans encouraged Japanese rearmament and industrialisation to create a zone of stability for the Western world. Although the Japanese never rearmed to the extent that the US desired, the US had secured the Asian ally it desperately needed. In 1956 Japan joined the UN and by 1965 its economic miracle had produced the first of its many international balance of payments surpluses.

However, important though Japan was, it is unlikely that it was the fear of a communist South Korea inspiring Japanese neutrality that triggered the US conduct of the Korean War. A much more compelling explanation is that Korea was the war that Truman needed to calm domestic critics, demonstrate US resolve in the face of communist aggression, and to forge ahead with his globalisation of containment. Korea seemed so opportune from this perspective that some scholars have suggested that US diplomacy invited the North Korean attack.[4] This is a matter of debate, but it is certain that, with Mao preparing to move once more against Chiang, McCarthyism in full spate and an uncooperative Congress concerned about defence expenditure, Truman desperately needed to sell NSC-68 to America. North Korean aggression gave him that opportunity. Furthermore, the Korean conflict was used to push through the remilitarisation of West Germany and a build-up of US forces in Europe. Kim Il Sung was portrayed as Stalin's crony and Mao's simultaneous build-up against Taiwan seemingly confirmed US assumptions about both the Sino-Soviet alliance and the unity of international communism.

Capitalising upon the Soviet boycott of the Security Council, on account of the US refusal to allow the PRC to take the China seat at the UN, Truman secured the moral high ground by obtaining a 9–0 condemnation of the North Korean offensive. US countermeasures were put swiftly into place. On 26 June 1950, the Truman Doctrine was formally extended to Asia, the Seventh Fleet was used subsequently as an interdiction force to counter Mao's challenge to Taiwan, and military aid was extended to the French, who had engaged Ho Chi Minh's communists in Indochina.

As for the Korean conflict itself, much was risked for little direct reward. The US committed its own troops to save Rhee as his corrupt and deeply unpopular regime failed to stem the North Korean onslaught. Under the lead of MacArthur, United Nations troops, predominantly American and South Korean, outmanoeuvred the communists with the Inchon amphibious landings and drove the communists back. Then, instead of stopping at the declared objective of restoring the 38th parallel, Truman authorised the military liberation of Korea. This was a high-risk strategy based on the calculation that neither the USSR nor China would intervene. The Americans were wrong. After the US ignored repeated Chinese warnings communicated via India, on 25 October China dispatched thousands of 'volunteers', in effect fully equipped regular troops, to repel MacArthur's push towards its border. It was a highly effective Chinese campaign and, with their point made, they withdrew and agreed to attend a UN meeting to resolve the crisis.

However, General MacArthur launched a counter-offensive timed specifically to coincide with the Chinese mission to the UN. China and America's European allies were enraged. More importantly, Chinese forces intervened once more and drove MacArthur back far beyond the 38th parallel. Only after alarming bluster about atomic weapons, which sent Britain's Prime Minister Attlee scurrying to Washington to urge moderation, did MacArthur return in March 1951 to where he had started – the 38th parallel. Then, when he crossed it once more, Truman hastened to dismiss him. General Ridgway, MacArthur's successor, subsequently held the line for over two further years of fighting, including the legendary battles of Heartbreak Ridge and Pork Chop Hill, while the politicians wrangled over terms for an expedient peace. Truman had all that he wanted, other than the objectives articulated by the unrealistic 'roll-back' rhetoric of NSC-68. He had put to rest Western fears of appeasement, held the line in Asia, and won over Congress for a policy of global containment. In July 1953, his successor, Eisenhower, finally concluded an armistice that de facto brought the war to an end with the boundaries between North and South Korea little different to those before it had started.

Vietnam: the arrogance of power challenged

As Korea wound down so another, even more important, issue in Asia began to gather momentum. When the French, with US support, reoccupied Vietnam after the Second World War, the Viet Minh went into active resistance. Ho Chi Minh, their leader, was an ardent nationalist and told the US of his desire for Vietnamese independence, democracy and land reform. The Cold War prevented a sympathetic American response. There was too great a risk that Ho Chi Minh was influenced overly by communism and, in any case, French support was much more important to Cold War containment. Thus, the US gave France financial and military aid. By 1954, it covered all French costs in Vietnam, which amounted to almost $800 million. This was still insufficient, however, either to secure the French position in Vietnam or to buy its approval of the European Defence Community (see Chapter 5).

In 1954 the Viet Minh commander, General Giap, defeated French forces at Dien Bien Phu and broke the French will to continue. The subsequent Geneva Accords partitioned Vietnam along the 17th parallel between communist and Western elements. Laos and Cambodia were to be neutral and Vietnam's fate was to be determined by a national election in 1956. The American problem was that Ho Chi Minh was liable to secure up to 80% of the vote. Consequently, the US not only refused to sign the Geneva Accords but also flouted them by giving military support to the leader of South Vietnam, Ngo Dinh Diem. Furthermore, the US turned a blind eye to his persecution of opposition elements and sanctioned his indefinite postponement of elections. By 1958, the US looked set for a long-haul Cold War campaign. It championed an unpopular dictator against both national aspirations and the will of the international community. It also paid most of Diem's military costs, heavily subsidised his economy, and stood in clear contravention of Geneva as it established a US Military Mission of over 1,000 troops in South Vietnam. Yet Diem still seemed to be losing, and the US faced a difficult choice of what to do next.

When J.F. Kennedy inherited Vietnam from Eisenhower, the US commitment was still relatively small and limited strictly to economic and technical assistance. There was every possibility that Kennedy could have used the change of presidency to pull the US out of Vietnam in much the same way that Eisenhower had done in Korea. Key European allies thought this worth considering. French experience in Indochina unsurprisingly led Charles de Gaulle to advise Kennedy against becoming sucked deeper into Vietnam. Harold Macmillan, too, was concerned about this prospect, although British words of caution were tempered by unwillingness to risk improvements in the special relationship and qualified by the hope that a strong US stance in Vietnam might complement and reinforce Britain's own substantial commitment to Malaysia in its struggle against Indonesia.[5]

Kennedy was not inclined to heed Old World caution. He had come to office promising a bold new foreign policy and, as the first Democrat president since Truman, he was vulnerable to charges of being soft on communism. Besides, he regarded Vietnam as being pivotal to the interests of the free world in South-east Asia. It had little intrinsic value but was vitally important in the interrelated context of the domino theory and of US assumptions about its vested interest in the world economic system. If communism triumphed in Vietnam, then Burma, Thailand, India, Japan, the Philippines, Cambodia and Laos would all be threatened. This would devastate the interests of the free world because it needed Asian markets and friendship, especially Japan's, where, from the 1949 Dodge Plan onwards, the US had assumed that reindustrialisation would work only if it had suitable markets and access to cheap raw materials in the Asian rimlands. Moreover, the US faced a series of adverse international events, notably the 1956 Suez Crisis and the failed Hungarian uprising that year, the Soviet launch of Sputnik in 1957, the weakened state of the US economy, and the double setbacks in 1961 of the failed intervention in Cuba and the building of the Berlin Wall. US credibility seemed in question. This was particularly acute when it came to showing resolve in the fight against communism in non-Western countries because, as an East–West nuclear balance began to emerge, there were much greater restrictions on vigorous action directly between the superpowers. In short, the ideological blinkers of containment, domestic political considerations and adverse international events all combined to lead Kennedy on to a tragic misjudgement. He assumed that US credibility depended upon victory in Vietnam and mortgaged it accordingly.

Kennedy was keen to develop a flexible response initiative both to wage containment in the Third World, which was the new focus of American efforts, and to mitigate the problems created by Eisenhower's big bomb approach. In particular, he looked to combine nation-building with economic aid and the development of a counter-insurgency force, the Green Berets, to combat guerrilla warfare. Vietnam was Kennedy's testing ground. For two years Kennedy persisted with Eisenhower's choice of puppet in Saigon, Diem, and supplied the South Vietnamese Army (ARVN) with increasing amounts of military hardware and US advisers: 15,000 by 1963. However, as Diem's unpopularity grew, he became worse than an embarrassment to the US, and in November 1963 the CIA successfully encouraged ARVN generals to lead a military coup. Diem was murdered and the Americanisation of the Vietnam War had begun.

Ironically, Kennedy did not live to see the full consequences of his actions. Less than a month later he was also assassinated and it fell to Lyndon Johnson to deal with a strengthened US commitment to, and a badly deteriorating situation in, Vietnam. In many ways, Johnson was trapped by the actions of his predecessor and by an American political system that was not yet ready to abandon either the rigidities of anti-communism or the fallacies of the arrogance of power. What Johnson did was logical and almost universally supported: he escalated the conflict. In July 1964, UN Secretary-General U Thant joined Moscow, Hanoi and Paris in calling for the US to attend an international conference in Geneva to discuss Vietnam. Johnson refused and underlined American determination to stay in Vietnam by announcing a 30% increase in US military advisers to South Vietnam. The following month, Johnson used a minor skirmish between US warships and North Vietnamese PT-boats to push through Congress the infamous Gulf of Tonkin Resolution. By a vote of 416 to zero in the House of Representatives and 88 to two in the Senate, Congress surrendered abjectly its constitutional duty to restrain the Executive and bestowed upon Johnson a blank cheque to wage war upon Asia. In February 1965, he launched an intensive bombing campaign against North Vietnam, Operation Rolling Thunder, and when it became clear that the Air Force could not, after all, bomb Hanoi into submission, escalated the land battle dramatically. On 28 July 1965, he approved sending 100,000 US ground troops to Vietnam and by 1968 the US had committed half a million men to fight for a tiny country of no intrinsic strategic value.

Johnson withdrew from the 1968 presidential race amid growing domestic turmoil as the anti-war movement became stronger, the Cold War consensus began to disintegrate, and the US economy faltered. Worst of all, the Tet Offensive, which won the communists spectacular if short-lived physical gains, brought Hanoi a psychological triumph that destroyed the American will to win. His successor, the Republican Richard Nixon, was elected to extricate the US from Vietnam with honour. It was an unenviable task. The US public would not tolerate much more carnage. A \$20 billion gap in its balance of payments meant that the US economy imposed further limits on policy options, and a guilt-ridden Congress was looking to redeem its credentials by transferring blame for Vietnam to the Executive.

Nixon and his NSA, Henry Kissinger, set about a carefully crafted strategy to deny North Vietnam foreign support, gradually reduce American commitment to the South, and build a position from which to negotiate a peace. The isolation of North Vietnam from its allies was pursued through developing *détente* with the Soviets and opening relations with the PRC. To liberate room for manoeuvre, Nixon abandoned the draft at home and introduced Vietnamisation abroad, which effectively substituted South Vietnamese for politically sensitive American troops. On 8 June 1968, Nixon announced the first withdrawal of 25,000 troops and by 1972 US forces were down to 70,000. Over the same period South Vietnamese forces rose from 700,000 to over 1 million. With the sting taken out of the protest movements, Nixon moved simultaneously to create the illusion of American ascendancy in Vietnam while engaging Hanoi in peace negotiations in Paris. In April 1970, Nixon announced that US forces had invaded Cambodia to cut off communist supply lines, and for similar reasons the US provided air cover for an ARVN invasion of Laos in February 1971. However, the Cambodian invasion was an illegal act that provoked Congress to reassert itself. On 31 December 1970, it repealed the Gulf of Tonkin resolution and, when Nixon ignored this, stated specifically that no future monies appropriated for military expenditure could be used to widen the war. In 1973, Congress also passed the War Powers Act.

However, all of this was too late either to deter Nixon or redeem US credibility. On 23 January 1973, Nixon claimed peace with honour as a ceasefire
ended all US participation in the war. This was undoubtedly the best that
Nixon could have hoped for under the circumstances. The fact remained,
though, that despite dropping more bombs on Vietnam than Johnson and
making the ARNV technically the fourth-ranking military power in the world
by 1975, Nixon oversaw the first war that the US had lost in modern history.
The peace treaty was not worth the paper it was written on and Thieu, the
ultimate US choice to head South Vietnam after Ky and Diem, was quickly
embroiled in conflict once more. Congress refused President Ford's request for
money to help him. In April 1975, Thieu fled the country, South Vietnam
surrendered unconditionally on 30 April, and Saigon was renamed Ho Chi
Minh City.[6]

Post-Vietnam US policy in Asia: trusted ally and the strategic triangle

In July 1971, Nixon revealed new US thinking that had in part emerged from
the débâcle of Vietnam. In future, calculations of power had to be much more
sophisticated and based primarily upon economics, because this was the key to
all other forms of power. He and Kissinger also saw an advantageous systemic
shift from a bipolar to a multipolar configuration of power that would reduce
dangerous rigidities and facilitate greater opportunities for developing a
shared concept of a world order. Although there were many *loci* of power,
five were overwhelmingly important – America, the Soviet Union, Western
Europe, China and Japan. Asia thus remained the primary focus of US foreign
policy, even after Vietnam.

In January 1973, Kissinger embraced trilateralism, which identified the US,
Western Europe and Japan as the powerhouses of liberal capitalism. Japan
was now a key centre of world power and had to be given the same attention as
Western Europe. Although the US had presided over the birth of the new
Japan, this was a relationship in need of work because it did not automatically
follow that the Japanese would follow the American line. Indeed, neither
Nixon nor Kissinger had good relations with the Japanese. In 1971 they
inadvertently upset them, first by not telling them of a proposed visit by
Kissinger to Peking in July and then by imposing both an import surcharge
and a temporary ban on converting dollars into gold. In the aftermath of the
1973 oil crisis, Japan pursued a policy in contradiction of the American line.
And Carter had little success in securing Japanese cooperation when in 1978–
79 the US annual trade deficit totalled some $40 billion, of which $12 billion
was derived from the Japanese trade surplus. Corrective measures were
imperative and required Japan to help more in managing the global economy
and to relieve some US expenditure overseas by increasing its security
spending. On both counts the Japanese refused.

Nevertheless, the US managed to retain Japan as a vital geostrategic ally
and an increasingly important trading partner. In 1972, Okinawa reverted to

Japanese sovereignty, but it was agreed that the enormous US base there should remain. Likewise, the Japanese avoided confrontation with the US when the latter drove down the value of the dollar which resulted in the 1986–88 'high yen shock'. Furthermore, in the 1980s Japan agreed with the US about its 'third opening to the world'. This was symbolised by the Structural Impediments Initiative designed to make Japanese markets more accessible to American goods in order to redress their trade imbalance. All things considered Japan remained a trustworthy ally throughout the Cold War, even if its growing economic power potentially rivalled that of the US.[7]

In stark contrast to the robust US friendship with Japan was its fragile relationship with China. Mao's alliance with the Soviet Union in 1950 had been reluctant and by 1960 was over. The Soviets withdrew all technical and economic advisers, refused to give Mao a nuclear capability, and withheld support in the 1962 India–China border skirmish. China denounced the USSR after Krushchev's unilateral revision of communist orthodoxy in 1956 and laid claim thereafter to ideological pre-eminence in the socialist world. In 1958, China embarked upon the Great Leap Forward, a new economic policy to harness its greatest natural resource – people power – and, by 1966, Mao had become embroiled in both the Cultural Revolution and a bitter border dispute with the Soviets. All of this, coupled with Chinese moderation concerning Vietnam, finally revealed the error of the 1949 US treatment of communism as a monolithic monster to be slain wherever it raised its head. New opportunities were at hand and Nixon, faced with a reassertive Congress, serious questions about US leadership of the global economy and a no-win position in Vietnam, needed desperately to capitalise upon them.

Between 1969 and 1972, 32 countries recognised the PRC and in 1971 it was finally admitted to both the UN and its Security Council. There was no point resisting the inevitable and, even though it represented one of the most startling U-turns in the history of US foreign policy, Nixon jumped aboard the Chinese bandwagon. In February 1972, he made an historic visit to China. Diplomatic contact was established, both countries renounced hegemonic ambitions in East Asia and an agreement was reached to defer the divisive issue of Taiwan. Nixon's principal objective was to give the US sufficient leverage amid the Sino-Soviet schism to force both to abandon support of North Vietnam and allow the US to extricate itself with what credibility it had left intact. There is little evidence to suggest that this 'strategic triangle' worked. Hanoi was never controlled by either China or the USSR and the outside support it received was negligible compared to that which the US gave to South Vietnam. Nevertheless, Nixon's legacy was a new era of Sino-American relations, which was formalised in January 1979 by President Carter when he opened formal diplomatic relations.

After normalisation, relations developed at an unprecedented pace. In contrast, US–Soviet relations underwent a significant downturn when the Soviet Union invaded Afghanistan in 1979, and this decline continued once Reagan reinvigorated fears about Soviet military power. Consequently, strategic considerations became paramount in America's China policy. An agreement was struck to share intelligence information on the Soviet Union and Carter's Secretary of Defense, Harold Brown, made successful overtures about defence cooperation. In September 1980, 20 licences were granted for US exports of military support equipment, a blind eye was turned towards Chinese engagement of Vietnamese forces in Cambodia, and in 1985 the Peace Pearl programme was initiated to upgrade China's new F-8 II interceptor. Once China had been granted MFN trading status, significant economic and cultural exchanges also began to take place. In addition, both the Carter and Reagan administrations were keen to cooperate with China on arms sales, drug enforcement, environmental protection and nuclear nonproliferation.

However, not everything in the 1980s augured well for future Sino-American relations. The Reagan administration jeopardised the nuclear balance by announcing the SDI initiative, appropriating funds for the MX ICBM and the B-1 bomber, and obtaining the agreement of key Western allies to deploy Pershing II missiles. This downgraded the importance of the strategic triangle and, coupled with Reagan's Sinophobia, led the US to take greater risks with Sino-US relations. For example, in 1982 Reagan sparked a major diplomatic row when he sold F-15 E/F aircraft to Taiwan. Although China was somewhat mollified in August, when America agreed gradually to reduce such arms sales in return for Chinese acceptance of a peaceful settlement of the PRC–Taiwan relationship, the issue was not resolved and simply transferred to the backburner. The Reagan administration also kept a very close check on both US liberalisation of technology transfers to China and the activities of COCOM members. Furthermore, the fact remained that China was a communist country with a culture and principles that the US found difficult to condone without compromising its self-pronounced moral superiority and its own doctrines. At times this led to provocative US behaviour such as in 1985 when Congress terminated funding to a UN agency that supported China's family planning programme.[8]

Conclusion

Asia witnessed the arrival of the American arrogance of power and subsequently dispatched it for the rest of the Cold War with devastating repercussions for US foreign policy and American society. Korea was as much, if not more, about Truman's battle at home and with his Western allies as it was with communism. America's intervention was initially unilateral and without prior consultation with its allies. The fig leaf of legitimacy accorded their action by the US-dominated UN Security Council scarcely disguised American ambitions: Korea was a war both to justify and signal the arrival of global containment. It justified the consolidation of the US position in Japan, the role of the seventh fleet as Chiang's lifeline against Mao, and the rearming of West Germany against the wishes of key US allies. It helped to formalise US primacy in the Pacific when the ANZUS security pact was signed in 1951 with Australia and New Zealand. It also brought about congressional approval of the remilitarisation that was required if NATO were to have sufficient muscle to back its objectives.

Korea also sold NSC-68 to America and secured for the presidency awesome powers. Selective service was reintroduced, a $50 billion defence budget was waved through Congress, six divisions were dispatched to Europe, massive expansion of the armed forces took place, new bases were secured in countries such as fascist Spain, and talks began to allow Greece and Turkey into NATO. Moreover, patterns in American society and in its economy were changed radically. Global containment gave a tremendous fillip to the economy through the development of an enormous industrial–military complex and, coupled with McCarthyism, helped to perpetuate the neglect of many domestic problems, such as poverty and institutionalised racial discrimination. Furthermore, Korea heralded the arrival of the Imperial Presidency. Truman waged war without the sanction of Congress and accumulated massive powers in the hands of the Executive.

For the next 20 years the American constitutional system was undermined as the Imperial Presidency prosecuted global containment. That ended for a while when Asia, in the form of Vietnam, restored the balance. American intervention in Vietnam was consistent with containment and the escalation of the conflict was frighteningly logical. American failure provoked an 'agonising reappraisal' of a sort very different to that with which Dulles threatened Europe during the EDC negotiations. The humbling of the world's greatest superpower by a tiny, backward, Asian country cost America its unquestioned leadership of the Atlantic Alliance and leant succour to new Third World challenges to the West. It also cost it bipartisan foreign policy support, the Imperial Presidency and the unconditional support of the American people for containment.

The Vietnam War Memorial stands in Washington DC as an austere, but unspeakably moving, tribute to those who died for their country. They did not win in the jungles of Asia, but they bequeathed important lessons that marked a watershed in the Cold War. Congress, with the added spur of Watergate, was provoked into doing what it was supposed to do: check the Executive. Vietnam also brought home to the American people the hypocrisy of US foreign policy. What sort of society could justify a military campaign, in a distant and insignificant country, which involved such indiscriminate and ultimately rather pointless violence? Finally, Vietnam demanded a rethinking of the blinding simplicity of containment and of calculations of power based predominantly on military might. As neither China nor the USSR controlled Vietnamese communism, the war exploded myths about the solidarity of international communism and wreaked havoc upon assumptions that vital US interests were at stake everywhere. Likewise, newfound vulnerability, particularly when Japan and Europe prospered while fears developed about US overstretch and relative economic decline, challenged assumptions about the global economic system.

After Vietnam, the US approach to Asia was markedly more circumspect, be it during *détente* or Reagan's reinvention of the Cold War. Containment remained the guiding principle, but it was far more nuanced as the US assessed its priorities, tactics and responses more carefully. Communism was engaged, first in the strategic triangle and later on a bilateral basis with China. Economics became the overriding concern and relations with Japan became ever more important, particularly as the US continued its relative decline. Yet, even this modified approach had only limited success and, as the Cold War ended, the US faced both old and new problems in Asia. Japan's security free-ride continued at American expense while its economic miracle ensured trading surpluses with the US. In addition, the reversion of Okinawa to Japanese sovereignty did not remove it as a difficult issue in American–Japanese relations. As for US–China policy, this remained even more delicate. The Taiwan Relations Act of 1979 was an unsatisfactory compromise between China hawks and doves, and the clause that allowed continued arms sales to Taiwan had potential to flare up in the future.[9] Moreover, China remained communist and resolved upon domestic policies that the US found difficult to condone. Indeed, as the decade closed the Chinese government sent troops into Tiananmen Square where they massacred pro-democracy dissidents and embarked subsequently on a period of repression. The 1990s promised little respite for US Asian strategists, even without Cold War considerations.

8 The US, Africa and the Middle East, 1945–89

There could be no greater contrast between the treatment of two regions than that accorded by the US to Africa and the Middle East. For instance, Israel was designated as a developed state in 1963 and therefore beyond the need of aid, but America gave it $2.6 billion in 1983 – twice the amount of aid given to the whole of sub-Saharan Africa.[1] US African policy was largely one of benign neglect, except for South Africa, which raised political difficulties because of apartheid. Similar problems arose with the white supremacist regime of Ian Smith in Southern Rhodesia from 1965 to 1979. For much of this period the US expected its West European allies to handle Africa, particularly as the Soviets did not mount a serious challenge there until the 1970s. In contrast, the Middle East was a theatre of fierce rivalry and high stakes. Policy struggled to keep pace with American economic expansionism and to cope successively with containment, fears of overextension and for oil supplies, discordant allies, decolonisation, nationalism, Zionism and Islamic fundamentalism. It was the region in which the limits of both cohesion within the Western Alliance and of US power were most evident. Furthermore, boundaries between blocs were most insecure here and occasioned seven of the 20 US nuclear alerts during the Cold War.

There were, however, some similarities between Africa and the Middle East. The US was often found wanting in terms of power in both theatres and faced difficulties in dealing with European retrenchment and different belief systems and stages of economic development. Also, from the insider's point of view, non-Cold War issues dominated these regions: race and decolonisation in Africa and religion and independence in the Middle East. How successful were US policy-makers in dealing with these regions' problems? What was the guiding light of their policies? How did they try to project adequate power to both regions? And what lasting effects did their policies have?

The US and Africa: discovering interests

The US had little traditional involvement in Africa and spent much time during the Cold War trying to identify American interests there and how to develop them. These exercises ebbed and flowed, largely in response to each other and to Soviet pressure, decolonisation and, sometimes, indigenous

African politics. Six broad collections of American interests in Africa, which received different emphases at different times, were: anti-colonialism, strategic minerals, Africa's place in the Western European security system, bases, proxies and 'signal-sending'.

The first of these reflected the long-established idealist tradition in American foreign policy of championing self-determination and democratic transition and therefore inclined policy-makers to favour African decolonisation. However, this disposition was tempered by consideration of the other five groupings of interests, all of which favoured either the status quo or only gradual transition to independence.

A redefinition of national security during and after the Second World War stressed the centrality of strategic raw materials to developing and sustaining modern conventional warfare and to manufacturing nuclear weapons. Materials in demand included oil, titanium, chromium, cobalt, bauxite, copper, iron ore, lead, manganese, phosphates, tin, uranium and zinc. Added to this were precious materials such as gold and diamonds. In 1951, 73% of America's strategic materials were estimated to come from underdeveloped regions. By 1960 the US imported, mainly from developing areas, 32% of its iron ore, 46% of its copper, 60% of its zinc and 98% of its bauxite. Africa assumed an increasingly significant part within this import pattern. In 1956 the US imported 25% of its iron ore requirements – much of it from Liberia – and by 1977 Africa provided 38% of US crude petroleum imports. The importance of African raw material sources was underlined during the oil shocks of the 1970s and the second Shaba crisis in Zaire in 1978, which forced the temporary closure of mines then producing the majority of internationally traded cobalt.[2] Passage by Congress of the Byrd Amendment in 1971 sent a similar message. This partially lifted UN-mandated American economic sanctions on Southern Rhodesia to enable the importation of Southern Rhodesian chrome and 72 other strategic minerals.

Strategic minerals were closely entwined with wider US concerns for the Western European security system. It was vital that Europe rearm and economically rejuvenate in order to deter a conventional Soviet attack and resist communist subversion. US policy-makers assumed that Europe's African colonies and former colonies would be a key part of their rehabilitation as sources of raw materials, trade opportunities and manpower. The colonies were also an important corollary to the Marshall Plan, especially in helping to ameliorate the post-Second World War dollar gap. They would earn dollars from US purchases of raw materials and by providing markets to compensate for those lost in Eastern Europe, bring dollars into Western Europe. Furthermore, there was a tacit assumption that support for European efforts to maintain influence in Africa would encourage both stability there and commitment to defending Europe. For instance, Washington seemingly accepted French rule in Algeria, Morocco and Tunisia in order to strengthen French support for containment in Europe.[3] The European Community's Lomé conventions that aimed from the 1970s to assist African development were valuable supplements to under-resourced American objectives in Africa.

The fourth consideration was Africa's usefulness in providing military bases that protected lines of communication that traversed or ran close to the continent. The US cultivated Emperor Haile Selassie's regime from the 1940s to the 1970s because of Ethiopia's strategic location and cooperation in a global telecommunications surveillance network targeted at the USSR. It also supported successive authoritarian dictatorships in Liberia in return for a series of military and intelligence assets. These included landing and refuelling facilities for aircraft and ships, the 'Omega' navigation station (one of eight globally that guided US ships and aircraft in the Atlantic Ocean) and two communication relay stations that carried the vast majority of US diplomatic and intelligence transmissions (including Voice of America) throughout sub-Saharan Africa.[4] The importance attached to African bases increased with the end of *détente*, which ushered in the 'Second Scramble for Africa' and the Second Cold War. In 1978 Sudanese President Numeiri afforded the US facilities at Port Sudan to help patrol the Indian Ocean and in 1980 President Carter acquired base rights in Kenya at Mombasa, Embakasi and Nanyuki and in Somalia at Mogadishu and Berbera. Three years later Caspar Weinberger argued in his 1983 Defense Guidance Plan that the US should maintain and expand still further access and transit rights in pro-Western African states for deployment of US forces to Africa, the South Atlantic and contiguous areas.[5] Foremost among the latter was the Middle East, which accentuated the importance of the Horn of Africa. This was especially pressing as the refusal of all but Oman and Bahrain of the Persian Gulf states to host US military bases meant reliance on Diego Garcia and an arc of African bases, including Morocco, Egypt, Somalia and Kenya.

The fifth consideration was Africa's importance in sourcing pro-Western proxy states that would form bulwarks against communism, provide bases and help undermine neighbouring communist-backed regimes. This encouraged a US classification of African states as state socialist or capitalist and whether or not they were resource-endowed. From this classification the US tended to cultivate those states that had both resources and capitalism. In 1977 the US identified Nigeria, Sudan, Ivory Coast, Kenya, Zaire and South Africa as outstanding investment climates. US trade with Nigeria of $5.7 billion in 1976 was two-thirds of total US trade with Black Africa, and a healthy US–Nigerian relationship developed from Carter's visit to Nigeria in 1977 and the conclusion of a technical assistance agreement.[6] Similarly, Mobutu Sese Seko's Zaire and successive administrations in South Africa were supported as regional bulwarks against communism and as proxy fighters in neighbouring countries, including support for US efforts to back guerrilla forces of the National Union for the Total Independence of Angola (UNITA).

Finally, there was the consideration of signal-sending to allies, the non-aligned and to the Soviet Union and its clients. This became increasingly significant from the 1960s onwards once American perceptions of Africa changed from its being an extension of European security considerations to its being part of 'an indivisible security system based on global containment and world stability'.[7] A good example of this was the proxy war in Angola that followed Portugal's withdrawal in 1974–75 and the onset of a bitter power feud between UNITA, the National Liberation Front of Angola (FNLA) and the Popular Movement for the Liberation of Angola (MPLA). The Soviets supported the MPLA and, when 250 Cuban military advisers arrived to help it, South Africa sent 2,000 troops to aid UNITA. The US backed both UNITA and the FNLA. Cuba responded by sending a further 14,000 troops. The US had no great strategic interest in Angola but the Nixon administration was still alarmed when a nervous post-Vietnam Congress forced it to accept a 'defeat' by passing the Clark Amendment in December 1975 that terminated aid to the FNLA and UNITA.

This superpower proxy war was a blow to *détente* but Kissinger was more concerned about the message it conveyed: 'If the United States is seen to emasculate itself in the face of massive, unprecedented Soviet and Cuban intervention . . . what will be the perception of leaders around the world as they make decisions concerning their future security?'[8] The loss of Angola so soon after Vietnam might encourage further Soviet adventurism and American client states and allies in Africa to doubt US resolve. This could in turn encourage non-alignment policies and embolden communist groupings across the continent. Angola might also become a communist cancer that actively and ideologically undermined neighbouring states – a danger graphically illustrated in 1977 when America provided Zaire with assistance to repel an attack by Angolan-based opponents of the Mobutu regime.

From neglect to limited activism

US administrations differed significantly in responding to these considerations. Truman and Eisenhower neglected African affairs, largely ascribing to Hans J. Morgenthau's argument in 1955 that the US had no specific political or military interests in Africa and that other interests were 'somewhat marginal'.[9] Europe, the Middle East and Asia were more pressing theatres and the escalation of containment from a Eurocentric to a global commitment denied American resources to peripheral regions. This, coupled with the connection made between European recovery and Europe's African colonies, predisposed both administrations to delegate responsibility for Africa to Europe's colonial powers and generally to lend support to their ability to remain there. Apathy was such that the State Department did not create an Africa Bureau until 1958 and the CIA created a separate Africa Division within the Deputy Directorate of Operations only in 1960. The Eisenhower administration also downplayed support for African nationalists as Dulles especially became concerned about newly independent states pursuing Cold War non-alignment. These fears were encouraged by the 1955 Bandung meeting of the Asian–African Conference and by the 1958 Accra Conference of the eight independent African governments. Cold War considerations and sensitivity to allies' vested interests therefore inclined Washington to view radical change as a threat to its interests and to favour either the status quo or carefully managed transitions to independence under colonial tutorage. Assistant Secretary of State for African Affairs Joseph Satterthwaite reflected this ambivalence in 1959: 'We support African political aspirations when they are moderate, non-violent, and constructive and take into account their obligations to and interdependence with the world community. We also support the principle of continued African ties with Western Europe.'[10]

The Reagan administration was at the opposite end of this spectrum, pushing for an activist, albeit still limited, African policy that emphasised Nixon's use of proxies and a more militaristic approach. Reagan's inclination to see Africa in colours of red versus the star-spangled banner rather than the more widely perceived black versus white prompted a series of controversial initiatives. Since Congress's intervention in 1975, UNITA had had to manage with assistance from American allies such as Saudi Arabia, Morocco and South Africa. However, matters changed once Reagan was elected and Cuba and the USSR stepped up their support of the MPLA. UNITA became a prime candidate for support under the Reagan Doctrine, which assumed that at low risk and relatively little expense the US could support groups fighting Soviet-backed regimes and make the cost of communist expansionism prohibitive to Moscow. In 1985 the Clark amendment was repealed. In 1986, UNITA leader Jonas Savimbi met Reagan in Washington and secured a pledge of substantial military help. By the following year UNITA was countering the MPLA's sophisticated Soviet weaponry with advanced American equipment, including Stinger anti-aircraft and TOW anti-tank missiles.[11]

Soviet retrenchment was not, though, immediately forthcoming. In fact, a renewed UNITA–South African military offensive prompted Cuba to send the Angolan government substantial additional combat forces, raising its commitment to around 50,000 troops. Against this background the US brokered a deal in December 1988 that provided for the withdrawal of Cuban and South African troops and a regional settlement. But Angola remained a live issue. Bush promised to continue covert military aid to UNITA and reportedly concluded an agreement in October 1989 with the Mobutu regime to channel supplies to UNITA through Zaire. Also Congress somewhat ironically now wanted guarantees that UNITA would be included within a final Angolan settlement before authorising US funding for prospective UN peacekeeping functions in the country.

Reagan's uncompromising approach also led him to resume aid to Somalia when it again locked horns with Mengistu's Marxist Ethiopia in 1982 and to target communist 'cancers'. Weinberger also argued that the US should develop plans to 'counter militarily Soviet, Cuban and Libyan forces operating from Libyan bases which pose a threat to US or NATO forces' and 'counter Libyan subversive actions throughout Africa by assisting friendly African states militarily, and by weakening Libya's ability to intervene'.[12] Pressure on Colonel Muammar Qaddafi's Libya was soon evident. In August 1981 the US held naval exercises off the Libyan coast. These included aerial operations within the Gulf of Sidra, over which Libya claimed sovereignty, and predictably provoked a minor dogfight in which the Libyan airforce lost two aircraft. Similarly, although Reagan apparently told French President Mitterand that any intervention required in the 1983 Chad crisis was France's 'historic responsibility', the US nevertheless assisted Chadian leader Hissène Habré with military advisers and $25 million of military aid – including 30 Redeye heat-seeking anti-aircraft missiles. Also, the aircraft carrier *Eisenhower* dropped anchor off the Gulf of Sidra and two AWACS radar planes, eight F-15 fighters and 600 Air Force personnel were deployed to Sudan – Chad's eastern neighbour.[13]

Still more controversial was the administration's policy of 'constructive engagement' towards South Africa. This was a significant retreat from Carter's strong support for 'black nationalism', majority rule and independence for Namibia from South Africa. To the discomfort of some within the Reagan administration, constructive engagement linked it with the white supremacist regime in Pretoria. For instance, Reagan's controversial resumption of US military aid to UNITA helped South African regional ambitions, as did the later tying of support for Namibian independence to Cuban withdrawal from Angola in the accords agreed in 1988 between South Africa, Cuba and Namibia. Reagan similarly used the Pretoria government to reduce Soviet influence through sponsoring security accords in February 1984 between South Africa, Angola and Mozambique. Even after the Free South Africa movement mobilised American public opinion sufficiently to force Reagan to impose punitive sanctions in March 1985 and Congress to override a presidential veto to pass the 1986 Comprehensive Anti-Apartheid Act, the administration maintained de facto support of Pretoria and the CIA continued to maintain extensive contact with South African military intelligence.[14]

Patterns and contradictions

Just as interesting as the specifics of US Cold War policy towards Africa are the policy patterns and contradictions across time. In some respects the progressive, if limited, increase in US involvement in Africa followed patterns of decolonisation elsewhere: colonial powers faded and the US either voluntarily or involuntarily filled the vacuum lest the Soviets did. Commitment was thus often incremental and without clear design. Consider, for instance, US policy towards resource-rich Zaire. Washington largely ignored the country as a Belgian responsibility prior to its planned independence in 1960. Independence, though, sparked civil war, a Belgian reoccupation and secessions by the diamond-rich province of South Kasai and by the wealthiest province, Shaba (Katanga). The Kennedy administration sponsored a controversial UN Security Council resolution calling for withdrawal of Belgian and other foreign forces and the reconvening of the Zairian Parliament. At the same time, the CIA was instructed to ensure that moderates dominated the Parliament. The American-backed African nationalist, Cyrille Adoula, duly became head of the newly independent state in 1961 and, after initial hesitation because of the influential Washington Katanga lobby and Western allies' objections, the Kennedy administration supported UN forces forcibly ending the Shaba secession in 1963.

However, the question of Zaire's stability was unresolved on the UN's withdrawal. Kennedy's decision to conclude a bilateral military agreement with Zaire marked the beginning of what would be a long-standing American commitment. Moreover, continuing instability caused both this commitment to escalate quickly and American support for moderate nationalists to wane in favour of military leadership by Mobutu – especially once Johnson assumed the presidency. CIA-sponsored counter-insurgency activities and American military aid expanded, and in November 1964 two US–Belgian military operations were conducted to rescue hostages held by rebel forces in Kisangani. Thereafter the US repeatedly supported economically and militarily Mobutu's efforts to enforce stability, and, particularly after the 1975 Angolan crisis, Zaire effectively became a regional pillar of US Africa policies. Carter did encourage Mobutu to adopt political and economic reforms – on principle and to assuage Congressional criticism – but Zaire was partially insulated from US pressure by alternative sources of support and trade (notably France and Belgium) and by its usefulness to wider American concerns. This was underscored during the Reagan administration by its cooperation vis-à-vis Chad and Angola and, as the Cold War wound down, was symbolically reinforced by Bush making Mobutu his administration's first African guest at the White House.[15]

Accompanying this rather ad hoc increase in selective American commitment to Africa was a blinkered Cold War focus on the continent's priorities. Its racial issues were generally subjugated to Cold War concerns, especially by Republican administrations. Eisenhower largely ignored white supremacy in South Africa; Nixon, in the December 1969 National Security Study Memorandum 39, famously accepted it as a fact of life unlikely to change; and Reagan dealt extensively with the Pretoria regime, regardless of domestic and international criticism. The US also refused to reconceptualise Africa's problems as constitutive of a North–South rather than East–West division. This was reflected in its rejection of the Group of 77 demands for a NIEO, whereby it opposed what it considered unrealistic positions on resource transfer, debt, commodity prices, technology transfer and the reorganisation of the world's primary financial institutions.[16]

Yet the peripheral nature of US interests meant also that Africa was the continent across which containment had least hold on American policy-makers. Repercussions were interesting. First, the permeability of the African agenda threw up fascinating contradictions, none more so than when the Reagan administration, after images of Ethiopian famines in the mid-1980s hit American television, became 'the largest official donor to the most doctrinaire marxist government on the African continent'.[17] Second, it allowed limited superpower cooperation and a lesser degree of zero-sum calculus. For instance, the US could afford to accept its 'loss' in Angola in 1975 and, when Ford and Carter supported black majority rule in Southern Rhodesia (Zimbabwe), they found themselves aligned with China and the USSR. Third, African containment was pursued with a pragmatic flexibility reminiscent of Kennan's original concept. The US and USSR even swapped proxies in the

Somali–Ethiopian conflict. The USSR initially responded to American culti-vation of Ethiopia by doing the same with Somalia. However, when Somalia occupied the Ogaden territory of Ethiopia in 1978, the USSR decided to back Ethiopia and the US supplied arms to Somalia as a counterweight, thus uncomfortably supporting the aggressor. Furthermore, Carter was able to accept a 'loss' to reduce East–West tensions when the arrival of 10,000 Cuban volunteers in Ethiopia, coupled with South Yemen's friendship with the USSR, raised the spectre of Soviet manoeuvring to strengthen their position in the Red Sea, through which oil flowed from the Middle East. By reducing military aid to Somalia, Carter accepted a minor loss for America's new client in return for forcing it to abandon its aggression and thereby preventing an escalation of the conflict.[18]

Finally, American administrations lacked the will and resources to match idealistic rhetoric with policy reality. During the Second World War, Roosevelt argued that, under point three of the Atlantic Charter, the peoples of the African colonies were entitled to choose their own leaders and run their own affairs. Kennedy pledged in his inauguration address help to the 'peoples in the huts and villages of half the globe struggling to break the bonds of mass misery . . . not because the communists may be doing it, not because we seek their votes, but because it is right'.[19] And Carter put more emphasis on human rights and partnership with mainstream forces within the African concert of states. Yet American weapons still found their way to Belgian military bases in the Congo. Portugal used US-supplied napalm and chemical weapons in Angola, Mozambique and Guinea. And Carter largely failed to follow through on promises to reduce US reliance on authoritarian dictatorships – something exemplified by his Somali bases deal in August 1980.

The New Frontier saw a more active African policy that recognised internal sources of instability and the importance of accommodating nationalist forces. Kennedy was also the first American president to impose sanctions on South Africa in response to apartheid, placed restrictions on Portuguese diver-sion of US-supplied NATO weaponry to counterinsurgency operations in Africa, and in 1961 supported a UN vote that encouraged an end to Portu-guese rule in Angola. Nevertheless, the proclaimed moral rather than strategic imperatives of his policies sit awkwardly with his election campaign claim that Africa was the objective of 'a gigantic communist offensive'. On his watch, too, investments by US banks and multinationals in South Africa increased and by late 1962 Kennedy had reverted to favouring the Angolan status quo and Portuguese interests.[20] Explanations proffered for the latter include Portu-gual's threat to terminate US and NATO access to key bases in the Azores and that Africa's low priority allowed Kennedy to sacrifice principles there to interests elsewhere. Indeed, Kennedy may have accommodated Portugal in part because he feared electoral losses should a pending nuclear test ban coincide with the loss of the Azores base to enable the Republicans to portray him as being weak on communism.[21]

The US and the Middle East: setting the trend

The Truman administration made three lasting contributions to US Middle Eastern policy. It abandoned traditional US non-involvement, endorsed the existence of Israel and followed a pattern of diplomatic schizophrenia that characterised American policies in the region for much of the Cold War. The Middle East was initially low on the list of Cold War priorities, despite the 1946 Iranian dispute being one of the first Cold War crises. NSC-68 changed that insofar as the US became more concerned about protecting its interests in the region. These interests were driven neither by history nor moral conviction. The Americans had no tradition of enmity with the Soviet Union in the Middle East, had little identification with the people there whose religious and socio-cultural values were very different from Western liberalism, and were frequently critical of the corrupt, backward and dictatorial regimes that littered the region. Instead, US policy was justified by ideology and driven by considerations that were not necessarily Cold War related. By far the most important of these was the economic interdependence of the Western world and the Middle East. As President Eisenhower put it in 1956, they were 'together the most strategic areas in the world – Western Europe requires Middle Eastern oil and Middle Eastern oil is of importance mainly through its contribution to the Western European economy'.[22] What Eisenhower did not mention, but which was uppermost in American calculations, was that most of that oil was either produced by American oil companies or coveted by them. Indeed, in 1954 the Eisenhower administration was instrumental in their obtaining, at Britain's expense, a major share of the Anglo-Iranian Oil Company's (AIOC) concession in Iran.[23] Such expansionism had Cold War justification in terms of the oil companies generating economic prosperity as a counterweight to communism and acting as stabilising forces within concession granting nations. Similarly, American geostrategic planning for the Middle East was couched in terms of denying the Soviets oil resources and potential bases from which to launch an assault upon the Persian Gulf. Nevertheless, American economic interests were the primary beneficiaries of US policy and the repatriation of enormous profits from oil operations smacked heavily of neo-imperialism.

Almost as important as the new attitude towards the Middle East was Truman's intervention in the question of the Palestine Mandate. This was a British responsibility and erratic American policy sorely tested Anglo-American relations. It was also an issue heavily charged by US domestic politics. When Truman connived in the UN with the Soviets to force a partition of Palestine into Arab and Jewish states on 29 November 1947, British Foreign Secretary Ernest Bevin accused him of pandering to the US domestic Jewish vote. Above all else, though, Truman's was a policy that imposed enormous constraints on subsequent US administrations.

On 14 May 1948, Israel declared its independence. America and the Soviet Union hastened to recognise it but the surrounding Arab nations refused and instead launched an invasion. Egyptian, Iraqi, Lebanese, Syrian and Jordanian armies inflicted heavy casualties on Israeli forces before the US and the Soviet Union sponsored a four-week UN truce. This respite gave Israel time to buy large quantities of weapons from communist Czechoslovakia and when hostilities resumed it drove the Arab armies back deep into their own territories. By the time the US sponsored another peace deal, Israel had expanded its borders far beyond those envisaged by the original UN partition of Palestine. The Truman administration consequently helped bring about the creation of Israel at the enormous cost of alienating the Arab world and creating the Palestinian refugee problem. The latter was a festering sore that determined the later conduct of Middle Eastern states far more than did the Cold War. Moreover, the Truman administration's actions hindered American ability to contain communism in the Middle East. Washington's de facto special relationship with Israel undermined US efforts to establish regional collective security arrangements, allowed the Soviets to champion Arab countries against Israel, and created an explosive situation. The issues involved were not of the Cold War but, nevertheless, threatened to feed off them as US and Soviet proxies embroiled the superpowers in their internecine disputes. In 1956, 1967, 1973 and 1982–84, the Arab–Israeli conflict burst into open warfare with the potential to escalate wildly out of control into a major Cold War conflict.[24]

Truman's final legacy was an inchoate policy incapable of fully meeting US rhetoric and ambitions in the Middle East. There were two principal threats to Western interests: direct Soviet intervention and communist subversion from within, or at least its collusion with radical Arab nationalism, which could bring about regimes inimical to the West. The former was considered unlikely, but it still had to be catered for. As the US had little power in the region and the Pentagon was strongly averse to overextending into the Middle East, policy-makers chose to rely upon the colonial powers of Britain and France to act as guarantors of regional security. At the same time, the US sought to align itself with Middle Eastern nationalism, which was staunchly opposed to Western colonialism, and to develop its own influence and economic interests, often at the expense of its European allies. This produced both a grossly oversimplified view of the Middle East and a debilitating kind of US diplomatic schizophrenia. Policy-makers recognised the existence of religious divides, deep social unrest and the clash between modernisation and traditionalism. They also identified the running sore of Israel within the body of Arab states, the rising tide of nationalism and the grave intra- and inter-state tensions – such as between Iran and Iraq, Egypt and Saudi Arabia, Turkey and Syria, Turkey and Greece, and North and South Yemen. Nevertheless, they superimposed a Cold War framework upon this complex mosaic that distorted the realities of the situation and encouraged inappropriate responses. Moreover, they tried to ride five horses simultaneously – nurturing direct US economic interests and expanding US political influence, Cold War containment, support for colonial powers, a special relationship with Israel, and the championing of Arab nationalist movements. At various times these all ran in different directions and left in their wake a confusing array of inconsistent short-term decisions that defied any explanation other than expediency.

From denial to surrogates

When Truman left office in January 1953, US Middle Eastern policy was already in deep trouble. Hopes that nationalism and Islam could be harnessed against communism had been replaced by fears that the communists had hijacked them first. Likewise, hopes were fading that Britain could hold its Middle Eastern position. It had withdrawn from Greece, was in dire financial straits, and was under serious nationalist attack in Iran and Egypt – the former hosted the AIOC's enormously important oil operations and the latter the bulk of Britain's Middle Eastern military presence near the geostrategically vital Suez Canal. Together with the quickening pace of decolonisation, this threatened a power vacuum in the Middle East, the loss of traditional Western bases, and great opportunities for the Soviets to expand their interests into the Persian Gulf.

Eisenhower continued established trends. Moral claims, the intellectual preferences of policy-makers and international law were all sacrificed as US fears of rampant nationalism led it to ally increasingly with conservative forces. In August 1953, the CIA manufactured a coup in Iran to topple the democratically elected Mohammed Mosadeq in favour, ultimately, of the autocratic Shah and his brutal police, the Savak, around whom the Americans built a client state.[25] In January 1957, the Eisenhower Doctrine also implied a firm commitment to the existing order. For example, the US offered military aid to friendly governments and withdrew its efforts to resolve the Arab–Israeli issue; that poisoned chalice was handed to the UN. Furthermore, in July 1958, Eisenhower sent US marines to preserve the status quo in the Lebanon when pan-Arab radicalism threatened to spill over from the overthrow of the Hashemite monarchy of Iraq.

The Eisenhower administration also looked to regional organisations to reconcile its desire for Middle Eastern security with reduced defence budgets and the Pentagon's obsessive reluctance to commit US forces. Apart from Israel the bulk of US expenditure went to Turkey and Iran in the hope that these, along with Pakistan, would form a Northern Tier to deter Soviet expansionism. The Americans hoped, too, to bring these countries together with Britain to coordinate regional defence. The basis for this was secured on 24 February 1955 with the signing of the Baghdad Pact, but a combination of the US refusal to join and intense Arab opposition meant that it ultimately failed. Iraq withdrew in March 1959, the subsequent Central Treaty Organisation (CENTO) did nothing much and, importantly, British power waned palpably.

The US had long known of British decline but had refused to act upon it because the only answer was one that American policy-makers did not want to hear – the US must fill the power vacuum. However, the Suez Crisis brought matters to a head. On 26 July 1956, Egyptian President Gamal Abdul Nasser nationalised the Anglo-French-owned Suez Canal Company. Britain and France collaborated with Israel to teach the Egyptians a lesson. On 19 October, Israeli forces drove into the Sinai peninsular. Britain and France pressed a stage-managed ultimatum upon Israeli and Egyptian forces to withdraw from the Suez Canal Zone. Shortly afterwards, they bombed Egyptian bases, dropped paratroopers and launched an amphibious assault. Eisenhower was dismayed. The timing, on the eve of American elections, was politically embarrassing because he was running for re-election on a peace ticket. It also made it difficult to make propaganda capital out of the brutal Soviet repression of the 1956 Hungarian uprising. More importantly, the Anglo-French intervention pulled the US back into the Arab–Israeli quagmire. The US could not be seen to support blatantly the forces of colonialism. Nor did it want to forfeit the goodwill it had been trying to regain with the Arab states by siding with Israel yet again. Furthermore, it did not want to give the Soviets a pretext for intervention. Eisenhower decided to prioritise US Cold War concerns over the vested interests of his major allies, and applied sufficient economic and diplomatic pressure to force Britain and France to withdraw. However, this was not before the Soviets had won a Third World propaganda coup by brandishing their atomic weapons at the imperialist Western powers.[26]

Although the Eisenhower administration scored some short-term successes, notably in Iran, it left a power vacuum in the Middle East which it had first tried to ignore, particularly with regard to the waning British position, and had then made worse by humiliating Britain and France over Suez. The short-lived Kennedy administration achieved little and it fell to Presidents Johnson and Nixon to deal with the problem. Both were preoccupied with Vietnam and realised that the US could ill-afford a sufficient build-up of power to play a balancing role in the Indian Ocean and the Persian Gulf. However, neither could they indulge themselves in the illusion that Britain could fill a regional power vacuum. This became self-evident in 1968 when it announced its intent to withdraw its military forces from east of Suez. The US now resorted increasingly to the use of surrogates to hold the status quo.

Interestingly, the US used both state and non-state actors. Of the latter, by far the most important were the US oil companies operating in the Middle East. These held privileged positions that made them effectively ambassadors of the West. They also became vehicles through which, using powerful tax incentives, US administrations could channel foreign aid without congressional approval. State surrogates were often less compliant, but more numerous. In the Six Day War in 1967, Johnson moved US policy decisively towards supporting Israel against the Arabs. In a brilliant military campaign, the Israelis inflicted a humiliating defeat upon the Arab states. Johnson made no attempt to force an Israeli withdrawal. Instead, he sponsored UN resolution 242, which proposed a land for peace deal whereby Israel would return occupied territory in exchange for security guarantees, and in December 1968 he supplied Israel with F-4 Phantom jets. Nixon's approach took the idea of using surrogates even further as he developed the Twin Pillar strategy whereby Iran and Saudi Arabia would police the Persian Gulf. To facilitate this and, conveniently, to help the ailing American economy, the US sold them vast quantities of sophisticated weaponry. In 1972, Nixon told the Shah that he could purchase any non-nuclear weapons and, in 1974 alone, the Foreign Military Sales (FMS) agreement saw the US supply him with over $3,950 million of arms. Similar offers were made to Saudi Arabia. In 1975, US–Saudi FMS agreements were worth almost $5,776 million and later that year Secretary of State Kissinger persuaded President Ford to allow it to purchase F-15 fighters.

Out of the ashes

American hopes that surrogates would be able to guarantee regional stability proved to be short-lived once their Middle Eastern policy was struck a series of blows in the 1970s. Three stand out in particular. The first came in 1973 when the Yom Kippur War erupted. Egypt and Syria, with Soviet backing, attacked Israel and won a series of stunning victories. The US supplied Israel with replacement arms necessary to repel Arab forces and, by 15 October, the Israelis had reversed the situation and were poised to annihilate the Egyptian Third Army. The Soviets announced their intent to intervene militarily, either as part of a combined operation with the US or unilaterally. However, the Americans saw this as a pretext for the Soviets to establish a foothold in the region. Accordingly, US nuclear forces were put on alert and NSA Henry Kissinger pushed through UN resolution 338 that called for the full implementation of UN resolution 242. Ultimately, another begrudging peace was restored, but by then the spirit of *détente* and the American position had incurred serious damage. Contrary to the 1972 US–Soviet summit declarations, the US had pursued unilateral advantage and demonstrated its unwillingness to treat the Soviets as an equal in the Middle East. Also, US championship of Israel against the Arab world had serious consequences. It damaged the Atlantic Alliance because the US failed to secure the support of its NATO allies for its action, most of them being disenchanted with the intolerant Israeli attitude and preoccupied with their need for Arab oil. It also awakened the Arab states to the power that they could wield against the US, which by 1973 had become a net importer of oil. The Organisation of Arab Petroleum Exporting Countries imposed an oil embargo on supporters of Israel, notably the US and the Netherlands. It imposed, too, a crippling price hike on oil, which threw Western Europe's economy into chaos and ruined early attempts at economic and monetary union. The only real consolation for the US was that its resolute action persuaded Egyptian leaders that it would never allow Israel to be destroyed and, therefore, that their flirtation with the Soviets would bring them less reward than would an improved relationship with Washington.

Two further blows were struck to US Middle Eastern policy in 1979. First, the Soviets dealt a fatal blow to *détente* and threatened to destabilise the region when they invaded Afghanistan. The subsequent Carter Doctrine heralded a new hard line, warning as it did that the US would take military action to keep the Soviets away from the Persian Gulf. Meantime, Carter imposed economic sanctions on the USSR and the CIA began covert support of Afghan resistance fighters. Second, the fundamentalist Ayatollah Khomeini led the Iranian revolution that deprived the US of one of its closest collaborators and destroyed the Twin Pillar strategy. In fact, the US reaped the rewards of an Iranian policy that had been delegitimised from the moment the CIA toppled Mosadeq in August 1953. Successive presidents championed an Iranian regime bent upon popular repression and by doing so sacrificed the democratic aspirations of a nation to a Cold War threat that was more imagined than real. Thereafter, in the most intensely media-covered US foreign policy crisis of all time, Iran humiliated the Carter administration during the bungled attempt to rescue American embassy staff held hostage in Teheran. Just as importantly, Iran became an embittered bastion of anti-Americanism, a haven for what the US labelled terrorists, and a focal point for Islamic fundamentalism and anti-imperial fanaticism.[27]

Although there were differences in rhetoric, the policies of US administrations from Nixon through to Reagan were consistent. All of them made efforts to rebuild the tattered US relationship with the Arab states. Kissinger's shuttle diplomacy during 1973–74 succeeded both in stopping the Middle East war and beginning the peace process.[28] Capitalising upon President Sadat's move away from the Soviets, President Carter mediated the Camp David Accords that led in March 1979 to an Egyptian–Israeli peace treaty. Whereas on many issues Carter's idealism and concern for human rights ran foul of US national security considerations, this was undoubtedly his greatest foreign policy success. Likewise, in 1988 the US began to tackle the Palestinian problem once the Palestine Liberation Organisation (PLO) leader, Yasser Arafat, had finally accepted UN resolution 242 and the legal existence of Israel.[29]

All administrations sought, too, to preserve America's established pattern of allies in the Middle East, most notably with the Saudis and the Israelis. In the immediate aftermath of the Yom Kippur War, the US provided the latter with more than $3 billion of weapons. In the early 1980s, Washington also turned a blind eye to Israel's invasion of the Lebanon in the hope that this would bring them into conflict with Syria, which was regarded as a Soviet client state. Furthermore, there was an increasing willingness to combat Middle Eastern terrorism, particularly after the ill-fated deployment of a US peace-making force of marines in 1982 to Beruit resulted in 241 men being killed in a truck bomb attack. Consider, for instance, Reagan's air strike in April 1986 against Qaddafi's Libya.

The single most important development in US Middle Eastern policy, though, was its move away from reliance on either colonial or indigenous allies. The collapse of imperial power and the Twin Pillar strategy gave impetus to a major review of US policy in the Indian Ocean and Persian Gulf. Nationalism, fundamentalism, decolonisation and communist machinations meant that land bases were increasingly unreliable and temporary assets. From Nixon onwards, US emphasis was on sea and air power, particularly once the wind-down in Vietnam released materials and the Yom Kippur War emphasised the need for military guarantees of precious oil shipments. In

1980, the Carter Doctrine committed the US to military action should any force seek to control the Persian Gulf and frantic efforts were made to back this promise with credible firepower. The island of Diego Garcia became the focal point of an enormous expansion of US capabilities in the Indian Ocean area and a Rapid Reaction Force was created to fight 'brush-fires', the funding for which Reagan increased by 85% – an additional $2 billion. In fact, Caspar Weinberger confirmed that from lowly beginnings the Middle East had, by the time that the Cold War closed, finally achieved 'top-billing' in US security considerations. As far as Reagan's Defense Secretary was concerned, the Persian Gulf had become the centre of conflict for the foreseeable future.[30]

Conclusion

US policy-makers struggled throughout the Cold War to manage their relationships with Africa and the Middle East. The latter was by far the more pressing. There the Americans variously deluded themselves by relying upon European imperial power that simply was no longer sufficient, developed surrogates to fight their battles for them, and finally accepted the burden of building up the force necessary to arbitrate the balance of power in the Indian Ocean and Persian Gulf. In the process they toppled progressive governments, supported dictators, turned a blind eye to Israeli atrocities in the Lebanon and, when it suited them, abandoned their closest allies, as with Britain and France during the Suez Crisis. The lens of containment through which policy-makers so often viewed the region distorted its problems into zero-sum calculations of profit or loss vis-à-vis the Soviets. The concern above all else was the economic dependence of the Western world on Middle Eastern oil.[31] The US therefore emphasised military security and, too often, the preservation of the status quo to protect Western, not Middle Eastern, interests. Indeed, its treatment of progressive and infant democracies raises significant issues regarding both the conduct of US foreign policy and democratic peace theory (see Chapter 9).

It is ironic that the Americans practised containment better in Africa than in the Middle East. In fact, it was precisely because the US cared less for Africa that policy-makers were, in relative terms at least, freed from the constraints of 'cult containment' to practise the flexible version proposed by Kennan. Carter's sanction of a 'loss' in Somalia in 1978 and quiet acceptance of a subsequent 20-year Treaty of Friendship and Cooperation between Ethiopia and the USSR would have been unthinkable in other parts of the world. However, the mantle of US moral supremacy was no less tarnished there than elsewhere. American arms facilitated proxy and civil wars that soaked Africa in the blood of countless thousands and, as American leaders poured out rhetoric stressing the plight of Black Africa, their actions and US economic interests underwrote white supremacy in South Africa.

Three interesting similarities between the US experience in Africa and in the Middle East help explain some of the problems policy-makers faced and the sometimes inappropriate nature of their actions. First, both regions demonstrated the blurring of US foreign and domestic policy. This was evident in the

Middle East with the Jewish lobby, but was also pronounced in Africa where limited US strategic interests allowed a more flexible agenda. Thus, African policy more than any other Cold War theatre revealed the conflicting strands of US foreign policy thinking, the impact of political creed within the White House, and the influence of public opinion, especially on human rights issues. Second, the US most probably made the problems of Africa and the Middle East, and thus of itself, much worse. Its quest for stability led successive American presidents to sponsor regimes that denied the peoples of these regions those rights and freedoms for which the US stood. Similarly, the substitution of American economic expansionism for collapsing imperial power, especially in the Middle East, created a new form of dependency and another focal point for extremist agitation, and the use of proxies justified the supply of vast quantities of arms that caused carnage to little Cold War end. Indeed in Africa, unlike in more geostrategically important areas of the world, there was little correlation between success and strategies of either the USSR or America. For instance, the Soviets capitalised upon decolonisation to win influence in a series of states, such as Ghana, Guinea, Mali, the Sudan and Somalia. That this influence often proved ephemeral, and that by the early 1970s former allies such as Mali and Ghana were reorienting towards the West, was due less to US action than to the internal dynamics of a fragmented continent struggling to adjust to a post-colonial world.

Finally, the US superimposed upon both regions a containment strategy designed to combat communism while the peoples of Africa and the Middle East were little concerned with the Cold War. The Americans and Soviets played a superpower game using native states as pawns, and the native states fought their own internecine battles and used the superpowers to press their interests. Racism and independence rather than 'red peril' dominated African thinking, and the Arab–Israeli conflict preoccupied Middle Eastern minds. To make matters worse, the US was integrally involved in these problems too – particularly because of its special links with Israel, white South Africa and repressive autocracies in both regions. By the time the Cold War ended the principal change in these regions was that the US had partially filled the colonial vacuum in Africa and had become the Middle East's hegemon. Otherwise there was a depressing continuity in their problems. Western interest remained focused principally on supplies of energy and raw materials. The plight of Black Africa was little improved. Apartheid remained in South Africa. The Arab–Israeli conflict was unresolved. And poverty, marginalisation and disenfranchisement continued to be so widespread that both regions were fertile breeding grounds for radicalism and militant Islam.

9 Power and purpose
The end of the Cold War and new challenges for American foreign policy

What caused the Cold War to end so abruptly? Gaddis has pointed out with ill-disguised relish the failure of international relations theory to predict its demise and the intellectual bankruptcy that this appeared to display.[1] And if theorists could not predict its end, what credence should we give to their hastily concocted and often mutually contradictory explanations about what caused it? For example, the two most common but seriously incompatible answers are: it was a carefully crafted victory by the US; and, it was the result of internal corrosion of the Soviet system with Gorbachev acting as a catalyst for further decay rather than for the renewal that he intended. While bearing these cautionary observations in mind, we nevertheless need to examine the different perceptions about why the Cold War ended, not least because they influence answers to the following cluster of questions. Was the world now unipolar? Was it threatened by a 'clash of civilisations'? Was it a 'back-to-the-future' scenario of less stable multipolarity? Was it a world in which US relative power would continue to diminish as many had suggested it would in the late 1970s and early 1980s? What would now be more important to the US, hard military and economic, or soft economic, cultural and normative power?[2] Did the end of the Cold War demote the importance of security in US foreign policy objectives? Is it appropriate to talk of a post post-Cold War era after 9/11? In other words, did 9/11 radically alter the international system and re-elevate the importance of security, or did it simply highlight dangers that had long been recognised but ineffectually addressed? And, finally, how did these dramatic changes affect those most contentious of all foreign policy questions: how, when, why and at what cost should the US intervene militarily in the affairs of other states?

The different answers successive administrations gave to these questions largely determined the way they tried to craft grand strategies to replace Cold War containment.

The end of the Cold War: not with a bang but a whimper

According to a NSC official: 'the first Reagan administration adopted, designed, and successfully implemented an integrated set of policies, strategies, and tactics specifically directed toward the eventual destruction (without war) of the Soviet Empire and the successful ending of the Cold War with victory for the west.'[3] However, one of the Reagan administration's key papers on the Soviet Union gives little hint of such a victory strategy, but instead speaks of long-term coexistence: 'the U.S. must demonstrate credibly that its policy is not a blueprint for an open-ended, sterile confrontation with Moscow, but a serious search for a stable and constructive long-term basis for U.S.–Soviet relations.'[4]

Were the Reagan administration's policies designed to defeat or draw the Soviets into negotiation? Views on this are influenced by political values and the neo-conservatives have notably reinterpreted Reagan's actions to suit their own ideological predilections.[5] According to them, Reagan followed an aggressive agenda dictated by his right-wing views.[6] His military build-up, the momentum he created for Western renewal and SDI, were, they claim, part and parcel of a carefully crafted strategy aimed at, and which in their view achieved, victory over the Soviet Union.[7] Reagan's strategic embargo policy, however (see Chapter 4), was far more pragmatic and closer to the much reviled policy of *détente* than such Cold War victory theses allow. The idea that the US military build-up was a major factor that led to the demise of the Cold War and Western 'victory' is rejected by Russian insider experts such as Georgi Arbatov, and by leading Western theorists such as Frederich Kratchowil. Close scrutiny of the chronology of Soviet policy developments leads Beth A. Fisher to likewise raise substantial doubts about cause and effect from both the US arms build-up and the early Reagan administration hard line. Gaddis's succinct view is that: 'President Reagan, who may have had cynical advisers was not cynical himself . . . took the principle of "negotiation from strength" literally: once one had built strength, one negotiated.'[8] A report from the congressional Office of Research Coordination on Reagan's Cold War strategy also provides a picture of pragmatic manoeuvring to draw the Soviets into negotiation for long-term coexistence.[9]

These views, that emphasise the Reagan administration's willingness to accommodate, open trade and communicate with the Soviets, do not reject entirely, but entertain different emphases about, the importance of America's contribution to the demise of the Soviet Union. They are compatible with explanations that rely on the importance of long-standing structural flaws in the Soviet economy and the corrosive influence of Western ideas in an ever more interdependent world. Seductive Western ideas began to take hold because of enhanced communications, the aggressive propaganda of the Roman Catholic Church, and the forums established by the Helsinki Accords for economic, political and human rights reforms, at the CSCE in 1975.[10]

Whatever line of interpretation one adopts, the facts make clear that 1983 was a crucible for change. On 8 March, Reagan made his most notorious speech on the Soviet Union in front of the National Association of Evangelicals in Florida. He was widely reported as having condemned the Soviet Union as an 'evil empire'.[11] Later that month, he announced the SDI. The tone was harsh at the outset of the year and in the autumn events cast an even deeper pall over US–Soviet relations. On 1 September there was the KAL-007 outrage. On 6 October, to the severe embarrassment of the Soviets, Lek Walensa, leader of the Polish Solidarity labour movement, was awarded the Nobel peace prize. That same month the US suffered heavy casualties to its peacekeeping force in the Lebanon when a terrorist truck bomb exploded in the marine barracks, and in the Caribbean there was the US invasion of Grenada. In early November the NATO exercise Able Archer was seen temporarily by the Soviets as being potentially a pre-emptive Western strike against the Soviet Union. And finally, in November, the US started to deploy Pershing II and Cruise missiles in Europe and the Soviets walked out of arms talks in Geneva. It was against this backdrop of rising tensions that Reagan began to shift his stance and look for negotiation rather than confrontation.

Exactly when this shift took place is not easy to determine. However, there were signs throughout the year that the US position was not thoroughly hostile. On 15 February, Reagan had his first formal discussion with a senior Soviet official when he met with Ambassador Dobrynin. Economic sanctions were eased and the US did not embark upon new sanctions after KAL-007, nor did it walk out of the Geneva talks in protest. At the height of US–Soviet tensions on 10 November, the ailing Soviet leader Leonid Brezhnev finally died. When Reagan visited the Soviet Embassy to pay his respects he projected a friendlier image. Dobrynin even notes in his memoirs: 'There are some who say that the historic turn in our relations began with this visit.'[12] The President's language was certainly more restrained after March 1983 and less than a year later Dobrynin noted the moderation and more friendly tone in a major speech about US–Soviet relations that Reagan gave on 16 January 1984.[13] By September 1984 Reagan was forthright in his call for talks. 'America has repaired its strength. . . . We are ready for constructive negotiations with the Soviet Union.'[14] Although repairing US strength, or, perhaps more importantly, perceptions of US strength, was very important for Reagan, there were other factors at work that point towards November 1983 as the crucial turning point.

In 1983, Oleg Gordievsky, the Committee for State Security (KGB) number two at the Soviet Embassy in London, provided evidence that the Soviets suspected that the CIA had contrived the whole KAL-007 episode and that they feared that Able Archer could be the real thing. Reagan was horrified that the Soviets could be so dangerously paranoid and swiftly moved to improve relations, particularly after March 1985, when Gorbachev became leader of the Soviet Union. Despite all the violent criticisms of *détente*, in the end, Reagan practised something similar himself. At Geneva in November 1985 Reagan and Gorbachev held the first US–Soviet summit for six years. Dobrynin later described it in Churchillian terms as 'the beginning of the end of the Cold War'.[15] Over the next three years the two leaders made substantial progress on disarmament and in generally improving East–West relations. At the time no one quite understood just how radical the changes were to prove. They ended what was already by then a very low-key Cold War, and soon afterwards the Soviet Union collapsed. From one perspective this was victory for the US. It was the only contender left in the ring. But it was not a victory that had come about primarily because of US actions. Increased economic, political and cultural penetrations from the outside world combined with the USSR's own growing economic inefficiency, corruption and self-recognition of at least some of its shortcomings to cause an internal unravelling of the Soviet empire. These were the crucial factors. US policy exacerbated some of the difficulties for the Soviet Union and its diplomacy provided a negotiated pathway that eased the passage of transition to something else.

Now came the job of trying to conceptualise where this left the US, what the new world order was, and what it might or should become.

Capability and power

As the Cold War faded away Paul Kennedy wrote *The Rise and Fall of the Great Powers*, which elaborated a theory of inevitable imperial overstretch. The book intensified arguments about US relative decline and fed into a wider debate about hegemony.

In 1945 the US had 40% of the world's wealth and was painlessly able to devote 9–10% of GDP to defence during the 1950s and 1960s. This declined to 6–7% by the 1980s, but its relative wealth slumped more dramatically from 40% to 20–24% of the world total. As a result, Paul Kennedy announced: 'decision makers in Washington must now face the awkward and enduring fact that the sum total of the United States' global interests and obligations is nowadays far larger than the country's power to defend them all simultaneously.'[16]

Economic omens were certainly not good. High-technology trade slipped from a US surplus of $27 to $4 billion between 1980 and 1985. US strength in agricultural exports was undermined by the EC CAP and by rising Third World productivity. At the same time, supply-side economics, or Reaganomics as it was called at the time, cut taxes and tried to diminish government in the hope of both releasing entrepreneurial dynamics and creating a trickle-down effect of increased demand from the wealthy. When the effects of these policies combined with the rather contradictory Keynesian-style deficit spending on Reagan's massive rearmament programme, the result was turbulence in national finances, high interest and inflation rates and an overvalued dollar, which crippled exports. By 1985 the annual trade deficit was over $200 billion and the national debt stood at $1.8 trillion, which carried interest charges of $129 billion a year. The US, it seemed, was fated to go the way of all empires: it would decline.

Responses to Kennedy came most notably from Joseph S. Nye.[17] He pointed out that if Kennedy had taken a pre-war baseline for calculating US wealth, then its relative decline would have been insignificant. It was only because the economies of other industrial nations had not recovered from the devastation of the Second World War that the relative power of the US was so unnaturally inflated in the late 1940s. Nye also claimed that other largely symbolic features of decline, such as the burning with impunity of the Stars and Stripes in

Teheran in 1980, had been grossly overexaggerated. The US did have a substantial problem in the form of debts bequeathed to the nation by the Reagan administration, but there was a remedy. Resources should be shifted from consumption to investment in industry and education. That would enable Americans to afford both social and international security. Above all, they should not cut themselves off from the international environment because it is a vital factor for both US strength and security. In short, the US must not lose faith because it is still 'bound to lead'.

By the end of the millennium, it looked as if Kennedy had got things drastically wrong and Nye more or less right. The Soviet Union imploded in 1991 and Russia has been in various stages of disarray ever since. In 1989 the US economy, with a GDP of $5.2 trillion, was still 1.8 times the size of Japan's, its nearest rival. By 1995 it had grown 30% to $7 trillion and by 2004 to $11.7 trillion while Japan's stood at $3.7 trillion. The US trade deficit was $100 billion in 1995, but that was partly offset by an $80 billion surplus on services, banking and royalties. Furthermore, US factories abroad command a greater share of world exports than their domestic counterparts, which means that the US overall, on these calculations, makes a modest profit on its dealings with the global economy. When these traditional indicators of economic power are added to the new forms of power identified by Susan Strange – production, financial and knowledge structures – then, one begins to realise the overstated nature of Kennedy's thesis. And there is more. In 1997, the US devoted 4% of its GDP to defence, but the total was equivalent to the defence expenditure of the next ten biggest military powers added together. By 2004 the US was spending $455–462 billion on defence and had stretched its lead by matching the total combined expenditure of the next 32 or so largest military spenders, depending on whose analysis and figures you take.[18] The gap between the US and even its closest and most militarily powerful allies, Britain and France, became painfully obvious in the military action to force Serbian President Milosovic to abandon his intervention in Kosovo in 1998. Interoperability between US and other forces became a serious issue. Allies simply could not keep up with the US. Their weapons systems, intelligence gathering, surveillance and logistical capabilities were years behind those of the Americans. The US military from this point on would try to avoid military operations with its allies, not just because of efficiency of command issues, but because allies were a liability in the field. On top of all this, the US has a flexible economy, a political, social and cultural environment that continues to attract many of the world's best and brightest, and positions of established influence and power in all the world's great organisations.

The US is unlikely to be substantially less important or less powerful in world affairs for the foreseeable future. Without doubt, it has the wherewithal to intervene with great power anywhere in the world. So, rumours of decline seem to have been grossly overexaggerated, but it should also be noted that US strength is now intertwined inextricably with the fortunes of the world outside its boundaries. The neo-isolationist option is not real. US power depends not only upon the continuing health of its domestic economy, but also its ability to function effectively in the international economy. Unfortunately for Americans developments in both spheres have recently raised concerns.

Since the arrival of the George W. Bush administration many of the positive trends established during Clinton's time have stalled or gone into reverse. Since 2000 the federal budget has swung from a surplus of $189.5 billion to a deficit of $412.3 billion in FY 2004. The economy is looking very vulnerable again as Figure 1 indicates. What it does not indicate are two further important and potentially weakening factors. The first is the dramatic decline in the value of the dollar, over 30% against other major currencies between 2002 and 2005. This also needs to be seen in the context of a long-term trade deficit (see Chapter 4). There has been little alternative to holding dollars abroad until recently, even though the US has run massive balance of payments deficits. However, that situation is changing as a consequence of the emergence of the euro as a potential rival currency, notwithstanding the 2005 crisis in the EU caused by the rejection of the European Constitution by France and the Netherlands. The development of the euro could pose serious difficulties for the dollar and the US economy as a whole in the not-too-distant future. If downward pressure on the dollar spirals out of control, the US may find itself having to seek multilateral help from the other leading world economies in the same way that Britain had to as sterling declined in the 1950s and 1960s and was unable to perform the role of the leading world currency that it had for so many years. In return for multilateral help, the US would be required to demonstrate more multilateralism of its own. Matters have been made worse by 9/11 and America's response. Although America's soft power remains potent and its hard power is far greater than any other likely combination of states, its unilateralism has lost it much goodwill, provoked much hostility in the world and in many areas has diminished its fund of soft power. This could have long-term negative consequences for its ability to promote the American economic model and democracy as a key strategy in regions such as Asia and the Western Hemisphere.

New and not so new conceptions of the world out there

American power may not have been as suspect as Kennedy *et al.* suggested but US foreign policy-makers still had to match appropriate power to objectives. This proved to be deeply problematic because Cold War certainties were replaced by varied, confusing and contradictory interpretations of the nature of the post-Cold War world. All we can show here is the spectrum range: Charles Krauthammer's unipolar era is challenged by Joseph Nye's *The Paradox of American Power*, or *Why the World's Only Superpower Can't Go It Alone*. Samuel Huntington's *The Clash of Civilisations* is opposed by the optimism of Francis Fukuyama's democratic triumphalism, mapped out in his *The End of History and the Last Man*, which in turn is complemented by Michael Doyle's argument, derived from Kantian philosophy, that democracies do not go to war with each other. John Mearsheimer's 'Back to

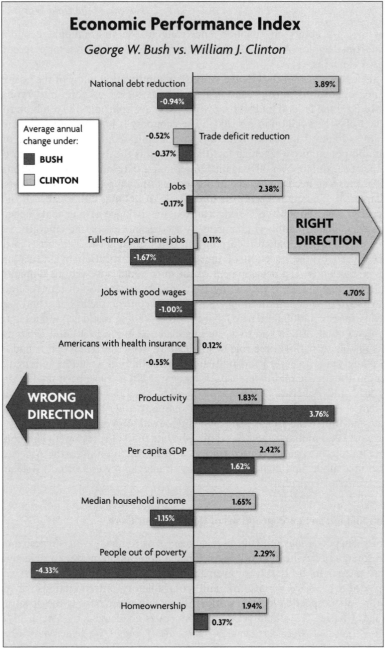

Figure 1
© The Progressive Policy Institute (PPI)[19]

the Future' unstable world of multipolarity contrasts with Kenneth Waltz's world of stability through nuclear proliferation. And finally there is the picture of the world in renewed disorder challenged by terrorism, rogue states and WMDs.[20] Such characterisations of the world out there notably do not deal directly with global distributive justice, sustainable economic growth, health or environmental issues, though as we shall see this does not mean to say that successive US administrations have been silent about these issues.

Optimism came first. There was much talk of the peace dividend, and indeed during the 1990s US defence spending was cut back dramatically with commensurate contraction in the defence industry, particularly in southern California. Then dramatically in the First Gulf War, as the USSR now cooperated with the US and a great coalition was formed to repel Iraq from Kuwait, President George H. Bush spoke of a New World Order. To many this suggested an era of collective security and multilateral cooperation in the UN and other organisations to bring good governance, peace and prosperity to the world. Notwithstanding the force of arguments from more pessimistic schools of thought, ideas of a democratic and multilateralist New World Order spread. For liberal democratic idealists, the systemic constraints of the realist and neo-realist models are not binding – namely, the imperative to maximise state power to ensure security, and the supremacy of state and communitarian values over cosmopolitan and universal values. For those, like Francis Fukuyama, such constraints were transcended with the demise of ideological dialectics and its result 'the end of history'. There was now the potential to spread democracy and the free market throughout the world: there were no longer any credible alternatives. According to Michael Doyle this was also likely to bring peace because democracies in their respect for individuals exercise restraint and have peaceful intentions in their foreign policies.

This agenda both operates from a number of assumptions, which beg important questions at the heart of an ongoing debate between cosmopolitan and communitarian theorists, and identifies the position of the US with the collective or universal good. In *Pax Democratica*, James R. Huntley articulated these views in terms of proposals for an alliance of democracies that should work together to foster economic and security communities that could act multilaterally to promote an enlarging peaceful democratic community. But, it would be one that would have to intervene to police non-democratic states. In considering how a democratic security community might do this, Huntley stumbled against the persistent realist obstacle to multilateralism: such problems were later made manifest in the world of practice in 2003 when George W. Bush ordered the invasion of Iraq.

> At least initially, the United States probably would not accept a situation in which it could be committed to war against its will; the voting must be carefully calculated. On the other hand, it should not be possible for Luxembourg, or Portugal, or even France or Britain alone, to immobilize the Alliance in the face of a preponderant majority.[21]

Bush, of course, did not have a preponderant majority in 2002–03, but even when one does pertain, it seems rather anomalous in Huntley's idealistic democratic-led world that respect for *force majeure* could trump what is right (assuming that the US is not infallible) and that there should be one rule for the strongest and another for all the rest. In fact, this new idealism is premised on three shaky foundations: first, that there are no alternatives to Western liberal democracy worthy of serious consideration; second, that democracies do not go to war with each other; and, third, that under US leadership there will be a growth of multilateral actions. The first assumption exhibits a closed mind that seems alien to the very tradition of thought that has spawned it. The second ignores the criticisms of theorists such as Mearsheimer, and, even if it were true that democracies do not go to war with each other, there would still be the problem of their relations with other non-democratic states. And the third assumption runs contrary to the evidence of history.

One possible conclusion from all this is that the US does not live up to its own ideals. It looks to outsiders as if the US is manipulating the language of idealism to further its own interests, and its purpose is thus no different from that which uses traditional forms of power for achieving security in an anarchical world order. On the other hand, rhetoric suggests that realism and idealism are reconciled by the implicit claim that US ideals are universally valid – engagement and democratic enlargement and promotion of the free market – and by the implicit assumption that the US has the power to realise this New World Order and create a viable new strategy to replace the legacy of uncertainty bequeathed by the end of the Cold War and the death of containment. From this perspective it was possible both for some conservative realists in George H. Bush's administration and for some liberal idealists in Clinton's to espouse the promotion of the free market and American-style democracy as panaceas for the world's problems. These attitudes, however, not only dismiss the cosmopolitan and communitarian debate too lightly, they also raise important practical questions as they fuel the desire for US intervention abroad.

Standing somewhat between the liberal idealists on the one hand and the conservative realists/neo-realists on the other is what we might call a liberal realist, Joseph S. Nye (though these categories do not exhaust the possibilities as we shall see shortly). Nye places great emphasis on power. Indeed as we noted earlier he believes that the US is 'bound to lead' because of its range of powers. However, unlike many other realists who emphasise America's economic and military hard power, Nye asserts the importance of what he calls soft power – the appeal of US culture, the attractiveness of the liberal democratic international regimes that it leads, and the fact of its centrality as the hub of the international communications and media systems. America's greatest mistake he claims would be to 'fall into one-dimensional analysis and believe that investing in military power alone will ensure our strength'.[22] This, no less than the liberal idealist and realist power pictures of the internationalist system, is a characterisation of what is important in foreign policy-making. Power cannot be divorced from statecraft and depends upon it. And statecraft is as much, if not more so, about persuasion than coercion, about a state's perceived moral integrity, the attractiveness of its culture and values and its ability to disseminate them abroad. America's consistent attempts to promote democracy abroad, its concerns over foreign states' restrictions on icons of American culture and way of life – be they on MacDonald's in France, or films in Europe and Canada – and its ongoing promotion of free trade for security as well as prosperity reasons, all indicate the growing sensitivity to the potency of soft power.

Charles Krauthammer was quick to dub the end of the Cold War the 'unipolar moment'. He argued that the world in 1990 was unipolar, not multipolar, cautioned against the dangers of conservative isolationism, and asserted that the world was less, not more, safe in the aftermath of the Cold War because of aggressive small states armed with WMDs. By 2003 it looked as if he had got things right. No country came within sight of the US in terms of defence expenditure and capabilities, and conservative isolationism never became the power that he feared. Just as it looked as if isolationism might have developed into something potent, 9/11 transformed things. In that transformation came for many the ultimate justification of Krauthammer's fears of increased, rather than diminished, dangers after the Cold War. It also made America's power dominance palpable and turned the moment into the unipolar era.

No state or grouping of states can match the US in any category of power, according to Krauthammer. Since the end of the Cold War putative challengers have not materialised: Japan has suffered economic decline; Germany stagnated and responded ineffectively to the challenge of the First Gulf War; Russia became drastically weakened; and the EU turned inward preoccupied with integration. Only China forged ahead and appeared as a possible contender, but its starting point was so low on the scales of power that it would take a very long time for its potential to materialise into an actual challenge: in 2003 it spent $50–70 billion on defence compared with around $386 billion by the US. On top of all this, 9/11 has made US latent military power fully palpable. It demonstrated US economic resilience as its economy soon returned to normality, and broadened the US alliance base, for example, with China, Pakistan and Russia all moving into a more cooperative mode with America. Krauthammer argues for a benignly directed unilateralism that should seek to preserve unipolarity and this he believes is the best way to preserve peace. He claims that there are two basic approaches to world order: paper and power. The former relies on law and morality, the latter on power. And only power can be relied on in a world characterised by the realist as insecure chaos. 'The new unilateralism defines American interests far beyond narrow self-defense. In particular, it identifies two other major interests, both global: extending the peace by advancing democracy and preserving the peace by acting as a balancer of last resort.'[23]

Krauthammer, like his fellow neo-conservatives, is often vague about how American and non-American interests are to be reconciled. Offering the platitude that unipolarity should be managed benignly is hardly likely to reassure those who hold different values and priorities from the US; for example, regarding the environment and global warming among other Western powers, and regarding religious and family values among many non-Western societies that are at odds with either America's secularism, or its Christianity, and extreme individualism. Also, the intriguing mixture of realism and conservative idealism do not always blend smoothly together. After professing the value of realism and power and denigrating the effectiveness of 'paper' in the form of law and values in the international realm, we are told that the spread of democracy is a useful strategy for keeping the peace. Thus, when Krauthammer claims that the unipolar moment has metamorphosed into the unipolar era, not everyone sees such a coherent picture as he, nor is everyone as reassured about its desirability. Neo-conservatives in the George W. Bush administration have largely followed Krauthammer's prescriptions by trying to square the realist–idealist circle by adopting a strategy that would spread democracy and the free market (American idealism) by the use of force where necessary (American realism).

Huntington offers an alternative realist vision where civilisations replace states. His hypothesis is that 'the fundamental source of conflict in this new world will not be primarily ideological or primarily economic. The great divisions among humankind and the dominating source of conflict will be cultural.'[24] He identifies eight major civilisations: Western, Confucian, Japanese, Islamic, Hindu, Slavic Orthodox, Latin American and possibly (!) African. He believes that conflict will occur along these fault lines, especially between the West and Islam, because of differences of history, language, culture and 'most important, religion'. Just how plausible this is depends on the credibility of Huntington's categories. Why should there be such distinctive differences between the West, Latin America and Slavic Orthodox civilisations when Christianity is a common thread and Huntington claims religion to be the most important defining factor of civilisations? Does he overexaggerate the reaction against Western values and overemphasise the impact of religious fundamentalism? If it is so difficult for cultures to assimilate or coexist, how is it that the American experience has been, although not without its difficulties, so successful? Are his categories really as impermeable as he suggests? Are they pitted one against the other? Do not the things that comprise a common humanity override the cultural differences? Or are these points simply the cant of over-optimistic idealism? Whatever one might think, the fearful image of clashing civilisations has impacted on public opinion, especially on the West's view of Islam, and on US policy-makers.

A third realist interpretation is offered by Mearsheimer who warned in 1990 that the situation at the end of the Cold War made Europe more not less dangerous. To many this seemed absurd, but Mearsheimer and the idea of absurdity do not go easily together. He is a neo-realist who believes that first-order causes of war 'lie more in the structure of the international system than in the nature of individual states. . . . This competitive world is peaceful when it is obvious that the costs and risks of going to war are high, and the benefits of going to war are low. Two aspects of military power are at the heart of this incentive structure: the distribution of power between states, and the nature of power available to them.'[25] The Cold War peace in Europe was thus the result of a bipolar distribution of roughly equal power based ultimately on nuclear weapons. With the disappearance of that structure the distribution of power will become multipolar and thus unstable because it is more complex. There are more possibilities for shifting alliances. Calculations of power are more difficult to make and there is greater scope for misunderstandings. In short, Europe has become a potentially volatile sub-system in which costs and risks of going to war are lowered and benefits of going to war enhanced. To counteract these dangers, Mearsheimer proposes that there should be a managed proliferation of nuclear weapons (at least to Germany) in order to create a system of complex deterrence, that the US should remain in Europe to help manage the system, and that it should take steps to prevent the re-emergence of hyper-nationalism.

The key problem with Mearsheimer's analysis is vagueness about the relationship between the domestic (second-order) and international systemic (first-order) causal factors of war. Just how important second-order causes are and how the line should be drawn separating them from first-order causes is never clearly stipulated. If domestic second-order causes such as hyper-nationalism turned out in fact to be first-order causes, as they seem to have been in the Serbian-Kosovo tragedy, then in other situations democracy might be similarly elevated in the causal chain. Perhaps the picture is not quite as Mearsheimer represents it. Neo-realism needs to take account of other dimensions. One would be foolish not to take on board Mearsheimer's arguments, which punctured the naive optimism of liberal idealists at the end of the Cold War, but it might also be less than wise not to give more weight to the impact of democracy and economic interdependence on the way that the international system operates.

Finally in the realist mould, Kenneth Waltz offers undiluted neo-realist assumptions about systemic explanations of international relations, and arrives at a slightly more optimistic scenario than Mearsheimer. Waltz believes that nuclear weapons are the great levellers, which create equality among states because of deterrence. He looks for proliferation to sustain order and allow states to pursue economic competition. States will continue to prioritise their own selfish national interests, but in a world where anarchy and competition are moderated and ordered by nuclear deterrence.[26] Unfortunately, this of course overlooks both the problem of irrational rogue states, which might be willing to use nuclear weapons irrespective of the consequences for themselves, and terrorists acquiring nuclear weapons, and using them immune from retaliation, and thus liberated from the constraints of deterrence, because they own no physical space that can be targeted for retribution.

The realist/neo-realist picture of the post-Cold War world is on the one hand very much 'back-to-the-future', in that a multipolar system has re-emerged after the stability of the bipolar Cold War, but it is governed by the same basic variables of international anarchy, power and the need for each state to defend itself. For Huntington, the problem is clashing civilisations rather than states but in the same anarchic type system. For Mearsheimer, the problem is the inherent instability of multipolarity. And, for Waltz, the key is the stabilising effect of nuclear deterrence, which leads him to advocate pro-liferation. However, he still sees dangers in an uncertain world where security competition continues much as before. On the other hand, there is Kraut-hammer's novel unipolar era in which the US should act benignly, but sustain its unipolarity and use its power to spread democracy and balance any aggressive regional power. For none of them is there a New World Order in the way Bush spoke of it or in the way liberal idealists conceptualise things.

Legitimacy and interventionism

But She Goes Not Abroad In Search Of Monsters to Destroy
John Quincy Adams, 1821

How, when, why and at what cost should the US intervene militarily in the affairs of other states? These questions are perennial, but they came into sharp focus at the end of the Cold War. The reason for that was twofold: first, the ready-made justification for interventions provided by containment and anti-communism was no longer available and legitimacy and authority for action had to be found elsewhere; second, opportunities for intervention beckoned strongly as America now had unchallengeable power and there seemed to be a real prospect for collective security responses in a world no longer troubled by a Manichean divide. Questions about military intervention have a lengthy progeny stretching back through the ages and connect with the long-standing debate about the nature of just wars. War, or military intervention that would likely lead to de facto if not de jure war, has traditionally been seen as an action of last resort. The theory of just war stipulates that there has to be proportionality between the level of violence used and the goals to be achieved. The cure must not be worse than the original affliction. There are two standard forms of justification that lend legitimacy to military interventions: humanitarian grounds to save many lives that would otherwise be lost; and a clear and present danger to the state from a potential aggressor that justifies pre-emptive action. It is important to note that neither of these conditions, if they pertain, justifies a disproportionate use of force: there are still standards of care and duties that need to be met if the action is to sustain its legitimacy. There must also always be concerns about and answers to the question: what comes next? By definition an intervention is temporary and at some point affairs have to be handed over to the indigenous population. Will they sustain the remedy imposed by force? Is an effective exit strategy available that leads to a peaceful withdrawal and a satisfactory long-term outcome?[27]

When the simplicities of the Cold War were replaced by the complexities of the post-Cold War world questions about intervention became more difficult to answer. No longer did Cold War certainties provide easy answers. George H. Bush and Clinton were troubled by these new complexities and the ongoing debate and disputes about the nature of the new international system. The merging of domestic and foreign policy compounded the problem by raising new questions about the nature of security.

The end of the Cold War accelerated a trend to reconceptualise security and this had an impact on questions about military interventionism. Liberated from the constraints of bipolarity, which had been bedrocked, in security terms, on the respective nuclear deterrents of the two superpowers, less traditional notions of security began to gain currency. All of a sudden security studies was able to consider more broadly cast definitions that had previously been pushed to the periphery, or totally excluded from consideration by the imperative of survival in a nuclear perilous bipolar world. According to scholars such as Buzan in his widely read *People, States and Fear*,[28] it was important to incorporate crime, drugs, health, economics and identity among other factors into the study of security communities. Such ideas further complicated conceptions of the international terrain, especially when others such as David Baldwin and Lawrence Freedman challenged the new security studies, alleging that it was conceptually confused and ill-focused.[29] These are exactly the same kinds of criticism that the authors of the new security studies had levelled at the traditionalists.

US policy-makers responded to all this by establishing three priorities: emphasis on the importance of engagement and democratic enlargement; the promotion of the free market; and concern about regional security problems, which incorporated some of the new security thinking. Bush and his Chairman of the Joint Chiefs of Staff, General Colin Powell, directed the consequent reorientation of US foreign policy to regional conflicts. The key question was: under what circumstances should the US intervene? The new strategy envisaged by Bush and Powell built on the Weinberger Doctrine promulgated in November 1984:

1. Our vital interests must be at stake.
2. The issues are so important for the future of the United States and our allies that we are prepared to commit enough forces to win.
3. We have clearly defined political and military objectives, which we must secure.
4. We have sized our forces to meet our objectives.
5. We have some reasonable assurance of the support of the American people.
6. U.S. forces are committed to combat only as a last resort.[30]

Powell added to this that intervention by US military force would take place only where full and overwhelming US power could be brought to bear. At the end of Bush's presidency, Powell recited a litany of successful US missions and claimed the reason 'for our success is that in every instance we have carefully matched the use of military force to our political objectives'.[31] But just how accurately does this sum up the US experience during these crucial hinge years of the closing of the Cold War and the opening on to a new world order? Had the Bush administration actually crafted a repeatable strategy to solve the problem of interventionism as Powell's self-satisfaction seemed to suggest?

Interventionism in the 1990s was still suffused with the Vietnam Syndrome. Bush was determined to lay this to rest because he believed it imposed restraints on US foreign policy that undermined its effectiveness. In Panama in 1989 and in the Gulf War in 1991 the US acted largely in accordance with the Weinberger/Powell criteria, though in the latter case there was lingering doubt about a clean exit strategy as the US continued to police the skies over Iraq. In Panama, the US acted decisively and successfully in a unilateral operation. In the Gulf War, the US acted decisively and successfully in a multilateral operation at the head of an impressively large coalition. This success prompted Bush's New World Order rhetoric and raised hopes of some form of robust collective security, especially as the demise of the Cold War enabled Moscow to cooperate with Washington against Iraq. For Bush, these interventions also finally appeared to dispel the Vietnam Syndrome, but a humanitarian intervention in Somalia, Operation Restore Hope, which he bequeathed to his successor, soon resurrected the problem he thought that he had put to rest. It also indicated that while interventions might have been well handled by the Bush administration, this was no guarantee of success in the future.

In the 1992 election campaign Clinton had been critical of Bush and had spoken out in favour of a more positive policy for dealing with the tragedy unfolding in Bosnia as the old Yugoslavia fragmented and ethnic slaughter became commonplace. Secretaries of State Warren Christopher and Madeleine Albright spoke of assertive multilateralism with the US taking the lead, supported by other members of the international community, to intervene in order to right or prevent the wrongs of genocide, failing states and famines. However, it took a long time and many deaths in Bosnia before Clinton made action match rhetoric. In his first year in office he concentrated on domestic affairs and even when, in 1993, he and his advisers affirmed that the US must remain internationalist, it was unclear how this would be translated into action. While Secretary of State Christopher gave a forceful exposition of the Doyle democratic peace theory,[32] Clinton set in motion a policy review on humanitarian interventions that resulted in PDD-25, but in between the initiation and the promulgation of the report, American Rangers were killed in Somalia. After that the Congress and the administration began to backtrack on interventionism. Somalia undermined faith in assertive multilateralism and there was a move away from the UN and complicated command structures to US leadership through NATO. But this again raised the questions about when, where and how the US should intervene.

Bosnia and the Serb leader, Slobodan Milosevic, soon provided a test case for Clinton's more cautious pragmatism. Until 1995, the US maintained a distance between itself and the Bosnian crisis, notwithstanding Clinton's criticisms of his predecessor's inaction. Clinton averred that there were no US interests directly involved and public opinion did not mandate a more vigorous line. Nevertheless, while both rhetoric and policy prevaricated, the Bottom-up Review of military strategy initiated by the President was released in September 1993 and appeared to confirm the internationalist and Wilsonian idealist facet of Clinton. Apart from predictable conclusions, such as the need to restrict the spread of nuclear weapons, the emphasis was on regional conflicts. The US needed the ability to deal with two major ones simultaneously. In addition, it should seek to foster democratic values and be prepared to 'participate effectively in multilateral peace enforcement and unilateral intervention operations that could include peacekeeping, humanitarian assistance, counterdrug and counterterrorism activities'.[33] So, regional intervention policy was still the main focus with a stronger commitment than Bush's to democratic enlargement. Was it for these reasons that US policy in Bosnia was transformed in 1995 with the launching of the Holbrooke mission, which led to the Dayton Peace Accords and the commitment of 20,000 US troops?[34] Not according to one scholar:

> The State Department's Bosnia study confirms that most senior foreign policy officials, most notably the president himself, were surprised to learn in June 1995 that U.S. troops might soon be on their way to Bosnia whether the administration liked it or not. The confusion stemmed from an earlier presidential decision that, should the situation on the ground become chaotic . . ., NATO would intervene to help the blue helmets flee. . . . While an intervention to limit U.N. failure would be dangerous and humiliating, the White House figured that reneging on its promise to NATO would destroy the remains of its credibility and devastate an already frayed alliance. . . . What one Clinton adviser called 'the single most difficult decision of [Clinton's] presidency – to send troops to Bosnia' has been made without anyone realizing it.[35]

Neither ideology nor realist self-interest seem able to explain this. Instead US intervention was the result of contingency and a lack of careful consideration of what appeared to be a limited engagement (to help UN forces pull out). Clinton had declared that there were no directly threatened US interests. Democratic enlargement was hardly a primary consideration and humanitarian concerns emerged only rather belatedly. Nothing more than lip-service was paid to either exit strategy, or to the cautionary language of PDD-25.

No sooner was the Bosnian crisis contained than Milosevic posed a new problem. Richard Holbrooke again entered the fray and tried to persuade Milosevic to stop the Yugoslav Serb army from attacking the Albanian minority in Kosovo. He failed. In the crisis that ensued, ambiguities in US intervention strategy, contradictions in its policies and difficulties with allies all impacted on the way US policy developed in the future. The US responded much more quickly to Kosovo than it had to the original Balkan crisis because of fear that the Dayton Accords might unravel and US prestige be undermined. But this raised the dangers and difficulties of mission creep and of establishing effective exit strategies. The NATO bombing campaign that now followed, conducted predominantly by the US, exposed serious interoperability and effectiveness of command problems. After Kosovo, the Pentagon viewed military operations in the field with allies as a burden not an advantage, and the US also vowed not to wage war again by committee. Both of these factors fed into a growing preference for unilateralism in Washington.

When the air war was slow to achieve results, British Prime Minister Blair urged President Clinton to consider committing ground troops. Clinton was most reluctant to do that, partly because of the kind of doubts long fostered by the Vietnam Syndrome. In the end, after a longer period of air strikes than many had expected and with a growing threat that ground troops might go in, Milosevic eventually gave way and Serbia withdrew from Kosovo. The US now urged that Milosevic should be arrested and tried for war crimes at the International Court of Justice in The Hague and that the UN should engage with reconstruction efforts in the Balkans. Neither of these demands sat well with the facts that the US and NATO acted in Kosovo without a UN mandate and that the US had insisted that US military personnel would not be subject to international jurisdiction. International law, it seemed, applied only when it was convenient for the US.

Clinton flexed American military muscle in Haiti in 1994 (see Chapter 12) and successively in Bosnia and Kosovo, but these were pragmatic and ad hoc actions that revealed his administration's failure to answer satisfactorily the major questions about interventionism in the post-Cold war era. George W. Bush addressed these questions, particularly after 9/11, in a rather different, though not necessarily more successful, way.

According to Arthur Schlesinger Jr, who has been preoccupied for many years with the war-making capability of presidents, the George W. Bush administration has taken the attitude that waging war is not a policy of last resort to be declared by the Congress, but a question of presidential choice.[36] The strategic doctrine now in place calls for preventative military action against rather opaque and distant dangers, not pre-emptive action against clear and present dangers. They are dangers that simply might prove to be a threat in the future to the security of the US, rather than being an actual palpable present danger. This doctrine was applied to Iraq.

Cold War containment's justification for military intervention has now been replaced by the justification that rogue states and terrorists may need to be preventatively struck before they can strike. Furthermore, the US has made it clear that it does not require the approval of the international community in the guise of the UN, nor even broad multilateral support, to launch such strikes. Questions of prudence, proportionality, legitimacy, authority and about what comes next have been subordinated to a new overriding priority to engage robustly in the war on terrorism. This is a more pro-active policy than containment and places a great burden on the judgement that the danger of a future threat to US security justifies sending the US military into situations of de facto war in order to prevent that danger from materialising. There is logic to the strategy, which addresses the difficulty of dealing with terrorists who elude the scope of deterrence, but it is contrary to the long tradition of just war, which allows for pre-emptive strikes against clear and present dangers, but is silent on preventative strikes. It is contrary to international law. It devalues the worth of multilateral acts and the legitimacy and authority that accompany them. Such a strategy could also be unconstitutional if it stretches the inherent powers of the CIC to commit US troops to combat too far. Thus, for the sake of apparently solving the problem of how to deal with terrorists who have no territorial base and who are thus immune to retaliation and hence deterrence, the Bush administration has opened a Pandora's Box of problems.

Conclusion

The end of the Cold War changed the world. American power may not have been primarily responsible for the end of the Soviet regime, but it had successfully contained it and the US abides as the one remaining world superpower. Its power and its capabilities are truly awesome, but it has struggled to devise a clear picture of the world out there and for a coherent strategy for dealing with it. For a while, at least for Americans, these problems did not appear too pressing as there was no ostensible threat to US national security. Under George H. Bush, the US spoke conservatively, but adjusted and adapted to a radically changing world and practised a multilateralism in the First Gulf War that embraced both the UN and the old foe, the Soviet Union. Under Bill Clinton, the US initially turned more inwards, but spoke strongly of assertive multilateralism and after much prevarication shouldered the burden of dealing with the tragedy in the Balkans. There were still many uncertainties about how US policy would evolve, but US leadership seemed comfortable with a US-led form of multilateralism, cooperation with the UN, and with appropriate inhibitions about the use of force. Then came 9/11 and the Bush administration's response: unilateralism and the doctrine of preventative strike.

There is no doubt that military intervention is sometimes justified, but it always endangers that most precious of all rights, the right to life. The Founding Fathers tried to ensure this would never happen without congressional approval through a declaration of war, or, if the US were actually under the threat of invasion, then the CIC would have the authority to order the armed forces into combat. In 2003, even if Iraq had possessed WMDs, no one claimed that they could be launched against the US. Under these circumstances it is difficult to see what could justify the US launching a preventative war against Iraq. But the past has always gone. It is in the future that the problem of interventionism will return again. If the current security doctrine of preventative strike remains unmodified then it will provide a logical strategy to deal with the challenge of terrorism. However, the key question that has to be addressed is whether the cost of that logic in terms of undermining international law, weakening the UN, creating disarray in the community of Western and friendly states, diminishing US soft power, eroding American domestic liberties, weakening the integrity of the US constitution, and sacrificing lives both American and non-American, is proportional to the objective to be achieved. How the present and future administrations deal with these issues will largely determine the extent to which 9/11 is seen as a catalyst for radical change in US foreign policy. Certainly, the US's new-found unilateralism and the deployment of a strategy of preventative strike are radical and could have even more far-reaching effects than have already emerged from the war in Iraq, both within the US and the international community.

10 The US and post-Cold War Europe

No relationship shaped post-Second World War American foreign policy more decisively than that with the USSR and no relationship was more important to America than that with Western Europe. Bush's incipient New World Order begged the question of how America would transform long-standing US–USSR enmity into peaceful and cooperative coexistence and demanded that the transatlantic bargain be successfully renegotiated. The US and EU combined enjoyed economic and military preponderance and structural empowerment, having largely initiated and dominated the world's principal multilateral forums, including the UN, NATO, G-7, IMF and GATT. Moreover, Europe was still home to America's most natural allies given the combination of historical ties, shared values, interdependence and belief that exporting the values underpinning the North Atlantic security community best provided for developing peace and security elsewhere.

In the mid-1990s Boris Yeltsin spoke of a 'Cold Peace' in US–Russia relations and analysts asked whether the US even had a Russia policy. Speculation also developed about the health of the US–EU relationship as NATO entered an existential crisis, American strategic priorities shifted to Asia and the Middle East and the EU became ambitious of developing a hard security capacity to complement its established soft power resources. Long before George W. Bush assumed office some observers talked of transatlantic drift or even of divorce. How can these apparently deteriorating relationships be accounted for? What factors have shaped US policy? Is Kagan right to depict the US and EU in his 'Power and Weakness' essay as inhabiting different worlds of Mars and Venus?[1] Has the Bush administration's proclivity for unilateralism set America apart from the EU and Russia too often and with too little thought for the consequences?

American calculations and structures of US–EU cooperation[2]

The end of the Cold War reinforced America's self-perception as leader of the civilised world but its unipolar moment was clouded by influential predictions of relative decline, pressing domestic issues and uncertainty about how to lead the world and to what ends. Washington's interest in renegotiating the US–EU relationship was thus underscored by apprehension and opportunity. Potential

European introspection played on lingering fears from the Reagan administration of a 'Fortress Europe' that discriminated against American exports and left the US burdened with unsustainable international commitments. Conversely, it was important to guard against EU 'over-assertion'. The EC had increasingly challenged American leadership during the 1980s and US influence over its erstwhile protégé could now weaken further given the relative downgrading of mutual defence considerations, NATO's uncertain future, German reunification and prospective EU enlargement. The latter also threatened to incur for America involuntary additional de facto security guarantees. New EU members would be able to join the WEU and, even without becoming members of NATO, they might secure its protection through interlocking collective security obligations created by EU states that were members of both institutions. Any attack on a WEU state would be taken as an attack on all WEU states and that would include some members of NATO, which would then also have to activate its own collective security obligations, which would draw in the US.

More optimistically, a more capable EU might better share the burdens of international leadership and allow the US to shed some of its European commitments in favour of emerging priorities elsewhere. Disproportionate American security contributions were ever less justifiable to Congress and the electorate. Hence President Bush welcomed Chancellor Kohl in 1989 as a 'partner in leadership' and supported German reunification – itself 'contained' by NATO membership and deeper integration within the EU. He also agreed in July 1989 that the European Commission should coordinate financial assistance to Central and Eastern Europe. The EU's normative and economic power was a potential stabilising force in Europe and twin intergovernmental conferences in readiness for the Treaty on European Union promised to improve its capacity for purposive security action.

The Bush administration sought to renegotiate a bilateral relationship built on years of cooperation, shared interests and common values. Bush worked hard to assuage European concerns about German reunification and to develop modalities for improved consultation. He met European Commission President Jacques Delors five times during 1989, the Commission's Delegation to Washington was upgraded to full diplomatic status and in December 1989 Secretary of State James Baker called for a 'New Atlanticism'. On 20 November 1990 the Declaration on EC–US Relations was concluded, which among other things formally recognised the EC's developing identity in economic and monetary matters, in foreign policy and in the domain of security.

The Clinton administration redoubled efforts to embed further the transatlantic relationship against a backdrop of deepening crisis in the Balkans and mutual fears of transatlantic drift. Most significant was the New Transatlantic Agenda (NTA) and its accompanying Joint Action Plan (JAP). Adopted at the Madrid Summit on 3 December 1995, the NTA was hailed by US Ambassador to the EU Stuart Eizenstat as 'the first time we have dealt comprehensively with the EU, not simply as a trade and economic organization, but as a partner in a whole array of foreign policy and diplomatic initiatives'. In the economic field ambitious moves were made in the direction of establishing a common transatlantic market and in the security domain by the development of a joint transatlantic security agenda and measures for collaboration and burden-sharing. The US and EU were to exercise joint leadership in the consolidation of democracy in Russia and Central Europe and in the reconstruction of Bosnia and Herzegovina, and to concert their efforts in preventative diplomacy, provision of humanitarian assistance and promotion of multilateral free trade.[3] The George W. Bush administration subsequently drove a NTA upgrade at the June 2001 Gothenburg Summit by developing six strategic themes. The emphasis was on clear and sustainable political priorities and more streamlined, political and results-orientated methods of cooperation.

US–EU economic relationship

American interest in the transatlantic relationship was sustained in part by profound economic interdependence with Europe. Statistics capture some of this. In 2004 the EU accounted for 21.1% of US merchandise exports and 19.2% of its imports. In terms of services it took 34% of American exports and provided 37.3% of American imports. And there is more, for it is important to consider other linkages too, such as capital flows – especially foreign direct investment (FDI). In 2004, $83.3 billion net flowed from US residents to EU countries in direct investments and $48.2 billion net flowed the other way. At the end of 2003, 47.2% of all US FDI was vested in the EU and the EU held 62% of FDI stocks in the US.[4]

US businesses and investors have contributed much to the vitality of the transatlantic economic relationship. Although critical of 'continental corporatism', these interests remain convinced of Europe's stability, general commitment to trade liberalisation and value in terms of risk-adjusted returns. The size of the EU market, prospective further enlargement and comparative advantages of the Single Market programme all attract US inward investment – between 1995 and 2001 this increased sevenfold. However, positive government action boosts business confidence, and the JAP, under the headline 'Contributing to the Expansion of World Trade and Closer Economic Relations', set out objectives that included creating a New Transatlantic Marketplace by progressively reducing or eliminating barriers to the free flow of goods, services and capital. This was augmented in May 1998 by the decision at the London Summit to launch the Transatlantic Economic Partnership and in December 2002 by agreement of the Positive Economic Agenda, complete with its own roadmap. Moreover, the economic relationship has assumed increasing political importance. Against the backdrop of profound transatlantic differences over US-led intervention in Iraq, American Under-Secretary of Commerce for International Trade, Grant Aldonas, declared that '[i]f there was ever a time when we really needed to . . . try and remove . . . obstacles to trade between the United States and Europe now is the time'.[5]

The EU is also America's most important partner in shaping the global economic agenda and institutions of governance. Their economies are vital to the global economy. Between 1995 and 2003 the US accounted for 60% of cumulative growth in world output and the EU for approximately a further 10%. In 2003 they accounted for 29% of world merchandise exports and 35.4% of imports. That same year they accounted for 43% of world service exports and 38.2% of imports. And in 2001–03 they accounted for 48.9% of world FDI inflows and 73.9% of outflows. Moreover, combined they have un-rivalled institutionalised economic power. The US and EU25 account for five of the G-8 and enjoy voting power of 48.97% in the IMF and 44.37% in the World Bank. They are also instrumental in driving free trade – as in the Doha Development Round – and in determining trade patterns through 'competitive liberalisation', meaning the contemporaneous pursuit of bilateral, regional and global free trade agreements. Furthermore, their exchange rates can pro-foundly affect global economic performance. Dollar–euro volatility has impinged negatively on employment and domestic investment in Argentina and Brazil, and exchange rate volatility across the G-3 currency areas (euro-zone, US and Japan) can severely affect Third World countries. G-3 exchange rate volatility and misalignments, especially the strength of the dollar, coupled with inflexible exchange rate regimes, played a significant part in the build-up to the spectacular Asia and Argentine economic crises.[6]

Despite and even because of the volume of shared trade, FDI and interests as technologically advanced economies, US policy-makers have found the EU to be an increasingly difficult post-Cold War economic partner. This is due principally to three factors: the EU is an intense economic rival as well as a partner; the EU has pooled sovereignty sufficiently in trade matters to speak as a powerful bloc; and the EU has capitalised upon US membership of the WTO, which constitutes a major exception to US general unwillingness to surrender sovereignty. The pattern of trade disputes demonstrates US–EU friction and the latter's growing willingness to confront the US. In the 1960s and 1970s the US had just three serious trade disputes with the EU; between the establishment of the WTO in 1995 and July 2003 this rose to 55 disputes. Of disputes during the 1980s the US initiated 85.7%; between 1995 and July 2003 it initiated 52.7%. US-initiated action includes the Clinton adminis-tration's championship of Chiquita Brands International in the so-called banana war and its appeal against EU bans on hormone treated beef and genetically modified crops on public health and environmental grounds. The Bush administration has likewise protested 'unfair' EU practices, including the European Commission's decision to allow de facto subsidisation of the AirBus 380. Conversely the EU successfully appealed US foreign sales corpor-ations as being illegal tax concessions, forced the Bush administration to abandon highly controversial three-year safeguard tariffs of up to 30% imposed on steel imports in March 2002, and in June 2003 initiated WTO action against allegedly discriminatory 'zeroing practice' – a method for calculating penalties for dumping goods at below cost price.

Other recurrent sources of transatlantic economic friction include mutual application of extraterritorial measures and the euro's emergence as a world currency. The US has reacted angrily to increasingly assertive European

Commission scrutiny of, and intervention in, mergers and acquisitions in other countries – despite this essentially being the counterpart of US anti-trust legislation. Relations became particularly tense once the Commission established a precedent in June 2000 for blocking mergers of purely American companies by refusing to approve the takeover of the US's third-largest telecommunications company Sprint by its rival WorldCom. In this, and other cases such as its blocking of General Electric's proposed takeover of Honeywell in 2001, Americans have often seen the Commission's interpretation of 'market domination' as a means to prevent US companies from dominating markets through their technological leadership. The US, though, also uses extraterritorial measures for advantage or as part of its wider foreign policy. For example, Helms-Burton legislation provided for the extraterritorial application to EU companies and individuals of the US economic isolation of Cuba, and the Iran–Libya Sanctions Act (ILSA) contained extraterritorial provisions designed to increase the economic isolation of these countries without disadvantaging American companies. The ILSA empowered US presidents to impose two countermeasures, drawn from a substantial list, upon any foreign company that invested more than $40 million annually in either the Iranian or Libyan energy sectors.

As for the euro, some analysts initially feared that its launch in 1999 would feed transatlantic tension because it might be seen as a challenge to the American dollar's hegemony.[7] In the event, the exchange rate has so far proven more controversial. The euro plummeted from its launch value on 1 January 1999 of $1.17 to $0.84 on 24 November 2000. This made eurozone exports steadily cheaper on world markets traditionally dominated by the US dollar and disadvantaged American exports. As early as 1999 the first American complaints were heard about insufficient EU effort to support the euro. Five years on the position has reversed. On 21 September 2005 the euro was worth fractionally more against the dollar than its original launch price. This meant a depreciation of the dollar against the euro since November 2000 of approximately 31%, and it has been European exporters complaining during this adjustment about the dollar's weakness and American talking-down of their currency.[8] Further weakening of the dollar against the euro could extinguish what sluggish growth exists within the eurozone – a risk exacerbated by the extent of the US deficit.

The US–EU security relationship

While US administrations fretted about EU economic competition and struggled to impose their will upon the world's most powerful trading block, in the security domain they worried more about the asymmetry of US–European relations and the future of NATO. The George H. Bush, Clinton and George W. Bush administrations have pursued relatively consistently three objectives herein. First, they have wanted the EU to accept greater international security commitments. All have thus welcomed its roles in exporting security to Central and Eastern Europe and in Balkan reconstruction, especially through the stabilisation and association process. They have also broadly supported the EU's development of the Common European Security and Defence Policy (CESDP) and a limited hard security capacity that is designed to meet responsibilities accepted in the Amsterdam Treaty (1997) for the Petersberg Tasks, which include humanitarian and rescue tasks and peacekeeping.

Successive Helsinki Headline Goals have sought to develop the capabilities necessary to fully equip the EU Rapid Reaction Force (EURRF), which envisages EU member states being able to deploy 60,000 troops within 60 days and to sustain them operationally for a year. US administrations intended that these developments should complement NATO and free up American forces from peacekeeping in the Balkans and Afghanistan. Evidence of developing EU capabilities and EU–NATO cooperation includes Operations Concordia, Artemis and Althea. Concordia was the EU's first military peace support operation and followed on from NATO's Operation Essential Harvest and Task Force Fox in support of the Ohrid Framework Agreement in the Former Yugoslav Republic of Macedonia. In Operation Althea the EU succeeded SFOR in Bosnia in December 2004, and Artemis demonstrated the Union's potential usefulness in areas further afield and of limited US interest – France serving as framework nation for intervention in the Democratic Republic of Congo in 2003.

The second key objective of all three US presidencies has been to ensure that NATO, as America's primary instrument of influence in Europe, retains its primacy within the European security architecture. Washington thus supported NATO outreach programmes such as Partnership for Peace (PFP),[9] expanding the organisation's remit, breaking the out-of-area taboo, and, under the Clinton and George W. Bush administrations, two rounds of enlargement that increased its membership to 26 countries – many new members being former communist nations. US officials have also repeatedly insisted upon NATO primacy. The Dobbins *démarche* set out the George H. Bush administration's opposition to the development of the WEU outside NATO; Madeleine Albright warned in December 1999 against the so-called 'three Ds' of delinking, duplication and discrimination in the development of a European Security and Defence Identity (ESDI); and Secretary of Defense Rumsfeld cautioned in February 2001 against reducing NATO's effectiveness by confusing duplication or by perturbing the transatlantic link. Furthermore, US administrations have consistently sought maximum influence over the structure, objectives and missions of first a European pillar within NATO and subsequently CESDP. The Clinton administration's Combined Joint Task Force initiative tried to head off an autonomous European military capability by giving the US a de facto veto through Europe effectively having to borrow key American assets in a military operation. The same premise runs through the current Berlin Plus arrangements, which set out provisions for assured EU access to NATO planning facilities for the conduct of crisis management operations. Secretary of State Colin Powell outlined in December 2003 what, in the American view, the so-called Berlin Plus road meant: 'When a mission comes along, if NATO for one reason or another is not prepared to accept that mission, then the EU should consider it first drawing on NATO assets. But if that also is not appropriate and the mission is within the capacity of the EU to handle alone without drawing on NATO assets, then the EU should certainly take a look at that.'[10]

The third consistent aspect of US policy towards the EU in the security domain has been to underscore its leadership claims by emphasising its military superiority and continuing European dependency. Slow US commitment to Bosnia and Clinton's failure to support the Vance–Owen peace plan were 'as if there was a need to demonstrate that the Europeans could not succeed without US help'. Military intervention in Bosnia and later in Kosovo highlighted European limitations. US aircraft flew 65.9% of the 3,515 sorties during Operation Deliberate Force; four years later in Operation Allied Force this proportion increased to almost 79% of the 38,004 sorties flown. Meantime, from a potential two million military personnel European NATO members struggled to provide just 40,000 troops for Kosovo and to maintain thereafter 50,000 peacekeepers in the wider Balkans.[11]

Successive US administrations have also criticised heavily EU and NATO Europe military spending, capabilities and investment in military-related research and development. They have a valid point. In 2004 the US dedicated 3.9% of GDP to defence spending, which totalled approximately $462 billion – equivalent to the next 32 most powerful nations combined. Estimates suggest that pushing ahead with Joint Vision 2020 and absorbing spiralling costs in Iraq will lead US defence expenditure to equal the rest of the world combined by the end of 2006. In the meantime, in 2004 NATO Europe collectively spent $235 billion at an average 1.83% of GDP, well below the world average of 2.6%. The US neither expects nor wants the EU or NATO Europe to match its defence spending. It does, though, want more effective European spending at least to enable it to delegate tasks such as peacekeeping. The European Commission indicated in March 2003 Europe's limited military potency per $ expenditure, estimating that EU15 military capability was just 10% of America's.[12]

America's approach to European security and to the EU's development as a security actor has thus been seemingly consistent and clear: it wants greater European burden-sharing and military capabilities, an informal US seat at the EU table and guaranteed NATO primacy. However, matters are not so straightforward. These objectives run into EU ambitions and the resentment of some of its member states about perceived US arrogance and/or lack of consultation. This long predates the current Bush administration. European Commission Vice-President Leon Brittan explicitly warned in September 1998 'that co-operation with the European Union does not mean simply signing up the European Union to endorse, execute, and sometimes finance, United States foreign policy'. More recently the Bush administration's sidelining of NATO in its Afghan and Iraqi interventions inflamed the running debate about NATO and its relationship with the EU's CESDP. In February 2005, Gerhard Schröder, Chancellor of traditionally staunch NATO supporter Germany, controversially declared that NATO was 'no longer the primary venue where transatlantic partners discuss and coordinate strategies'. This followed both French President Chirac's claim in October 2003 that 'There cannot be a Europe without its own defence system' and the so-called 'chocolate summit' in April that year at which France, Germany, Belgium and Luxembourg agreed deepening defence collaboration and proposed the creation of a permanent EU operational military planning cell (as an alternative to NATO) in Tervuren. US Ambassador to NATO Nicholas Burns bluntly described developments in CESDP as 'one of the greatest dangers to the transatlantic relationship'.[13]

Neither are the three broad American objectives necessarily compatible. US administrations have demanded better European capabilities to burden-share, but when the EU has responded they fear discrimination against US defence companies, French-led drives for a more autonomous Europe, and the undermining of NATO. When the EU introduced a European Defence Agency in 2004 American interests cried foul, fearing intra-European defence industry consolidation and Euro-centred procurement. Similarly, the Bush administration responded to the EU's development of CESDP, the Helsinki Headline Goals and the EURRF by announcing in 2002 a parallel capability enhancement process within NATO – the Prague Capability Commitments – and the creation of a NATO Response Force (NRF). NATO emphasises that these initiatives complement the EU's but the NRF both nullified the EURRF's potential range advantage by ending the out-of-area debate and is likely to take a large share of Europe's limited resources.

Inconsistency is apparent too in US warnings of a de facto technological decoupling of the Atlantic Alliance and loss of interoperability. These dangers could be mitigated by greater technology transfer, more coordinated procurement and reduced protectionism of defence markets. Indeed, on 24 May 2000, Madeleine Albright announced the Defence Trade Security Initiative to improve US technology and arms transfers to America's closest allies. Nevertheless, the US spends under 2% of its defence budget beyond its borders – of which half is concentrated in Britain – and champions its domestic industry. The Clinton administration subsidised its post-Cold War reconfiguration by $16.5 billion, including $1.3 billion within the Technology Reinvestment Programme designed to promote dual-use technologies. Protective measures also remain against FDI, joint ventures and exports to third parties – including the Buy American Act, the Arms Export Control Act and the International Traffic in Arms Regulations.[14]

Even more fundamental challenges to transatlantic security cooperation are posed by differences over multilateralism, the rule of law and readiness to use military force. These issues are at the heart of heated debate about crisis and value gaps in transatlantic relations, especially during the George W. Bush era. Unlike the US, the EU is a multilateral and predominantly civilian power actor that emphasises by choice and default soft security measures and policies of engagement. Hence it has clashed with Washington's confrontational approaches to Iran, Cuba and North Korea and has repeatedly criticised

US refusal to accept multilateral commitments such as the Kyoto Protocol, Comprehensive Test Ban Treaty, Ottawa Convention and the International Criminal Court (ICC). The EU remains deeply concerned about the implications for international law and nuclear stability of US abrogation of the ABM Treaty and its commitment to Ballistic Missile Defence (BMD) and the Bush Doctrine. Security discourses can be quite different on either side of the Atlantic. US officials tend to talk of security threats, protecting national sovereignty and interests, interventionism, forced disarmament and, most recently, of war upon terrorism and preventative strikes. European counterparts generally prefer the non-combative, consensual language of security challenges and talk of collective endeavours such as promoting global governance, managing globalisation, projecting stability and developing conflict prevention.

Post-9/11 US–EU anti-terrorism cooperation illustrates the importance of this debate about transatlantic values. On 20 September a joint ministerial statement pledged efforts to 'work in partnership' on a 'worldwide' scale to combat terrorism. Areas targeted for cooperation included aviation and other transport security, police and judicial cooperation, export controls and non-proliferation, financial sanctions, border controls and exchange of electronic data. EU measures to improve its own security coordination – such as a common arrest warrant – also facilitated transatlantic cooperation. Legal cooperation was improved, agreement was concluded with Europol on 6 December 2001 to share best practice and strategic information in criminal matters, and information was exchanged on travel documents and migration issues to boost border security. Combined US–EU pressure forced an International Civil Aviation Organisation security audit and, in line with UN resolution 1373, the US and EU developed measures to fight funding of terrorist organisations. EU officials also cooperated in steering US action against the Taliban through UN auspices and invested considerable diplomatic effort in assuring Islamic capitals that American retribution for 9/11 was not a crusade against Islam. This commitment followed through into reconstruction of Afghanistan, with the US and EU being prominent collaborators at the UN-backed Bonn conference.

All of this indicated continued strength within the transatlantic relationship but creeping value differences still undermined the effectiveness of cooperation. Two controversial areas were the US death penalty and the balance drawn between security and individual liberty. The former meant some European reluctance to extradite suspected terrorists to the US. The latter meant both that the EU refused to collect and share the amount of personal data authorised in the US under the Patriot Act and that European officials were highly critical of US classification of Afghan prisoners as unlawful combatants, which denied them prisoner-of-war rights during their incarceration at Camp X-Ray in Guantanamo Bay. A more general difference also developed in anticipation of what would happen after the Taliban was destroyed. Europeans wanted the US to act multilaterally in its wider war on terrorism. Bush's principal European ally, British Prime Minister Blair, sought desperately to steer intervention in Iraq through the UN Security Council. US refusal to wait for a second resolution in March 2003 duly sparked one of the worst-ever transatlantic rows.

Is Kagan therefore right to depict the US and EU as inhabiting different worlds, Hobbesian-Mars and Kantian-Venus respectively? Certainly there is some justification, and the Bush administration has hardened the impression of a unilateralist America that has exchanged its 1990s benign hegemon image for that of an assertive twenty-first-century hyperpower. Intervention in Iraq demonstrated its willingness to jeopardise transatlantic relations for priorities elsewhere – perhaps on the assumption that everything would work out in the end. Its interest in developing US–European relations on its own terms was reflected also in its threat in 2002 to veto the UN mission in Bosnia unless the Security Council gave US troops prior exemption from ICC jurisdiction. However, it is important to recognise that Kagan's distinctions are crude generalisations. The EU may be a type of Kantian sub-system but its December 2003 Security Strategy embraced robust intervention when necessary and identified threats similar to the US. The EU or one of its member states has sometimes been more anxious than the US to use military force. Clinton's unwillingness to commit US ground troops in the Balkans badly strained US–EU relations twice. And EU states have not been averse to taking unilateral action when it has suited them: French policy in Rwanda and Algeria, Greek flaunting of EU policy towards Macedonia, German unilateral recognition of Croatia, and both Britain's break with the EU to support Clinton's military strikes against Iraq in 1998, and its military intervention in Sierra Leone in 2000.

As for intervention in Iraq in 2003, this should not be miscast as a transatlantic divide. It was not. Rather it was a deeply problematic question that divided countries worldwide over what to do about a regime that routinely abused its own people and had defied UN resolutions and weapons inspectors for over a decade. Neither were the positions of key states informed by moral virtue or Kantian and Hobbesian prescriptions. Countries such as France and Russia that opposed the war had significant economic interests in Iraq and, together with China and Germany, saw an opportunity to bind America through international law. Atlanticists such as Britain perceived grave dangers to their own interests, to NATO and to hopes of encouraging American multilateralism if they deserted the Bush administration over Iraq. Damage to transatlantic relations was consequently substantial but that done to intra-European relations was arguably greater. Indeed, the Bush administration exacerbated the latter through a crude disaggregation policy that, in Rumsfeld's words, divided Europe into 'Old' and 'New'.

The US and Russia

Transforming US–USSR relations from antipathy to collaboration promised to be more problematic than dealing with traditional European allies. George H. Bush embraced the USSR as a partner in stability after testing Gorbachev's intentions through 'status quo plus'. However, an attempted *coup d'état* in August 1991 threw this policy into turmoil.

Gorbachev survived but with diminished authority his efforts to preserve the Communist Party and the USSR were doomed. By January 1992 an earthquake in the geostrategic topography of Europe was underway. Gorbachev had been replaced, the Soviet Union was formally dissolved, and in place of this stabilising Eurasian force were an unstable Russia and the Commonwealth of Independent States (CIS). US relations with Russia became relatively less important but more unpredictable. Members of the CIS pressed their national interests and some inherited substantial Russian diasporas and nuclear weapons. Russia's new leader, Boris Yeltsin, was an unknown quantity and ostensibly more radically democratic than Gorbachev. Moreover, he was besieged domestically by rising nationalism and disillusionment with market reform and confronted abroad by a security vacuum between Russia and a powerful reunified Germany, and by a need to stabilise the Russian periphery, the so-called 'Near Abroad'.

American core interests had somehow to be promoted and ripple effects of Russian weakness guarded against. This reinforced the Bush administration's determination to promote NATO's primacy in European security. It thus supported the North Atlantic Co-operation Council and NATO's announcement on 8 November 1991 of a New Strategic Doctrine that laid claim to responsibilities far beyond collective defence. The administration was otherwise largely content for the EU to take the lead in exporting security to the Balkans and Central and Eastern European countries, which left the US free to deal with Russia and, especially, the nuclear question. This was particularly pressing for three reasons. First, Russia's ageing nuclear reactors might create another Chernobyl disaster and its economic weakness risked inability to either satisfactorily maintain or safely decommission its WMDs arsenal and nuclear-powered fleet. Second, Russia might haemorrhage nuclear know-how or lose control over WMDs materials, both scenarios advantaging terrorist groups and/or rogue states. Third, Russia had a nuclear arsenal capable of threatening the US, and the independent republics of Belarus, Ukraine and Kazakhstan now also had nuclear weapons.

The Bush administration needed someone in Russia to deal with in order to progress its agenda. It thus pragmatically switched from supporting Gorbachev to cautiously embracing Yeltsin, began to de facto equate American interests with his political stability and assumed that these two things would develop hand in hand through Russia's democratic transition, economic improvement and integration into the global economy. The 1992 Freedom Support Act encouraged market economies, democratic politics and sustainable systems of social protection in the newly independent states. The Bush administration also helped Russia secure membership of the IMF and World Bank, accorded it MFN status, concluded an investment treaty and agreed cooperation on fuel and energy development. These measures provided opportunities for US businesses in Russia, encouraged Yeltsin's pro-Western policies and paved the way for dealing with the Soviet nuclear legacy. This was addressed in part by the Cooperative Threat Reduction Program. Better known as the Nunn-Lugar program, this ongoing initiative provided $410 million assistance in FY 1992 to Russia, Belarus, Kazakhstan and Ukraine to prevent proliferation and aid their storing, safeguarding and dismantling of WMDs.

In the meantime there was debate within the administration about how to address the multiplication of nuclear-capable states as a consequence of the USSR's collapse. Hardliners such as Secretary of Defense Cheney and Director of the CIA Robert Gates favoured using a nuclear-capable Ukraine as a counterweight to Russia. This reflected distrust of Yeltsin and smacked of Waltz's ideas for stability through limited nuclear proliferation. Bush and Baker, though, favoured the transfer of strategic weapons from the republics to Russia and further arms control negotiations with Yeltsin. The latter's views prevailed. On 23 May 1992 the US and Russia signed the Lisbon protocol, along with Ukraine, Belarus and Kazakhstan, which provided for all signatories to become party to START, and the three former Soviet republics pledged to join the Non-Proliferation Treaty (NPT) as non-nuclear states in the shortest possible time. This restored the US–Russia relationship as the single nuclear dyad from the wreck of the Soviet Union and the two subsequently worked on further arms reduction talks. These culminated on 3 January 1993 in START II (albeit not ratified by the Russian Duma until 14 April 2000), which aimed to reduce their deployed strategic forces to 3,000–3,500 ballistic missile warheads by 2003.

When the Bush administration left office in January 1993 five major nuclear arms control initiatives had been accomplished, providing for a 66% reduction on 1990 levels of US strategic nuclear forces and a 75% reduction in the overall American nuclear arsenal.[15] None of this, however, saved Bush from Clinton's allegations during the 1992 presidential election race that he should have embraced Yeltsin quicker, that he had betrayed the rights to self-determination of the peoples in the Soviet Union, and that his lack of imagination threatened to lose America the Cold War peace. Instead of this drift, Clinton pledged to deliver a US–Russia strategic partnership and international leadership to the world. Once given the mandate, that same world watched to see how he would do this.

Secretary of State Warren Christopher provided the answer. In 1993 he hailed facilitating Russia's transition to a free society and market economy as 'the greatest strategic challenge of our time' and an endeavour that 'will serve our highest security, economic, and moral interests'. Conversely, failure would exact a frightening price: 'Nothing less is involved than the possibility of renewed nuclear threat, higher defense budgets, spreading instability, the loss of new markets, and a devastating setback for the worldwide democratic movement.'[16] However, this rhetoric raised false expectations because ambivalence rather than imagination characterised Clinton's initial Russia policy. The Republicans laid the foundation of his $2.5 billion aid programme in 1993/94. Concessions from the West on rescheduling Russia's foreign debt were scarcely revolutionary. And Clinton's decision to mortgage US Russian policy to Boris

Yeltsin's ability to deliver successful domestic reform was little different to Bush's reliance upon Gorbachev to hold the Soviet Union together. The conspicuous absence of Clinton's customary rhetoric about democratic enlargement and human rights when Yeltsin unconstitutionally dissolved the Russian Parliament in September 1993 and invaded Chechnya in December 1994 was strikingly reminiscent of Bush's toleration of Soviet troops in Azerbaijan in January 1990 and Gorbachev's intimidation of Lithuania when it declared independence two months later.

All of this lends weight to the conclusion that 'the Clinton administration appeared to take charge of American post-Cold War foreign policy with a single assumption in mind: Russia was now benign, a basket case, or both, and could therefore be taken for granted'.[17] Under pressure from allies and needing to divert attention from domestic affairs, Clinton subsequently revised a policy that fell haplessly between his idealism and Bush's pragmatism. Focusing on Washington's core Russian concern he moved to accelerate ratification of START. On 1 January 1994 he, Yeltsin and Ukrainian President Kravchuk signed the Trilateral Accord in Moscow that committed Ukraine to eliminate all nuclear weapons, including strategic offensive arms, in its territory. Clinton and Yeltsin agreed too in January 1994 provisions for detargeting strategic weapons away from each other's homelands. In the meantime, the administration sought to control Russian WMD expertise and to offer economic incentives for Russian nuclear cooperation. Schemes such as the Nuclear Cities Initiative and Bio Redirection assistance aimed to help provide new employment opportunities to workers displaced by Russia's shrinking WMDs complex. Similarly, in 1994 the Clinton administration concluded a 20-year deal worth $12 billion for Russia to dilute approximately 20,000 warheads of uranium for sale to utilities in the US.[18]

Still, though, the notion of a US–Russian strategic partnership was being rapidly exposed for what it was – a policy lacking both strategy and partnership. At home Clinton's aid for Russia ran into increasing opposition from Congress, particularly once the Democrats lost control of both Houses of Congress and erstwhile pillars of moderation such as Senator Lugar argued that the administration should stop treating Russia as a 'partner' and recognise it instead as a 'tough rival'. Abroad, the administration was damaged by misadventures in Somalia and Haiti and mired in disagreements with European allies over Bosnia. Still worse, leading Russians were attacking its Russia policy. In 1994 Russian Foreign Minister Kozyrev bemoaned that the US–Russia partnership was failing and attributed this 'not to a wrong strategy, but to the fact that we have no strategy at all'. If partnership were to emerge, the strength of American idealistic optimism must enable the US to 'see beyond narrowly perceived national interests for the sake of major strategic goals'.[19]

Rather than accepting Kozyrev's challenge the Clinton administration quietly retreated from strategic partnership to a more modest normalisation of US–Russia relations. This was encouraged by three factors. First, Russia assumed ever-less relative importance in US foreign policy as its economy shrank and it ceased to be a major threat. Second, Russia's declining importance encouraged unwillingness in the Clinton administration to battle an unsympathetic Congress for more aid to, and tolerance of, Russia. Other issues were more important. Third, the disappointing pace of Yeltsin's reforms suggested that US–Russia interests would not coincide as much as had been hoped in the honeymoon period of the early 1990s. For instance, Russia's sympathies for Milosevic's Serbia and opposition to NATO military action put the two at loggerheads during the Bosnian conflict. NATO outreach programmes and potential formal enlargement fuelled Russian resentment at their strategic displacement in Central and Eastern Europe. Russia also resented criticism of its interference in its Near Abroad and resisted American pressure not to export missile and nuclear technology to countries such as India and Iran.

From the mid-1990s the Clinton administration continued to engage Russia but prioritised other US interests. A pattern developed whereby it pursued policies contrary to Russian interests while also making gestures to mollify Russian sensitivities. Clinton finally agreed the first formal enlargement of NATO in 1997 and to courting the Ukraine as a counterweight to Russia through PFP and the 9 July 1997 Charter on a Distinctive Partnership with NATO. Concomitantly, in part to assuage Russian concerns, this enlargement was restricted to Poland, Hungary and the Czech Republic, and Russia was given a special relationship with NATO through the NATO–Russia Founding Act and creation of the Permanent Joint Council (PJC). The Clinton administration led military interventions in Bosnia and Kosovo against Russian opposition. In the latter Moscow suspended cooperation in the PJC and dispatched Russian troops to Kosovo to occupy Pristina airport before NATO forces could get there. Afterwards, though, the administration engaged Russia in peacekeeping in the Balkans and reconstruction through the Contact Group and involvement in the Kosovo Peace Implementation Force (KFOR).

This type of American 'light-switch diplomacy' in its Russia policy harked back to the Cold War and Yeltsin made Russian resentment clear when in mid-1995 he characterised the US–Russia relationship as one of 'Cold Peace'. An increasing number of US–Russia disputes reflected the failure of strategic partnership. For instance, the Clinton administration became increasingly annoyed about Russian frustration of its Middle Eastern policy. Between 1997 and 2000 Russian–Iraqi trade quintupled and Madeleine Albright called Russian diplomats 'Saddam's lawyers' for shielding his regime in the UN Security Council and providing de facto assistance to undermine the UN Special Commission's efforts to oversee the elimination of Iraq's WMDs and ballistic missiles. Similarly the Clinton administration imposed sanctions on Russian entities thought to be assisting Iran's nuclear and missile programmes, and Vice-President Gore bluntly told Prime Minister Primakov in November 1998 that he had to choose between 'a piddling trickle of money from Iran or a bonanza with us'.[20] Conversely Russia recalled its ambassadors from Washington and London in protest against Anglo-American military strikes on Iraq in 1998 and bitterly denounced, in the aftermath of Russian economic collapse that same year, the 'economic imperialism' of IMF criteria attached to its largest-ever financial assistance package – some $17.1 billion. Russia also reacted hostilely to the first formal enlargement of NATO in 1999, to Clinton's authorisation of BMD research and to fresh American criticism of its handling of renewed insurrection in Chechnya – criticism that prompted Yeltsin to remind Clinton crudely that Russia still had nuclear weapons. Moreover, Russian pro-Western enthusiasm had been replaced by distrust and a search for alternatives. Russian diplomacy increasingly opposed US unilateralism and sought options to balance US power and reduce Russia's Western dependency. Prime Minister Primakov mooted ideas in 1998 for a Moscow–Bejing–Delhi 'strategic triangle' and Russia became interested in collaborating with the EU's CESDP. Russia's Medium-term Strategy for Development of Relations between the Russian Federation and the European Union made clear initial Russian hopes that an ESDI might counterbalance the 'NATO-centrism' in Europe.

Successive national leadership changes did not immediately auger well for improved US–Russia relations. After twice sacking Russian prime ministers in 1999 to preserve his leadership Yeltsin finally resigned on 31 December. His eventual successor, Vladimir Putin, quickly harkened back to Russia's great past, promised to strengthen Russia's armed forces through a 57% increase in defence spending, and developed his election campaign around the need to recreate a strong centralised state. That this was not mere rhetoric was evident in the revised National Security Concept and the New Military Doctrine, ruthless prosecution of the Chechen war, and the retention of the missile-orientated Igor Sergeyev as Defence Minister. At the same time in the US the Republicans launched an election-year blitz against Clinton's Russia policy. Clinton had allegedly overly personalised US–Russia relations and invested too much in trying to promote internal Russian political and economic reform at the expense of the US–Russia security agenda, including Russia's dealings with rogue states and its role in weapons proliferation. Condoleezza Rice indicated a prospective hard line. She argued in 2000 that Russia's determination to assert itself was haphazard and threatening to US interests. Rumsfeld and Paul Wolfowitz were less diplomatic, calling Russia an 'active proliferator' and accusing the Russians of being 'willing to sell anything to anyone for money'.[21]

George W. Bush's initial principal interest in Russia again lay in the nuclear sphere but this time in overcoming opposition to BMD and his intention to abrogate the ABM Treaty. Within months, however, 9/11 provided the basis of a new positive agenda for cooperation and encouraged a series of similar reactions that made it more difficult for the Bush administration to criticise Russian conduct. Russia was an important potential ally in the battle against terrorism. Its predominant religion was Christianity, but it had Islamic fundamentalist problems of its own and could provide and help arrange forward bases, offer valuable intelligence and bring influence to bear on states over which the US had limited purchase, such as Iran. The 9/11 attacks also demonstrated shared US–Russian state-centric views of the world that emphasise national interests, sovereignty, territorial integrity and national

security. Furthermore both governments reacted domestically by using 9/11 to centralise power, limit basic civil liberties and tighten immigration law.[22]
Putin grasped quickly how Russian interests might be advanced as the US responded to the terrorist attacks. He was the first head of state to call the White House after 9/11 to pledge support in finding those responsible, offered assistance in the US Afghan campaign and overrode opposition from the Russian military to facilitate US troop deployments in Central Asia. By driving out the Taliban the US essentially did for Russia what it had been unable to do through years of support for the Northern Alliance. Neither was American cooperation in tackling the Islamic Movement of Uzbekistan unwelcome. Instability in the Middle East also offered an opportunity to convince America of Russia's importance as an alternative reliable source of oil, having a projected production of 9.5 million barrels per day by 2010. In the meantime, Putin used precedents set by the Bush administration to shield Russia from American criticism as he began reasserting Russian influence, especially in the CIS. The long-running Chechnya conflict was largely reinvented, especially after the Beslan massacre, as an anti-terrorist war designed to prevent Islamic destabilisation of the Russian Caucasus. Also, in October 2003 the so-called Ivanov Doctrine staked out Russian preventative strike 'rights', including in CIS countries, which were arguably more expansive than those claimed by Bush's 2002 National Security Strategy.

This new functional dynamic revitalised US–Russia relations. After their first meeting in Slovenia in June 2001 Bush hailed Putin as 'an honest, straightforward man who loves his country. He loves his family. We share a lot of values.' By May 2002 this personal relationship had so broadened that the US and Russia professed to be 'achieving a new strategic partnership'. Emphasis on common values stretched credulity given Russia's developing 'illiberal democracy' but there was substance to shared interest in a 'benign security environment', including in ensuring energy security, promoting non-proliferation and combating terrorism and organised crime. US criticism of Russian domestic affairs temporarily became muted and Russia's response to NATO's announcement in November 2002 of another enlargement – including the Baltic states – was 'almost anti-climactic'.[23] Cooperation also continued concerning WMDs. In August 2002 the US and Russia cooperated in removing enriched uranium from Serbia's Vinca reactor, and in January 2003 the Bush administration authorised $450 million within the Nunn–Lugar Program to facilitate work on a chemical weapons destruction facility at Shchuch'ye in Russia.[24] A deal was also struck in May 2002 that gave Putin some political cover for US withdrawal from the ABM Treaty and pursuit of BMD. The US–Russian Strategic Offensive Reductions Treaty (SORT) committed both sides to reduce their strategic nuclear warheads to 1,700–2,200 by 31 December 2012.

Yet for all the Bush administration's criticism of Clinton's approach there have been marked similarities. Bush has placed considerable weight upon his personal relationship with Putin – just as Clinton did with Yeltsin. His administration's embrace of the market and democratisation has led to renewed criticism of Russia's internal practices, especially since the start of its second term. In 2005 the State Department accused Russia of 'backsliding' in its commitments to democracy, civil liberties and the conduct of its forces in Chechnya. And the pattern has continued of prioritising US interests while offering olive branches to soothe Russian irritation. NATO's announced second enlargement was accompanied by establishment of the NATO–Russia Council, with the so-called 'NATO at 20' agreement according Russia equal status in discussions of issues relating to terrorism, WMDs, rescue operations and so forth. Likewise, the SORT was clearly a political sop to Putin. The cuts offered were consistent with those outlined in the US Nuclear Posture Review, there was a lack of verification conditions, and warheads would have only to be dismantled rather than destroyed.

The Bush administration seems no closer to realising a genuine strategic partnership with Russia than did its predecessor. It is odd that the US–Russia Joint Declaration emphasised in May 2002 that the two countries were achieving a strategic partnership when the following month Richard Haas, Director of the Policy Planning Staff, contended that 'the most important and challenging task at this stage is to *define* a long-term positive agenda for the bilateral relationship'.[25] Selective engagement is not a strategic partnership and while some consider that Putin's support against the Taliban and al-Qaeda confirmed 'a more basic strategic decision to throw Russia's lot in with West', others are less convinced.[26] Putin took care not to derail the US–Russia relationship but nevertheless opposed strongly US intervention in Iraq in 2003 and accused the Bush administration of double standards in condemning the initial election result in Ukraine in late 2004 but insisting on the legitimacy of those held in Afghanistan and Iraq. Likewise Russia moved to counter perceived enhanced strategic vulnerability consequent upon US withdrawal from the ABM Treaty and pursuit of BMD. On 13 June 2002 Russia withdrew from START II. It is thus no longer banned from deploying land-based missiles with multiple warheads and the formidable Soviet-era SS-18 and SS-19 missiles can remain at the core of its arsenal. Moreover, it has since developed the submarine-launched SS-NX-30 Bulava missiles, which Russia claims are indestructible by modern ABM systems.[27]

There are signs, too, of emerging US–Russia strategic competition rather than cooperation in Eastern Europe and Central Asia. The 2004 NATO enlargement again raised Russian dissatisfaction with the outdated CFE Treaty and encouraged fears of BMD facilities being located upon their borders. The Ukrainian 'Orange Revolution' and tacit US support of Viktor Yushchenko, the ultimately successful opponent of Russia-backed Yanukovich, strengthened Russian resistance to the democracy-promotion schemes of foreign governments and non-government organisations (NGOs). And Russia's promotion of the Shanghai Cooperation Organisation as the premier stabilising force in Central Asia indicates resolve to limit American influence. Indeed, Russia has developed a series of initiatives to strengthen its Central Asian influence and counter that of the US. These include efforts to develop a special relationship with Kazakhstan, which is key to developing a southern buffer and providing crucial military and economic routes to the heart of Asia, and the establishment of Russia's first new base abroad for many years at Kant in Kyrgyzstan – just kilometres from a new US base at Manas.[28] Also, Russia orchestrated the setting up in May 2002 of a Collective Security Treaty Organisation that included itself, Kazakhstan, Kyrgyzstan, Tajiikistan, Belarus and Armenia, and which has plans for a joint military command in Moscow, a rapid reaction force for Central Asia, a common air defence system and coordinated action in foreign, security and defence matters.[29] The following month Putin was party to the Almaty Act that set up another new 16-nation-strong Asian security organisation – the Conference on Interaction and Confidence Building Measures in Asia.

The Bush administration's selective engagement of Russia and penetration of Central Asia in its war against terrorism risks encouraging Russian resistance and deepening Moscow's relations with countries unsympathetic to Washington. In 2000 the US National Intelligence Council conceded that Russia might seek a de facto geostrategic alliance with China and India in an attempt to counterbalance US and Western influence. Prospects of this have since improved. Russia, India and China face common threats in Central Asia – religious extremism, terrorism, the drugs trade and a potential American challenge to their spheres of influence. They also approach similarly issues such as the Middle East Peace Process (MEPP), Iraq, non-proliferation, regional security, the role of the UN and aspirations for a multipolar world. Moscow is working hard to develop these relationships. Russian links with India have warmed significantly since Putin's arrival in office, Russia remains India's major arms supplier, and the Russian and Indian navies hold regular joint war games in the Indian Ocean. The Russia–China relationship is deepening apace too. In 2001 they signed a Treaty of Good-neighbourliness, Friendship and Cooperation. Their border disputes have been resolved and military cooperation reached a new milestone in August 2005 when their armed forces commenced war games. Trade between the two countries has been increasing at around 30% per annum since 1999 and China remains a major consumer of Russian military exports – not least to deter Taiwan's drive for independence and counter the US seventh Fleet.[30]

One further potential complication arising from the Bush administration's relative neglect of Russia and Russian interests is that Moscow will strengthen ties with Teheran – the premier target of Bush's 'axis of evil' following the toppling of Saddam Hussein. Iran is Russia's principal foothold in West Asia and provides a buffer against American encroachment and strategic hemming in from the south. It is also a significant consumer of Russian arms and has strong energy links with Moscow. The growing strength of the Russian–Iranian relationship was indicated in February 2005 when Putin refused to bow to US pressure and agreed to supply fuel to the Bushehr reactor on condition that Iran return spent nuclear fuel rods. Moreover, other members of Primakov's reviving 'strategic triangle' share Russian interest in Iran. India signalled its interest in a strategic partnership with Iran in the Teheran (2001) and Delhi (2003) Declarations. Iran offers India export markets, much-needed energy sources, land access to markets in Afghanistan and Central Asia and a potential partner in ensuring the political independence of Afghanistan. As for China and Iran, the US provides a commonality by identifying them as a strategic threat and rogue state respectively. Iran is also China's only meaningful potential ally in West Asia and military and economic ties are deepening. China sources the majority of supplies for the Iranian Navy's combat craft and missiles, and two oil and gas deals were recently completed worth approximately \$100 billion.[31] This helps China meet its soaring energy needs and Iran to offset US sanctions.

Conclusion

The post-Cold War US relationship with Europe has been full of possibilities, contradictions and difficulties. From an economic perspective the US relationship with the EU especially is one of accelerating and profound interdependence. US prosperity depends heavily on this relationship, as do its efforts to shape the instruments of global economic governance and to set the agenda of global free trade. For all the differences over trade practices, anti-trust measures and exchange rates the EU is likely to remain a strong partner, provided Washington heeds its concerns. Yet both Europe and Russia have fallen dramatically as focuses of American strategic concern. The end of the Cold War stripped Europe of its front-line status and Clinton's eventual commitment to the Balkans was driven largely by secondary concerns for NATO and to support wider claims to US leadership of a strategy of democratic enlargement. Russia's demotion is starkly demonstrated by NATO enlargement and by US military intervention in Bosnia and Kosovo, withdrawal from the ABM Treaty and development of BMD. Russia's primary importance to the current Bush administration seems to be as a facilitator in Central Asia, the states of which have assumed unusual strategic significance as the front-line of the war on terrorism. As for Europe, the US looks to the EU and NATO to perform some of the less demanding security tasks, especially peacekeeping and reconstruction, and to provide coalitions of the willing as and when necessary for material but especially legitimacy purposes.

The US has achieved a number of its post-Cold War objectives in Europe. It concentrated Soviet nuclear capabilities in Russia and subsequently dramatically and securely reduced mutual arsenals. It developed strong collaborative US–EU structures, especially through the NTA. It has so far successfully insisted on the primacy of NATO over the respective preferences of France and Russia for a more autonomous European military capability and an enhanced Organisation for Security and Cooperation in Europe. Successive NATO and EU enlargements have given Central and East European Countries (CEECs) a security home, brought both organisations to Russia's borders and ensured a stronger Atlanticist contingent within the EU. And the application of overwhelming military superiority in the Balkans underscored Washington's message that even in their own backyard, Europeans need to improve their military capabilities and develop them in ways approved by the US.

However, these 'successes' have thrown up strange ironies and exacted potentially high prices. First, they have been achieved largely because of unquestionable American power rather than because of consistent or well-constructed strategies. Clinton and George W. Bush both asserted but failed (thus far at least) to deliver strategic partnership with Russia, and the general approach to the EU contains contradictions that are potentially unmanageable in the long term. Second, throughout the Cold War common values underpinned the transatlantic relationship and helped define the Soviet Union as the enemy. Now America disagrees with Russian illiberal democracy but has more in common with Moscow than Brussels in terms of state-centric world views that prioritise national interests, sovereignty, territorial integrity and national security. America still shares more with the EU than Russia in terms of democratic values but now finds differences evolving in these values: the relative weight attached to security and individual liberty, state sovereignty and human rights, the sanctity of international law and so forth. Furthermore, America finds that the EU and Russia often have more in common on foreign policy issues than the US does with either of them, including the MEPP, attachment to multipolarity, the importance of the UN and how to deal with Iran.

As for the 'price' of success, doomsayers of imminent transatlantic divorce and Kaganesque caricatures are overstated. The Bush administration has tried in its second term to rebuild relationships badly damaged by intervention in Iraq, and this ongoing construction work is laid on still solid foundations of interdependence and decades of close cooperation. Nevertheless, there is a danger that differences over unilateralism/multilateralism, preferred security tools, policies of engagement or confrontation and especially pre-emptive or preventative strike will translate into enduring differences about what values to embed in structures of global governance and how to enforce and protect them. The Bush administration also risks pushing the EU and Russia into counterbalancing moves through lack of consultation and continuous engagement. In the EU's case this is unlikely to be hostile but might be sufficient to thwart or compromise US objectives. Russia is more likely to become less accommodating if not better rewarded for its cooperation in fighting terrorism. The Bush–Putin Bratislava summit in February 2005 failed to bridge differences on democracy, the CIS and Iran, and on 22 February 2005 the Director of the Moscow Carnegie Centre argued that the US–Russia relationship 'is quickly transforming from partnership to cold peace at best'.[32] US policy has already forced Russian withdrawal from START II and encouraged Russia's further investment in nuclear missile technology, which it may or may not share with other states. NATO enlargement and the US military presence in Central Asia are squeezing Russian interests and have already provoked a response in the CIS and Central Asia. If this continues the US might counter-productively push Russia further into a triangular relationship with India and China, developing its arms exports to countries such as Syria and consolidating its relationship with Iran.

11 The US and post-Cold War Africa and the Middle East

What are the drivers of American foreign policy in these regions? Was Huntington right about African and Islamic challenges to Western civilisation? Would the 'end of history' see democracy spread across the African continent and the Middle East and assimilate even Islam? Would regional insecurity drive states to develop WMDs and create a 'back-to-the-future' scenario, particularly in the Middle East? And would post-Cold War US presidencies be able to formulate and execute coherent strategies or would they be inconsistent, event driven and circumscribed by domestic actors and interests influencing foreign policy? How, too, would the US seek to exercise its power in these regions and to what ends? Could a Middle East peace settlement be secured? Could Africa be brought from the periphery to the centre of international concern? And could the US finally reconcile its promotion of universal values with policy on the ground?

The US and Africa – mind the gap?

The close of the Cold War seemingly bequeathed the US opportunity and moral imperative to lead the world in shining the beacon of hope and liberty across the 'Dark Continent'. Statistics graphically demonstrate the enormity of that challenge. Sub-Saharan Africa is the only major underdeveloped region whose per capita income has declined since 1980.[1] Africa's share in world trade fell from 5% in 1980 to 2.2% in 1995. In 1993, 40% of sub-Saharan Africans lived on less than $1 a day. And between 1975 and 1995 annual growth rates for the African continent fell from about 5% to 3% – marginally higher than population growth.

Pro-African administration officials, such as Clinton's first NSA Anthony Lake, complemented moral considerations with the identification of three sets of American interests in Africa. Pre-emptive measures were required to help obviate the need for hasty emergency responses to recurrent African humanitarian crises. Africa was also a key source of transnational threats, including drug, arms and human trafficking, environmental degradation, disease and terrorism. The latter was demonstrated starkly by terrorist attacks in 1998 on US embassies in Kenya and Tanzania and reinforced a further fear, namely that Islamic fundamentalism might fill the Soviet vacuum in Africa. Rapidly deteriorating US–Sudanese relations following a successful military coup in 1989 were potentially a case in point. Al-Bashir enforced strict adherence to Islamic law, leaned on the support of the National Islamic Front and allegedly provided Iranian-sponsored bases for training Islamic militants. Lake's third set of American interests constituted the economic opportunity dimension. Africa still possessed important strategic minerals and other primary goods, offered potential for American investment and in the more distant future could become an important market for US goods. To this list can also be added calculations of political advantage. A pro-African policy might garner support for American foreign policy within the UN – both in the General Assembly and, more importantly, from Africa's three seats in the Security Council. It could also influence positively the African-American vote and interests in the US.

The US was now freer to promote democratic reform in Africa and to abandon authoritarian regimes that it had formerly supported to help combat communism. Yet at the same time, its strategic interest in Africa and its levers of influence over indigenous states diminished once the continent ceased to be a theatre of superpower competition. US aid to Africa had already been hard hit following the 1986 Gramm–Rudman–Hollings Deficit Reduction Act. Seen through an evolving lens of national interest rather than global strategy, residual American interests in African primary products, trade, sustainable development, human rights and so forth were relatively less compelling. Former Soviet bloc countries emerged as alternative providers of strategic minerals and, as Congress and popular demands for a peace dividend squeezed foreign policy resources, Asia and the Middle East had first call on diminishing funds. The voice of poverty is always weak and Black Africa especially lacked a Washington lobby powerful enough to secure and maintain the attention of Congress and the Executive, despite TransAfrica and the Congressional Black Caucus. South Africa was a notable and initially controversial exception to the general lack of engagement, the Clinton administration including it in its Big Emerging Markets programme.

These contradictory trends begged questions about how to reconcile universal American values, African expectation and optimism for a New World Order and the realities of US domestic constraints and diminished American strategic interest in Africa. The continent's becoming one of the first casualties of the debate about power and purpose in US foreign policy compounded this dilemma. Somalia had been a significant Cold War client state, due not least to the Berbera air and port facilities that enabled the US Navy to monitor Soviet submarine movements through the narrow Straits of Bab el-Mandeb. When it descended into intensified civil war following the April 1988 Ethiopian–Somali accord, the US Defense Department duly provided military aid to the established Siad regime. However, Congress, liberated by the receding Cold War and growing evidence of Soviet cooperation in Africa, opposed aid on grounds of widespread abuses by Somali armed forces. In 1989, the Bush administration reluctantly reprogrammed $2.5 million of military aid and $21 million of Economic Support Funds earmarked for Somalia. In 1990 the Siad regime fell. Early in 1991, the US evacuated embassy personnel and American appetite for dealing with Somalia diminished proportionately to the country's waning strategic significance and spiralling crisis. The Bush administration looked to offload political responsibility for Somalia on to Britain and Italy – as former colonial powers in the affected territories – and on to the UN to meet humanitarian needs. Even former champions of Somalia among the Defense Department, the CIA and State Department regional specialists opposed forcible American intervention. Somalia was no longer a vital US interest, American casualties were probable, and the anarchic situation on the ground denied a clear exit strategy. However, this approach was compromised politically by heavy media coverage of the deepening crisis in Somalia, the impending US presidential election and slow progress within the UN Security Council. It was also possible to view Somalia as a test of Bush's aspirations for a New World Order as well as a humanitarian crisis, which put the onus on Washington to take the lead. On 4 December, Bush announced he would send American troops to Somalia under a UN mandate to create a secure environment for the distribution of famine-relief aid. The terms of deployment reflected the globalist thinking of Secretary of State Baker and NSA Brent Scowcroft in particular. Once the immediate humanitarian objective of alleviating famine conditions was met then the UN should assume responsibility for political reconstruction and provide a peace-keeping force to keep aid moving. Bush underscored this message shortly before leaving office by authorising the withdrawal of approximately 550 US troops on 19 January 1993.

The deployment of US combat troops, who constituted two-thirds of Operation Restore Hope's 36,000-man strong force, seemingly heralded a turning point in US Africa policy. Thomas Friedman commented in the *New York Times*: 'for the first time American troops are entering a country uninvited, not to shore up an anti-communist regime, protect American wealth or stifle a strategic threat, but simply to feed starving people'.[2] This optimism was short-lived. The Clinton administration quickly found an exit strategy to be predictably elusive. Still worse, when UN peacekeepers came under sniper attack from supporters of Mohammed Farah Aidid the Security Council requested American assistance in capturing the Somali warlord. This exemplified the dangers of mission creep and the results were both disastrous and formative in US Africa policy. On 3 October 1993, US Army Rangers and the Delta Force, plus helicopter gunships, were sent to capture Aidid. Eighteen Rangers were killed and images were broadcast on prime-time television of a dead American soldier being dragged through the streets of Mogadishu.

The backlash in America against the Clinton administration, the UN and American commitment to multilateralism was severe. Congress instructed Clinton to withdraw all US troops from Somalia, which he did over the coming months – and the remaining UN peacekeepers withdrew in early 1995. Congress also cut US foreign aid, especially once the Republicans seized both Houses in 1994, and sought to limit future US commitment to peacekeeping operations. US economic aid to Africa fell by 25% from 1995 to 1996; in FY

1997/98 US foreign aid reached an all-time low of 0.16% of GDP; and in 1995 Congress passed the National Security Revitalization Act that limited American contributions to peacekeeping and restricted US soldiers from serving under foreign commanders. Vital national interest criteria returned to centre stage of the power and purpose debate in US foreign policy and under intense pressure the Clinton administration signalled in PDD-25 a reduced commitment to multilateral peacekeeping. The effect of this was serious in Europe's troubled Balkans, but decisive in Africa where the national interest case was harder to advance to a sceptical Congress and public. The Clinton administration's Africa policy thereafter generally eschewed participation in multilateral interventionism and peacekeeping, delegating such tasks primarily to Europe's former colonial powers in Africa. US standing aside while genocide swept through Rwanda epitomised this retreat. That it would continue under Clinton's successor was quickly apparent when Bush, asked on 23 January 2000 what he would do if confronted with another Rwanda, declared, 'We should not send our troops to stop ethnic cleansing and genocide in nations outside our strategic interests.'[3]

Somalia cut short US adventurism in Africa in pursuit of a New World Order, effectively returned it to the political backwater of American foreign policy and contributed to the shrinking of US aid to the continent during the 1990s. This did not mean, though, complete US disregard for Africa. Clinton actually devoted more time and energy to it than any previous US president. His administration launched numerous initiatives orientated around themes of conflict resolution, democratisation and economic development. US mediators were directly and indirectly involved in seeking resolutions to numerous crises (including in Mozambique, Angola, Liberia, Ethiopia, Eritrea and the Sudan) and, shorn of the option of American military intervention, the US developed a capacity to act by proxy. The African Crisis Response Initiative prepared African troops for deployment to crisis situations and was complemented by US provision of training and communications equipment to select African armies (including those of Ethiopia, Ghana, Malawi, Mali, Senegal and Uganda). Democracy promotion was embedded in conditions attached to US foreign aid and economic incentives. Later in the administration, as disillusion grew with the corruption of some of the African political elites and manufacture of 'pseudo-democracies',[4] emphasis switched to promoting civil society as a vehicle to deliver programmes as diverse as health, education, democratisation, environmentalism and the rule of law.

As for the economic dimension, the Clinton administration's solution to Africa's plight was for it to embrace neo-liberal economics and become integrated into the globalising economy. Emphasis was laid on the IMF and World Bank to oversee painful structural adjustment measures, which the US supported through a combination of development assistance, debt reduction, trade incentives and investment promotion. The centre-piece of this strategy was the Africa Growth and Opportunity Act (AGOA) to expand US–Africa trade and investment, which passed through Congress in 2000 and enabled participant African countries to export selected products tariff-free to the US.

George W. Bush subsequently extended this agreement and in July 2005 hailed its success, noting that the previous year American exports to sub-Saharan Africa had increased by 25% and imports from AGOA countries had risen by 88% (albeit from a very low base).[5]

The Clinton administration's flourishes suggested a pan-African approach, including the first-ever White House conference on Africa in July 1994, signature of the Global AIDS and Tubercolosis Relief Act, the Leland initiative, design of the first 'Month of Africa' at the UN, and Clinton's visit to Africa in 1998 and participation the following year in the National Summit on Africa. However, there remained heavy overtones of the selective engagement of the Cold War years as efforts focused particularly on sub-regional power centres and high GDP growth countries. These criteria often conveniently coincided with, and encouraged, the selective engagement that NSA Lake foreshadowed in his warning to the Organisation of African Unity in 1994: pro-African policy-makers 'are confronting the reality of shrinking resources and an honest scepticism about the return on our investments in peacekeeping and development'.[6]

Two key examples of this approach are South Africa and Nigeria. The US national security institutions especially were never reconciled to the 1986 Comprehensive Anti-Apartheid Act. The Bush administration consequently smoothed Congress by signalling sympathy with the anti-apartheid movement while also citing sufficient evidence of South African reform to lift sanctions on 10 July 1991. Thereafter the US progressively deepened relations with a South Africa that is strategically well located and enjoys vast mineral wealth, a strong industrial base and a diverse and productive agricultural sector. South Africa's privileged status was reflected in its aid allocation in FY 1994 of $900 million. This made it one of just two African states in the top 15 of US aid destinations in FY 1994 (the other being famine-stricken Ethiopia), despite its having an overall standard of living much higher than most African countries.

As for Nigeria, it was, and remains, attractive for three key reasons. First, it is mineral rich, a magnet for US multinationals, and a source of non-Middle Eastern oil. It currently has proven oilfields of around 25 billion barrels, natural gas reserves of over 100 trillion cubic feet, provides 7–9% of US oil imports, and carries a US investment stock of $7 billion, mainly in the energy sector. Second, Nigeria is a key power centre that can serve as a stabilising regional force and deliver American power by proxy, as reflected in the Clinton administration's train-and-equip programme to prepare at least five Nigerian battalions for peacekeeping duties in Sierra Leone. Third, Nigeria could be a catalyst for democratisation if it accomplished a successful political transition, albeit critics have seen this as a lesser American priority. The US imposed limited sanctions on Nigeria in the mid-1990s after its failure to make democratic progress – including visa restrictions and termination of military aid – but quickly removed these after General Abacha's death in June 1998. When Clinton travelled to Nigeria in August 2000 in support of democratic transition, he emphasised the country's role in regional peacekeeping and international crime cooperation. Despite ongoing human rights problems, the

George W. Bush administration subsequently recognised Nigeria as playing a leading role in forging an anti-terrorism consensus among states in sub-Saharan Africa.[7]

Bush's election was greeted with some trepidation by African countries and pro-African policy-makers and pressure groups, especially given his assertion in February 2000 that Africa did not fit into US national strategic interests. In the event it was 9/11 rather than the Bush administration's arrival that most changed US Africa policy. Prior to this the administration moved to refocus aid around three pillars of economic growth, agriculture and trade; global health; and democracy, conflict prevention and humanitarian assistance. Actual policy, though, broadly followed the established contours of trade and aid concessions to countries that undertook economic and political reforms; promoting African capacity for conflict resolution; and pursuit of privileged relationships with selected countries of strategic and/or economic importance. Hence the Bush administration continued to back peace initiatives, such as in Sierra Leone and the conclusion of the Comprehensive Peace Agreement in Sudan in 2005. Its African Contingency Training and Assistance Program was designed to train over 40,000 peacekeepers within five years. And the continuing 'Mogadishu syndrome' was evident in the Bush administration's preference during the Liberia crisis for Nigeria to take a leading peacekeeping role rather than deploy US peacekeepers.

9/11 returned Africa to a situation somewhat akin to the Cold War whereby it was addressed as a part of something else – anti-terrorism being substituted for superpower competition. The principal changes have been threefold. First, African leaders have seen danger and opportunity in the Bush administration's 'for us or against us' dichotomy in the war on terror. Sudan seized the chance to restore diplomatic relations with the US by handing over secret files on Osama bin Laden, who had lived there during the 1990s, and surrendering Abu-Anas al-Liby, who was implicated in the 1998 embassy bombings in Dar es Salaam and Nairobi.[8] The reaction of Qaddafi's Libya was likewise accommodating. Referred to by one US official as in the 'junior varsity axis of evil' – along with Syria and Cuba – it was bound to attract unwanted attention, especially as it had been a Cold War American enemy and subsequently a rogue state that supported terrorism and developed a rudimentary WMDs programme and short-range Scud missiles. Qaddafi decided to appease the US and the international community.[9] Libya condemned the 9/11 attacks and, given its own problems with Islamic militants, emphasised their connections with al-Qaeda and the Jihad in Afghanistan. It also finally settled with Britain over the Lockerbie bombing and renounced terrorism and WMDs. In 2004, once caught shipping nuclear material, Libya accepted the 'inspections-as-verification' model of inspectors witnessing the dismantling and destruction of prohibited weapons.[10]

Second, the allocation of aid has acquired a renewed strategic focus as a means to secure resource interests, garner support for US policy in the UN Security Council and stabilise key vulnerable states. For instance, African oil currently accounts for 15% of US oil imports, is projected to grow to 25%

within ten years and has the double advantage that it reduces dependence on the volatile Middle East and that African producers are likely to be more malleable as few are OPEC members. Also, the Bush administration threatened to withhold military aid from 35 countries that refused to sign an agreement with the US exempting Americans from potential prosecution by the ICC. Furthermore, FY 2004 US aid figures reveal that Ethiopia, Kenya and Uganda – important African allies – were among the top 15 recipients as a consequence of their being focus countries for the Global AIDS initiative. Figures for 2001–03 suggest, though, that these were not the worst affected countries and that the AIDS infection rate was actually falling faster in Uganda and Kenya than elsewhere in Africa.[11]

Third, there has been an increased securitisation of US Africa policy. The 2002 National Security Strategy for the first time identified global development as a pillar of US national security,[12] and in January 2004 USAID designated five core operational goals of American foreign assistance, two of which were supporting US geostrategic interests and strengthening fragile states.[13] Washington has thus, for instance, stepped up initiatives to train and secure influence over African, especially South African, military and police forces through the construction of new war colleges and security police academies. It has been instrumental in crafting new domestic anti-terrorism legislation in Kenya, Tanzania and Uganda – countries at the centre of the war on terrorism in the Horn of Africa.[14] Moreover, it is keen to establish bases in African countries to help with crisis response in the Persian Gulf and Middle East. For example, American military units were stationed in Djibouti in December 2002, from where anti-al Qaeda strikes in Yemen were launched; US naval forces are using ports in Kenya and Eritrea to patrol the Indian Ocean and Red Sea; and Ethiopia has been helping to combat Islamist terrorists based in Somalia.[15]

To its credit the Bush administration has resourced development policy far beyond that secured by Clinton. The New Compact for Development promises a 50% increase in US development assistance and includes new funds for famine and emergency relief, an Emergency Plan for AIDS relief, increased contributions to the World Bank and the creation of the flagship Millennium Challenge Account (MCA). At the G-8 summit in July 2005 Bush agreed to a series of measures to advance global poverty reduction, including cancellation of all bilateral and multilateral debt for qualifying heavily indebted poor countries. And his administration has endorsed collaborative African ventures, such as the New Partnership for Africa's Development, the Economic Community of West African States (ECOWAS) and the African Union.

Nevertheless, doubts remain that Bush will, or can, deliver on his promises, and expansive rhetoric fuels the gap between Africa's expectations and the realities of American policy. His administration's trade policies were a major cause of the collapse of the WTO Cancun meeting and American subsidies damage key African primary exports and undermine potential benefits of the AGOA. Also, the US lags at the bottom of OECD rankings of major aid donors as a percentage of gross national income (GNI), and Congress remains unconvinced of overseas development aid as a funding priority – as indicated by its repeated slashing of MCA funding requests.[16] Multiple criticisms have been voiced too about the style and objectives of the MCA. Its bilateral basis increases US leverage over participants and would-be participants and reflects ongoing reservations about multilateralism. Also, MCA qualifying criteria, organised around ruling justly, investing in people and encouraging economic freedom, have been seen as blatant export of the American model. Critics regard this as likely to maintain the majority of African states in a condition of dependency and as cynical manipulation of American trade advantage, particularly as over 70% of US development aid is conditional upon purchase in America of the goods and services involved.[17] Furthermore, there is renewed danger that the global war on terrorism will maintain Africa at the margins of American policy and lead development priorities to be subordinated to a country's stability, economic value and willingness to cooperate in, especially, the war on terrorism.

The US and the Middle East – return of the 'vision thing'?

It was never in doubt that America would remain intimately involved in the Middle East after the Cold War. The US could not afford to jeopardise its special relationship with Israel and the secure flow of Middle Eastern oil into the world economy, or abandon its allies to a dangerous security environment, especially as 'new' threats emerged such as state-sponsored terrorism, proliferation of WMDs and the growing power of Islamic fundamentalism. Yet it also faced new problems in acting because removal of Cold War overlay better revealed the region's multiple fracture points, necessitated new means of legitimising US policies, and compromised administrations' freedom of manoeuvre by allowing domestic actors greater influence in foreign policy. Key questions were how would Washington fulfil its role as regional hegemon? What would be the key objectives of its policies? And what level of political and resource commitment would it make?

The George H. Bush administration quickly had opportunity to demonstrate US determination to remain the regional hegemon and that its power and, potentially, its willingness to use it, were undiminished. The speed, nature and intensity of its response to Saddam Hussein's disastrously miscalculated invasion of Kuwait on 2 August 1990 caused great discussion. Was it motivated by concern for oil (the Persian Gulf accounted for 65% of known world oil reserves), human rights, non-proliferation of WMDs, territorial integrity of Kuwait, or by revenge for the Iraqi leader's 'betrayal' of American support during the Iran–Iraq war? Most probably there were elements of all these factors. Even more importantly, US leadership of an international coalition operating under UN auspices to repel Iraq lent credence to American determination to safeguard Middle Eastern stability and encouraged hopes for assertive multilateralism and a New World Order. It also sent important messages to Middle Eastern states. First, it encouraged Saudi Arabia and vulnerable Gulf mini-states to continue their policy since the Iran–Iraq war of drawing closer to the US. Second, it suggested that Russia was no longer a significant restraint on American Middle Eastern policy. This increased US regional influence, enhanced the possibility of an interventionist American policy, and signalled to former Soviet client states a need to redevise and reorientate their foreign policies. The Bush administration also developed strategic contours and focuses that shaped US policy throughout the 1990s. It initially continued the Reagan administration's policy of engagement of Iraq, which was encouraged by fear of Iran's Shiite revolution and lingering resentment over the Iranian hostage crisis. After favouring Baghdad in the Iran–Iraq war that ended in August 1988, Washington assumed that it could 'tame' Saddam Hussein because of Iraqi domestic reconstruction priorities and continuing American assistance in helping the regime to develop an impressive arsenal and to access loans and high technology. However, the Bush administration jettisoned engagement once Hussein proved this assumption wrong by using chemical weapons against Iraqi Kurds and invading Kuwait. History had turned full circle. Nixon had supported Iran as part of the Twin Pillar strategy; Reagan and Bush had supported Iraq as balancer of post-revolutionary Iran. Now both countries were regional malcontents and American enemies, and playing them off against one another could no longer provide regional stability. The Bush administration thus adopted a strategy of 'comprehensive containment' designed to prevent the rise of any regional power hostile to American interests. This was underpinned by an expanded post-Gulf War military deployment in the region – especially in the Gulf monarchies – that was itself backed by the formidable US 'over-the-horizon' military presence that Reagan developed in the wake of the Carter Doctrine.

Denied the legitimisation of anti-communism the Bush administration evolved a new justification for comprehensive containment, namely the rogue state. The pejorative classification of states not conforming to the 'rules' of the established order was not new. Nevertheless, categorising states as 'rogue' played well to US domestic constituencies and appealed to the long-established Manichean strand of American foreign policy that cast international affairs in simplistic terms of the battle between good and evil. The moral force of US arguments benefited, too, from hopes of a norm-based New World Order. States designated as 'rogue' were thus cast as a threat not only to US interests but also to the aspirations of the international community. The Bush administration further developed this notion of shared threat by advancing a highly dubious but compelling link between certain states and the issues of terrorism and WMDs proliferation. Secretary of State-designate James Baker told Congress in September 1989 that 'chemical warheads and ballistic missiles have fallen into the hands of governments with proven records of aggression and terrorism'.[18]

It is now known that the US helped to put such weapons into the hands of Saddam Hussein. Also, the definition of rogue state has been notoriously soft, frequently reflecting the political predilections of the US and replete with glaring inconsistencies. For instance, during its first term the

Clinton administration cited Cuba as a rogue state but refused to so designate the objectively more justifiable Syria. This selectivity reflected the contemporaneous influence of the American Cuban émigré community and then ongoing attempts to engage Damascus in a comprehensive peace settlement with Israel. Yet in some respects these criticisms miss the point of the rogue state concept. It was less an exercise in intellectual rigour than a strategy of mobilisation and justification for American actions and overseas commitments. It also encouraged international cooperation and burden-sharing. The selection of specific targets might cause friction with allies, but those same countries shared fears about issues such as WMDs proliferation and wanted to keep the US multilaterally engaged. Hence, for example, to contain Saddam Hussein a comprehensive international sanctions regime was imposed under UN Security Council resolution 661 – relieved only by the oil for food programme – and multilaterally enforced no-fly zones were established to protect Kurds in southern Iraq and Shiite Muslims in the north.

Leadership of the Gulf War, the shift to comprehensive containment and the emerging emphasis on rogue states all indicated that the Bush administration generally favoured the status quo in the Middle East. This conformed with its strategic conservatism elsewhere and was epitomised by its Gulf War decision to stop short of Baghdad and refrain from forcibly removing Saddam Hussein's regime. In the meantime the Bush administration worked quietly with established partner states in the Middle East and with the Soviet Union/ Russia to address some of the region's other sources of instability. For instance, in January 1992 multilateral talks on Middle Eastern issues were held in Moscow focusing on water resources, the environment, economic development, refugee issues and arms control.[19] Still more significantly the Bush administration sought to capitalise on propitious post-Gulf War conditions to advance the MEPP. Iraq was contained, a Syria-enforced peace in the Lebanon was holding, the PLO had lost its Soviet backing and Israel recognised the implications of its diminished strategic importance in the post-Cold War era. In October 1991, Bush and Gorbachev launched a new initiative and at the Madrid Conference brought together all the major Middle Eastern parties to begin a series of bilateral and multilateral talks aimed at reaching a comprehensive peace settlement. An elaborate multi-track negotiation structure was laid out and hopes of success rose, especially once Yitzhak Rabin's Labour Party was elected in Israel in June 1992.

The Clinton administration reaffirmed existing US Middle Eastern priorities and policies: 'Securing a just, lasting and comprehensive peace between Israel and its neighbours . . . preserving Israel's security and well-being; maintaining security arrangements to preserve stability in the Persian Gulf and commercial access to its resources; combating terrorism and weapons proliferation; assisting U.S. businesses, and promoting political and economic reform.'[20] Rather like in Africa, the Clinton administration talked up the prospects of engaging the region in the global economy, stressed the importance of trade liberalisation and hoped that supporting civil society and promoting economic development would encourage bottom-up reform in authoritarian regimes. Hence, for example, USAID funded programmes in Egypt, Jordan and the Palestinian territories to develop civic groups; funding also went to good-governance schemes in Egypt and to developing industrialisation in Jordan. However, the pattern of US funding suggested that these programmes were designed foremost to shore up key partners such as Saudi Arabia, Egypt and Jordan against domestic discontent and potential challenge from Islamic fundamentalists rather than to effect serious change in the politics of the region.

The prioritisation of stability also ran through the reconstitution of comprehensive containment into 'dual containment'. The Clinton administration's overarching strategy of engagement and enlargement rested on the assumption that enlarging the family of nations committed to democracy, free markets and peace would protect American strategic interests and stabilise the international system. NSA Lake argued that states that chose to remain outside this 'family' were on 'the wrong side of history'. These were the 'rogue' or 'backlash' states, characterised by their promotion of radical ideologies, suppression of basic human rights and a 'siege mentality' that drove them to pursue ambitious and destabilising military programmes, including the development of WMDs and missile delivery systems. The US had a 'special responsibility for developing a strategy to neutralise, contain and, through selective pressure, perhaps even transform these backlash states into constructive members of the international community'.[21]

Classifying Iran and Iraq as rogue states legitimised dual containment in the Middle East, albeit that the Clinton administration regarded these regimes in slightly different ways. It was hoped that pressure would persuade Iran to end its support of international terrorism, its efforts to undermine the MEPP, and its drive to acquire WMDs and the means to deliver them. Saddam Hussein's Iraq was simply to be contained for it was considered irredeemable. The administration initially pursued rigorous containment and isolation policies towards both countries. Comprehensive sanctions against Iraq were routinely renewed and in late 1994 the US airlifted military forces to Kuwait in response to Iraqi forces moving towards the Kuwaiti border. On 30 April 1995 Clinton banned all American economic relations with Iran and the following year Congress passed the ILSA, which provided for extraterritorial sanctions against foreign commercial entities conducting business with Iran and Libya.

The demonisation of Iran and Iraq as rogue states, coupled with memories of the Gulf War and the Iranian hostage crisis, made the costs inherent in dual containment an easy sell to Congress and the American people. However, the strategy soon ran into trouble. Some feared it would push Iran and Iraq into a Faustian pact. More importantly, it depended on a willingness to deploy American troops to combat, which in turn partly depended on the willingness of Middle Eastern countries to afford facilities for such operations – a willingness that often fluctuated in response to US policy towards Israel and the MEPP. Dual containment also demanded that the US keep Iran and Iraq isolated from their neighbours and forge an international consensus on maintaining comprehensive sanctions. The Clinton administration achieved neither of these objectives. European allies favoured constructive engagement with Teheran and disputed the effectiveness of economic sanctions. This undermined unilateral US sanctions, increased the cost to America of maintaining them and, when the Clinton administration sought to offset the latter through the ILSA, inspired a major transatlantic dispute. Soon, dual containment became a strategic cul-de-sac, neither offering a solution to indefinite resource expenditure nor allowing the flexibility to pursue different US objectives in Iran and Iraq.

Increasing domestic and international criticism and American inability to control events on the ground forced a policy shift. Regime change became the objective in Iraq. The administration ruled out large-scale military action to forcibly depose Saddam Hussein but did increasingly seek to undermine him. It resisted pressure from France and Russia especially to rethink Iraqi sanctions. It conducted military strikes to degrade Iraq's military capacity – such as Operation Desert Fox in December 1998 in response to Iraqi obstruction of UN weapons inspectors. And it worked with domestic and exiled opposition groups – including measures such as Clinton's signature in October 1998 of the Iraq Liberation Act to provide up to $97 million of military aid to Iraqi opposition elements. Meantime, with its Iranian policy collapsing and encouraged by the inauguration of the more moderate Mohammed Khatami as Iran's president, the Clinton administration softened its approach to Teheran. It was domestically constrained, especially by Congress, as to how far it could relax economic sanctions, but the administration nevertheless signalled a shift in 1997 by indicating that it would not oppose a planned 2,000-mile pipeline to carry gas from Turkmenistan to Turkey through Iran.[22] The following year it waived extraterritorial sanctions against a large consortium of foreign firms that agreed a deal to develop Iran's natural gas reserves. On 17 June 1998, Secretary of State Albright enunciated as policy the de facto development of differentiated containment, suggesting a roadmap to a normalisation of US–Iranian relations subject to Iran acting upon Khatami's denunciation of terrorism.

The complement to dual containment, and purportedly the cornerstone of the Clinton administration's Middle Eastern policy, was a resolution of the Israeli–Palestinian conflict. Here too levels of engagement and policy coherence oscillated between benign neglect and diplomatic overdrive. Initially it did little but strengthen US relations with Israel and neglect the peace process. Secret negotiations between the PLO and Israel, mediated by Norway rather than the US, provided the breakthrough that enabled Clinton to preside in September 1993 over a momentous meeting at the White House between PLO Chairman Yasser Arafat and Yitzhak Rabin. In the Oslo Accord the PLO acknowledged Israel's right to exist in peace in return for Israel recognising the PLO as the official representative of the Palestinian people and allowing Palestinians in the Gaza Strip and Jericho on the West Bank to begin self-government. This was followed in 1994 by another historic meeting at the White House that saw Rabin and King Hussein of Jordan normalise Israeli–Jordanian relations.

Clinton then surprisingly stood back from the MEPP, declaring in March 1994 that 'the United States should refrain from intervening in these peace talks'.[23] Despite the conclusion of the Oslo II agreement in September 1995 momentum predictably stalled without sufficient US prodding amid political disagreement and the activities of extremist groups such as Hezbollah, Hamas and Islamic Jihad. In November 1995, Yitzhak Rabin was assassinated for his part in the peace process and his replacement, Shimon Peres, put security before peace. In January 1996, the Israeli secret service conducted a highly incendiary assassination in Gaza of 'The Engineer', Yehiya Ayash – a legendary Islamic terrorist responsible for the deaths of dozens of Israelis. Peres responded to waves of retaliatory bus bombings with both the harshest blockade ever on Palestinians in the West Bank and Gaza and, in April 1996, 'Operation Grapes of Wrath', a military operation against civilian areas in southern Lebanon. The aim was to punish Hezbollah fighters but the ensuing massacre appalled world opinion and tarnished the US by association with Israel.

The Clinton administration belatedly moved to rescue the peace process. To stabilise the security environment it pledged intelligence and technical assistance to Israeli efforts to combat bombings and offered resources to the Palestinian Authority (PA) to help professionalise its security services so that it could better control terrorist activities within its territories. In 1997–98 Clinton held two summits with Peres's successor, Benjamin Netanyahu, and two with Arafat. Secretary of State Albright visited Israel and the PA three times and met senior officials elsewhere at least six times. Middle East Envoy Dennis Ross shuttled back and forth to the Middle East at least seven times.[24] Constant 'hand-holding' finally brought Arafat and Netanyahu to revive the MEPP with the signature on 23 October 1998 of the Wye Memorandum in Washington. However, when Ehud Barak replaced Netanyahu and failed to implement the Wye agreement the US response was again feeble.

The pinnacle of Clinton's personal investment in the MEPP, and a complete reversal of his earlier hands-off approach, was his convocation on 11 July 2000 of a trilateral summit at Camp David. This followed an accord signed by Barak and Arafat at Sharm el-Sheikh on 4 September 1999 that promised a framework agreement and then a full peace treaty within the year. However, 14 days of negotiation failed to deliver an agreement and the blame game began. Clinton and Barak blamed Arafat and the Palestinians. There was some truth in this, but it was not the whole story. Barak adopted a take-it-or-leave-it approach and Clinton apparently did little to moderate it. Clinton also made matters worse by searching for an administration-defining final settlement rather than nudging the process forward. Moreover, precedent suggested to both Israelis and Palestinians that US rhetorical pressure on Israel to meet commitments and make concessions – such as settlement policy and negotiated Israeli withdrawals – was rarely followed by action, due not least to the power of the US pro-Israeli lobby led by the American-Israel Public Affairs Committee and the Christian Religious Right.[25]

Clinton left office with the US firmly embedded as the Middle Eastern hegemon and having largely preserved a status quo that seemingly suited

American vested interests. The rogue state concept had also rallied domestic and international constituencies against, essentially, enemies of American regional interests. Yet core objectives remained unfulfilled and strategy seemed increasingly adrift and event driven. Saddam Hussein still clung to power, international support for Iraqi sanctions was crumbling, and indigenous groupings seemed incapable of overthrowing the regime. The thaw in US–Iranian relations was potential rather than material, especially once fears grew that its WMDs programme was further developed than originally thought: Clinton had responded by signing the Iran non-proliferation act on 14 March 2000. The MEPP had collapsed amid the post-Camp David blame game and the onset in September 2000 of the al-Aqsa intifada. American standing in the Muslim world had fallen as a consequence of perceived double-standards vis-à-vis US treatment of Iraq and Israel, Clinton's cruise missile strikes in 1998 against alleged terrorist targets in Afghanistan and Sudan, and alleged pro-Israeli bias in the peace process. In turn, terrorism was an as yet under-addressed but rising threat to US interests and personnel – as evidenced by the bombings of US military barracks at Al-Khobar in June 1996 and the attack on the USS *Cole* in Aden on 12 October 2000.

The George W. Bush administration initially demonstrated general policy continuity but leading neo-conservative advisers and officials had long been dismayed by Clinton's allegedly weak handling of Middle Eastern policy and, especially, by Saddam Hussein's continuing grasp on power. 9/11 provided the catalyst that enabled them to operationalise preconceived ideas. The result was an astonishing reversal of established American Middle Eastern policy and of things for which the Bush administration professed to stand for and against. An administration sceptical of nation-building and peacekeeping commitments in the Balkans and elsewhere turned volte-face to attempt precisely this in Afghanistan and Iraq. An administration that promised to rectify its predecessor's alleged confusion of foreign policy and morality prosecuted a war in Iraq in the name of American national security and subsequently reinvented it as a war for Wilsonian liberalism. And a conservative Republican administration launched an unprecedented and potentially high-risk assault on the status quo in the Middle East and on 60 years of American foreign policy.

Five key facets of the Bush administration's new approach to the Middle East are: shock and awe; a confrontational approach to rogue states; an uncompromising embrace of democratisation and the market; an emerging emphasis under Secretary of State Condoleezza Rice on public diplomacy; and the Israeli–Palestinian conflict. The mighty American military machine easily delivered shock and awe once unbound by 9/11 and the emerging doctrine of preventative strike. 9/11 and connections drawn between the Afghan Taliban leadership and al-Qaeda allowed the Bush administration to steer retaliatory action through the UN and its allies to rally behind the US position and to support efforts to counter Osama bin Laden's claim of the West waging war upon Islam. The Afghan campaign began on 7 October 2001 and employed a potent combination of precision weapons, indigenous allies and special operational forces. The Taliban was rapidly routed and by December

2001 the Bonn accord had been signed under UN auspices to establish a roadmap to the establishment of a stable and democratic Afghanistan. An Afghan Interim Administration was established under the leadership of Hamid Karzai; an International Security Assistance Force was deployed to assist stabilisation; NGOs increased relief activities; and in Tokyo in January 2002 the international community pledged $4–5 billion of aid over five years. A new democratic constitution was subsequently agreed and, on 9 October 2004, landmark, if flawed, presidential elections were held. National elections to elect a lower house of parliament followed in September 2005, with one-quarter of the 249 seats being reserved for women.

No sooner had American and mujahidin guns dispatched the Taliban than Bush locked Saddam Hussein in US sights. Military planning began in November 2001 and Bush made the decision in principle to remove Hussein forcibly as early as January 2002.[26] In March 2003 the military campaign began, despite failure to secure specific UN approval of military intervention, profound transatlantic divisions, deep disquiet in the Arab Middle East and a worldwide popular protest involving an estimated 10 million people. A barrage of cruise missiles and thousands of satellite-guided bombs decimated Iraqi defences and within two weeks US troops reached Baghdad. The capital quickly succumbed and Saddam Hussein fled, eventually being captured in December. A military occupation was established and run by a Coalition Provisional Authority (CPA), which subsequently appointed and delegated limited power to the Iraq Interim Governing Council. On 28 June 2004 a transitional constitution came into effect, the CPA and the Governing Council were disbanded and restricted sovereignty was transferred to Iyad Allawi's Iraqi interim government. A new government came into power in January 2005 as a result of elections and a referendum was set for 15 October 2005 on a controversial new constitution. Security, however, still depended heavily on American-dominated coalition forces.

The Bush administration's more confrontational approach to the Middle East's rogue states was evident in the way that it swept away Clinton's enfeebled strategy of differentiated containment with a torrent of dubious conflations between rogue states, WMDs proliferation and international terrorism. The President told a joint session of Congress in September 2001 that the US would regard as hostile any state that harboured or supported terrorism. He extended this in his 2002 State of the Union address to include unfriendly states seeking to develop WMDs. In the same speech he named Iran, Iraq and North Korea as representatives of an 'axis of evil'. In December 2002, NSC Presidential Directive-17 added Libya and Syria to the list of rogue states allegedly developing WMDs and sponsoring terrorist activities. Iraq was the vanguard of a new interventionist Middle Eastern policy but shock and awe sought also to persuade other potential targets to amend their ways. As Richard Perle, Assistant Secretary of Defense in the Reagan administration, put it, 'We could deliver a short message, a two-word message . . . You're next.'[27]

The message had impact. Syria, for instance, moderated its position as the Bush administration accused it of supporting terrorist groups including

Hezbollah and Hamas, of sheltering Iraqi insurgents, of possessing chemical and biological weapons, and of facilitating Iranian assistance to extremist groups in Lebanon and the Palestinian territories. Newly surrounded by American occupied or allied states, Damascus closed its borders – officially at least – with Iraq, toned down its anti-American rhetoric and in 2005 withdrew its armed forces from Lebanon. Iran was less easily swayed and Bush administration policy towards it has been inconsistent, unconvincing and, to date, largely unsuccessful. In June 2001 it issued an indictment identifying Saudi Hezbollah as responsible for the June 1996 bombing of US military barracks at Al-Khobar and claimed that Iran had inspired, supported and directed Hezbollah organisations in Bahrain, Kuwait, Lebanon and Saudi Arabia since the early 1980s.[28] In 2002 it signalled that it had lost patience with Khatami's reforms and advanced a strengthened combined WMDs, proliferation and terrorism case against Teheran. The 9/11 Commission identified contacts between the Iranian clerical regime and al-Qaeda members. Much play was made of the interception in early 2002 of an arms shipment from Iran that was destined for the Palestinian leadership. Washington also began to criticise Iran for promoting Islamic fundamentalist groups in post-invasion Afghanistan and Iraq.

On 2 August 2002 Zalmay Khalilizad, senior White House official with responsibility for Iran, explained the administration's approach as 'a dual track policy based on moral clarity: tell the world specifically what is destructive and unacceptable about Iran's behaviour: sponsorship of terror; pursuit of weapons of mass destruction; and oppression of the clearly expressed desires of the Iranian people for freedom and democracy while laying out a positive vision of partnership and support for the Iranian people'.[29] The administration has been much better at demonising Iran than developing positive support of either the Iranian people or the international community. For much of its first term this produced merely a US–Iranian stand-off reminiscent of the predifferentiated containment era. Sabre-rattling directed at Iran also alarmed American allies and exacerbated an impression that the Bush administration was intent upon a crusade against Islam. In 2005 the administration swung behind EU attempts to incentivise Iran into reform and abandoning its nuclear programme. However, this is probably less a conversion to soft power multilateralism than a tactical shift driven by preoccupation with Iraq, a lack of alternatives and the hope that if talks break down the Europeans might finally join a hardline approach to Teheran.

The third component of Bush administration Middle Eastern policy is a conscious and overt break with 60 years of American foreign policy. In November 2003 Bush argued that 'it would be reckless to accept the status quo' because for 'as long as the Middle East remains a place where freedom does not flourish, it will remain a place of stagnation, resentment, and violence ready for export'.[30] He also rejected America's traditional trade of stability for tolerating oppression: 'Long-standing ties often led us to overlook the faults of local elites ... this bargain did not bring us stability or make us safe. It merely bought time, while problems festered and ideologies of violence took hold.'[31] The new prescription was a healthy dose of democratisation and zealous embrace of the market to drain popular support from extremist groups. Bush seemingly dismissed at a stroke the clash of civilisations thesis and the perceived incompatibilities of democracy and Islam that throughout the Cold War underpinned the so-called 'Middle Eastern exceptionalism' and justified the US collaborating with autocracies.

Bush encapsulated this policy revolution in his announcement of the Reaganesque 'Forward Strategy for Freedom'[32] on 6 November 2003, which foresaw political and economic reform advancing hand-in-hand across the Middle East. Some groundwork was in place. On 12 December 2002 the US–Middle East Partnership Initiative was established to promote education reform, private sector development, civil society, rule of law and economic opportunity. This was organised around four pillars of economic, political, educational and women's empowerment and designed to include governments, academic institutions, the private sector and NGOs. The region was also eligible for the MCA programme and in May 2003 Bush proposed the establishment of a US–Middle East Free Trade Area by 2013. In June 2004 the G-8 agreed a 'Partnership for Progress and a Common Future with the Broader Middle East and North Africa'. Initiatives therein included democracy assistance dialogue, promoting education reform, training in microfinance, promotion of entrepreneurship, developing measures to encourage investment and a 'Forum for the Future' that brings together the G-8 and regional partners.

An emerging emphasis on public diplomacy to win Middle Eastern hearts and minds has complemented these initiatives. It would be an enormous challenge in the best of circumstances to convince Middle Eastern regimes and peoples that, after 60 years of supporting autocratic rule in exchange for regional stability, America had suddenly changed. This task was made much harder by the invasion of Iraq, which destroyed the 1990s impression of the US as a relatively benign regional hegemon. And America's reputation was further tarnished by a series of disastrous events and scandals – including failure to find WMDs in Iraq, heavy-handed counter-insurgency operations and high-profile American human rights violations against Iraqis. In a heavily mediatised world this has, in the Bush administration's view, provided an opportunity to those who deliberately misrepresent or misinterpret American policy and contributed to a disconnection between American policy and message. It is consequently developing an office of global communications in the White House and a rapid response unit designed to counter 'misinformation and misinterpretation' of US policies and to enhance 'information channels' in the Middle East. These measures echo the Cold War preoccupation with sending signals and messages and include increased Voice of America broadcasting and a new Middle East television network called Alhurra – Arabic for 'the free one'.

This leaves the MEPP as the fifth element of the Bush administration's Middle East strategy. Bush showed interest only once 9/11 allowed the Israel–Palestine conflict to be seen as encouraging terrorism and hatred of Israel's Western backers. His response was potentially a significant step forward. Bush became the first US president to articulate support for a two-state solution with an independent Palestinian state in the West Bank and Gaza Strip contiguous with Israel.[33] In September 2002, together with other Quartet members (the EU, UN and Russia) and following on from UN Security Council resolution 242, the US unveiled a performance-based and goal-driven roadmap. There would be three phases, progress from one to the next being contingent upon fulfilment of a series of conditions and events and with the ultimate objective a comprehensive settlement by 2005.

The commitment of the Bush administration to the MEPP should not, though, be overstated. The surprising speed with which the roadmap was developed owed much to its prior European authorship.[34] In practice the administration's approach has been even less balanced than its predecessor, owing not least to the combined influence of neo-conservatives, Christian fundamentalists and the Israel lobby. Bush effected a major pro-Israeli shift in American policy by accepting, during the 2004 presidential election campaign, the legitimacy of major Israeli settlements in east Jerusalem and the West Bank.[35] His administration continued to blame the Palestinians for the collapse of the Camp David talks and largely accepted Israeli Prime Minister Ariel Sharon's conflation of Palestinian resistance and terrorism. Indeed, Bush effectively made Palestinian regime change a prerequisite for progress on the roadmap by declaring in 2002 that Arafat was an unacceptable negotiating partner. Furthermore, he has thus far largely failed to realise his pledge to invest political capital during his second term to make a Palestinian state a reality, despite Arafat's death and the election in January 2005 of Mahmoud Abbas as head of the PA, someone far more acceptable to the US than Arafat ever was. Sharon's disengagement from Gaza in 2005 was largely unilateral and US efforts to link it to the roadmap have been low-key at best. In the meantime the US emphasis on Israeli security continues with Bush offering the PA the assistance of General William Ward to help restructure its security services and Condoleezza Rice stressing the PA's need to 'tackle the infrastructure of terrorism'.[36]

The Bush administration's record in the Middle East is a complex mixture of grand ideas, inadequate planning, unforeseen consequences, unknown destinations and controversy. Saddam Hussein's removal was the centre-piece of its decision to rearrange the politics of the region but it was horribly mistaken in thinking that it could invade Iraq without creating massive and intractable problems. It was not fanciful to believe that conventional military victory would come quickly, but it was to believe that armed resistance would be brief, that Iraqis would welcome liberation, that a new Iraqi regime could be quickly installed and that ex-post-facto international consensus would emerge as a result of success on the ground and proof positive that Saddam Hussein had WMDs. American moral authority was strong when Bush struck at the Taliban in Afghanistan. It subsequently ran into the Middle Eastern sands due to US failures to bring the international community behind its invasion of Iraq, to find WMDs there, and to observe what it preached for the defence of rights and rule of law. The controversial detention practices in Guantanamo, human rights abuses at Abu Ghraib and refusal to sign up to the ICC damned the US in the eyes of many. Democratisation is an attractive strategy, a US–Middle East Free Trade Area might progressively reduce the attraction of extremist politics and strengthen US influence through socialisation and the inherent hub-and-spoke arrangement, and to its credit the administration has not absolved traditional US allies from its pressure to reform. In June 2005 Condoleezza Rice welcomed demands for political reform in Egypt and Saudi Arabia, and hailed as 'impatient patriots' pro-democracy people in Baghdad, Beruit, Riyadh, Ramallah, Amman, Teheran and Cairo.[37] It is doubtful, though, that the surge for American-style democratic reform is as strong or as widespread as the Bush administration would like to believe. Bahrain's experiment with political liberalisation in 2002 was marred by the closure of the country's leading human rights organisation and the imprisonment of its leader. The new constitution in Qatar conferred some greater political rights upon the people in 2004 but also institutionalised the absolute power of the emir and his family. Iran has seen a recent tightening of conservative control and, although a step forward, the conduct of Egypt's first contested presidential election in September 2005 fell far below accepted international standards.

Furthermore, basing the 'Forward Strategy for Freedom' on democratisation and economic liberalisation exposes the US afresh to charges of exporting the American model and of hypocrisy as it continues to deal with autocratic regimes in the seemingly higher priority of anti-terrorism. For instance, to secure success in Afghanistan the US embraced two powerful dictators, Islam Karimov of Uzbekistan and Pervez Musharraf of Pakistan. The latter was also vital in dismantling Abdul Qadeer Khan's network marketing nuclear weapons components to countries including Iran. It has also to be questioned whether democratisation and the focus on civil society and economic liberalisation as agents of reform is the best strategy for remaking the Middle East or a headline-grabbing and politically expedient initiative. External pressure for democratisation might have quick surface effects and therefore deliver political and public relations advantages. Alternatives such as modernisation and human rights advocacy are slower and therefore less likely either to play well in American domestic politics or create the impression of active US leadership. However, these approaches are certainly less antagonistic and arguably more effective. US interest in democratisation diverges from the interests of most of the region's regimes, and significant changes in Middle Eastern culture and society are probably needed before democracy can take root. For instance, unless civil society is first liberalised – freedom of expression, association and so on – then elections might simply maintain privileged groupings in power, gift them an added veneer of legitimacy and assist them in co-opting civic groups into existing rather than reformed structures. It is possible too that radical Islam might consolidate its position rather than atrophy in open elections without prior changes in society and human expectation. Consider, for example, the political success of Hamas in the Palestinian territories and that Syrian withdrawal from Lebanon creates a vacuum that might be filled by sectarian nationalism and enable Hezbollah to come into the political process without first surrendering its arms.

Finally, it remains uncertain whether the Bush administration can achieve the nation-building in Afghanistan and Iraq that it initially wanted to extract the US from in the Balkans. Surface democracy seemingly shone when millions of Afghans lined up on 9 October 2004 to vote in the historic election but Afghanistan's economic, political and security realities suggest a long haul ahead, for which an Iraq-distracted Bush administration has lost appetite. Large parts of Afghanistan beyond Kabul remain unsafe and effectively ruled by warlords. The US is complicit in this because it has relied on the same mujahidin militias – many little less extreme than the Taliban – that wrought havoc upon the country between the USSR's withdrawal and the Taliban government's arrival in 1996. Also, despite large aid pledges, the Afghan government still struggles to finance essentials. Regional warlords withhold customs revenues and foreign assistance funds predominantly UN operations and specific reconstruction projects. Kabul's limited reach is indicated by a limited Taliban reassertion in the south-east especially and by considerable increases in opium production. Indeed, in 2003 the opium harvest was worth over $1 billion – around 25% of the country's GDP[38] and Afghanistan risks degenerating into a Colombia-style narco-state.

The situation in Iraq is even worse, despite the massive commitment of American personnel, equipment and money. At the time of writing the Bush administration had 140,000 troops in Iraq, had already spent $250 billion on military operations and reconstruction, and was spending a further $6 billion per month on basic running costs. If American troops remain for a further five years estimated costs are around $1.3 trillion.[39] The administration seems to have grievously underestimated the political and religious complexity of Iraq, the strength and resilience of the insurgency, the difficulties in preventing foreign fighters and arms seeping through the country's porous borders, and the sheer scale of the task of rebuilding the instruments of governance and law and order. Conversely, it appears to have overestimated the willingness of the international community to finance and assist rebuilding Iraq. The latter has not been helped by controversial US distribution of reconstruction contracts and the very nature of its intervention. Even close allies have begun to desert – Spain, for example, pulled military forces out of Iraq following Aznar's election defeat by Zapatero in the aftermath of the Madrid train bombings in March 2004. Political progress in Iraq is therefore painfully slow, violence and insecurity are rife and an exit strategy is difficult to discern. Moreover, Bush's 'for as long as it takes' stance is increasingly difficult to sustain as bombings and firefights in Iraq regularly fill television screens worldwide, the American body and injury counts rise and events such as Hurricane Katrina, which devastated New Orleans in September 2005, lead the American people to ask why so much is being sacrificed in Iraq when the US has so many problems at home.

Conclusion

The Cold War's end reinforced rather than changed the different relative importance attached by the US to Africa and the Middle East. American policy towards the former has remained driven by considerations of primary products, economic opportunity and desire to maintain relations with key preferred partners. To this has been added a forced spasmodic engagement consequent upon Africa's numerous heavily media-exposed humanitarian crises. Clinton's good intentions for Africa struggled after the Somalia débâcle, and without a strong lobby in Washington it was all too easy to let African policy drift and take solace in the hope that economic development and indigenous activities would slowly ameliorate things. George W. Bush has better resourced Africa policy but the focus is less Africa-centred than on the value of certain nations and collections of countries to the war on terror.

The contrast in the levels of political, economic and military engagement dedicated to Africa and the Middle East by all post-Cold War American administrations is stark. America has continued to look to the UN and other nations to deal with Africa while becoming more firmly entrenched than ever as the Middle Eastern hegemon. Since Somalia, the US has sought to develop surrogates and eschew even peacekeeping duties in Africa but in the Middle East it has undertaken enforcement action in support of post-Gulf War UN Security Council resolutions, fought two wars in Iraq and one in Afghanistan, and complemented its 'over-the-horizon' military presence with expanded regional deployment. And, although George W. Bush has slightly amended his view that Africa does not register in US strategic interests, he has pledged a generational commitment to the Middle East and mortgaged both US credibility and the war on terror to a successful rearrangement of the region's economic and political structures – starting with somehow making Iraq a triumph of nation-building.

Finally, whereas it is difficult to discern a post-Cold War US Africa strategy there have been numerous strategies developed for the Middle East: engagement of Iraq, comprehensive containment, dual containment, differentiated containment and the Forward Strategy for Freedom. The common denominators of the first four are that they were designed primarily to preserve a status quo considered to be in US interests and that they were all qualified failures. The last is a sudden rejection of the status quo and is both incomplete and a monumental gamble that unleashing agents of political and economic reform will deliver a Middle East more rather than less amenable to US interests. Indeed, it is difficult to avoid the conclusion that the George W. Bush administration is, to an extent at least, making up strategy as it goes along. A war of national security in Iraq became a war of Wilsonian liberalism. The Forward Strategy for Freedom was announced only once US forces got bogged down in Iraq and realisation dawned that US power alone might be insufficient to remake the region. Engagement with the pivotal issue of the Israeli–Palestinian conflict only began once 9/11 allowed it to be seen as a part of the war on terror. And the emphasis on strengthened public diplomacy only came after the humiliation of finding no WMDs in Iraq and damaging scandals about US detainee practices and human rights abuses by American troops.

12 The Western Hemisphere and Asia in the post-Cold War world

What defined US policy in these two important regions? In the Western Hemisphere and in Asia, as elsewhere, the end of the Cold War reduced the preoccupation with narrow security issues. More emphasis was placed on trade and economics and the development of democracy, though these also took on a security perspective, especially in the Western Hemisphere, as successive administrations came to view prosperity and democracy overseas as closely interlinked with US security. How appropriate and successful were such assumptions? The end of the Cold War also removed from the policy shelf readymade justifications for military interventions. Nevertheless, they continued on a regular basis in the Western Hemisphere, sometimes with highly traditional justifications as with Panama, and with new patterns of justification as with Haiti. Did these interventions conform to a coherent policy? In Asia there was also a concern with spreading the free market and democracy, but other serious challenges also confronted the US. China's growing economic might and a commensurate growth in its military capabilities worried the Pentagon and has been the cause of much speculation about future relations.

Academics, such as Mearsheimer, have warned that China poses a serious military and economic challenge to US hegemony in the twenty-first century, but are these warnings justified? North Korea's nuclear threat has been of more immediate and pressing concern. Unlike US strategy for dealing with rogue states with the potential to develop WMDs in the Middle East, US policy for North Korea has been almost a model of multilateral cooperation, embracing Japan, China, South Korea and Russia. Should this, rather than the unilateralism so evident in policy towards Iraq, provide the model for US foreign policy? Differences with Japan, America's most important ally in Asia, have elicited an array of often rather contradictory approaches to try to move the alliance forward. George H. Bush's vomiting into the lap of Prime Minister Miyazawa Kiichi in January 1992, at a state function in Tokyo, cannot be marked up as a diplomatic success for that strategy, but, despite the embarrassment, relations were generally good during his term in office. They deteriorated under a more economically aggressive Clinton administration, and then warmed again as George W. Bush and Prime Minister Junichiro Koizumi established good personal relations. But, as Japan emerges from a decade of recession and stagnation, will personal friendships be enough to carry the US–Japanese relationship forward constructively?

The Americas: military interventions and free trade panaceas

The end of the Cold War brought little change to US–Canadian relations. This is noteworthy because they are probably the most extensive in the world with a transborder flow of over \$1 billion a day in goods, services and investment income, with more than 200 million border crossings every year, and with the closest of defence cooperation, including, since 1958, continental air defence within the framework of the North American Aerospace Defense Command (NORAD). Most significantly, there are few high-profile foreign policy issues between Canada and the US. Minor territorial boundary disputes rumble on from the nineteenth century, and periodic trade problems erupt over timber and agricultural trade, and Canadian cultural restrictions on US films and magazines. But, more importantly, the 1989 Canadian-American Free Trade Agreement blazed the trail for broader free trade initiatives that led to the North American Free Trade Agreement (NAFTA) and other multilateral developments. Canada maintains its own identity, an independent line on international issues – it opposed the non-UN-sanctioned invasion of Iraq in 2003 – and is generally more supportive of UN norms and multilateralism than the US, but relations are so close that the thought of disruptive trouble between the two is unthinkable.

Latin America is a more complex challenge. The US talked much about economic development during the Cold War, but, caught within the constraints of containment, too often it collaborated with right-wing dictatorships and launched military interventions against what it deemed to be communist threats. Such collaboration and intervention compromised America's position and the effectiveness of economic help, and often prevented the emergence of political regimes that could have nurtured appropriate environments for development. After the Cold War, America's ability to use its soft power more effectively in the Western Hemisphere was greatly enhanced. Anti-Americanism and the opprobrium of the term 'gringo' diminished, the US became more discriminating about Latin American regimes, a stronger coincidence of interests emerged, and a new page turned, though it still contained some well-established themes from the past. Cold War Manichean dichotomies began gradually to fade and the fading was helped by the defeat of the Sandinistas in the Nicaraguan elections in 1990. Latin American regimes generally, not just those with previous communist leanings, now had more room to manoeuvre and many recognised their own failures and shortcomings of the 1970s and 1980s. They became more amenable to engaging with the US and working with it to achieve prosperity and stable democratic governments, but with the emphasis on increased trade rather than aid. Political cooperation was also galvanised, most notably between traditional rivals Brazil and Argentina. They reduced defence expenditure and the 1990 Foz do Iguazu declaration terminated their nuclear weapons programmes. However, as important as these developments were, it was and is economics that holds centre stage throughout the region.

Latin America has remained poor and, more significantly politically, the region of the world with the largest differential between rich and poor. This recipe for political instability, crime and disorder has posed a difficult challenge. However, even before the 1992 presidential election and Clinton's aphorism 'it's the economy stupid', President George H. Bush grasped the reality that international economic issues would help turn the key for both doors of prosperity and security in Latin America. Contemporary migration patterns helped to reinforce this conviction as people from Latin America poured into the US legally and illegally in search of a decent life: Latin America accounted for a mere 4% of emigrants arriving in the US in 1920, but by 1996 that figure was 50% and still rising.

Impetus for change seemed to be developing fast. In 1991 $40 billion of private investment flowed into Latin America, twice the amount of the previous year, and in June 1991 the Santiago Declaration gave the OAS a new lease of life, moving it away from some of the anti-communist security clichés of the Cold War and committing itself to the protection of democracy, free markets and inter-American cooperation. The search for freer trade and economic growth, and through that security and stronger democracies, became a major theme of US post-Cold War policy towards Latin America. Those policies were generally reinforced by 9/11.

The early 1990s saw measurable economic improvement in the region and an increase in, and a strengthening of, regimes trying to embrace democracy. Pinochet's dictatorship in Chile came to an end and centre-left governments steered the country back to prosperity with an average annual growth rate of 6% in the 1990s. In 1994, President Clinton inaugurated a series of Summits of the Americas, which provided a hemisphere-wide framework for focusing on economic and development issues. Nevertheless, in several countries the improvements of the early 1990s were short-lived. Monetary and economic problems reappeared in mid-decade, tensions mounted – particularly between the US and Venezuela which criticised US policies and adopted a populist left-leaning reform programme. Political and civil turmoil has troubled Bolivia and Peru over recent years and 1998–2002 was a lost half decade for Latin American economies. Thus fledgling democracies still flounder amid political turmoil, massive external debt and enormous disparities in wealth and land ownership – in 2005, 5% of the population still owned 80% of the land in Venezuela. And, as if man-made problems were not enough, Latin America is also often plagued by natural disasters, such as the hurricane that ripped catastrophically through Honduras at 208 miles per hour in 1998.

Nevertheless, positive economic change gained momentum again in 2002 as Chinese and Indian demand for raw materials from Latin America expanded, and tighter fiscal policies and floating exchange rates encouraged exports. The region in the period 2002–05 experienced an average growth of 4% a year.[1] 9/11 re-emphasised security priorities for the US and impacted on its policies, but the clock did not turn back to Cold War days. The US goal of prosperity through free trade and targeted aid to establish a virtuous circle of democratic regimes committed to the same principles as the US and with the same, or similar, security priorities continued.

Free trade abides as the key US foreign policy prescription for the Western Hemisphere, but, even under this dispensation, desires to promote democracy and enhance American security, construed more broadly than containment, are never far distant from American minds. Problems with communism and fellow travellers linger on symbolically in Cuba, and in more violent form with guerrillas such as the Revolutionary Armed Forces of Colombia (FARC), and instability and disorder continue to beckon US intervention, as in Panama and Haiti with military force, in Colombia with military aid and advisers, and in Venezuela with political pressures. However, the overriding rationale for intervention is no longer communism, but populism, anti-democratic disorder, economic instability, humanitarian concerns, crime and narco-terrorism. The story is complex and US policy lacks the consistency of Cold War certainties: in Panama US intervention was of a traditional kind; in Haiti it was not, as the US deferred more to international norms than had ever been the case in the Cold War.

Interventions in the post-Cold War era

In Panama, the problem was General Manuel Noriega, a one-time recruit of the CIA when George H. Bush had been Director in the 1970s. Noriega in the late 1980s was now no friend of the US. In 1989, he clung to power regardless of US sanctions and defeat in the May national election. Bush was both personally embarrassed by Noriega and anxious to signal that, despite the end of the Cold War and President Carter's Panama Canal treaty, the US would still not tolerate challenges to its predominance in the Western Hemisphere.[2] He was also eager to lay to rest the Vietnam Syndrome. Deputy Secretary of State Lawrence Eagleburger warned Noriega that action would be taken against his 'illegal' government unless it stood down by 1 September. When this did not happen, the US itself duly embarked on what many saw as illegal action. In October, America backed a coup to depose Noriega. It failed. On 15 December, Panama declared a state of war with the US. The Bush administration, after a car carrying American officers was shot at, began to consider what later became known as Operation Just Cause.

In the discussions about what the US should do, Colin Powell records that 'George Bush sat like a patron on a bar stool coolly observing a brawl while his advisers went hard at it'.[3] NSA Brent Scowcroft wanted to know possible casualty numbers and what would happen if Noriega escaped. No one could answer. But it was anticipated that a lot of 'real estate would get chewed up' and that there would be 'chaos' in the early stages. In other words, there was no guarantee that if American forces went in they would be able to control the situation. Powell noted:

The key issue remained whether we had sufficient provocation to act. We had reasons – Noriega's contempt for democracy, his drug trafficking and indictment, the death of the American Marine, the threat to our treaty rights to the canal with this unreliable figure ruling Panama. And, unspoken, there was George Bush's personal antipathy to Noriega, a third-rate dictator thumbing his nose at the United States. I shared that distaste.

. . . The questions continued thick and fast, until it started to look as if we were drifting away from the decision at hand. . . . But then Bush, after everyone had had his say, gripped the arms of his chair and rose. 'Okay, let's do it,' he said. 'The hell with it.'[4]

So much for careful and objective application of the rules of engagement! Old fashioned hegemony over the Western Hemisphere and the long US tradition of unilateral military action there tell us more about the invasion of Panama than the new security agenda, the rules of engagement for regional security crises, democratic enlargement and the desirability of multilateral operations. But then is this really surprising because, for all his talk of the New World Order, Bush remained stubbornly conservative. The invasion involved the deployment of 25,000 troops, six days of fighting and contravention of both OAS and UN charters. The OAS and the UN General Assembly condemned the invasion and called for the immediate withdrawal of American troops. This appeared to be yet another case of intervention as and when necessary in conformity with the long-standing Corollary to the Monroe Doctrine and habitual Cold War behaviour. However, there were differences. In particular there was no possibility of automatically invoking anti-communism as a blanket justification and, as the tensions of the Cold War dissipated and the widespread acknowledgement of common interests between the US and Latin American countries noted above strengthened, American inhibitions about intervention grew. Those inhibitions were strengthened later by the tragedy in Mogadishu, Somalia. Significantly, Clinton intervened in Haiti multilaterally not unilaterally and in conformity with the wishes and authorisation of the UN.

Haiti has had a turbulent history from the slave rebellions of the eighteenth century to the chaos and disorder of recent times. After elections in December 1990, Jean-Bertrand Aristide in February 1991 became only the second-ever president of Haiti to come to power through any semblance of democratic choice. Seven months later, his fragile democracy was overturned by the military and the island fell into disarray with paramilitaries bringing fear and brutality to the people. The US was swift to condemn the overthrow of Aristide, but President Bush was equally swift to pursue a far less noble policy in respect of 41,000 fleeing refugees whom the US Coast Guard picked up between 1991 and 1992: he ordered their return to Haiti. Clinton lambasted this approach as 'cruel' and inhumane, yet, once in office, he acted little differently until pressures for action mounted. The Executive Director of Trans-Africa, Randall Robinson, went on hunger strike to publicise the plight of refugees, the Black Caucus in Congress took Haiti up as an issue, and adverse publicity increased because of the fleeing refugees. Other developments outside the US also accelerated the momentum for action. The OAS and the UN condemned the coup and economic sanctions were applied. Measures were taken to pressurise the military government led by General Cédras to stand down, but in October 1993 when the USS *Harlan County* tried to dock in Port-au-Prince, as part of the campaign to remove Cédras, it was prevented by protesting paramilitaries and had to beat an embarrassing retreat. In July 1994 the Security Council took the unprecedented step of authorising the US to lead a forceful intervention. Clinton, for the first time ever, had a UN sanction for the use of US force in the Western Hemisphere. An interesting turn of events now followed. As substantial US military forces approached Haiti, ex-President Jimmy Carter led a negotiating team comprised of General Colin Powell and Senator Sam Nunn to attempt to resolve the crisis peacefully. With less than 36 hours to go before the invasion, the military government remained truculent and defiant. It was not until Powell spoke as one military man to another that Cédras stood down:

> I began ticking off on my fingers: two aircraft carriers, two and a half infantry divisions, twenty thousand troops, helicopter gun ships, tanks, artillery. I kept it up, watching the Haitians' spirits sink under the weight of the power I was describing.[5]

Once again the US had flexed its military muscle in the Western Hemisphere, but this time with the authorisation of the UN and the backing of the OAS. To some at least this seemed to be in line with, and an affirmation of, the Santiago Declaration, and an augury of less arrogant future US behaviour in the Western Hemisphere.

Whether or not the US has become more respectful of the sovereignty of its neighbours and more inhibited about interventions is difficult to judge. If the democratic credentials of Latin American countries strengthen and economic stability and growth continue to take hold, then one might expect US intervention to become less necessary and certainly more difficult, especially without OAS and UN authorisation. And Clinton's intervention in Haiti may thus be seen as an important precedent here. On the other hand, the 2002 Bush Doctrine asserts the right of the US to intervene preventatively anywhere to counter terrorism and WMDs and the 2004 episode in the Aristide saga was not propitious. After standing down as president in 1996, as constitutionally required, he was re-elected in 2000. However, political fragmentation and schism, accompanied by ongoing violence and rebellion, placed him out of favour with the US. He was denounced by right-wing members of the US Congress for consorting with anti-democratic elements and narco-traffickers, and in February 2004 his regime was roundly condemned by both the US and France. Early on 29 February, Aristide was flown out of the country to the Central African Republic on a US plane. According to official American accounts he went voluntarily to exile. According to Aristide and unofficial US accounts, he was effectively, if temporarily, kidnapped by US armed forces. In June 2004 a UN Stabilisation Mission took responsibility for Haiti and elections were scheduled for November 2005. This most recent scene in the Haitian drama epitomises the 'as and when necessary' doctrine, albeit with a thin veneer of UN respectability for camouflage.

Part of Aristide's problem was that he was more populist than democratic – this does not go down well in Washington, even though one might point out that George W. Bush's 'caring conservatism' was at least an attempt at populism in the 2000 presidential election campaign and that in Aristide's presidential election that same year he got more of a popular mandate than Bush. Populism is also the problem with the left-leaning President Hugo Chavez of Venezuela. Chavez has not curried favour in Washington. He has cut oil production to raise prices, sold oil to Cuba, supported radical reform movements in Latin America, and opposed the US anti-narcotics programme because it is too intrusive. Venezuela soon slipped from being the largest supplier of oil to the US to the fourth largest in 2001 and the US continued to nurture close relations with the Venezuelan military and appeared to be disappointed, to say the least, when a coup failed to topple Chavez in April 2002. The OAS made it clear that it disagreed with US sentiments concerning the coup. Chavez continues to rule on a populist mandate, attempting to redistribute wealth and land in a country that epitomises the rift between the rich and poor. A strange twist was given to US relations with Chavez on 23 August 2005, when televangelist Pat Robertson recommended his assassination by the US. The Bush administration responded by saying Robertson was a 'private citizen' whose remarks were 'inappropriate': a rather modest reproach for someone advocating political murder.

In contrast to Venezuela, Colombia has been cooperative and has welcomed US assistance with open arms to counter the FARC and narco-traffickers. Throughout the 1990s the US staunchly supported successive regimes in Colombia in an effort to strangulate the cocaine flow into the US: estimates indicated that 80% of cocaine on the streets in the US came from Colombia. This support continued even though the human rights record in Colombia was often wanting. Between 1996 and 1998 the US suspended aid to the Colombian military because of concerns about that, but simply funnelled aid to the Colombian police instead. In October 1998, US aid to Colombia tripled to $289 million and in 2000 Clinton proposed a $1.6 billion aid package. George W. Bush continued this strong support for counter-narcotics operations, though there was a distinct lack of enthusiasm for President Pastrana's attempts at a peace process with the guerrilla forces. The election of Alvaro Uribe in May 2002 was warmly welcomed in Washington as he was determined to take a much more robust line and this coincided with the post-9/11 policy of the Bush administration, which dictated the abandonment of distinctions between narco-traffickers and terrorists such as the FARC. Military aid could now be used against the FARC and other left- and right-wing guerrilla groups in Colombia. This aroused concern that the US might be slipping into a new Vietnam, but so far the administration has successfully negotiated that slippery slope. Currently Uribe's campaign against guerrillas is gaining ground, there is some semblance of stability returning and growth has averaged about 4% a year in 2003–05. The overall judgement of one scholar on US security policy, taking into account the effect of 9/11, in Latin America is:

> unlike the situation in the Cold War, the fight against terrorism is now compatible with US interests in strengthening democracy and market economies and pursuing further economic integration and political cooperation in the Western hemisphere.[6]

Free trade panacea?

The centre-piece of America's post-Cold War approach in the Western Hemisphere has been NAFTA and subsequent promises to extend it into a free trade area for the Americas (FTAA). President Reagan endorsed the idea of a Mexico–US free trade area in the early 1980s and similar thoughts were behind the thrust of George H. Bush's Enterprise for the Americas initiative set out in June 1990, whereby Central and Latin America were to 'trade not aid' their way out of the debt crisis and low economic growth. This message was clearly in line with US policy that drastically cut US aid programmes to the region: between 1992 and 1995 aid was almost halved to $760 million. In 1990, after Mexico's efforts to develop stronger economic links with Japan and the EU faltered, it approached the US for talks and the free trade strategy began to promise fruit. President Bush, the NSC and the Commerce and State Departments were all enthusiastic, but there were problems with American organised labour and agricultural and textile interests concerned about cheap competition and loss of jobs. Nevertheless, on the back of the popularity generated by success in the First Gulf War, Bush managed to obtain fast-track authority from Congress in May 1991 to enable him to negotiate for NAFTA with Mexico and Canada. Talks began in June, and once Mexico acknowledged that it had the most closed economy and would have to make the most concessions, progress was made. In October 1992 the 2,000-page agreement was signed. It would now have to be approved by the US Congress under the auspices of the new president, Bill Clinton. However, during the presidential election campaign the Texas billionaire Ross Perot had entered as an independent candidate who, among other things, strongly opposed NAFTA and he garnered 19% of the total vote, the best showing by an independent since Theodore Roosevelt and his Bull Moose Party in 1908. NAFTA with the intertwining of foreign trade, the new security agenda, jobs and economic growth at home came to epitomise the ascendancy of the intermestic agenda of the period between the end of the Cold War and 9/11.

Clinton handled the issue masterfully. He saw that the House of Representatives was the key to success and focused closely, though not exclusively, on that. Cabinet colleagues were assigned key individuals to work on, and Vice-President Gore was delegated to take on what had become the public face of opposition to NAFTA – Ross Perot. In a televised debate on 9 November,

Gore destroyed Perot's credibility in a carefully crafted performance. A week later Perot's favourable public opinion rating had declined from 66% to 29% and on 17 November the House voted 234–200 in favour of NAFTA. Between 9 and 11 December 1994, Clinton hosted the First Summit of the Americas in Miami Florida. It was the first hemispheric summit since 1967 and the agenda was clear: poverty alleviation, education, human rights, strengthening democracy and, most significantly of all, a commitment to create a FTAA by 2005. Ironically, the previous April, Clinton had lost his fast-track trade-negotiating authority and was never to regain it. This now restricted the potential for further dramatic developments of the free trade strategy.

Economic problems also arose that interrupted progress, but the way that Latin American states coped with them was indicative of new resilience. Within the overall scheme of free trade for the Americas, Mexico was targeted to demonstrate the virtues of the 'American way'. If Mexico's internal reform and closer ties with the US were seen to work, then it would catalyse other reform-minded states to follow suit. In 1995 came a major test with the Mexican peso crisis. The US and the IMF stitched together a $50 billion package, of which the US provided $20 billion. It worked, and in fact the US made $500 million profit on the ahead-of-time Mexican repayments. Notwithstanding such economic turbulence, NAFTA brought political and economic rewards and, as anticipated, acted as a stimulant for regional cooperation and a general, if rather slow, move towards freer trade. The hemisphere has become by far the fastest growing US export market and between 1991 and 1995 Latin America reduced its trade barriers by 80%. Also Mercosur, a free trade agreement between Brazil, Argentina, Uruguay and Paraguay, was established, along with a similar style Andean Pact. Better political cooperation has also accompanied these developments.

The economic improvements that took place in the early 1990s were challenged once again at the end of the decade: the Asian financial crisis that began in Thailand in April 1997; the weakening of the Japanese economy; the 1998 Russian financial crisis; and the diminishing impetus for free trade emanating from Washington. How did the resurgent economies of Latin America deal with all this and the recession that followed between 1998 and 2002? Brazil by 1998 had taken over from Mexico as the economy *par exemplar*. After the introduction of the *real plan* – a new unit of currency linked to the US dollar, but floating in value – by President Cardoso in July 1994, Brazil sustained moderate economic growth. It achieved unprecedented low inflation, attracted foreign investment and weathered economic turbulence, especially in 1999 and 2002 when depreciation of the currency raised the cost of servicing its $250 billion debt. Unlike in previous times there was no catastrophe. The economy, like others within the region, soon bounced back: in 2004 Brazilian GDP growth was over 5%.

In the midst of this recession in Latin America, George W. Bush became president with a renewed commitment to vigorous policy in the Western Hemisphere. In the election campaign, Condoleezza Rice wrote of the priorities to 'promote economic growth and political openness by extending free trade and a stable international monetary system . . . including in the western hemisphere, which has too often been neglected as a vital area of national interest'.[7] Trade and following the American model was the recipe marketed for success, and the election of Vicente Fox in Mexico in 2000 brought an iconic politician to power with whom Bush was able to establish a warm and comfortable working relationship. Mexico helped to publicise the benefits of free trade and the American-style free market.

Bush pushed the free trade agenda. In the 2002 Trade Act he wrestled trade promotion (fast-track) authority from the Congress and this gave him the power to develop both bilateral and multilateral initiatives. In July 2003 the House approved a free trade agreement with Chile and in August 2005 the Central American–Dominican Republic Free Trade Agreement (CAFTA–DR) was signed, which effectively consummated the aspirations of Reagan's Caribbean Basin Initiative. These developments by no means exhaust the initiatives currently underway, including the ambitious FTAA. A recent official State Department document succinctly summarises the free trade panacea for economic and security problems. Taken in conjunction with economic benefits garnered for US corporations, banks and consumers, in many ways it captures the essence of recent US policy in the Western Hemisphere.

> It [CAFTA–DR] also enhances our security here in the United States. Crushing poverty is one of the root causes of political instability, migration and crime in Central America and the Dominican Republic. It is better to attack these problems at their source than to have to deal with them when they reach our shores through illegal immigration, the drug trade or terrorism.[8]

While there has been progress, huge problems still remain in trying to nurture economic growth and develop regional cooperation at the same time as integrating very different economies into the global economy. Recent Latin American responses to US policy have begun to be more critical and indicate a waning of US soft power, which was potent in the 1990s. At the Summit of the Americas in Mar del Plata, Argentina, in November 2005 there was unrest about the general character of US foreign policy; countries such as Venezuela and Argentina opposed the American economic model; and popular demonstrations raised the anti-globalisation placard against continuing US attempts to spread freer trade in the Western Hemisphere. Increased US subsidies for agriculture and sporadic, but worrying, moves by the US Congress to revert to a policy of selective protectionism for beleaguered traditional manufacturing industries also pose a threat to the integrity of the American economic model that successive administrations have tried so hard to sell to Latin America. Whether the US retains sufficient soft power, successfully to consummate its free trade ambitions, remains to be seen.

Asia

Asia was the nemesis of Cold War US foreign policy: Vietnam was its epitome. After the Cold War the threats were different, but little easier to deal with. Asia's economic fortunes raised new issues as Japan's economic miracle faltered and became overshadowed by a greater one in China and by impressive growth in India, which lifted the latter to fourth in the world GDP league table in 2005 according to purchasing power parity (tenth by US dollar exchange rate). South-east Asia continued to prosper, but then went into dramatic reverse with the currency and finance crisis that erupted in Thailand in 1997 and spread throughout the region. This was directly linked with contemporary globalisation, which, in its broader context in Asia, posed a threefold challenge to the US. First, as the Asian tiger economies boomed, they challenged US economic interests and influence. Second, when they went into spiralling recession, shockwaves were felt throughout the world's financial markets and US fears grew of Asian protectionism. And third, the remedy, widely imposed by the IMF to try to stabilise the free-falling economies, was seen by many Asians as inappropriate. The 'Washington consensus' on fiscal conservatism, deregulation, privatisation and trade and capital flow liberalisation was foisted on a reluctant Asia by proxy via the IMF. Joseph Stiglitz, sometime senior official at the World Bank, and no disruptive radical by any means, wrote a devastating critique of IMF, and thus by direct implication of Washington's, remedies. It had a major political impact around the world.[9] The growing economic interdependence of the US and Asia thus posed important challenges for bilateral trade relations, for cooperation through multilateral organisations such as the IMF, the Association of South East Asian Nations (ASEAN) and Asian Pacific Economic Cooperation (APEC), and for the dominant Washington economic consensus.

Chinese economic growth financed military modernisation, which troubled the Pentagon. Also, matching the importance of the general security concerns posed by China, were fears of both North Korean nuclear ambitions and terrorism. In his State of the Union Address to Congress, 29 January 2002, George W. Bush declared of North Korea (and of Iraq and Iran): 'States like these, and their terrorist allies, constitute an axis of evil, arming to threaten the peace of the world.'[10] These fears were contextualised by potentially dangerous cultural, religious and economic divisions emerging, both between Asia and the US and within Asia. Malay and Indonesian reformers embraced a revitalised Islamic identity and there are major tensions about disproportionate Chinese commercial influence, most notably in Indonesia where, in 1998, the Chinese totalled 4% of the population, but controlled 80% of the assets of the top 300 companies. Similarly, anti-Western imperialist sentiment periodically breaks out over the US military presence in the region, over inappropriate economic policies championed by Washington, and over episodes such as the Australian-led UN peacekeeping mission that went into East Timor in 1999. America's ability to project its military power throughout the region is based on three important platforms: the US Navy, bases throughout the Pacific and

Asia, and intelligence networks that incorporate important agreements with Australia, New Zealand and Japan.

In the early 1990s America's role in Asia was characterised by Defense Secretary Richard Cheney as that of a 'balancing wheel'.[11] Occasionally that balancing wheel still operates, for example, during the December 2001 to July 2002 nuclear capable military confrontation between India and Pakistan. On 13 December 2001, Islamic militants struck at the Indian parliament in Delhi sparking off a crisis that led to a provocative Indian military deployment along the frontier with Pakistan. With one million men mobilised either side of the Kashmir Line of Control and the potential for nuclear conflict, this was a complex and difficult issue for the US. Pakistan is an authoritarian Islamic state, but President General Musharraf cooperated with the US in the aftermath of 9/11 and was still a crucial ally in the war on terrorism. In contrast India, while blemished with some human rights failings, is nevertheless a democracy and from the early 1990s has embraced the American liberal economic model of development. For different reasons, therefore, America had to maintain good relations with both. Washington successfully trod the fine line between them and talked them down from possible military aggression.

However, this balancing wheel role has become increasingly difficult in the absence of bipolar discipline and with relative US economic decline. George H. Bush and more especially Clinton supported regional cooperation through organisations such as the ASEAN but also aggressively and unilaterally pursued US economic interests. An APEC meeting in November 1998 revealed increasing tension between the eastern and western edges of the Pacific as Asia was unwilling to accept the American economic model wholesale. Dr Mahathir, Malaysia's Prime Minister, specifically warned at the meeting of the dangers for Asia posed by too much economic liberalisation. This has and continues to clash with US determination to prescribe the model for Asia and prise open its markets by setting ambitious targets for trade liberalisation and exporting American/IMF-style capitalism. The attention of George W. Bush was somewhat distracted from Asia by 9/11 and its aftermath, but continuities in many policies are discernible and nowhere more so than in the drive for free trade and economic reform. At the November 2004 APEC Summit in Santiago Chile, Bush noted America's support for the Doha Round and for Russian and Vietnamese membership of the WTO and went on to proclaim:

> We're going to be aggressive about our bilateral trade agreements and our regional trade agreements. We've completed trade agreements with nations throughout Asia and the Americas, including Australia, Singapore, Chile, the five nations of Central America and the Dominican Republic. We are working on new agreements with Thailand, Panama, the Andean nations of South America. We're moving ahead with the enterprise for the ASEAN initiative, which is lowering trade barriers and strengthening economic ties in Southeast Asia. We're committed to the Bogor goals, which call for free trade among developed nations of the

Asian Pacific region by 2010, and free trade among all APEC economies by 2020.[12]

The similarity with the US grand strategy for the Western Hemisphere and its assumptions about links between free economies, democracy and security hardly needs to be pointed out.

Japan

In the early aftermath of the Cold War conflicts of interest were particularly pronounced with Japan – America's foremost Asian ally. They remained 'inextricably intertwined, economically, politically, and militarily',[13] but the end of the Cold War gave Japan more room to manoeuvre and beckoned it to take a more assertive international role. At the 1995 Osaka summit of APEC, Tokyo split with the US over the pace and style of economic liberalisation in East Asia. This was problematic for American strategy, especially as Japan's share of the Asian market had grown more rapidly than that of the US. Another important factor in their cooling relationship was Clinton and the aggression with which he attacked Japan's 'closed' market and the fortitude with which the Japanese defended it. George H. Bush's approach to Japan had been moderate. There was talk of voluntary import expansion (VIE) targets, but the US was careful not to antagonise the Japanese government. Clinton had a different approach, signalled by 'hawkish' appointments such as Mickey Kantor as USTR and Lawrence Summers as Deputy Secretary of the Treasury. In February 1994 the Hosokawa summit became deadlocked as Japan resisted American demands to deregulate and to expand its imports. Matters hit a flashpoint in the 1995 'car crisis'. The preceding year the auto and auto parts industry accounted for 58% of America's $66 billion trade deficit with Japan, equivalent to 23% of the total global US trade deficit. Clinton threatened 100% punishment tariffs on 13 models of Japanese car if Japan did not accede to US VIE demands. Such assertive US unilateralism was clearly at odds with its declared support for multilateralism. More importantly, Japan refused to buckle and, although some points of compromise were eventually reached, the American assault caused such damage to American–Japanese relations that US trade policy was described as 'almost a disaster area'.[14]

American–Japanese tensions in trade in the 1990s were mirrored in part in fluctuations in the warmth of their security relationship. In 1995 the US Defense Department released a report 'United States Strategy for the East Asia Pacific Region', which stressed the importance of Japanese cooperation. The Americans were therefore heartened by Japan's 'Modality' report in 1994, which reaffirmed its strategic alliance with the US. At the same time America and Japan no longer shared such an identity of security interest now that the Soviet threat was gone. Tokyo had seemingly little appetite for shouldering the security burdens that Washington expected, which was demonstrated in October 1995 by its Self-Defence Agency recommending cuts of 10–20% in Japan's defence forces. Symbols of Japan's continuing reliance on the US also became increasingly unpopular among the Japanese public. In this respect, the gang-rape of a teenage girl by American servicemen on Okinawa was particularly damaging. In 1995 public support for the US security treaty fell to 42%; in 1997 the Japanese public ranked the US as a threat second only to North Korea; and American demands in the midst of the Asian finance and monetary crisis in 1998 that Japan should reinflate and act as an economic motor for regional recovery caused friction and resentment.

Matters never ran out of control but it was important that in 2001 the human dimension of diplomatic relations injected a renewal of amity. George W. Bush and the mercurial Prime Minister Junichiro Koizumi came to power and established a close personal relationship that acted as a catalyst to bring economic and security ties into greater prominence and halt the temporary deterioration in their bilateral relations. By the 2004 US presidential election this relationship was so close that Koizumi indiscreetly spoke out in favour of a Bush victory over Democrat candidate John Kerry. It is also true to say that Japanese leaders tend to get on better with the business-oriented Republicans: this was very notably the case with George W. Bush after the bruising Japanese experience with the Clinton administration.

Koizumi's efforts to address the stalled Japanese economic miracle through structural reforms and the liberalisation and privatisation of dysfunctional parts of the Japanese economy resonate of American-style capitalism. Likewise harnessing American economic growth to kick-start Japanese recovery underscores the importance of US–Japanese trade relations. Japan in 2005 was the fourth largest of the US's trade partners and though the trade gap remained stubbornly wide – $55 billion exports and $130 billion imports in 2003 – tensions were eased by converging economic practices and increasing American preoccupation with China. Japan still has strong diplomatic and security reasons too that encourage close relations with the US. Washington will undoubtedly be central to Japan's ambition, shared with Brazil, Germany and India, to achieve a permanent seat on the UN Security Council. Japan would also be fearful of dealing alone with either the North Korean nuclear threat or the rise of China, which continues to develop its military capabilities and with which Japan has ongoing friction over undersea resources and over the Second World War and how it is accounted for in the history books.

Washington reciprocates this interest in a re-energised security partnership. Japan is a key Asian partner and has played an important role in the six-power talks trying to resolve the North Korean nuclear problem. Washington also benefits overall from a change in traditional Japanese reluctance to participate in foreign affairs. As former Prime Minister Morihiro Hosokawa argued, global conditions force Japan to play a greater international role. This means first that a new generation of political leaders, less affected by the legacy of the Second World War, is looking to develop a more independent Japanese role and is willing to accept greater international responsibilities, as illustrated by Japan's contribution from its Strategic Defence Force (SDF) to UN peace-keeping missions in Cambodia, Mozambique, Rwanda and East Timor. Also, Japan is sensitive to the horrors of terrorism, especially after the sarin gas outrage perpetrated by religious fanatics on the Tokyo underground in 1995 killed 12 people and hospitalised thousands. These two factors combined have brought the US tangible benefits. After 9/11 Koizumi quickly declared support for the US war on terrorism and Bush went out of his way in February 2002, at what was their fourth meeting since he came to office, to speak of Japan's staunch support. Japan supplied oil for US Navy ships during Operation Enduring Freedom and more controversially sent over 500 military engineers, members of the SDF, to help reconstruction in Iraq in 2005.

US–Japanese relations thus appear to be stronger than at any time since the Cold War, especially as in 2005 Koizumi took a major gamble and won. After failing to push through reform of the postal service he called a general election in the summer and, to the surprise of some, secured a resounding victory. However, there are clouds on the horizon for Koizumi and his successor (according to the constitution, Koizumi must soon stand down). Popular feeling in Japan remains stubbornly critical of the US over the Okinawa military base, environmental and a raft of multilateral issues, as well as the war in Iraq. Being closely associated with Washington carries risks too. The relationship attracts disfavour from Islamic extremists in Asia and is domestically unpopular. There is also danger should Japan respond to pressure to increase its military capabilities. With a GDP of over $3.7 trillion (2004), and a population of more than 127 million, Japan is a reasonably secure regional economic power and Japan's leaders are very conscious that any concerted move to strengthen their military capability might decrease their security by provoking others into an arms race. All of this demands that Japanese leaders tread a cautious path between close and overly close relations with the US and makes it difficult to predict with any certainty the likely tenor of US–Japanese relations as Japan emerges from its lost decade and begins to make economic progress again.

China

The US balancing role in Asia has been complicated further by China, the country singled out in 1996 by Warren Christopher as an increasingly important market and as being potentially decisive in tipping the balance between regional stability and conflict. China's marriage of market economy with authoritarian leadership has produced an average growth rate of 9% between 1978 and 2005. It has also attracted massive direct foreign investment (over $60 billion in 2004 alone); created a trade surplus that now dwarfs Japan's (US Commerce Department figures for June 2005 put the monthly deficit with Japan at $6.9 billion and with China at $17.6 billion); and secured the reversion of prestigious Hong Kong from British control. China's rise has put it at the heart of Asian security too. Sino-American cooperation has significantly eased some difficulties, such as with the US–North Korean agreement of 1994 to stop the latter's military nuclear programme. As a permanent member of the UN Security Council, a nuclear power and a leading international arms supplier, China's cooperation is also of great importance in arms control, nuclear non-proliferation and the promotion of multilateral cooperation in Asia. The obverse of this is China's potential to create major regional instability. Its posture of non-aggression is often difficult to reconcile with its claims to large parts of the South China Sea, its 40% increase in military expenditure between 1990 and 1995, and its provocative acts, such as testing missiles in July 1995 near Taiwan. Pentagon estimates put China's defence spending by 2005 as third in the world behind the US and Russia at $50–70 billion a year and that caused concern about how that military strength might be used. China also continues to develop nuclear capabilities – a particularly sensitive issue in light of revelations in April 1999 of Chinese espionage in America's nuclear programme. And in 2003 it demonstrated its missile prowess by launching Shenzhou 5, the first Chinese manned space flight. There are also fears that China might adopt similar policies towards Taiwan to those used to reclaim Hong Kong and the Portuguese territory of Macau, which reverted to China on 20 December 1999.

The US response to the 'China challenge' has been marked by George H. Bush pragmatism, Clinton's betrayal of electoral promises, and George W. Bush's renewal, at least initially, of a significantly harder line. The honeymoon period in Sino-American relations coincided with Deng Xiaoping's programme of economic reform and international engagement during the 1980s and was largely over even before the Cold War ended. American calculations of the strategic triangle were replaced by concern for regional stability and an anxiety to expand trade links. Bush therefore advocated 'constructive engagement' with China and made a very pragmatic, muted response to the human rights issue epitomised by the Tiananmen Square government massacre of advocates of political democracy on 4 June 1989. Clinton attacked Bush for this *realpolitik* approach, promised to pursue with all vigour US principles in his dealings with China, and expressed a desire to link human rights with China's MFN status. Such idealism proved to be empty rhetoric and Clinton later admitted that 'it would be fair to say that my policies with regard to China have been somewhat different from what I talked about in the [1992 presidential] campaign'.[15] Constructive engagement continued to dominate Sino-American relations, with Clinton anxious both to accommodate and contain China. There is no automatic Sino-American coincidence of either economic or security interests. China has developed a strategic partnership with Russia and they conducted joint military exercises in 2005. It continues to posture over Taiwan, has developed closer relations with Iran, and has embraced an authoritarian developmental model ill-suited to US international trade liberalisation. US responses included reaffirming its commitment to Taiwan, albeit initially through a policy of strategic ambiguity that left the Chinese wondering what the US would do if they were to invade Taiwan. The US also tried to consolidate its relationship with Japan and other ASEAN members and vigorously to defend its economic interests. However, while George H. Bush and Clinton were not prepared to pursue engagement at any price, they were prepared to do so at the expense of human rights and American principles. In 1994 Clinton renewed China's

MFN status and, against the tide of American public opinion, decoupled the issues of trade and human rights. Two years later his conversion from idealist to pragmatist was confirmed when the US refused to apply sanctions on China for its export of M-11 missiles and strategically important ring magnets to Pakistan.

George W. Bush brought a renewal of acrimony and tension in the early days of his administration. Two incidents in particular in April 2001 stand out: first, the emergency landing on Chinese soil of a US EP-3 reconnaissance plane, and second, comments by Bush that punctured the film of ambiguity surrounding the response the US would make to a Chinese invasion of Taiwan. The EP-3 incident raised tensions and took weeks to resolve as the Chinese refused to allow the plane to fly out of China. In the end, it was dismantled and flown out as cargo, and American service personnel were eventually repatriated. Regarding Taiwan, Bush claimed that if China invaded then the US would defend it with whatever power was required. Subsequently he moderated his position by emphasising that Taiwan should not declare its independence. Matters remained difficult especially as Chen Shui-bian, President of Taiwan since 2000, continued in 2005 to talk the language of Taiwanese independence, though US influence kept him from constitutional reforms that would have legalised such a position.

Troubling issues therefore abide and are fed by the near-paranoia that many of the neo-conservatives in Bush's administration harbour towards China. Presidents Bush and Hu Jintao have failed to ignite warm personal relations despite several encounters. The US remains nervous about Chinese military cooperation with Russia. It would also like Beijing to explain its rising defence spending, act more responsibly in various areas of economic activity and grant a broader array of human rights to its people. Yet this is by no means the whole story.

China, Taiwan and the US all agreed on China and Taiwan entering the WTO. China insisted on entering first and did so formally on 11 December 2001; Taiwan followed on 1 January 2002. There has been substantial growth in Taiwan–China trade and over time the issue of Taiwan's status has cooled. China has established relations with its political opposition parties and, if a peaceful reintegration into China were negotiated, the US would not intervene. Sino-American economic relations have also continued to grow. Trade has risen from $17.8 billion in 1989 to over $245 billion in 2004 with the US shouldering a massive annual deficit of over $175 billion. Part of the reason for this deficit is the fact that China pegged the renminbi to the dollar, and was thus unaffected by the dollar's recent depreciation. As the dollar went down so did the renminbi, and Chinese exports to the US remained cheap. After much US pressure the Chinese revalued the renminbi by 2% in 2005 and it is now pegged to a basket of currencies, but still with the dollar the most influential. All of this indicates emerging Sino-American interdependencies, which particularly benefit China and tend to moderate its traditional truculent style. Indeed, China has achieved a position where it would lose much from hostile or near-hostile relations with the US and its interest in cooperation has been evident in its important and constructive role in US-led attempts to control North Korea's nuclear ambitions.

North Korea and the war on terrorism

The reclusive and totalitarian communist regime of the Democratic People's Republic of Korea (North Korea) has long been a thorn in America's side. Technically, the two remain at war because the division of the Korean Peninsular at the 38th parallel during the Korean War was established in 1953 by armistice rather than by peace treaty. Thereafter the US could do little about North Korea during the Cold War, not least because it received support from the Soviet Union and China. After the Cold War, North Korea became a complex problem and a potentially major source of regional and wider instability. It sells missiles to Middle Eastern countries including Egypt and Iran. In 1997–98 it exchanged No-Dong missiles with Pakistan in return for gas-centrifuge uranium enrichment technology, thus fuelling Indo-Pakistan nuclear tension. Its successful ICBM test-launch over Japan in 1998 delivered security shockwaves, not least because, much to Chinese chagrin, it prompted Tokyo to agree to cooperate with Washington in developing a regional missile defence system. A sustained North Korean drive to stockpile nuclear weapons, coupled with its proven capacity to deliver them, might even provoke South Korea, Japan and Taiwan into reconsidering their non-nuclear status.[16]

The Clinton administration regarded North Korea as bearing all the hall-marks of a rogue state and in 1993–94 gave serious consideration to a pre-emptive military strike against its nuclear facilities. However, a combination of the high risk involved and evidence of easing North–South Korean tensions led Clinton to a less aggressive path. Kim Dae Jung's South Korean sunshine policy of reconciliation and engagement with the North seemed to be bearing fruit. For instance, in 1991 the North–South Agreement on Reconciliation, Non-Aggression, Exchanges and Cooperation was concluded, followed in 1992 by a North–South Declaration on a Non-Nuclear Korean Peninsular. Pyongyang also became slightly more flexible as a result of severe economic problems and reduced external support from Russia and China, the latter being epitomised by China's normalisation and subsequent consolidation of relations with South Korea from August 1992.[17] All of this helped the Clinton administration to conclude a Framework Agreement with North Korea on 21 October 1994, a key part of which were measures to combat the destabilising consequences of the latter's decision to withdraw from the NPT. The Korean Peninsular Energy Development Organisation (KEDO) was subsequently set up in March 1995, whereby in return for closing down nuclear operations that could be used for weapons development North Korea would be assisted in the production of energy for civilian purposes.

The Korean problem subsequently retreated to the margins of US strategic concern, especially as Kim Jong-il's beleaguered regime took tentative steps towards opening up to the outside world. It became party to the UN Covenant on Economic, Social and Cultural Rights and the Convention on the Rights of the Child. In June 2000 the first-ever inter-Korean Summit was held and Kim Jong-il pledged to extend a moratorium on missile testing, to restrain missile technology exports and to open discussions on human rights. In 2000 North Korea attended the seventh meeting of the ASEAN Regional Forum; in July 2002 it formally abrogated its command economy; and in September 2002 Kim Jong-il opened the way for improving relations with Japan. He admitted to and apologised for the North Korean kidnapping of Japanese citizens during the 1970s. Japanese Prime Minister Koizumi reciprocated by apologising for the harshness of Japanese inter-war colonisation of Korea and offered a multi-billion-dollar aid package as part of the normalisation process.[18]

However, US–North Korean relations turned sour once more with the arrival of the George W. Bush administration. North Korea met pretty much every tick box on the neo-conservative hit list: an established connection between its leader Kim Jong-il and terrorism; possession and delivery capability of WMDs; documented use of WMDs and missile technology to raise funds and to bargain with regional powers; and being a potential supplier of materials and delivery systems to state and non-state actors, including international terrorist groups. Evidence of a new hardline American approach came quickly. In November 2001 Under-Secretary of State for Arms Control and International Security, John Bolton, accused North Korea of having broken the Biological and Toxin Weapons Convention. The following month the Bush administration specified North Korea in its Nuclear Posture Review as an 'immediate contingency' for which the US must be prepared to respond with nuclear force. In January 2002 North Korea was demonised in Bush's State of the Union Address as a member of the 'axis of evil'. And matters took a further dramatic downturn on 16 October 2002 when the US announced that North Korea had admitted enriching uranium for nuclear weapons in contravention of its obligations under the NPT, North–South Declaration on a Non-Nuclear Korean Peninsular and the Agreed Framework underpinning KEDO. On 12 December Pyongyang announced that it was restarting its 5-MW reactor and resuming construction of its 50 and 200 MW reactors. It subsequently expelled International Atomic Energy Authority inspectors on 27 December, formally withdrew from the NPT on 10 January 2003 and pulled out of the 1992 agreement on a nuclear-free Korean Peninsular.

In Washington councils were divided along similar lines to the simultaneous debate about military intervention in Iraq, but there were three major differences: the North Koreans almost certainly possessed nuclear weapons by November 2002 and intermediate range means of delivering them; key regional American allies were potentially vulnerable, especially South Korea and Japan; and the US was itself vulnerable because it had over 35,000 troops in South Korea who could become victim to a North Korean nuclear strike. The US resolved upon a policy of tailored containment and developed a multilateral response through six-party talks between itself, North and South Korea, China, Russia and Japan. In August 2005 they were renewed after more than a year's break and more talks are scheduled for the near future.

The contrast between American treatment of Iraq and North Korea creates an image of the US under the George W. Bush administration as a respecter of hard power only. Failure to find a solution to the North Korean problem also demonstrates the lack of an East Asian security system that is acceptable to the leading regional powers. North Korea is a concern to countries throughout Asia and beyond but American policy towards it has limited support. The European Commission has criticised the Bush administration's hardline attitude and consequent blocking of North Korean membership of key international financial institutions as an impediment to the socialisation of Pyongyang through integration into the world economy.[19] In the meantime Russia and China do not want to see North Korea's nuclear programme controlled at the expense of seeing American power increase in the Korean Peninsular and Asia. The 1996 US–Japan Security Agreement strengthened these concerns. China especially sees North Korea as a useful communist buffer between itself and American influence flowing from South Korea. Indeed, it is telling of Great Power differences in Asia that so far China has made but limited use of its unrivalled potential economic leverage vis-à-vis Pyongyang.[20]

While US concerns about North Korean nuclear weapons and China's defence spending abide, much of America's security attention since 9/11 has switched to trying to curb terrorism. This strategy stretches out throughout the region, but with particular focus on Indonesia as the country with the largest Muslim population in the world and one that suffered the Bali discotheque outrage in October 2002, on the Philippines where combined US and Philippine operations have been conducted against Islamic terrorists, and on the most sensitive area of all – the Central Asian states of Kazakhstan, Kyrgyztan, Tajiikistan, Turkmenistan and Uzbekistan. This area became geopolitically important with the launch of the war on terrorism in Afghanistan and then later the invasion of Iraq. However, these states also used to be part of the Soviet empire and Russian relations with them remain a possible and at times an actual source of controversy between Russia and the US (see Chapter 10). US military positioning here also impacts on China. Nevertheless, the US was swift to move in the aftermath of 9/11 and opened a military base at Manas in Kyrgyzstan in 2001 and formalised close relations with Uzbekistan in 2002, which enabled the opening of military facilities at Karshi-Khanabad to service the campaign against Afghanistan.

There have been frequent criticisms about the US consorting with these corrupt and oppressive regimes, notwithstanding the standard US line that it tries to encourage reform, economic growth and democracy. This looks the same as the *realpolitik* Cold War justification for consorting with brutal dictators, except this time they have to be anti-terrorist rather than anticommunist. Ex-British Ambassador to Uzbekistan, Charles Murray, roundly condemned the corruption and brutal and undemocratic behaviour of the Uzbekistan government in 2005 and equally savagely condemned the US for sacrificing its principles for security priorities and consorting with it. Instability in the region is clearly fraught with danger given the strategic involvement of both Russia and the US and their vying for favour among the states there.

The 'Rose Revolution' in Georgia in 2003 and the 'Orange Revolution' in the Ukraine in 2004, when popular protest brought reformist governments to power, were emulated in nearby Kyrgyzstan in the summer of 2005 with the collapse of the incumbent government and the coming to power of President Bakiyev, though his reforming fervour swiftly diminished once he was in power. These unsettling times, concerns about Russia's position, and fear of a backlash by their Muslim populations, have resulted in waning support among the central Asian republics for close ties with the US and doubts about the wisdom of a US military presence on their soil. This prompted a visit by US Secretary of Defense Rumsfeld in July 2005. Most critical in the region was a commitment by Kyrgyzstan that US forces could continue operations at Manas, and while Rumsfeld managed to get this renewed it was not open-ended. The general understanding is that once the situation in Afghanistan improves then the US military must withdraw.

Conclusion

Post-Cold War US policies towards the Western Hemisphere and Asia have some common denominators, especially spreading democracy and American-style capitalism as guarantors of American prosperity and facilitators of international security. In both regions successive administrations have felt freer since the Cold War to advance aggressive trade liberalisation policies and to push allies to share more of the security burden. In practice US dominance of the Western Hemisphere has enabled greater success there than in Asia in the development of competitive liberalisation. Although the American model has faced limited resistance in the Western Hemisphere by countries such as Cuba and Venezuela and ran into more serious difficulties at the Mar del Plata Summit of the Americas in November 2005, this pales next to that encountered in Asia, both within forums such as ASEAN and bilaterally. Interestingly this resistance comes from allies and strategic competitors alike, such as Japan and China respectively. Moreover, economic growth in China, India and the Asian tiger economies, and the possibility of a resurgent Japanese economy, suggests that the economic balance of power in the world will gradually shift somewhat from the Atlantic, which currently encompasses over two-thirds of the world's GDP, to the Pacific. Such change will require careful management.

The security picture is somewhat similar. The Western Hemisphere hosts a number of weak and potentially failing states but even designated 'rogues' such as Castro's Cuba pose little threat to the US. Nor does the region harbour the Islamic fundamentalists that Asia does. The Central Asian republics have become the front-line in the war on terror. Asia also poses some of the most serious state-based immediate and medium-term threats to the US. China will continue to rise. Its regional ambitions and how it advances them will do much to determine the stability or otherwise of its locale and beyond. Kashmiri and other Indo-Pakistan tensions make their relationship currently the most plausible nuclear flashpoint, and the US will need to continue to

13 Conclusion

The US has come a long way since 1945. Its foreign policy has responded to immense foreign, domestic and technological challenges. The rapid transition from wartime planning for a UN-based security system to the Cold War forced a radical rethink of US strategy. Threatened again by totalitarianism, Americans drew lessons from the prelude to the Second World War. There must be no appeasement. The US must be strong and prepared to defend itself. And liberal democracies should not be divided as they had been by the dual threat of Nazi Germany in Europe and of Japanese militarism in Asia: the US would have to assume the mantle of leadership. In exercising that leadership, isolationism was pushed to the margins as the US crafted a grand strategy of containment that grew fitfully through stages, but all of them confronting the need to justify a willingness to use varying levels of force in order to ensure the survival of liberal democracy and capitalism. In doing so, it often adopted tactics that rested on the argument that the end justified the means and took decisions that skirted on, or occasionally transgressed, the borders of constitutionality. Cold War stakes were so high that they provided justification for such tactics and decision-making. But means-ends arguments that compromise civil and human rights and inadequately constrain executive power do not sit comfortably for long with liberal democracy and the value it places on the sanctity of the individual. By the end of the Cold War civil rights and constitutional integrity remained largely intact, but they had been periodically and severely battered.

Leadership of the Free World had other serious consequences too for the American body politic. New power centres arose, especially the military–industrial complex that Eisenhower warned against as he left office in 1961. Bipartisan anti-communist consensus drew the teeth of Congress until at least the Vietnam War. For some American leaders this was not an unwelcome development because democratic controls can hamper effective foreign policy-making, especially when there is too much influence from a Congress riven with political rivalries and vested interests, possessing little foreign policy expertise and having predominantly domestic priorities. As Dean Acheson lamented, 'Congress is too damn representative. It's just as stupid as the people are; just as uneducated, just as dumb, just as selfish.'[1]

Successive administrations upheld the US commitment to shouldering the burdens of Free World leadership and of maintaining its principal security and economic structures, though after the collapse of Bretton Woods the US management role in the world economy was reduced. Whether or not the US achieved hegemonic status, anywhere in the Free World, remains open to debate, but its Cold War efforts undoubtedly confronted it with problems similar to empires of the past. The enormous commitment overseas caused long-term neglect of serious domestic social and economic problems and often compromised efforts that were made to correct them, such as Johnson's Great Society programme.

The end of the Cold War beckoned American policy-makers to put right long-neglected domestic wrongs and to fashion a New World Order from a position of unrivalled power, as in 1945. This reignited traditional debates about the balance between isolationism and internationalism, the appropriate mix of idealism and realism, and the blend between multilateral and unilateral means. It also begged new questions about the purpose of American power, about the durability of alliances without a unifying common threat, and about the nature of the world 'out there'. Too often critics of post-Cold War American foreign policy, especially of the struggle to find a grand strategy to replace containment, neglect to take appropriate account of the enormous changes brought forth by the end of bipolarity. In their ways, each of the post-Cold War presidencies contributed to redefining America's role in the world.

George H. Bush was a conservative who uttered the rhetoric of New World Order whereby 'nations recognize the shared responsibility for freedom and justice, [in] a world where the strong respect the weak'.[2] Bush and his team, however, were not good on the vision thing. More to the point, Bush was sceptical of its value. His hallmarks were courage and caution. He was a cautious and pragmatic conservative realist, who gathered skilful men around him and saw the benefits of working and acting with allies in the pursuit of American interests, but would also act unilaterally if that were necessary.

This pragmatism produced some curious results. It seemed odd indeed, after 45 years of the US trying to destroy the Soviet Union, that Bush dedicated such energy to trying to prevent its collapse. In the process this threw up all sorts of unpalatable contradictions, notably his willingness to stand aside while Gorbachev sought to quash independence movements such as that led by Lithuanian leader Vytautas Landsbergis. No grand strategy shines through Bush's foreign policy and Dumbrell is right to characterise it as: 'little more than vague commitment to multilateralism, and a promise that foreign policy would be tied to US interests (themselves grounded vaguely in an asserted coincidence of free markets and liberal democracy)'.[3]

However, this does not mean that Bush was unsuccessful or that he did not leave important foreign policy legacies. Courage and caution can be virtues in times of great uncertainty, and Bush and his close advisers had these qualities in abundance. Bush's embrace of Gorbachev was logical, for the USSR was a great stabilising force and the bilateral nuclear relationship was far easier to manage than the proliferation that followed its collapse. Working in cooperation with Gorbachev also helped him achieve major foreign policy objectives, especially dramatic cuts in US and Soviet nuclear arsenals, Germany's reunification and entry into NATO, the CFE Treaty and successful leadership of the First Gulf War. None of this was at the expense of US interests for Bush did not hesitate to intervene militarily in Panama and to drive an aggressive foreign economic policy that dealt well with Japan and the EU and brought about the innovative NAFTA.

Bush also began the groundwork in reorientating focus and expectations. His administration initiated the switch in priorities from Europe to Asia and the Middle East and the drive both to rationalise American overseas commitments and offload some responsibilities on to other actors – hence his welcoming of Germany's Chancellor Kohl as a 'partner in leadership' and endorsement of the European Commission coordinating aid to Central and Eastern Europe. He also largely resisted temptation to abuse America's unipolar moment and even attempted to adopt guidelines that would limit US use of force in the post-Cold War world and confirm it as an option of last resort. If these did not work fully, it was due less to a failure of will than to the enormously difficult questions at the heart of interventionism. Furthermore, for all his *realpolitik* reflexes Bush contributed significantly to encouraging multilateralism in American foreign policy and hopes for a New World Order based on international law and policed by the UN. He valued allies and provided the UN with new prestige by steering the US response to Iraq's invasion of Kuwait under UN auspices and in leading an impressively large coalition force, which included the Soviet Union. And lest this be simply decried as cover for protecting American political and oil interests, it is important to remember his administration's commitment to UN humanitarian involvement in Somalia.

President Bill Clinton appeared likely to be radically different from his predecessor. Clinton's focus on domestic issues and the relative decline of security threats to the US shifted the focus of American foreign policy towards economics. The President created the NEC to play the same role in economic policy as the NSC did in security. His administration continued to support multilateral trade agreements, Congress approved NAFTA in November 1993 and the US signed up to the WTO, which constituted a major exception to its usual reluctance to cede sovereignty. At the same time Clinton vigorously pursued unilateral initiatives to protect American economic interests and to punish those such as the EU, Japan and China who were deemed to damage them.

In contrast to Bush's pragmatic and cautious realism, Clinton and his administration responded to new challenges by shifting along the spectrum towards liberal idealism. In September 1993 NSA Anthony Lake spoke eloquently of the importance of enlarging both democracy and free markets and this was very much in harmony with the positions of Secretary of State Warren Christopher, US Ambassador to the UN, Madeleine Albright, and President Clinton himself. Hallmarks of the Clinton administration's foreign policy approach became democratic enlargement, engagement and assertive multilateralism to deal with international problems and in particular humanitarian crises like the one in Somalia.

Clinton's vision had its weaknesses. It was difficult to identify the national interest and hard, as the world's sole superpower, to avoid expectation that the US should intervene everywhere that good cause was shown, which is why its standing aside during the Rwanda genocide was so damaging. More especially, neither the Clinton administration, nor Congress, nor the American public was prepared to lend the full weight of America to assertive multilateralism. This meant that the Clinton administration's idealism was shot through by pragmatism and hard realism. It was checked further by the Cold War's end, which brought domestic actors more forcibly into foreign policy and encouraged Congressional assertiveness, especially after the Republicans seized control of both houses in the 1994 mid-term elections. For example, Congress slashed the overseas aid budget and partially reversed the drive for peace dividends, which Clinton had sought through the downsizing of the defence budget and the military industrial complex.

Thus what emerges is an administration that felt more comfortable with the vision thing, but whose picture of a New World Order and America's role in it remained rather fuzzy. This was reflected in the administration's inconsistencies as it struggled to reconcile its idealism with the 'world out there' and with new constraints at home. PDD-25 was toned down in response to the death of US Rangers in Somalia, involvement in Bosnia was as much by accident as design, and experience in Kosovo indicated the practical as well as political limitations of multilateralism. At the same time, US interventions did continue in Haiti – notably with UN endorsement – and in Bosnia and Kosovo under the guise of NATO.

Nevertheless, Clinton did move American foreign policy forward. His administration articulated the vision thing in liberal and idealistic language and made progress in trying to evolve the basis of a coherent foreign policy strategy from the sensible but ad hoc policies of its predecessor. American prosperity and security could progress hand-in-hand through democratic enlargement and expansion of the free market. Where problems arose, they would be addressed through predominantly, though not exclusively, multilateral means. This demonstrated sensitivity to post-Cold War questions of the legitimacy of international action and the limits of US power and reflected continued anxiety to burden-share. Moreover, the Clinton administrations made three very important contributions to the future of US foreign policy. First was an insightful reading of the post-Cold War ascendancy of geo-economics. Second was the symbiosis seen between security and values, which was promoted in democratic enlargement and the free market. And third was Clinton's emphasis on the diminishing difference between foreign and domestic policy. In short, he soon acknowledged, in a way that his predecessors had not, that the US was in a deeply interpenetrated state system of complex interdependence. The water's edge, where traditionally foreign policy ended and began, had disappeared.

The 2000 election and early months of the Bush administration gave little indication of what was to come. In the lead-up to the election there was much talk about re-establishing a hierarchy of American national interests and reducing overseas commitments, which caused great consternation among US allies in Europe lest America pull out of the Balkans. Bush presented a profile of caring conservatism, came across as more moderate and pragmatic than many he subsequently appointed and initially conducted his presidency little different from a conventional, albeit right-of-centre, pragmatist. 9/11 changed matters. It demonstrated American vulnerability to WMDs and international terrorism and just how far foreign and domestic policy had merged. It also made crafting a grand strategy for foreign policy somewhat easier because it gave clear priority to security, enabled a reversion to defending the American way of life, and provided a new enemy to defeat, all of which facilitated the mobilisation of support from domestic constituencies. Finally, the crisis provided opportunity for the ready-crafted agenda of the ideologically charged neo-conservatives and their fellow-travellers – Paul Wolfowitz, Donald Rumsfeld, Dick Cheyney, John Bolton, Richard Perle, Stephen J. Hadley and Condoleezza Rice.

The progeny of the neo-conservative agenda stretches back into the 1960s and the disillusion of highly moralistic left-leaning radicals who then tipped sharply to the right. By the 1990s their focus was the emergence of China; the troubling direction of political developments in Russia; threats from Iraq, Serbia and North Korea; and the consequences of the peace dividend for US military capabilities. While all this sounds like traditional realism, it is permeated with values that transform it into something else. In fact it is 'a new political animal born of an unlikely marriage of humanitarian idealism and brute force'. It differs from Wilsonianism's desire to make the world over in the image of American liberalism in that 'neo-conservatives prefer to act alone and heavily armed rather than work through the often laborious multilateral process'.[4] Furthermore, the moral dimension of neo-conservatism departs from realism as it emphasises the promotion of values as well as security.

The promotion of these values is informed by both strategic doctrine fathered by Albert Wohlstetter and the unipolar condition. In the aftermath of 9/11 this neo-conservative agenda provided a clear policy for Bush's response. However, it would not be directed in the first instance against terrorists, but against rogue states that could challenge the US and its security by harbouring terrorists, developing WMDs and even equipping terrorist proxies with WMDs for delivery against the US and its allies. Confronting this challenge, the neo-conservatives convincingly argued that the traditional deterrence option was impotent and that smart weapons must be used to intervene clinically and pre-emptively, or preventatively if deemed necessary, against rogue states. A major sub-theme of their strategy to deal with instability in the Middle East (and conveniently the oil access problem) was to spread democracy and the free market, first in Afghanistan, then in Iraq and then onwards throughout the region. The outcomes of these value positions were embodied in diplomatic exchanges and policy and strategy papers over the months that followed 9/11. Even while President Bush appeared initially to move multilaterally it was appearance rather than reality. The US military made it very clear to the French from the outset that they were not going 'to wage war by committee' – Kosovo had provided the salutary lessons.[5] In his January State of the Union Address in 2002 Bush spoke of an axis of evil. In June at West Point he spoke of the need for pre-emptive action against clear and present dangers, which soon developed into a policy of preventative action against less clear and less present dangers. And in September 2002 in *The National Security Strategy of the United States of America* three key concepts were embedded: the need for pre-emptive action; that the US must be the unchallengeable superpower; and that US democratic values should be trumpeted and spread abroad.[6] In many ways, even though NSA Rice determined much of the content, the ideas were a logical follow-on from the findings of the 1998 Commission to Assess the Ballistic Missile Threat to the United States chaired by Donald Rumsfeld and into which Paul Wolfowitz also fed ideas.[7]

Thus of the three post-Cold War administrations, that of George W. Bush has developed the clearest vision of America's role in the world. There is considerable continuity in economic statecraft with his two predecessors, but George W. Bush is the first post-Cold War president to craft a grand strategy to succeed containment. It is largely premised on an acceptance of Krauthammer's unipolar era, and borrows heavily from the Clinton administration's emphasis on democratic enlargement and free market economics. What is new is a greater willingness to act unilaterally and to bring the full weight of America to bear down upon its enemies and in support of its objectives. Cold War threats to the state have been replaced by the threats from terrorism and rogue states. These threats are real, but perhaps not in the same sense that the Soviet nuclear threat was real, and there are greater difficulties in persuading allies to share American views, prescriptions and even values – something popularised by Kagan's categorisation of Europeans as Venusians and Americans as Martians.[8] Moreover, these threats are much harder to combat because traditional nuclear deterrence has but limited purchase (e.g. North Korea) and non-territorial threats invite less conventional approaches that might well sometimes be at the margins of constitutionality. Indeed, the case of proving that the ends justify the means becomes more difficult to make when it relies on intelligence estimates of the strike capabilities of secret weapon development programmes, judgements that they will be used, and a decision to strike to kill before those judged to be your opponents strike first. Containment never embraced a preventative strike rationale.

The Bush administration's response to 9/11 does constitute a revolution in American strategy and can claim to have resolved traditional tensions within US foreign policy. Isolationist sentiment has once more been banished and idealism and realism squared in the merging of values and security. To its credit the Bush administration has spared neither foe nor friend from its crusade to liberalise and democratise, which was boldly demonstrated in its rejection of past US Middle Eastern policy. There is an engaging logic too in the invasion of Iraq. It removed a potential security threat to the US and its allies and provided an opportunity to nation-build and to establish a bastion of democratic government in the Middle East from where democratic ideas can be spread to others – a kind of democratisation domino effect.

Like all revolutions, though, the Bush administration's has released such powerful forces that it has been compelled to make much policy 'on the hoof' and the ultimate outcome is very uncertain. It may be that the spread of democracy, economic interdependence and a growing awareness of common security interests deradicalise the disenfranchised and encourage collective enterprise for the good of all. However, it is also possible that traditional competition for security and power will be exacerbated by the overlay of the war on terrorism, which might in turn encourage a 'clash of civilisations' or widen the new fault lines created by US preventative strike doctrine. It is further possible that the assumptions of democratic peace theory will be sorely tested should radical groups achieve power through the very democratic processes that the US is determined to encourage.

What is already certain is that the world can never be the same again, that super-terrorism demands new responses, and that the US is again confronted with enormous responsibilities and difficult balances to strike. Immediate issues are those perennial problems of how a democracy conducts an effective foreign policy and upholds the integrity of its underpinning principles, especially in a time of crisis. There are three vitally important issues here for the US: the first is to maintain the integrity of its constitutional democracy; the second is the importance of safeguarding America's moral authority; and the third is to ensure that when Americans are asked to lay their lives on the line for foreign policy goals this is properly justified. These issues are not separable, even though they seem to refer to the domestic and the foreign spheres, and they resonate strongly of similar dilemmas during the Cold War. There is much debate about whether the Imperial Presidency has returned in the aftermath of 9/11 and just how far the war on terrorism waged at home, symbolised by Homeland Security and the Patriot Act, justifies the erosion of American civil liberties – a debate similar to that of the McCarthy years. Just as in the Cold War, there are inconsistencies between US human rights rhetoric and policy practice, such as the treatment of detainees at Guantanamo Bay and the highly damaging abuses perpetrated by American troops in Iraq. And there is great contention in America and abroad about whether the sacrifice of American lives in Iraq is better justified than in Vietnam. There are some definite similarities between the wars too: for all its sophisticated weaponry, logistical and intelligence gathering capabilities, the US is struggling to control far inferior forces; its foot-soldiers are incurring growing casualties; the insurgency is stretching US troop capability; and recruitment is down and demands are up.

Critics of the Bush administration highlight a number of other dangers that result from its current policies and chosen means of executing them. Its policy towards the UN is characteristic of a broad preference for unilateral rather than multilateral action. This unilateralism feeds off America's unchallengeable hard power, its convictions about the need for vigorous action against terrorism and rogue states, and a long tradition that fears corruption of its constitutional integrity and its democratic procedures if it has to compromise and accommodate with other nation-states in the course of collective action. Many, most notably Nye, fear that obsession with unilateralism and America's hard power will so undermine America's soft power that it will only 'win' empty military victories and lose the more important battles for the hearts and minds of people around the world. In the long term such losses would be corrosive of American democracy and society in a way far more dangerous than anything that multilateralism might harbour. After all, US military hard power only ensured the West did not lose the Cold War: it did not win it. If it is possible to talk of the West winning, then it was because of its soft power and the cooperative multilateral institutions that the US did so much to found, such as the IMF, World Bank, GATT and NATO.

Advocates of multilateral action also stress that it is a companion of international law and that both are embedded in democratic practice. Western democracy has flourished through deliberation and due process. This can be cumbersome and slow, but multilateral action through international law might in fact achieve quicker and more authoritative results than those achieved without the UN and which involve the flouting of international law and the refusal to abide by international agreements, such as the US's unwillingness to submit its military personnel to the jurisdiction of the ICC. For many there is a tragedy-in-waiting here: the US risks discounting the soft power of its own democratic and free market model – with its civil rights, due process and wealth of cultural attraction – for the sake of a hard power unilateralist strategy that is incapable of consummating its goals and which endangers its soft power through apparent disregard and disrespect for international law and collective multilateral action.

America's soft power has been damaged by its refusal to abide by a raft of multilateral agreements, by its stance on climate change and by a growing dissatisfaction with the failure of its brand of capitalism to address the issues of distributive justice and the often economically disruptive and identity-challenging effects of globalisation. When one adds to this suspicions that American oil companies have too much say in official US policy on climate change and that US government aid overseas is relatively less than that of Japan or the EU (even though individual Americans remain outstandingly generous), then the authority of America's voice is further diminished and dissatisfaction increased with the way that the richest nation deals with the disadvantaged, the dispossessed and the debtors of this world.

These criticisms are well reasoned. It is important, though, to acknowledge also change and, especially, the efficacy of alternatives for US policy-makers. For a start there is evidence to suggest that, thus far at least, the Bush administration has toned down its unilateralism in its second term, as demonstrated in Bush's 'listening tour' to Europe in 2005, its greater cooperation with the EU over Iran and its multilateral approach to North Korea. There has been a retreat, too, from the crude disaggregation policy that divided Europe at the time of the Iraq War into the old and the new – a division that puzzlingly placed Britain in the latter camp.[9] This may well be the product of the administration becoming bogged down in Iraq and buffeted at home by the political storm that has followed in the wake of Hurricane Katrina. Even if this is the case, then it is a salutary lesson of the limits of American power and an opportunity for other nations to re-engage the US and persuade it that multilateralism can be effective rather than a means of either deferral or simply constraining the US. But to do this the onus is on US allies to 'walk the walk' as well as 'talk the talk'.

Thus we come to one final thought. Where, if anywhere, does the failure of imagination lie in the inability to craft a New World Order after the Cold War that delivers, in the words of Franklin D. Roosevelt, freedom of speech and religion and freedom from want and fear?[10] It is easy to blame America. George H. Bush seemed to think that the UN system, liberated from ideologically wielded vetoes in the Security Council, could fulfil its original promise and usher in a New World Order, but took things little further than to exploit the opportunity in the First Gulf War. The Clinton administration's rhetoric of assertive multilateralism certainly promised more, but did not always deliver. The George W. Bush administration has consciously turned away from the UN, has criticised its management and effectiveness, and is often unwilling to engage with it constructively. Here, maybe, is a failure of imagination to utilise what could be an effective device for promoting policies beneficial for the US and the wider world community.

However, this is too simplistic. Structures may, as neo-liberal institutionalists suggest, facilitate agreement, build confidence and blunt the impact of anarchy in the international system. Also, the UN must be used as a political forum as Roosevelt had always expected and intended it to be. But before any of this can take place there has to be some confidence in an organisation and common ground from which to begin. The US is no exception to this. Hence, despite sometimes strained relationships, the US remains an active and central actor within the WTO. It has even pooled some sovereignty here. The UN is different. It has a history of ineffectiveness and of attempts, by members of the Security Council especially, to frustrate rather than contribute to US policy, as France and Germany did in the lead-up to the Iraq War. Even UN Secretary-General Kofi Annan delivered a 'stunning institutional *mea culpa*' in 1999 of the UN's role in the Balkans,[11] and currently the organisation is mired in the scandal surrounding the oil for food programme.

Moreover, world order has to be forward-looking rather than rooted in the past, and the post-9/11 era is one of renewed and fundamental debate about sovereignty and legitimacy. This is reflected in the EU's continued move towards some sort of post-Westphalian sub-system, in the notion of humanitarian interventionism and, more controversially, in the US doctrine of preventative strike. All of these are logical evolutions in response to events but none of the assumptions that underpin them are universally shared. In this sense, therefore, it is not enough to criticise the US for its preventative strike doctrine as being contrary to international law because WMDs and the emergence of an international terrorism that seeks to exact maximum casualties rather than negotiation give this approach a clear rationale. Rather, the world has to offer the US viable alternatives to unilateralism and it may be that international law has to evolve too in response to contemporary dangers and, especially, super-terrorism.

Whatever the future holds, the women and men who run the foreign policy of the US will bear considerable responsibility. How they understand the world, cope with and direct it will fundamentally affect us all. Realist appreciation of problems that they will confront in dealing with terrorists or states concerned with power and security in a system where anarchy is still an important characteristic must be a part of their understanding. Likewise the effects of the growth of democracy, economic interdependence and non-state actors (including regional blocs such as NAFTA and the EU) and the idealist imagination, not bounded solely by Western values, have all got parts to play as well. Fukuyama's vision, of the monolithic triumph of the West, is flawed and a rank impoverishment of the richness of this world. Thus policy-makers will have to deal with complexity, value democratic controls and account-ability, recognise the worth and needs of others, strike appropriate balances between hard and soft power, and have imagination to work constructively across normative divides. And all this needs to be done without endangering the security of the US. Such qualities are not easily acquired, but the US has not lacked imagination in the past and it has now an established tradition, as Colin Powell once wrote, of recognising that with enormous power comes sobering responsibility.[12]

Notes

1 US foreign policy

1 Second Bush–Kerry debate, St Louis, Missouri, 8 October 2004.
2 M. Albright, 'The Testing of American Foreign Policy', *Foreign Affairs* 77:6, 1998, 50.
3 Alternative nomenclatures are states of concern and backlash states.
4 The Office of the President of the United States of America, *The National Security Strategy of the United States of America*, September 2002.
5 'Uniting and Strengthening America by Providing Appropriate Tools Required to Intercept and Obstruct Terrorism (US PATRIOT ACT) Act of 2001'.
6 On foreign policy see: H.J. Morgenthau, *Politics among Nations: The Struggle for Power and Peace*, 6th edn revised by K. Thompson, New York: Knopf, 1985; G.T. Allison, *Essence of Decision: Explaining the Cuban Missile Crisis*, Boston: Little Brown, 1971; L. Neack, J.A.K. Hay and P. J. Haney (eds), *Foreign Policy Analysis: Continuity and Change in Its Second Generation*, Englewood Cliffs NJ: Prentice Hall, 1995; S. Strange, 'Political Economy and International Relations', in K. Booth and S. Smith, *International Relations Theory Today*, Cambridge: Polity Press, 1995, pp. 154–175; M. Nincic, *Democracy and Foreign Policy: The Fallacy of Political Realism*, New York: Columbia University Press, 1992; R.N. Lebow, *The Tragic Vision of Politics: Ethics, Interests and Orders*, Cambridge: Cambridge University Press, 2003; D.K. Chatterjee and D.E. Scheid (eds), *Ethics and Foreign Intervention*, Cambridge: Cambridge University Press, 2003; and, for an insider's view in the aftermath of 9/11, see R.A. Clarke, *Against All Enemies: Inside America's War on Terror*, London: Free Press, 2004.
7 For more on democratic peace theory, see Chapter 9, and M.W. Doyle, 'Kant, Liberal Legacies and Foreign Affairs' Parts 1 and 2, *Philosophy and Public Affairs* 12:3, 1983, 205–35; 12:4, 1983, 323–53.
8 H.J. Morgenthau, *A New Foreign Policy for the United States*, London: Pall Mall Press, 1969; see also Chapter 7.
9 A. Wendt, *Social Theory of International Politics*, Cambridge: Cambridge University Press, 1998, p. 249.
10 For an introduction to international relations theory, see S. Burchill *et al.*, *Theories of International Relations*, 2nd edn, Basingstoke: Palgrave, 2001.
11 D. Lal, *In Praise of Empires: Globalization and Order*, Basingstoke: Palgrave, 2004. For another revisionist view of empire, see N. Ferguson, *Empire: How Britain Made the Modern World*, London: Penguin, 2004.
12 Washington's Farewell Address in H.S. Commager, *Living Ideas in America*, New York: Harper, 1951, pp. 143–47.

13 J.S. Nye, *The Paradox of American Power: Why the World's Only Superpower Can't Go It Alone*, New York: Oxford University Press, 2002.
14 S. Kull and I.M. Destler, *Misreading the Public: The Myth of the New Isolationism*, Washington DC: Brookings Institute, 1999.
15 A.P. Dobson (ed.), with S. Malik and G. Evans (assistant eds), *Deconstructing and Reconstructing the Cold War*, Andover: Ashgate, 1999.
16 Hereafter the Nationalist Chinese island is referred to as Taiwan.
17 A.M. Schlesinger Jr, *The Imperial Presidency*, New York: Popular Library, 1974.
18 http://www.whitehouse.gov/news/releases/2002/10/20021002–2.html.
19 Wohlstetter, a leading critic of MAD and a proponent of strategic flexibility, advocated the defeat of terrorism by the use of superior military technology just as he had advocated the maintenance of US superiority over the USSR and abandonment of arms limitation talks. See A. Wohlstetter, 'Bosnia as Future', in Wohlstetter *et al.*, *Lessons from Bosnia*, Santa Monica CA: Rand, 1993, pp. 1–34.
20 A.M. Schlesinger Jr, *War and the American Presidency*, New York: W.W. Norton, 2005, p. 21.

2 The US and the Cold War

1 M.P. Leffler, 'The American Conception of National Security and the Beginnings of the Cold War, 1945–48', *American Historical Review* 89:2, 1984, 364.
2 M. McGwire, 'National Security and Soviet Foreign Policy', in M.P. Leffler and D.S. Painter (eds), *Origins of the Cold War*, London: Routledge, 1994, pp. 63–68.
3 See, for instance, A. Bullock, *Ernest Bevin: Foreign Secretary*, Oxford: Oxford University Press, 1985; A. Deighton, *The Impossible Peace: Britain, the Division of Germany and the Origins of the Cold War*, Oxford: Clarendon, 1990; C.S. Maier (ed.), *The Cold War in Europe: Era of a Divided Continent*, Princeton: Marcus Wiener, 1996.
4 For an insight into this interpretative debate, see M.P. Leffler, 'The Interpretative Wars over the Cold War', in G. Martel (ed.), *American Foreign Relations reconsidered 1890–1993*, London: Routledge, 1994, pp. 106–24; H. Feis, *From Trust to Terror, 1945–50*, New York: W.W. Norton, 1970; W.A. Williams, *The Tragedy of American Diplomacy*, 2nd edn, New York: Dell Publishing, 1972; D. Yergin, *Shattered Peace: The Origins of the Cold War and the National Security State*, Boston: Houghton Mifflin, 1977; J.L. Gaddis, 'The Emerging Post-revisionist Thesis on the Origins of the Cold War', *Diplomatic History* 7:3, 1983, 171–90; Leffler, 'The American Conception of National Security'; J.L. Gaddis, *We Now Know: Rethinking Cold War History*, Oxford: Clarendon Press, 1997.
5 See: M. Hogan, *The Marshall Plan: America, Britain and the Reconstruction of Western Europe, 1947–52*, Cambridge: Cambridge University Press, 1987; I. Wexler, *The Marshall Plan Revisited: The European Recovery Program in Economic Perspective*, Westport CT: Greenwood, 1983; C.L. Mee, *The Marshall Plan: The Launching of Pax Americana*, New York: Simon & Schuster, 1984.
6 For details of the Berlin Crisis, see A. Shlaim, *The United States and the Berlin Blockade, 1948–1949: A Study in Crisis Decision-making*, London: University California Press, 1983; E. Morris, *Blockade: Berlin and the Cold War*, London: Hamilton, 1983.
7 G.F. Kennan, 'X', 'The Sources of Soviet Conduct', *Foreign Affairs* 25, July 1947, 566–82.
8 R. Chandler, 'Political Sufficiency of Nuclear Forces', *Air University Review*,

September–October, 1980, http://www.airpower.maxwell.af.mil/airchronicles/
aureview/1980/sep-oct/chandler.html.

9 L. Freedman, 'Henry Kissinger', in J. Baylis and J. Garnett (eds), *Makers of Nuclear Strategy*, London: Pinter Publishers, 1991, p. 103.

10 E. Luttwak, 'Perceptions of Military Force and US Defence Policy', *Survival* 19:1, 1977, 5.

11 L. Freedman, *The Evolution of Nuclear Strategy*, 2nd edn, London: Macmillan, 1989, p. 433.

12 Toynbee cited in G. Allison, J.S. Nye and A. Carnesale, 'Defusing the Nuclear Menace', *The Washington Post*, 4 September 1988, http://www.bcsia.ksg.harvard. edu/ publication.cfm?ctype=article&item_id868.

13 http://www.americanhistory.si.edu/subs/work/missions/deterrence.

3 Superpower collaboration and confrontation

1 Cited by E.R. May, *American Cold War Strategy: Re-interpreting NSC 68*, New York: Bedford Books, 1993, p. 9.

2 *Foreign Relations of the United States* 1, 1950, NSC–68, 14 April 1950, 243–44.

3 J.L. Gaddis, *Strategies of Containment*, Oxford: Oxford University Press, 1982, p. 95.

4 *Ibid.*, p. 151, source J. Shepley, 'How Dulles Averted War', *Life Magazine* 40, 16 January 1956.

5 K. Larres, *Churchill's Cold War: The Politics of Personal Diplomacy*, New Haven CT: Yale University Press, 2002.

6 Cited in P.G. Boyle, *American–Soviet Relations: From the Russian Revolution to the Fall of Communism*, London: Routledge, 1993, p. 134.

7 G.H. Chang, 'To the Nuclear Brink: Eisenhower, Dulles and the Quemoy-Matsu Crisis', *International Security* 12:4, 1988, 97.

8 J.F. Kennedy, Inaugural Speech, 20 January 1961.

9 W.W. Rostow, *The Stages of Economic Growth: A Non-Communist Manifesto*, Cambridge: Cambridge University Press, 1962.

10 For more on Kennedy, see M.R. Beschloss, *The Crisis Years: Kennedy and Krushchev, 1960–63*, New York: Edward Burlingame Books, 1991; A.M. Schlesinger Jr, *A Thousand Days: John F. Kennedy in the White House*, Boston: Houghton Mifflin, 1965; T.G. Paterson (ed.), *Kennedy's Quest for Victory: American Foreign Policy, 1961–1963*, New York: Oxford University Press, 1989.

11 J. Spanier, *American Foreign Policy since World War II*, New York: Holt, Rinehart, & Winston, 1985, p. 168.

12 H. Kissinger, *American Foreign Policy*, New York, W.W. Norton, 1977, p. 305. For more about Kissinger's *realpolitik* approach and the policy of *détente*, see R. Garthoff, *Détente and Confrontation: American–Soviet Relations from Nixon to Reagan*, Washington: The Brookings Institute, 1994; W. Isaacson, *Kissinger: A Biography*, New York: Simon & Schuster, 1992.

13 For the change in US policy towards China, see I.J. Kim, *The Strategic Triangle: China, the United States and the Soviet Union*, New York: Paragon House, 1987; H. Harding, *A Fragile Relationship: The United States and China since 1972*, Washington DC: Brookings Institute, 1992.

14 It has been argued that the US never had at its disposal the incentives and sanctions that were necessary to moderate Soviet behaviour. R.S. Litwak, *Détente and the Nixon Doctrine: American Foreign Policy and the Pursuit of Stability, 1969–1976*, Cambridge: Cambridge University Press, 1984, p. 93.

15 For discussion of Carter's dilemmas, see G. Smith, *Morality, Reason and Power: American Diplomacy in the Carter Years*, New York: Hill & Wang, 1986; L. Schoultz, *Human Rights and the United States Policy Towards Latin America*, Princeton: Princeton University Press, 1981; J. Muravchik, *The Uncertain Crusade: Jimmy Carter and the Dilemmas of Human Rights Policy*, London: Hamilton Press, 1986.
16 Garthoff, *Detente and Confrontation*, p. 573.
17 W. Newmann, 'The Structures of National Security Decision Making', *Presidential Studies Quarterly* 34:2, 2004, 288.
18 J.L. Gaddis, *The United States and the End of the Cold War: Implications, Reconsiderations, Provocations*, New York: Oxford University Press, 1992, p. 123.
19 J. Dumbrell, *American Foreign Policy: Carter to Clinton*, London: Macmillan Press, 1997, p. 74.
20 *Ibid.*, p. 87.
21 Gaddis, *The United States and the end of the Cold War*, p. 131.
22 For more on the Reagan approach to containment, see D. Mervin, *Ronald Reagan and the American Presidency*, London: Longman, 1990; R.A. Dallek, *Ronald Reagan: The Politics of Symbolism*, Cambridge MA: Harvard University Press, 1984; R.J. McMahaon, 'Making Sense of American Foreign Policy during the Reagan Years', *Diplomatic History* 19:2, 1995, 367–84.
23 Cited by S.J. Ball, *The Cold War: An International History 1947–1991*, Oxford: Oxford University Press, 1997, p. 228.
24 Quoted in D.E. Nuechterlein, *America Recommitted*, 2nd edn, Kentucky: University Press of Kentucky, 2001, p. 171.
25 Cited in M.A. Alexeev, 'From the Cold War to the "Cold Peace": US–Russian Interactions from Gorbachev to the Present', in S.P. Ramet and C. Ingebritsen (eds), *Coming in from the Cold War*, New York: Rowman & Littlefield Publishers, 2002, p. 153.
26 R.A. Melanson, *American Foreign Policy since the Vietnam War: The Search for Consensus from Nixon to Clinton*, 2nd edn, New York: M.E. Sharpe, 1996, p. 213.
27 A.L. Horelick, 'US–Soviet Relations: Threshold of a New Era', *Foreign Affairs* 69:1, 1989/90, 55.
28 http://www.policyalmanac.org/world/archive/usnato_cfe.shtml.
29 D.B. Cohen, 'From START to START II: Dynamism and Pragmatism in the Bush Administration's Nuclear Weapon Policies', *Presidential Studies Quarterly* 27:3, 1997, 412–29.
30 Quoted in Boyle, *American–Soviet Relations*, p. 234.
31 For more on Bush, see especially M.R. Beschloss and S. Talbott, *At the Highest Levels: The Inside Story of the End of the Cold War*, Boston: Little, Brown, 1993.

4 Economic statecraft, 1945–89

1 D. Horowitz, *Free World Colossus*, New York: Hill & Wang, 1971; I. Wallerstein, *The Modern World System*, 2 vols, New York: Academic Press, 1974; P. Kennedy, *The Rise and Fall of the Great Powers*, New York: Random House, 1987; J.S. Nye, *Bound to Lead: The Changing Nature of American Power*, New York: Basic Books, 1990; S. Gill, *American Hegemony and the Trilateral Commission*, Cambridge: Cambridge University Press, 1990; S. Strange, 'The Persistent Myth of Lost Hegemony', *International Organization* 41:4, 1987, 551–74.
2 J.E. Spero and J.A. Hart, *The Politics of International Economic Relations*, London and New York: Routledge, 1997, p. 1.

3 C.P. Kindleberger, *The World in Depression 1929–1939*, Berkeley: University of California Press, 1973.
4 A.A. Stein, 'The Hegemon's Dilemma: Great Britain, the United States, and the International Economic Order', *International Organization* 38:2, 1984, 384.
5 US Trade in Goods and Services – Balance of Payments Basis: 1960–2004, US Census Bureau, Foreign Trade Division. S. Newton, in *The Global Economy 1944–200: The Limits of Ideology*, London: Arnold, 2004, p. 156, puts US indebtedness to the rest of the world in 2002 at $2.2 trillion.
6 See A.P. Dobson, 'The US, Britain and the Question of Hegemony', in G. Lundestad, *No End to Alliance: The United States and Western Europe: Past, Present and Future*, London: Macmillan, 1998, pp. 134–67.
7 It was succeeded in 1967 by the European Community (EC) and in 1993 by the European Union (EU).
8 *John F. Kennedy Library*, NSF box 310, folder: Trade East–West Trade, Policy Planning Council Paper, 'US Policy on Trade with the European Soviet Bloc', 26 July 1963.
9 *Ibid.*
10 Gaddis, *United States and the End of the Cold War*, p. 125.
11 B.W. Jentleson, *Pipeline Politics: The Complex Political Economy of East–West Trade*, Ithaca: Cornell University Press, 1986, p. 210; P. Hanson, *Western Economic Statecraft in East–West Relations: Embargoes, Sanctions, Linkage, Economic Warfare and Détente*, London: Routledge & Kegan Paul, 1988, p. 43.
12 G.C. Hufbauer and J.S. Schott, *Economic Sanctions Reconsidered: History and Current Policy*, second edition with Ann Elliott, Washington DC: Institute for International Economics, 1990, pp. 683–711.
13 See A.P. Dobson, 'The Reagan Administration, Economic Warfare, and Starting to Close Down the Cold War', *Diplomatic History* 29:3, 2005, 531–57.
14 H. Magdoff, *The Age of Imperialism: The Economics of US Foreign Policy*, New York: Modern Reader Paperbacks, 1969. Magdoff was one of many New Left luminaries, which include W.A. Williams, G. Kolko, G. Alperovitz, L.C. Gardner, D.S. Clemens and a host of others.
15 F. Fanon, *The Wretched of the Earth*, translated by Constance Farrington, New York: Grove Press, 1968.
16 D. Calleo, *Beyond American Hegemony: The Future of the Western Alliance*, New York: Basic Books, 1987.
17 A.P. Dobson, *Flying in the Face of Competition*, Aldershot: Avebury, 1995.

5 The US and Europe, 1950–89

1 C.S. Maier, 'Alliance and Autonomy: European Identity and U.S. Foreign Policy Objectives in the Truman Years', in M.J. Lacey (ed.), *The Truman Presidency*, Cambridge: Cambridge University Press, 1989, pp. 273–98; G. Lundestad, *'Empire' by Integration: The United States and European Integration, 1945–1997*, Oxford: Oxford University Press, 1998, pp. 1–5.
2 For the Berlin Crisis see H.M. Catudal, *Kennedy and the Berlin Wall Crisis: A Case Study in US Decision Making*, Berlin: Berlin Verlag, 1980; J.C. Ausland, *Kennedy, Khrushchev, and the Berlin–Cuba Crisis, 1961–64*, Oslo: Scandinavia, 1996; J.S. Gearson, *Harold Macmillan and the Berlin Wall Crisis 1958–1962: The Limits of Interest and Force*, Basingstoke: Macmillan, 1998; J.M. Schick, *The Berlin Crisis, 1958–1962*, Philadelphia: University of Pennsylvania Press, 1971.
3 For details of the EDC–Indochina connection, see J. Aimaq, *For Europe or for*

222 *Notes*

Empire? French Colonial Ambitions and the European Army Plan, Lund, Sweden: Lund University Press, 1996. For the Anglo-American relationship, see A.P. Dobson, *Anglo-American Relations in the Twentieth Century*, London: Routledge, 1995; J. Dumbrell, *A Special Relationship: Anglo-American Relations in the Cold War and After*, Basingstoke: Macmillan, 2001. For Britain and integration, see E. Dell, *The Schuman Plan and the Abdication of British Leadership in Europe*, Oxford: Oxford University Press, 1995; C. Lord, *Absent at the Creation: Britain and the Formation of the European Community*, Aldershot: Dartmouth, 1996; S. George, *An Awkward Partner: Britain in the European Community*, Oxford: Oxford University Press, 1998; J. Young, *Britain and European Unity 1945–1999*, Basingstoke: Macmillan, 2000.

4 Public Record Office, FO 371/38523, 'The Essentials of an American Policy', 21 March 1944.

5 *FRUS* 1951, 4, record of State-Joint Chiefs of Staff Meeting held at the Pentagon, 21 November 1951, pp. 985–89.

6 M. Hogan, *The Marshall Plan: America, Britain, and the Reconstruction of Western Europe, 1947–52*, Cambridge: Cambridge University Press, 1987, p. 445.

7 S. Strange, *Sterling and British Policy: A Political Study of an International Currency in Decline*, London: Oxford University Press, 1971, p. 63.

8 C. Kelleher, 'US Foreign Policy and Europe, 1990–2000', *Brookings Review* 8:4, 1990, 5.

9 There are a number of good overviews of the development of general post-war European integration. These include R. McAllister, *From EC to EU: An Historical and Political Survey*, London: Routledge, 1997; M. Dedman, *The Origins and Development of the European Union 1945–95*, London: Routledge, 1996.

10 J.F. Dulles cited in Lundestad, *'Empire' by Integration*, p. 47. For the EDC controversy and West German rearmament, see E. Fursdon, *The European Defence Community: A History*, London: Macmillan, 1980; S. Dockrill, *Britain's Policy for West German Rearmament, 1950–1955*, Cambridge: Cambridge University Press, 1991; K. Ruane, *The Rise and Fall of the European Defence Community: Anglo-American Relations and the Crisis of European Defence, 1950–55*, Basingstoke: Macmillan, 2000.

11 Lundestad, *'Empire' by Integration*, p. 42.

12 G. Lundestad, *East, West, North, South: Major Developments in International Politics, 1945–1990*, Oslo: Norwegian University Press, 1994, p. 197.

13 D. Acheson, *Present at the Creation: My Years in the State Department*, London: Hamilton, 1970, p. 284.

14 A.P. Dobson, *The Politics of the Anglo-American Economic Special Relationship*, New York: St Martin's Press, 1988, p. 186.

15 See, for example, William Park, *Defending the West: A History of NATO*, Boulder CO: Westview Press, 1986.

16 P. Pitman, ' "A General Named Eisenhower": Atlantic Crisis and the Origins of the European Economic Community', in M. Trachtenberg (ed.), *Between Empire and Alliance: America and Europe during the Cold War*, New York: Rowman & Littlefield Publishers, 2003, p. 43.

17 Cited in Freedman, *The Evolution of Nuclear Strategy*, p. 312.

18 *Ibid.*, p. 429.

19 Pitman, 'A General Named Eisenhower', p. 52 and note 72.

20 Kennedy cited by Lundestad, *'Empire' by Integration*, p. 68.

21 For the MLNF, see P. Winand, *Eisenhower, Kennedy, and the United States of Europe*, London: Macmillan, 1997, especially pp. 203–45, 315–56. For rejection

of Britain's EEC membership application, see W. Kaiser, 'The Bomb and Europe: Britain, France, and the EEC Negotiations 1961–63', *Journal of European Integration History* 1:1, 1995, 65–85; R. Steininger, 'Great Britain's First EEC Failure in January 1963', *Diplomacy and Statecraft* 7:2, 1996, 404–35. For the trade dispute, R.B. Talbott, *The Chicken War*, Ames: Iowa State University, 1978.
22 H. Wilson, *The Labour Government 1964–1970: A Personal Account*, London: Weidenfeld & Nicolson, 1971, p. 264.
23 Kennan cited in G. McTurnan Kahin and J. Lewis, *The United States in Vietnam*, New York: Delta Books, 1967, p. 297.
24 See, for example, R.L. Rubenstein (ed.), *The Dissolving Alliance: The United States and the Future of Europe*, New York: Paragon House, 1987; J. Joffe, *The Limited Partnership: Europe, the United States and the Burdens of Alliance*, Cambridge MA: Ballinger, 1987; M. Smith, *Western Europe and the United States: The Uncertain Alliance*, London: Allen & Unwin, 1984.
25 P. Duigan and L.H. Gann, *The United States and the New Europe, 1945–1993*, Oxford: Blackwell Publishers, 1994, p. 76.
26 For further details, see H. Smith, *European Union Foreign Policy and Central America*, Basingstoke: Macmillan, 1995.
27 See, for example, W. Goldstein (ed.), *Reagan's Leadership and the Atlantic Alliance: Views from Europe and America*, London: Pergammon-Brassey, 1986; S. Gill (ed.), *Atlantic Relations: Beyond the Reagan Era*, New York: St Martin's Press, 1989; K. Featherstone and R. Ginsberg, *The United States and the European Union in the 1990s: Partners in Transition*, London: Macmillan, 1996; G. Lundestad, 'The United States and Western Europe under Reagan', in D.E. Kyvig (ed.), *Reagan and the World*, New York: Greenwood, 1990, 39–66.
28 A.P. Dobson, *US Economic Statecraft for Survival 1933–1991*, London: Routledge, 2002, p. 267. For further details of the pipeline crisis, see A.J. Blinkin, *Ally Versus Ally: America, Europe and the Siberian Pipeline Crisis*, New York: Praeger, 1987; M. Thatcher, *The Downing Street Years*, London: Harper Collins, 1993, pp. 253–56.
29 A. Milward, *The European Rescue of the Nation State*, Berkeley CA: University of California Press, 1992.
30 K. Schwabe, 'The United States and European Integration: 1947–57', in C. Wurm (ed.), *Western Europe and Germany: The Beginnings of European Integration 1945–60*, Oxford: Berg, 1995, p. 129; R.T. Griffiths, 'The European Historical Experience', in K. Middlemas (ed.), *Orchestrating Europe: The Informal Politics of European Union 1973–95*, London: Fontana Press, 1995, 1–70; A.P. Dobson, 'The USA, Britain, and the Question of Hegemony', in G. Lundestad (ed.), *No End to Alliance: The United States and Western Europe: Past, Present and Future*, London: Macmillan Press, 1998, pp. 134–66.

6 Hegemony and the Western Hemisphere

1 See T.J. McCormick, *America's Half Century: United States Foreign Policy in the Cold War*, Baltimore: Johns Hopkins University Press, 1989; Calleo, *Beyond American Hegemony*; Stein, 'Hegemon's Dilemma'.
2 President Theodore Roosevelt, State of the Union Address to Congress, 6 December 1904.
3 Williams, *The Tragedy of American Diplomacy*.
4 Allison, *Essence of Decision*; R.A. Divine (ed.), *The Cuban Missile Crisis*, New York: Marcus Wiener, 1988; Gaddis, *We Now Know*, ch. 9; L.V. Scott, *Macmillan,*

Kennedy and the Cuban Missile Crisis: Political, Military and Intelligence Aspects, Basingstoke: Macmillan, 1999.
5   Crisis management is at the heart of Allison's *Essence of Decision*, but students should compare that work with what Gaddis has to say in *We Now Know*, ch. 9. For an introduction to crisis decision-making, see P.R. Viotti and M.V. Kauppi, *International Relations Theory: Realism, Pluralism, Globalism, and Beyond*, Boston: Allyn & Bacon, 1999, ch. 3.
6   J.G. Blight and D.A. Welch (eds), *Intelligence and the Cuban Missile Crisis*, London: Frank Cass, 1998.

7 The US and Asia, 1945–89

1   For Korea, see M. Hastings, *The Korean War*, London: Michael Joseph, 1987; R.J. Foot, *The Wrong War: American Policy and Dimensions of the Korean Conflict*, Ithaca NY: Cornell University Press, 1985; B. Cumings, *The Origins of the Korean War, Vol. 2, The Roaring of the Cataract*, Princeton: Princeton University Press, 1992.
2   D.F. Fleming, *The Cold War and its Origins, 1917–1960*, 2 vols, London: Allen & Unwin, 1961, pp. 1067–68.
3   For evidence of Stalin's encouragement of North Korea, see D. Heinzig, 'Stalin, Mao, Kim and Korean War Origins, 1950: A Documentary Discrepancy', *The Cold War International History Project Bulletin* Issues 8–9, 1996/97, 240–43; S. Goncharov, J.W. Lewis and X. Litai, *Uncertain Partners: Stalin, Mao, and the Korean War*, Stanford: Stanford University Press, 1993, pp. 143–45; J.L. Gaddis, *We Now Know: Rethinking Cold War History*, Oxford: Clarendon Press, 1997, pp. 70–75.
4   D. Horowitz, *The Free World Colossus*, New York: Hill & Wang, 1971, p. 119.
5   H.G. Nicholas, *The United States and Britain*, Chicago: University of Chicago Press, 1975, pp. 167–68; P. Busch, *All the Way with JFK? Britain, the US and the Vietnam War*, Oxford: Oxford University Press, 2003.
6   Literature on Vietnam is enormous and riven by debate about the justification of US actions and why its intervention was unsuccessful. Among the best accounts is G.C. Herring, *America's Longest War: The United States and Vietnam 1950–1975*, New York: Wiley, 1979. For a clash over the morality of US actions, see T. Taylor, *Nuremberg and Vietnam: An American Tragedy*, Chicago: Quadrangle Books, 1970; G. Lewy, *America in Vietnam: Illusion, Myth, and Reality*, New York: Oxford University Press, 1978. For the 'winnability' debate, see B. Palmer Jr, *The 25 Year War: America's Military Role in Vietnam*, Lexington: Kentucky University Press, 1984; G. Kahin, *Intervention: How America became Involved in Vietnam*, New York: Knopf, 1986.
7   For more on US–Japanese relations, see W. LaFeber, *The Clash: A History of US–Japanese Relations*, New York: W.W. Norton, 1997; M. Schaller, *Altered States: The United States and Japan Since the Occupation*, New York: Oxford University Press, 1997; W.I. Cohen, *The United States and Japan in the Post War World*, Lexington: University Press of Kentucky, 1989; W.S. Borden, *The Pacific Alliance: United States Foreign Economic Policy and Japanese Trade Recovery, 1947–1955*, Madison: University of Wisconsin Press, 1984; A. Iriye, *Across the Pacific: An Inner History of American–East Asian Relations*, New York: Harcourt, Brace, & Brace, 1967.
8   For more on US–China relations, see G. Chang, *Friends and Enemies: The United States, China, and the Soviet Union, 1948–1972*, Stanford: Stanford University

Press, 1990; G.A. James, *The China Connection: US Policy and the Peoples Republic of China*, Stanford: Stanford University Press, 1986; A.X. Jiang, *The United States and China*, Chicago: Chicago University Press, 1988; J.G. Stoessinger, *Nations at Dawn: China, the United States, and the Soviet Union*, 6th edn, New York: McGraw Hill, 1994.

9 For details, see R.W. Meyers, *A Unique Relationship: The United States and the Republic of China under the Taiwan Relations Act*, Stanford: Stanford University Press, 1989.

8 The US, Africa and the Middle East, 1945–89

1 C. Young, 'United States Policy Toward Africa: Silver Anniversary Reflections', *African Studies Review* 27:3, 1984, 12.
2 R. Wood, 'The Marshall Plan', in Leffler and Painter (eds), *Origins of the Cold War*, p. 209; D. Merrill, 'The United States and the Third World', in Martel (ed.), *American Foreign Relations Reconsidered*, p. 168; G. Shepherd Jr, 'The Conflict of Interests in American Policy on Africa', *Western Political Quarterly* 12:4, 1959, 998; T. Shaw and M. Grieve, 'The Political Economy of Resources: Africa's Future in the Global Environment', *Journal of Modern African Studies* 16:1, 1978, 6; D. Gibbs, *The Political Economy of Third World Intervention: Mines, Money and US Policy in the Congo Crisis*, Chicago: University of Chicago Press, 1991.
3 S. Bills, *Empire and Cold War: The Roots of US–Third World Antagonism, 1945–47*, London: Macmillan, 1990.
4 P.J. Schraeder, *United States Foreign Policy Toward Africa: Incrementalism, Crisis and Change*, Cambridge: Cambridge University Press, 1994, p. 253.
5 Cited in D. Volman, 'Africa's Rising Status in American Defence Policy', *Journal of Modern African Studies* 22:1, 1984, 144.
6 For US–Nigerian relations, see R. Shepard, *Nigeria, Africa and the United States from Kennedy to Reagan*, Bloomington: Indiana University Press, 1991.
7 S. Metz, 'American Attitudes Toward Decolonisation in Africa', *Political Science Quarterly* 99:3, 1984, 527.
8 Kissinger cited by Schraeder, *United States Foreign Policy Toward Africa*, p. 36.
9 Cited in Metz, 'American Attitudes Toward Decolonisation in Africa', p. 517.
10 Cited in Young, 'United States Policy Toward Africa', p. 2.
11 J. Marcum, 'Africa: A Continent Adrift', *Foreign Affairs* 68:1, 1988–89, 162.
12 Cited in Volman, 'Africa's Rising Status', p. 144.
13 Schraeder, *United States Foreign Policy Toward Africa*, p. 27; Volman, 'Africa's Rising Status', p. 143.
14 For US–USSR rivalry in the Horn, see R.G. Patman, *The Soviet Union in the Horn of Africa: The Diplomacy of Intervention and Disengagement*, Cambridge: Cambridge University Press, 1990; P. Henze, *The Horn of Africa: From War to Peace*, London: Macmillan, 1991; C. Crocker, *High Noon in Southern Africa: Making Peace in a Rough Neighbourhood*, New York: W.W. Norton, 1992.
15 For more on the US–Zaire relationship and the Congo crisis, see C. Young, *Politics in the Congo: Decolonisation and Independence*, Princeton: Princeton University Press, 1965; Schraeder, *United States Foreign Policy Toward Africa*, pp. 51–113; M. Kalb, *Congo Cables: The Cold War in Africa from Eisenhower to Kennedy*, New York: Macmillan, 1982.
16 D. Newsom, *Diplomacy and the American Democracy*, Bloomington: Indiana University Press, 1988, p. 86.

17 Schraeder, *United States Foreign Policy Toward Africa*, p. 157.
18 J.A. Lefebvre, 'The United States, Ethiopia and the 1963 Somali–Soviet Arms Deal: Containment and the Balance of Power Dilemma in the Horn of Africa', *Journal of Modern African Studies* 36:4, 1998, 611–43; J.A. Lefebvre, *Arms for the Horn: US Security Policy in Ethiopia and Somalia, 1953–91*, Pittsburgh: Pittsburgh University Press, 1991; D. Petterson, 'Somalia and the United States 1977–83: The New Relationship', in G. Bender, J. Coleman and R. Sklar (eds), *African Crisis Areas and US Foreign Policy*, Berkeley: University of California Press, 1985.
19 Cited by L. Nwachuku, 'The United States and Nigeria, 1960 to 1987: Anatomy of a Pragmatic Relationship', *Journal of Black Studies* 28:5, 1988, 591.
20 Kennedy cited in Metz, 'American Attitudes Toward Decolonisation in Africa', p. 518. For more on Kennedy and Angola, see especially R. Mahoney, *JFK: Ordeal in Africa*, New York: Oxford University Press, 1983. For more on the US and South Africa, see T.J. Noer, *Cold War and Black Liberation: The United States and White Rule in Africa, 1948–68*, Columbia: University of Missouri Press, 1985; R.C. Coker, *The United States and South Africa 1968–85: Constructive Engagement and its Critics*, Durham North Carolina: Duke Press, 1986; R.K. Massie, *Loosing the Bonds: The United States and South Africa during the Apartheid Years*, New York: Nan A. Talese, 1997; T. Borstelmann, *Apartheid's Reluctant Uncle: The United States and Southern Africa in the Early Cold War*, Oxford: Oxford University Press, 1993.
21 Schlesinger, *A Thousand Days*, pp. 536–37.
22 Cited by W. Stivers, *America's Confrontation with Revolutionary Change in the Middle East, 1948–83*, London: Macmillan, 1986, p. 12.
23 S. Marsh, *Anglo-American Relations and Cold War Oil*, London: Palgrave, 2003.
24 For details, see R. Ovendale, *Britain, the United States, and the End of the Political Mandate*, Woodbridge: Royal Historical Society, 1989; R. Ovendale, *Origins of the Arab Israeli Wars*, London: Longman, 1984; C. Smith, *Palestine and the Arab–Israeli Conflict*, 5th edn, Boston: St Martin's Press, 2004.
25 See especially M.J. Gasiorowski, *US Foreign Policy and the Shah: Building a Client State in Iran*, Ithaca: Cornell University Press, 1991. For the coup, see S. Marsh, 'The US, Iran and Operation Ajax: Inverting Interpretative Orthodoxy', *Middle Eastern Studies* 39, 2003, 1–38; M.J. Gasiorowski and M. Byrne (eds), *Mohammad Mosaddeq and the 1953 Coup in Iran*, Syracuse: Syracuse University Press, 2004.
26 For early US defence planning for the Middle East, see M.J. Cohen, *Fighting World War Three from the Middle East: Allied Contingency Plans, 1945–54*, London: Frank Cass, 1997. Among the many books on the Suez Crisis, see W.R. Louis and R. Owen (eds), *Suez 1956: The Crisis and Its Consequences*, Oxford: Oxford University Press, 1989; W.S. Lucas, *Divided We Stand: Britain, the US and the Suez Crisis*, London: Hodder & Stoughton, 1991.
27 For details of the hostage crisis and the turbulent US–Iranian relationship, see J.A. Bill, *The Eagle and the Lion: The Tragedy of American–Iranian Relations*, New Haven: Yale University Press, 1988; G. Sick, *All Fall Down: America's Tragic Encounter with Iran*, New York: Random House, 1985; R.W. Cottam, *Iran and the United States: A Cold War Case Study*, Pittsburgh: Pittsburgh University Press, 1988.
28 See H.A. Kissinger, *White House Years*, London: Michael Joseph, 1979; H.A. Kissinger, *Years of Upheaval*, Boston: Little, Brown & Company, 1982; Isaacson, *Kissinger: A Biography*.

29 For details of the Camp David Accords, see J. Carter, *Keeping Faith: Memoirs of a President*, New York: Bantam Books, 1982; W. Quandt, *Camp David: Peacemaking and Politics*, Washington: The Brookings Institute, 1986. For a good overview of attempts to find a Middle East peace settlement, see I. Rabinovich, *Waging Peace: Israel and the Arabs, 1948–2003*, Princeton: Princeton University Press, 2004.

30 For more on US policy towards the Middle East, see B.I. Kaufman, *The Arab Middle East and the United States: Inter-Arab Rivalry and Super-Power Diplomacy*, New York: Twayne, 1996; S.L. Spiegel, *The Other Arab–Israeli Conflict: Making America's Middle East Policy from Truman to Reagan*, Chicago: University of Chicago Press, 1985; H.W. Brands, *Into the Labyrinth: The United States and the Middle East, 1945–1993*, New York: McGraw Hill, 1994.

31 R. Engler, *The Politics of Oil: A Study of Private Power and Democratic Direction*, New York: Macmillan, 1961; D. Yergin, *The Prize: The Epic Quest for Oil, Money, and Power*, New York: Simon & Schuster, 1991; D. Painter, *Private Power and Public Policy: Multinational Oil Companies and U.S. Foreign Policy, 1941–1954*, London: I.B. Taurus, 1986; F. Venn, *Oil Diplomacy in the Twentieth Century*, Basingstoke: Macmillan, 1986; S. Bromley, *American Hegemony and World Oil: The Industry, the State System and the World Economy*, Philadelphia: Pennsylvania State University Press, 1991.

9 Power and purpose

1 J.L. Gaddis, 'International Relations Theory and the End of the Cold War', *International Security* 17:3, 1992/93, 44.

2 Nye, *The Paradox of American Power*. Note that while economic power can coerce (hard power), it can also co-opt and socialise others into one's ways, for example, the free trade initiatives that the US has made in the Western Hemisphere; see Chapter 12.

3 *Ibid.*, p. 8.

4 National Security Decision Directive 75 (NSDD 75), *US Relations with the USSR*, 17 January 1983.

5 S. Halper and J. Clarke, *America Alone: The Neo-Conservatives and the Global Order*, Cambridge: Cambridge University Press, 2004.

6 Dallek, *Ronald Reagan: The Politics of Symbolism*; J. Krieger, *Reagan, Thatcher and the Politics of Decline*, Cambridge: Polity Press, 1986; G. Smith, *Reagan and Thatcher*, London: The Bodley Head, 1990; L. Cannon, *President Reagan: The Role of a Lifetime*, New York: Simon & Schuster, 1991.

7 P. Schweizer, *Reagan's War: The Epic Story of His Forty-year Struggle and Final Triumph over Communism*, New York: Doubleday, 2002; D. Leebaert, *The Fifty-year Wound: The True Price of America's Cold War Victory*, Boston: Little, Brown & Co. 2002. Members of the Reagan administration who have written in a similar vein include C. Weinberger, *Fighting for Peace: Seven Critical Years in the Pentagon*, New York: Warner Books, 1990; R. Gates, *From the Shadows: The Ultimate Inside Story of Five Presidents and How They Won the Cold War*, New York: Simon & Schuster, 1996; R. Pipes, 'Misinterpreting the Cold War', *Foreign Affairs* 74:1, 1995, 54–161; G.W. Weiss, *The Farewell Dossier: Strategic Deception and Economic Warfare in the Cold War – An Insider's Untold Story*, The American Tradecraft Society; and N.A. Bailey, *The Strategic Plan that Won the Cold War, NSDD 75*, Maclean VA: Potomac Foundation, 1999.

8 G. Arbatov, *The Soviet System: An Insider's Life in Soviet Politics*, New York:

Time Books, 1992; F. Kratchowil, 'The Embarrassment of Changes: Neo-realism as the Science of Realpolitik without Politics', *Review of International Studies* 19:1, 1993, 63–80; B.A. Fisher, *The Reagan Reversal: Foreign Policy and the End of the Cold War*, Missouri: Missouri University Press, 2000; Gaddis, *The United States and the End of the Cold War*, p. 125.

 9 Committee on Foreign Relations, *Soviet Diplomacy and Negotiating Behavior – 1979–88: New Tests for US Diplomacy*, Washington DC: US Government Printing Office, 1988.

10 R. Davy (ed.), *European Détente: A Reappraisal*, London: Sage/RIIA, 1992; K. Dawisha, *Eastern Europe, Gorbachev and Reform*, Cambridge: Cambridge University Press, 1990; D. Ryall, 'The Cross and the Bear: The Vatican's Cold War Diplomacy in East Central Europe' and R. Bideleux, 'Soviet and Russian Perspectives on the Cold War', in Dobson (ed.), *Deconstructing and Reconstructing the Cold War*, pp. 181–201 and 226–50 respectively. A closely associated approach emphasises the importance of the beliefs of Gorbachev and his associates: D. Oberdorfer, *The Turn from Cold War to a New Era*, New York: Poseidon Press, 1991; and M. Bundy, 'From Cold War to Trusting Peace', *Foreign Affairs* 69:1, 1990, 197–212.

11 The tone of the speech was more moderate than one might think from the reports. Ironically, Reagan used the phrase 'evil empire' in the midst of a plea for toleration for the opening of negotiations with the Soviets. Source: *The Greatest Speeches of All Time* (This speech certainly does not merit such an accolade), Jerden Records, 1996, Ronald Reagan, 'Evil Empire' extract.

12 A. Dobrynin, *In Confidence: Moscow's Ambassador to America's Six Cold War Presidents 1962–1986*, New York: Time Books, 1995, pp. 511–12.

13 *Ibid.*, p. 545; *Public Papers of the Presidents of the United States: Ronald Reagan 1984*, Washington DC: Government Printing Office, 1986, pp. 40–44.

14 Quoted from Garthoff, *Détente and Confrontation*, p. 1013, Reagan's speech to the UN General Assembly, citing *Presidential Documents*, vol. 20 (1 October 1984), p. 1356.

15 Dobrynin, *In Confidence*, p. 564.

16 Kennedy, *Rise and Fall*, p. 666.

17 J.S. Nye, 'Understating US Strength', *Foreign Policy* 72, autumn 1988, 105–29; and *Bound to Lead*. Strange and Gill have respectively argued that a US, and a capitalist hegemony centred mainly in the US, continue to grow: 'The Persistent Myth of Lost Hegemony', *American Hegemony and the Trilateral Commission*.

18 NATO–Russia Compendium of Financial and Economic Data Relating to Defence, 9 June 2005; Xinhua, 'US Defence Spending Almost Half of World Total', http://www.xinhuanet.com.

19 http://www.ppionline.org/ndol/print.cfm?contentid=252964, last accessed 18 October 2004.

20 C. Krauthammer, 'America and the World', *Foreign Affairs* 70:1, 1990/91, 23–33; Nye, *Paradox of American Power*; S.P. Huntington, 'The Clash of Civilizations', *Foreign Affairs* 72:3, 1993, 22–49; J. Mearsheimer, 'Back to the Future: Instability in Europe After the Cold War', *International Security* 15:3, 1990, 5–57; K. Waltz, 'The Emerging Structure of International Politics', *International Security* 18:2, 1993, 44–79; F. Fukuyama, *The End of History and the Last Man*, London: Hamish Hamilton, 1992; Doyle, 'Kant, Liberal Legacies and Foreign Affairs'.

21 J.R. Huntley, *Pax Democratica: A Strategy for the 21st Century*, Basingstoke: Macmillan, 1998, p. 164.

22 Nye, *Paradox of American Power*, p. 12.

23 C. Krauthammer, 'The Unipolar Moment Revisited', *National Interest* 70, winter 2002–03, 5–17.
24 Huntington, 'Clash of Civilizations', p. 22.
25 Mearsheimer, 'Back to the Future', p. 12.
26 Waltz, 'The Emerging Structure'.
27 A.P. Dobson, 'The Dangers of US Interventionism', *Review of International Studies* 28:3, 2002, 577–97.
28 B. Buzan, *People, States and Fear*, Hemel Hempstead: Simon & Schuster, 1991.
29 D. Baldwin, 'The Concept of Security', *Review of International Studies* 23:1, 1997, 5–26; L. Friedman, 'International Security: Changing Targets', *Foreign Policy* 110, spring 1998, 48–63.
30 Weinberger, *Fighting for Peace*.
31 C. Powell, 'US Forces: Challenges Ahead: Enormous Power, Sobering Responsibility', *Foreign Affairs* 71:5, 1992, 39.
32 W. Christopher, 'America's Leadership: America's Opportunity', *Foreign Policy* 98, spring 1995, 8.
33 Quoted from C.W. Kegley and E.R. Wittkopf, *World Politics: Trend and Transformation*, New York: St Martin's Press, 1995, p. 415.
34 The EU took over military responsibility from the Stabilisation Force (SFOR) in Bosnia in 2004.
35 W. Bass, 'The Triage of Dayton', *Foreign Affairs* 77:5, 1998, 99.
36 Schlesinger, *War and the American Presidency*, p. 21.

10 The US and post-Cold War Europe

1 R. Kagan, 'Power and Weakness', *Policy Review* 113, June 2002, 3–28.
2 This chapter draws in parts upon S. Marsh and H. Mackenstein, *The International Relations of the European Union*, Harlow: Pearson, 2005.
3 Eizenstat cited in T. Frellesen, 'Processes and Procedures in EU–US Foreign Policy Cooperation: From the Transatlantic Declaration to the New Transatlantic Agenda', in E. Philippart and P. Winand (eds), *Ever Closer Partnership: Policy-making in EU–US Relations*, New York, Oxford: Peter Lang, 2001, p. 333; 'Transatlantic Relations – The EU–US Partnership', http://www.useu.be/TransAtlantic/Index.html; 'Joint EU–US Action Plan', http://europa.eu.int/comm/external-relations/us/action-plan.
4 W.H. Cooper, 'EU–US Economic Ties: Framework, Scope and Magnitude', CRS Report for Congress, 15 April 2005; 'Bilateral Trade Issues', http://europa.eu.int/commm/trade/issues/bilateral/countries/usa/index_en.htm; UNCTAD WID country profile: United States.
5 US Mission to the EU, 'Commerce's Aldonas: Shoring up the U.S.–EU Trade, Economic Relationship', http://www.useu.be/Categories/Trade/Apr2803AldonasUSEURelationship.html.
6 http://stat.wto.org/CountryProfile/WSDBCountryPFView.aspx?Language=E&Country=US,G32/; http://trade-info.cec.eu.int/doclib/docs/2005/april/tradoc_122531.pdf; http://www.imf.org/external/np/sec/member/members.htm; http://www.worldbank.org; IMF (September 2003) 'World Economic Outlook', Chapter II, pp. 94–103.
7 M. Feldstein, 'EMU and International Conflict', *Foreign Affairs* 76:6, 1997, 60–73.
8 E.L. Andrews, 'Strong Dollar, Weak Dollar: Anyone Have a Scorecard?', *New York Times*, http://www.globalpolicy.org/socecon/crisis/2003/0924strongweakdollar.htm.

9 PFP was a confidence-building measure fostering cooperation between NATO and partner countries. For details of the original PFP process, see G. von Moltke, 'Building a Partnership for Peace', *NATO Review* 42:3, 1994, 3–7. The Implementation Force (IFOR) and SFOR in Bosnia were NATO's first joint operations with PFP and other non-NATO states.

10 M. Albright, 'The Right Balance will Secure NATO's Future', *Financial Times*, 7 December 1999; D. Rumsfeld, Munich Conference on European Security Policy, http://www.defenselink.mil/speeches/2001/s20010203-secdef.html; US Secretary of State Powell, 2 December 2003, http://www.useu.be/Categories/Defense/Dec0203PowellOSCE.html.

11 S. Hoffmann, 'The United States and Europe', in R.J. Lieber (ed.), *Eagle Adrift: American Foreign Policy at the End of the Century*, New York: Longman, 1997, p. 190. Statistics from 'Operation Deliberate Force', http://www.globalsecurity.org/military/ops/deliberate_force.htm.

12 Total defence spending figures based on current prices and exchange rates; GDP figures based on current prices. Both sets exclude Iceland and are calculated from 'NATO–Russia Compendium of Financial and Economic Data Relating to Defence', 9 June 2005, pp. 5 and 7. See also Xinhua, 'US Defence Spending almost Half of World Total: Swedish Report', http://english.people.com.cn/200506/08/print20050608_189129.html; European Commission, 'European Defence – Industrial and Market Issues', COM(2003) 113 final, 11 March 2003, p. 5.

13 L. Brittan, 'Europe and the United States: New Challenges, New Opportunities', September 1998, http://www.eurunion.org/news/speeches/1998/1998index.htm; 'Germany Urges NATO Reform and Rethink of Transatlantic Ties', *Agence France Presse*, 13 February 2005; Chirac cited in Angus Roxburgh, 'EU's Defence Plans Baffle NATO', 3 December 2003, http://news.bbc.co.uk/1/hi/world/europe/3287009.stm; Burns cited in 'Defensive Reactions', *Guardian*, 18 October 2003, http://www.guardian.co.uk/guardianpolitics/story/0,,1065708,00.html.

14 G. Anderson, 'US Defence Budget Will Equal ROW Combined "within 12 months" ', *Janes Defence Industry*, 4 May 2005, http://www.janes.com/defence/news/jdi/jdi050504_1_n.shtml; T. Lansford, 'Security and Marketshare: Bridging the Transatlantic Divide in the Defence Industry', *European Security* 10:1, 2001, 9; A. Moens, in collaboration with R. Domisiewicz, 'European and North American Trends in Defence Industry: Problems and Prospects of a Cross-Atlantic Defence Market', Ottawa: International Security Research and Outreach Programme, April 2001.

15 Cohen, 'From START to START II', pp. 412–29.

16 W. Christopher, 'Securing US Interests While Supporting Russian Reform', US State Department Dispatch, 29 March 1993.

17 R.F. Staar, 'A Russian Rearmament Wish List', *Orbis* 43:4, 1999, 605.

18 M. Alexseev, 'From the Cold War to the Cold Peace: US–Russian Interactions from Gorbachev to the Present', in Ramet and Ingebritsen (eds), *Coming in from the Cold War*, pp. 160–61. START came into effect on 5 December 1994 and upon its completion on 5 December 2001 constituted the largest-ever arms controls reduction.

19 Lugar cited in S. Sestanovich, 'Why the United States Has No Russia Policy', in Lieber (ed.), *Eagle Adrift*, p. 170; J. Rosner, 'Clinton, Congress and Assistance to Russia', *SAIS Review*, winter/spring 1995, 15–35; A. Kosyrev, 'The Lagging Partnership', *Foreign Affairs* 73:3, 1994, pp. 60 and 71.

20 S. Sestanovich, 'Dual Frustration: America, Russia and the Persian Gulf', *National Interest*, Winter 2002, 157.
21 C. Rice, 'Promoting the National Interest', *Foreign Affairs* 79:1, 2000, 45–63; 'U.S. Resurrect "Spirit of Cold War" ', *New York Times*, 21 March 2000.
22 M. Rykhtik, 'Why Did Russia Welcome a Republican Victory?', PONARS Policy Memo 330, November 2004, p. 2.
23 Press conference by President Bush and Russian Federation President Putin, Brdo Pri Kranju, Slovenia, 16 June 2001, www.whitehouse.gov/news/releases/2001/06/20010618.html; U.S.–Russia Joint Declaration, 24 May 2002, http://www.state.gov/p/eur/rls/or/2002/10469.htm; D. Trenin, 'Silence of the Bear', *NATO Review*, spring 2002, http://www.nato.int/docu/review.htm.
24 R. Legvold, 'All the Way: Crafting a U.S.–Russian Alliance', *National Interest*, winter 2002, 24; 'Bush Approves Resumed Funding for Destruction of Soviet Arms', 14 January 2003, US Office of International Information Programs. The Bush administration's FY2003 budget request for $1.04 billion for Cooperative Threat Reduction programmes marked a 37% increase on the previous year.
25 Author's italics. R.N. Haass, 'U.S.–Russian Relations in the Post-Post-Cold War World', RAND Business Leaders Forum, Tenth Plenary Meeting, New York, 1 June 2002.
26 Legvold, 'All the Way', p. 22.
27 J. Richter, ' "A Sense of His Soul": The Relationship between Presidents Putin and Bush', PONARS Policy Memo 329, November 2004, p. 5; M. Light, 'US and European Perspectives on Russia', in J. Peterson and M. Pollack (eds), *Europe, America, Bush: Transatlantic Relations in the Twenty-first Century*, London: Routledge, 2003, p. 79; http://www.missilethreat.com/missiles/ss-nx-30_russia.html.
28 R. Allison, 'Strategic Reassertion in Russia's Central Asian Policy', *International Affairs* 80:2, 2004, 284; T. Diamond, 'US Unilateralism Fuels Great Power Rivalry in Central Asia', *Eurasia Insight*, 10 January 2003; *Asia Times*, 24 September 2003.
29 Allison, 'Strategic Reassertion', p. 286.
30 National Intelligence Council, 'Global Trends 2015', December 2000. Between 1997 and 2001 Russia supplied 91.5% of China's import of major conventional weaponry. See Stockholm International Peace Research Institute, *SIPRI Yearbook 2002: Armaments, Disarmament and International Security*, New York: Oxford University Press, 2002, p. 376.
31 D. Ross, 'The Middle East Predicament', *Foreign Affairs* 84:1, 2005, 61–74; S. Kapila, 'Iran in the Strategic Matrix of Russia, China and India', South Asia Analysis Group, paper 1284, 9 March 2005; E. Ahrari, 'Iran, China and Russia: The Emerging Anti-US nexus?', *Security Dialogue* 32:4, 2001, 453–66; H. Pant, 'The Moscow–Beijing–Delhi "Strategic Triangle": An Idea Whose Time May Never Come', *Security Dialogue* 35:3, 2004, 311–28.
32 A. Kuchins, 'Getting Back to Business in Bratislava', *The Moscow Times*, 22 February 2005.

11 The US and post-Cold War Africa and the Middle East

1 A. Singh, 'The Year of Africa's Economic Turnaround?', *eAfrica*, 8 March 2005.
2 Friedman cited in Schraeder, *United States Foreign Policy Toward Africa*, p. 178.
3 Bush cited in I. Daalder and J. Lindsay, *America Unbound: The Bush Revolution in Foreign Policy*, Washington DC: Brookings Institute Press, 2003, p. 37.

232 *Notes*

4 L. Diamond, 'Is the Third Wave Over?', *Journal of Democracy* 7:3, 1996, 20–37.
5 Video remarks by the President, African Growth and Opportunity Act forum, 18 July 2005, http://usinfo.state.gov/af/Archive/2005/Jul/ 20–203196.html.
6 Cited in D. Rothchild and T. Sisk, 'Promoting Conflict Management in Uncertain Times', in Lieber (ed.), *Eagle Adrift*, p. 272.
7 US State Department, Bureau of African Affairs, 'Background Note: Nigeria, August 2005, http://www.state.gov/r/pa/ei/bgn/2836.htm.
8 D. Kenda and A. Kikaya, 'A Vulnerable Continent: Africa', in M. Buckley and R. Fawn (eds), *Global Responses to Terrorism*, London: Routledge, 2003, p. 171.
9 Cited in Daalder and Lindsay, *America Unbound*, p. 37.
10 D. Neep, 'Gadaffi May Find that the Goalposts have been Moved', *The Observer*, 21 December 2003; A. Moens, *The Foreign Policy of George W Bush: Values, Strategy and Loyalty*, Aldershot: Ashgate, 2004, p. 178.
11 2004 World Population Data Sheet, Population Reference Bureau, http://www.prb.org/Template.cfm?Section=PRB&template=/ContentManagement/ContentDisplay.cfm&ContentID=11320.
12 *National Security Strategy of the United States*, September 2002.
13 US AID, 'US Foreign Aid: Meeting the Challenges of the Twenty-first Century', January 2004.
14 G. Khadiagala, 'Seeking the "Grand Compromise" in Africa', http://www.sais-jhu.edu/pubaffairs/publications/saisphere/winter04/Khadiagala.html.
15 H. Cohen, 'The United States and Africa: Non-vital Interests Also Need Attention', 30 August 2003.
16 Congress cut MCA funding request FY 2004 from $1.3 billion to $994 million, FY 2005 from $2.5 billion to $1.488 billion and, prospectively, the 2006 request for $3 billion to $1.75 billion. Larry Knowles, 'Millennium Challenge Account: Implementation of a New Foreign Aid Initiative', CRS Report for Congress, 25 May 2005.
17 J. Steinhilber, 'Millennium Challenge Account', Briefing Papers, FES Berlin, p. 5.
18 Cited in M. Klare, *Rogue States and Nuclear Outlaws: America's Search for a New Foreign Policy*, New York: Hill & Wang, 1995, pp. 26–27.
19 F. Hartmann and R. Wendzel, *America's Foreign Policy in a Changing World*, New York: Harper Collins, 1994, p. 405.
20 US Assistant Secretary of State for Near Eastern Affairs, R. Pelletrau, cited in R.O. Freedman, 'US Policy Toward the Middle East in Clinton's Second Term', *Middle East Review of International Affairs* 3:1, 1999, n.p.
21 A. Lake, 'Confronting Backlash States', *Foreign Affairs* 73:2, 1994, 45–55.
22 S.G. Richter, 'America's Iran Policy Rethinks Itself', *New York Times*, 18 August 1997.
23 Cited in S.L. Spiegel, 'Eagle in the Middle East', in Lieber (ed.), *Eagle Adrift*, p. 306.
24 M.B. Mahle, 'A Political–Security Analysis of the Failed Oslo Process', *Middle East Policy* 12:1, 2005, 88.
25 For more on the failed Oslo peace process, see E.W. Said, *The End of the Peace Process: Oslo and After*, London: Granta Books, 2000; C. Enderlin, *Shattered Dreams: The Failure of the Peace Process in the Middle East, 1995–2002*, New York: Other Press, 2003.
26 Moens, *The Foreign Policy of George W Bush*, p. 163.
27 R. Perle, 'Next Stop Iraq', Foreign Policy Research Institute's annual dinner, 14 November 2001.

28 G. Sick, 'Confronting Terrorism', in A. Lennon and C. Eiss (eds), *Reshaping Rogue States*, Cambridge MA: MIT Press, 2004, p. 233.

29 Cited in G. Kemp, 'Confusion on the Middle East in Washington', 11 August 2002, http://www.nixoncenter.org.

30 President Bush, Twentieth Anniversary of the National Endowment for Democracy, US Chamber of Commerce, Washington DC, 6 November 2003.

31 President Bush, Royal Banqueting House, London, 19 November 2003.

32 On 26 August 1987 Reagan delivered a speech called 'A Forward Strategy for Peace and Freedom' in Los Angeles.

33 D. Makovsky, 'Gaza: Moving Forward by Pulling Back', *Foreign Affairs* 84:3, 2005, 52–62.

34 V. Perthes, 'America's "Greater Middle East" and Europe: Key Issues for Dialogue', *Middle East Policy* 11:3, 2004, 92.

35 M. Hudson, 'The United States in the Middle East', in Louise Fawcett (ed.), *International Relations of the Middle East*, Oxford: Oxford University Press, 2005, p. 302.

36 Condoleezza Rice, interview with the *New York Times*, 17 August 2005.

37 Condoleezza Rice, remarks at the American University in Cairo, 20 June 2005.

38 K. Gannon, 'Afghanistan Unbound', *Foreign Affairs* 83:3, 2004, 35–46; M. Galeotti, 'Narcotics Knot', *World Today* 59:12, 2003, 5.

39 'Washington May Pull Back 50k Troops by Dec: Talabani', Reuters, 14 September 2005; A. Moore, 'Costs of Iraq high', 29 August 2005, http://www.allheadlinenews.com.

12 The Western Hemisphere and Asia in the post-Cold War world

1 'The World in 2005', *The Economist*, special issue, 2005, 68–69.

2 See Dumbrell, *American Foreign Policy*, pp. 132–34.

3 C. Powell, *A Soldier's Way*, London: Hutchinson, 1995, p. 424.

4 *Ibid.*, p. 425.

5 *Ibid.*, p. 600.

6 S.K. Purcell, 'US Foreign Policy and Its Impact on Latin America', paper at conference on *Power, Asymmetry and International Security*, 6 September 2002, Buenos Aires, Argentina.

7 Rice, 'Promoting the National Interest', pp. 45–63.

8 'State Department Official Outlines US Diplomacy in Latin America', 27 July 2005, http://usinfo.state.gov.

9 J.E. Stiglitz, *Globalization and Its Discontents*, New York: W.W. Norton, 2002.

10 www.whitehouse.gov/news/releases/2002/01/20020129-11.html.

11 G. Evans, 'Asia Pacific in the Twenty-first Century: Conflict or Cooperation?', *World Today* 52:2, 1996, 52.

12 www.whitehouse.gov/news/releases/20041120-6.html.

13 K. Fukushima, 'The Revival of "Big Politics" in Japan', *International Affairs* 72:1, 1996, 65.

14 J. Bhagwati, 'The US–Japan Car Dispute: A Monumental Mistake', *International Affairs* 72:2, 1996, 261.

15 J.T. Rourke and R. Clark, 'Making U.S. Foreign Policy toward China in the Clinton Administration', in J.M. Scott (ed.), *After the End: Making US Foreign Policy in the Post-Cold War World*, Durham NC: Duke University Press, 1999, p. 201.

16 See S. Kim (ed.), *North Korean Foreign Relations in the Post-Cold War Era*, New

York: Oxford University Press, 1998; D. Albright and K. O'Neill (eds), *Solving the North Korean Nuclear Puzzle*, Washington DC: Institute for Science and International Security, 2000.

17 In 2001 China overtook the US to become South Korea's largest trading partner with two-way trade of over $40 billion. D. Shambaugh, 'China and the Korean Peninsular: Playing for the Long Term', *Washington Quarterly* 26:2, 2003, 49.

18 D. Kang, 'The Avoidable Crisis in North Korea', *Orbis* 47:3, 2003, 495–510; J. Laney and J. Shaplen, 'How to Deal with North Korea', *Foreign Affairs* 82:2, 2003, 17; D. Wall, 'North Korea and China', *World Today* 58:12, 2002, 21.

19 European Commission, The EC–Democratic People's Republic of Korea Country Strategy Paper 2001–2004.

20 China–North Korea trade exceeded $700 million in 2002 and China reportedly provides 30% of total outside assistance to North Korea, 38% of its imports and 70–90% of its energy supplies. V.D. Cha and D.C. Chang, 'The Korea Crisis', *Foreign Policy* May/June, 2003, 23.

13 Conclusion

1 Harry S Truman Library, Oral History no. 412, Dean Acheson, 1971, p. 9.

2 *Public Papers of the Presidents of the United States: George H. Bush: 1992–93, Book II*, Washington DC: Government Printing Office, 1993, pp. 2191–92.

3 Dumbrell, *American Foreign Policy*, p. 174.

4 J. Mann, *The Rise of the Vulcans: The History of Bush's War Cabinet*, New York: Viking, 2004, pp. 181 and 160.

5 *Ibid.*, p. 304, quoting interview by author with François Bujon de L'Estang, French Ambassador to the US.

6 The Office of the President of the United States of America, *The National Security Strategy of the United States of America*, September 2002.

7 A. Newman, 'Arms Control, Proliferation, and Terrorism: The Bush Administration's Post-September 11 Security Strategy', *Journal of Strategic Studies* 27:1, 2004, 59–88.

8 R. Kagan, *Of Paradise and Power: America and Europe in the New World Order*, New York: Knopf, 2003.

9 D. Puchala, 'The Atlantic Community in the Age of International Terrorism', *Journal of Transatlantic Studies* 3:1, 2005, 89–105.

10 Roosevelt's address to Congress, 6 January 1941; A.J. Williams, *Failed Imagination? New World Orders of the Twentieth Century*, Manchester: Manchester University Press, 1998.

11 D.H. Allin, *NATO's Balkan Interventions*, Adelphi Paper 347, London: Oxford University Press for the International Institute for Strategic Studies, 2002, p. 26.

12 Powell, 'US Forces: Challenges Ahead', pp. 32–45.

Bibliography

Note

The bibliography offers a brief guide to further reading. However, there are many other excellent sources of information on post-Second World War American foreign policy. We draw in parts upon primary materials from the US National Archives, Presidential Libraries and the British Public Record Office. Primary sources can also be accessed through *Foreign Relations of the United States* at http://www.state.gov/www/about state/history/index.html and then go to FRUS in the index; The Cold War International History Project at http:www.cwihp.si.edu; and *Public Papers of the Presidents of the United States* at http://www.archives.gov/federal-register/publications/presidential-papers.html#online.

For an excellent reference book, see B.W. Jentleson and T.G. Paterson (eds), *Encyclopaedia of U.S. Foreign Relations*, 4 vols, New York, US Council of Foreign Relations: Oxford University Press, 1997.

Numerous academic journals cover aspects of American foreign policy past and present and provide access to the latest research. Many of these are now available online. Good starting points include: *Cold War History, Diplomacy and Statecraft, Diplomatic History, Foreign Affairs, Foreign Policy, International Affairs, Journal of Cold War Studies, Journal of Strategic Studies, Journal of Transatlantic Studies, Middle Eastern Studies, National Interest, Orbis, Review of International Studies, Security Dialogue, Survival* and *Washington Quarterly*.

Books

Acheson, D., *Present at the Creation: My Years in the State Department*, London: Hamilton, 1970.

Aimaq, J., *For Europe or for Empire? French Colonial Ambitions and the European Army Plan*, Lund, Sweden: Lund University Press, 1996.

Albright, D. and K. O'Neill (eds), *Solving the North Korean Nuclear Puzzle*, Washington DC: Institute for Science and International Security, 2000.

Allin, D.H., *NATO's Balkan Interventions*, Adelphi Paper 347, London: Oxford University Press for the International Institute for Strategic Studies, 2002.

Allison, G.T., *Essence of Decision: Explaining the Cuban Missile Crisis*, Boston: Little Brown, 1971.

Arbatov, G., *The Soviet System: An Insider's Life in Soviet Politics*, New York: Time Books, 1992.

Ausland, J.C., *Kennedy, Khrushchev, and the Berlin–Cuba Crisis, 1961–64*, Oslo: Scandanavia, 1996.

Bailey, N.A., *The Strategic Plan that Won the Cold War, NSDD 75*, Maclean VA: Potomac Foundation, 1999.

Ball, S.J., *The Cold War: An International History 1947–1991*, Oxford: Oxford University Press, 1997.

Baylis, J. and J. Garnett (eds), *Makers of Nuclear Strategy*, London: Pinter Publishers, 1991.

Bender, G. with J. Coleman and R. Sklar (eds), *African Crisis Areas and US Foreign Policy*, Berkeley: University of California Press, 1985.

Beschloss, M.R., *The Crisis Years: Kennedy and Krushchev, 1960–63*, New York: Edward Burlingame Books, 1991.

Beschloss, M.R. and S. Talbott, *At the Highest Levels: The Inside Story of the End of the Cold War*, Boston: Little, Brown, 1993.

Bill, J.A., *The Eagle and the Lion: The Tragedy of American–Iranian Relations*, New Haven: Yale University Press, 1988.

Bills, S., *Empire and Cold War: The Roots of US–Third World Antagonism, 1945–47*, London: Macmillan, 1990.

Blight, J.G. and D.A. Welch (eds), *Intelligence and the Cuban Missile Crisis*, London: Frank Cass, 1998.

Blinkin, A.J., *Ally Versus Ally: America, Europe and the Siberian Pipeline Crisis*, New York: Praeger, 1987.

Booth, K. and S. Smith, *International Relations Theory Today*, Cambridge: Polity Press, 1995.

Borden, W.S., *The Pacific Alliance: United States Foreign Economic Policy and Japanese Trade Recovery, 1947–1955*, Madison: University of Wisconsin Press, 1984.

Borstelmann, T., *Apartheid's Reluctant Uncle: The United States and Southern Africa in the Early Cold War*, Oxford: Oxford University Press, 1993.

Boyle, P.G., *American–Soviet Relations: From the Russian Revolution to the Fall of Communism*, London: Routledge, 1993.

Brands, H.W., *Into the Labyrinth: The United States and the Middle East, 1945–1993*, New York: McGraw Hill, 1994.

Bromley, S., *American Hegemony and World Oil: The Industry, the State System and the World Economy*, Pennsylvania: Pennsylvania State University Press, 1991.

Buckley, M. and R. Fawn (eds), *Global Responses to Terrorism*, London: Routledge, 2003.

Bullock, A., *Ernest Bevin: Foreign Secretary*, Oxford: Oxford University Press, 1985.

Burchill, S. *et al.*, *Theories of International Relations*, 2nd edn, Basingstoke: Palgrave, 2001.

Busch, P., *All the Way with JFK? Britain, the US and the Vietnam War*, Oxford: Oxford University Press, 2003.

Buzan, B., *People, States and Fear*, Hemel Hempstead: Simon & Schuster, 1991.

Calleo, D., *Beyond American Hegemony: The Future of the Western Alliance*, New York: Basic Books, 1987.

Cannon, L., *President Reagan: The Role of a Lifetime*, New York: Simon & Schuster, 1991.

Carter, J., *Keeping Faith: Memoirs of a President*, New York: Bantam Books, 1982.

Catudal, H.M., *Kennedy and the Berlin Wall Crisis: A Case Study in US Decision Making*, Berlin: Berlin Verlag, 1980.

Chang, G., *Friends and Enemies: The United States, China, and the Soviet Union, 1948–1972*, Stanford: Stanford University Press, 1990.

Chatterjee, D.K. and D.E. Scheid (eds), *Ethics and Foreign Intervention*, Cambridge: Cambridge University Press, 2003.

Clarke, R.A., *Against All Enemies: Inside America's War on Terror*, London: Free Press, 2004.

Cohen, M.J., *Fighting World War Three from the Middle East: Allied Contingency Plans, 1945–54*, London: Frank Cass, 1997.

Cohen, W.I., *The United States and Japan in the Post War World*, Lexington: University Press of Kentucky, 1989.

Coker, R.C., *The United States and South Africa 1968–85: Constructive Engagement and its Critics*, Durham NC: Duke University Press, 1986.

Commager, H.S., *Living Ideas in America*, New York: Harper, 1951.

Committee on Foreign Relations, *Soviet Diplomacy and Negotiating Behaviour – 1979–88: New Tests for US Diplomacy*, Washington DC: US Government Printing Office, 1988.

Cottam, R.W., *Iran and the United States: A Cold War Case Study*, Pittsburgh: Pittsburgh University Press, 1988.

Crocker, C., *High Noon in Southern Africa: Making Peace in a Rough Neighbourhood*, New York: W.W. Norton, 1992.

Cumings, B., *The Origins of the Korean War, Vol. 2, The Roaring of the Cataract*, Princeton: Princeton University Press, 1992.

Daalder, I. and J. Lindsay, *America Unbound: The Bush Revolution in Foreign Policy*, Washington DC: Brookings Institute Press, 2003.

Dallek, R.A., *Ronald Reagan: The Politics of Symbolism*, Cambridge MA: Harvard University Press, 1984.

Davy, R. (ed.), *European Détente: A Reappraisal*, London: Sage/RIIA, 1992.

Dawisha, K., *Eastern Europe, Gorbachev and Reform*, Cambridge: Cambridge University Press, 1990.

Dedman, M., *The Origins and Development of the European Union 1945–95*, London: Routledge, 1996.

Deighton, A., *The Impossible Peace: Britain, the Division of Germany and the Origins of the Cold War*, Oxford: Clarendon Press, 1990.

Dell, E., *The Schuman Plan and the Abdication of British Leadership in Europe*, Oxford: Oxford University Press, 1995.

Divine, R.A. (ed.), *The Cuban Missile Crisis*, New York: Marcus Wiener, 1988.

Dobrynin, A., *In Confidence: Moscow's Ambassador to America's Six Cold War Presidents 1962–1986*, New York: Time Books, 1995.

Dobson, A.P., *The Politics of the Anglo-American Economic Special Relationship*, New York: St Martin's Press, 1988.

Dobson, A.P., *Flying in the Face of Competition*, Aldershot: Avebury, 1995.

Dobson, A.P., *Anglo-American Relations in the Twentieth Century*, London: Routledge, 1995.

Dobson, A.P., *US Economic Statecraft for Survival 1933–1991*, London: Routledge, 2002.

Dobson, A.P. (ed.), with S. Malik and G. Evans (assistant eds), *Deconstructing and Reconstructing the Cold War*, Aldershot: Ashgate, 1999.

Dockrill, S., *Britain's Policy for West German Rearmament, 1950–1955*, Cambridge: Cambridge University Press, 1991.

Duigan, P. and L.H. Gann, *The United States and the New Europe, 1945–1993*, Oxford: Blackwell Publishers, 1994.

238   *Bibliography*

Dumbrell, J., *American Foreign Policy: Carter to Clinton*, London: Macmillan Press, 1997.

Dumbrell, J., *A Special Relationship: Anglo-American Relations in the Cold War and After*, Basingstoke: Macmillan, 2001.

Enderlin, C., *Shattered Dreams: The Failure of the Peace Process in the Middle East, 1995–2002*, New York: Other Press, 2003.

Engler, R., *The Politics of Oil: A Study of Private Power and Democratic Direction*, New York: Macmillan, 1961.

Fanon, F., *The Wretched of the Earth*, translated Constance Farrington, New York: Grove Press, 1968.

Fawcett, L. (ed.), *International Relations of the Middle East*, Oxford: Oxford University Press, 2005.

Featherstone, K. and R. Ginsberg, *The United States and the European Union in the 1990s: Partners in Transition*, London: Macmillan, 1996.

Feis, H., *From Trust to Terror, 1945–50*, New York: W.W. Norton, 1970.

Ferguson, N., *Empire: How Britain Made the Modern World*, London: Penguin, 2004.

Fisher, B.A., *The Reagan Reversal: Foreign Policy and the End of the Cold War*, Missouri: University Press Missouri, 2000.

Fleming, D.F., *The Cold War and its Origins, 1917–1960*, 2 vols, London: Allen & Unwin, 1961.

Foct, R.J., *The Wrong War: American Policy and Dimensions of the Korean Conflict*, Ithaca NY: Cornell University Press, 1985.

Freedman, L., *The Evolution of Nuclear Strategy*, 2nd edn, London: Macmillan, 1989.

Fukuyama, F., *The End of History and the Last Man*, London: Hamish Hamilton, 1992.

Fursdon, E., *The European Defence Community: A History*, London: Macmillan, 1980.

Gaddis, J.L., *Strategies of Containment*, Oxford: Oxford University Press, 1982.

Gaddis, J.L., *The United States and the End of the Cold War: Implications, Reconsiderations, Provocations*, New York: Oxford University Press, 1992.

Gaddis, J.L., *We Now Know: Rethinking Cold War History*, Oxford: Clarendon Press, 1997.

Garthoff, R., *Détente and Confrontation: American–Soviet Relations from Nixon to Reagan*, Washington DC: The Brookings Institute, 1994.

Gasiorowski, M.J., *US Foreign Policy and the Shah: Building a Client State in Iran*, Ithaca NY: Cornell University Press, 1991.

Gasiorowski, M.J. and M. Byrne (eds), *Mohammad Mosaddeq and the 1953 Coup in Iran*, Syracuse: Syracuse University Press, 2004.

Gates, R., *From the Shadows: The Ultimate Inside Story of Five Presidents and How They Won the Cold War*, New York: Simon & Schuster, 1996.

Gearson, J.S., *Harold Macmillan and the Berlin Wall Crisis 1958–1962: The Limits of Interest and Force*, Basingstoke: Macmillan, 1998.

George, S., *An Awkward Partner: Britain in the European Community*, Oxford: Oxford University Press, 1998

Gibbs, D., *The Political Economy of Third World Intervention: Mines, Money and US Policy in the Congo Crisis*, Chicago: University of Chicago Press, 1991.

Gill, S. (ed.), *Atlantic Relations: Beyond the Reagan Era*, New York: St Martin's Press, 1989.

Gill, S., *American Hegemony and the Trilateral Commission*, Cambridge: Cambridge University Press, 1990.

Goldstein, W. (ed.), *Reagan's Leadership and the Atlantic Alliance: Views from Europe and America*, London: Pergammon-Brassey, 1986.

Goncharov, S. with J.W. Lewis and X. Litai, *Uncertain Partners: Stalin, Mao, and the Korean War*, Stanford: Stanford University Press, 1993.

Halper, S. and J. Clarke, *America Alone: The Neo-Conservatives and the Global Order*, Cambridge: Cambridge University Press, 2004.

Hanson, P., *Western Economic Statecraft in East–West Relations: Embargoes, Sanctions, Linkage, Economic Warfare and Détente*, London: Routledge & Kegan Paul, 1988.

Harding, H., *A Fragile Relationship: The United States and China since 1972*, Washington DC: Brookings Institute, 1992.

Hartmann F. and R. Wendzel, *America's Foreign Policy in a Changing World*, New York: Harper Collins, 1994.

Hastings, M., *The Korean War*, London: Michael Joseph, 1987.

Henze, P., *The Horn of Africa: From War to Peace*, London: Macmillan, 1991.

Herring, G.C., *America's Longest War: The United States and Vietnam 1950–1975*, New York: Wiley, 1979.

Hogan, M., *The Marshall Plan: America, Britain and the Reconstruction of Western Europe, 1947–52*, Cambridge: Cambridge University Press, 1987.

Horowitz, D., *Free World Colossus*, New York: Hill & Wang, 1971.

Hufbauer, G.C. and J.S. Schott, *Economic Sanctions Reconsidered: History and Current Policy*, 2nd edn with Ann Elliott, Washington DC: Institute for International Economics, 1990.

Huntley, J.R., *Pax Democratica: A Strategy for the 21st Century*, Basingstoke: Macmillan, 1998.

Iriye, A., *Across the Pacific: An Inner History of American–East Asian Relations*, New York: Harcourt, Brace, & Brace, 1967.

Isaacson, W., *Kissinger: A Biography*, New York: Simon & Schuster, 1992.

James, G.A., *The China Connection: US Policy and the Peoples Republic of China*, Stanford: Stanford University Press, 1986.

Jentleson, B.W., *Pipeline Politics: The Complex Political Economy of East–West Trade*, Ithaca NY: Cornell University Press, 1986.

Jentleson, B.W., *American Foreign Policy: The Dynamics of Choice in the Twenty First Century*, 2nd edn, New York: Norton & Norton, 2003.

Jiang, A.X., *The United States and China*, Chicago: Chicago University Press, 1988.

Joffe, J., *The Limited Partnership: Europe, the United States, and the Burdens of Alliance*, Cambridge MA: Ballinger, 1987.

Kagan, R., *Of Paradise and Power: America and Europe in the New World Order*, New York: Knopf, 2003.

Kahin, G., *Intervention: How America became Involved in Vietnam*, New York: Knopf, 1986.

Kalb, M., *Congo Cables: The Cold War in Africa from Eisenhower to Kennedy*, New York: Macmillan, 1982.

Kaufman, B.I., *The Arab Middle East and the United States: Inter-Arab Rivalry and Super-Power Diplomacy*, New York: Twayne, 1996.

Kegley, C.W. and E.R. Wittkopf, *World Politics: Trend and Transformation*, New York: St Martin's Press, 1995.

Kennedy, P., *The Rise and Fall of the Great Powers*, New York: Random House, 1987.

Kim, I.J., *The Strategic Triangle: China, the United States and the Soviet Union*, New York: Paragon House, 1987.

Kim, S. (ed.), *North Korean Foreign Relations in the Post-Cold War Era*, New York: Oxford University Press, 1998.

Kindleberger, C.P., *The World in Depression 1929–1939*, Berkeley: University of California Press, 1973.

Kissinger, H.A., *American Foreign Policy*, New York: W.W. Norton, 1977.

Kissinger, H.A., *White House Years*, London: Michael Joseph, 1979.

Kissinger, H.A., *Years of Upheaval*, Boston: Little, Brown & Company, 1982.

Klare, M., *Rogue States and Nuclear Outlaws: America's Search for a New Foreign Policy*, New York: Hill & Wang, 1995.

Krieger, J., *Reagan, Thatcher and the Politics of Decline*, Cambridge: Polity Press, 1986.

Kull, S. and I.M. Destler, *Misreading the Public: The Myth of the New Isolationism*, Washington DC: Brookings Institute, 1999.

Kyvig, D.E. (ed.), *Reagan and the World*, New York: Greenwood, 1990.

Lacey, M.J. (ed.), *The Truman Presidency*, Cambridge: Cambridge University Press, 1989.

LaFeber, W., *The Clash: A History of US–Japanese Relations*, New York: W.W. Norton, 1997.

LaFeber, W., *The American Age: United States Foreign Policy at Home and Abroad since 1750*, 2nd edn, New York: Norton & Norton, 1994.

Lal, D., *In Praise of Empires: Globalization and Order*, Basingstoke: Palgrave, 2004.

Larres, K., *Churchill's Cold War: The Politics of Personal Diplomacy*, New Haven: Yale University Press, 2002.

Lebow, R.N., *The Tragic Vision of Politics: Ethics, Interests and Orders*, Cambridge: Cambridge University Press, 2003.

Leebaert, D., *The Fifty-year Wound: The True Price of America's Cold War Victory*, Boston: Little, Brown, 2002.

Lefebvre, J.A., *Arms for the Horn: US Security Policy in Ethiopia and Somalia, 1953–91*, Pittsburgh: Pittsburgh University Press, 1991.

Leffler, M. and D. Painter (eds), *Origins of the Cold War*, London: Routledge, 1994.

Lennon, A. and C. Eiss (eds), *Reshaping Rogue States*, Cambridge MA: MIT Press, 2004.

Lewy, G., *America in Vietnam: Illusion, Myth, and Reality*, New York: Oxford University Press, 1978.

Lieber, R.J. (ed.), *Eagle Adrift: American Foreign Policy at the End of the Century*, New York: Longman, 1997.

Litwak, R.S., *Détente and the Nixon Doctrine: American Foreign Policy and the Pursuit of Stability, 1969–1976*, Cambridge: Cambridge University Press, 1984.

Lord, C., *Absent at the Creation: Britain and the Formation of the European Community*, Aldershot: Dartmouth, 1996.

Louis, W.R. and R. Owen (eds), *Suez 1956: The Crisis and Its Consequences*, Oxford: Oxford University Press, 1989.

Lucas, W.S., *Divided We Stand: Britain, the US and the Suez Crisis*, London: Hodder & Stoughton, 1991.

Lundestad, G., *No End to Alliance: The United States and Western Europe: Past, Present and Future*, London: Macmillan, 1998.

Lundestad, G., *'Empire' by Integration: The United States and European Integration, 1945–1997*, Oxford: Oxford University Press, 1998.

Lundestad, G., *East, West, North, South: Major Developments in International Politics, 1945–1990*, Oslo: Norwegian University Press, 1994.

Magdoff, H., *The Age of Imperialism: The Economics of US Foreign Policy*, New York: Modern Reader Paperbacks, 1969.

Mahoney, R., *JFK: Ordeal in Africa*, New York: Oxford University Press, 1983.

Maier, C.S. (ed.), *The Cold War in Europe: Era of a Divided Continent*, Princeton: Marcus Wiener, 1996.

Mann, J., *The Rise of the Vulcans: The History of Bush's War Cabinet*, New York: Viking, 2004.

Marsh, S., *Anglo-American Relations and Cold War Oil*, London: Palgrave, 2003.

Marsh, S. and H. Mackenstein, *The International Relations of the European Union*, Harlow: Pearson, 2005.

Martel, G. (ed.), *American Foreign Relations Reconsidered 1890–1993*, London: Routledge, 1994.

Massie, R.K., *Loosing the Bonds: The United States and South Africa during the Apartheid Years*, New York: Nan A. Talese, 1997.

May, E.R., *American Cold War Strategy: Re-interpreting NSC 68*, New York: Bedford Books, 1993.

McAllister, R., *From EC to EU: An Historical and Political Survey*, London: Routledge, 1997.

McCormick, T.J., *America's Half Century: United States Foreign Policy in the Cold War*, Baltimore: Johns Hopkins University Press, 1989.

McTurnan Kahin, G. and J. Lewis, *The United States in Vietnam*, New York: Delta Books, 1967.

Mee, C.L., *The Marshall Plan: The Launching of Pax Americana*, New York: Simon & Schuster, 1984.

Melanson, R.A., *American Foreign Policy since the Vietnam War: The Search for Consensus from Nixon to Clinton*, 2nd edn, New York: M.E. Sharpe, 1996.

Mervin, D., *Ronald Reagan and the American Presidency*, London: Longman, 1990.

Meyers, R.W., *A Unique Relationship: The United States and the Republic of China under the Taiwan Relations Act*, Stanford: Stanford University Press, 1989.

Middlemas, K. (ed.), *Orchestrating Europe: The Informal Politics of European Union 1973–1995*, London: Fontana Press, 1995.

Milward, A., *The European Rescue of the Nation State*, Berkeley CA: University of California Press, 1992.

Moens, A., *The Foreign Policy of George W Bush: Values, Strategy and Loyalty*, Aldershot: Ashgate, 2004.

Morgenthau, H.J., *A New Foreign Policy for the United States*, London: Pall Mall Press, 1969.

Morgenthau, H.J., *Politics among Nations: The Struggle for Power and Peace*, 6th edn revised by K. Thompson, New York: Knopf, 1985.

Morris, E., *Blockade: Berlin and the Cold War*, London: Hamilton, 1983.

Muravchik, J., *The Uncertain Crusade: Jimmy Carter and the Dilemmas of Human Rights Policy*, London: Hamilton Press, 1986.

Neack, L., J.A.K. Hay and P. J. Haney (eds), *Foreign Policy Analysis: Continuity and Change in Its Second Generation*, Englewood Cliffs NJ: Prentice Hall, 1995.

Newsom, D., *Diplomacy and the American Democracy*, Bloomington: Indiana University Press, 1988.

Newton, S., *The Global Economy 1944–200: The Limits of Ideology*, London: Arnold, 2004.

Nicholas, H.G., *The United States and Britain*, Chicago: University of Chicago Press, 1975.

Nincic, M., *Democracy and Foreign Policy: The Fallacy of Political Realism*, New York: Columbia University Press, 1992.

Noer, T.J., *Cold War and Black Liberation: The United States and White Rule in Africa, 1948–68*, Columbia: University of Missouri Press, 1985.

Nuechterlein, D.E., *America Recommitted*, 2nd edn, Kentucky: University Press of Kentucky, 2001.

Nye, J.S., *Bound to Lead: The Changing Nature of American Power*, New York: Basic Books, 1990.

Nye, J.S., *The Paradox of American Power: Why the World's Only Superpower Can't Go It Alone*, New York: Oxford University Press, 2002.

Oberdorfer, D., *The Turn from Cold War to a New Era*, New York: Poseidon Press, 1991.

Ovendale, R., *Origins of the Arab Israeli Wars*, London: Longman, 1984.

Ovendale, R., *Britain, the United States, and the End of the Political Mandate*, Woodbridge: Royal Historical Society, 1989.

Painter, D., *Private Power and Public Policy: Multinational Oil Companies and U.S. Foreign Policy, 1941–1954*, London: I.B. Taurus, 1986.

Palmer, B. Jr, *The 25 Year War: America's Military Role in Vietnam*, Lexington: Kentucky University Press, 1984.

Park, W., *Defending the West: A History of NATO*, Boulder CO: Westview Press, 1986.

Paterson, T.G. (ed.), *Kennedy's Quest for Victory: American Foreign Policy, 1961–1963*, New York: Oxford University Press, 1989.

Patman, R.G., *The Soviet Union in the Horn of Africa: The Diplomacy of Intervention and Disengagement*, Cambridge: Cambridge University Press, 1990.

Peterson, J. and M. Pollack (eds), *Europe, America, Bush: Transatlantic Relations in the Twenty-first Century*, London: Routledge, 2003.

Philippart, E. and P. Winand (eds), *Ever Closer Partnership: Policy-making in EU–US Relations*, New York, Oxford: Peter Lang, 2001.

Powell, C., *A Soldier's Way*, London: Hutchinson, 1995.

Public Papers of the Presidents of the United States: Ronald Reagan 1984, Washington DC: Government Printing Office, 1986.

Quandt, W., *Camp David: Peacemaking and Politics*, Washington DC: The Brookings Institute, 1986.

Rabinovich, I., *Waging Peace: Israel and the Arabs, 1948–2003*, Princeton: Princeton University Press, 2004.

Ramet, S.P. and C. Ingebritsen (eds), *Coming in from the Cold War*, New York: Rowman & Littlefield Publishers, 2002.

Rostow, W.W., *The Stages of Economic Growth: A Non-Communist Manifesto*, Cambridge: Cambridge University Press, 1962.

Ruane, K., *The Rise and Fall of the European Defence Community: Anglo-American Relations and the Crisis of European Defence, 1950–55*, Basingstoke: Macmillan, 2000.

Rubenstein, R.L. (ed.), *The Dissolving Alliance: The United States and the Future of Europe*, New York: Paragon House, 1987.

Said, E.W., *The End of the Peace Process: Oslo and After*, London: Granta Books, 2000.

Schaller, M., *Altered States: The United States and Japan Since the Occupation*, New York: Oxford University Press, 1997.

Schick, J.M., *The Berlin Crisis, 1958–1962*, Philadelphia: University of Pennsylvania Press, 1971.

Schlesinger, A.M. Jr, *A Thousand Days: John F. Kennedy in the White House*, Boston: Houghton Mifflin, 1965.

Schlesinger, A.M. Jr, *The Imperial Presidency*, New York: Popular Library, 1974.

Schlesinger, A.M. Jr, *War and the American Presidency*, New York: W.W. Norton, 2005.

Schoultz, L., *Human Rights and the United States Policy Towards Latin America*, Princeton: Princeton University Press, 1981.

Schraeder, P.J., *United States Foreign Policy Toward Africa: Incrementalism, Crisis and Change*, Cambridge: Cambridge University Press, 1994.

Schweizer, P., *Reagan's War: The Epic Story of His Forty-year Struggle and Final Triumph over Communism*, New York: Doubleday, 2002.

Scott, J.M. (ed.), *After the End: Making US Foreign Policy in the Post-Cold War World*, Durham NC: Duke University Press, 1999.

Scott, L.V., *Macmillan, Kennedy and the Cuban Missile Crisis: Political, Military and Intelligence Aspects*, Basingstoke: Macmillan, 1999.

Shepard, R., *Nigeria, Africa and the United States from Kennedy to Reagan*, Bloomington: Indiana University Press, 1991.

Shlaim, A., *The United States and the Berlin Blockade, 1948–1949: A Study in Crisis Decision-making*, London: University California Press, 1983.

Sick, G., *All Fall Down: America's Tragic Encounter with Iran*, New York: Random House, 1985.

Smith, C., *Palestine and the Arab–Israeli Conflict*, 5th edn, Boston: St Martin's Press, 2004.

Smith, G., *Morality, Reason and Power: American Diplomacy in the Carter Years*, New York: Hill & Wang, 1986.

Smith, G., *Reagan and Thatcher*, London: The Bodley Head, 1990.

Smith, H., *European Union Foreign Policy and Central America*, Basingstoke: Macmillan, 1995.

Smith, M., *Western Europe and the United States: The Uncertain Alliance*, London: Allen & Unwin, 1984.

Spanier, J., *American Foreign Policy since World War II*, New York: Holt, Rinehart, & Winston, 1985.

Spero, J.E. and J.A. Hart, *The Politics of International Economic Relations*, London and New York: Routledge, 1997.

Spiegel, S.L., *The Other Arab–Israeli Conflict: Making America's Middle East Policy from Truman to Reagan*, Chicago: University of Chicago Press, 1985.

Stiglitz, J.E., *Globalization and Its Discontents*, New York: W.W. Norton, 2002.

Stivers, W., *America's Confrontation with Revolutionary Change in the Middle East, 1948–83*, London: Macmillan, 1986.

Stockholm International Peace Research Institute, *SIPRI Yearbook 2002: Armaments, Disarmament and International Security*, New York: Oxford University Press, 2002.

Stoessinger, J.G., *Nations at Dawn: China, the United States, and the Soviet Union*, 6th edn, New York: McGraw Hill, 1994.

Strange, S., *Sterling and British Policy: A Political Study of an International Currency in Decline*, London: Oxford University Press, 1971.

Talbott, R.B., *The Chicken War*, Ames: Iowa State University, 1978.

Taylor, T., *Nuremberg and Vietnam: An American Tragedy*, Chicago: Quadrangle Books, 1970.

Thatcher, M., *The Downing Street Years*, London: Harper Collins, 1993.

Trachtenberg, M. (ed.), *Between Empire and Alliance: America and Europe during the Cold War*, New York: Rowman & Littlefield Publishers, 2003.

Venn, F., *Oil Diplomacy in the Twentieth Century*, Basingstoke: Macmillan, 1986.

Viotti, P.R. and M.V. Kauppi, *International Relations Theory: Realism, Pluralism, Globalism, and Beyond*, Boston: Allyn & Bacon, 1999.

Wallerstein, I., *The Modern World System*, 2 vols, New York: Academic Press, 1974.

Weinberger, C., *Fighting for Peace: Seven Critical Years in the Pentagon*, New York: Warner Books, 1990.

Weiss, G.W., *The Farewell Dossier: Strategic Deception and Economic Warfare in the Cold War – An Insider's Untold Story*, American Tradecraft Society, n.d.

Wendt, A., *Social Theory of International Politics*, Cambridge: Cambridge University Press, 1998.

Wexler, I., *The Marshall Plan Revisited: The European Recovery Program in Economic Perspective*, Westport CT: Greenwood, 1983.

Williams, A.J., *Failed Imagination? New World Orders of the Twentieth Century*, Manchester: Manchester University Press, 1998.

Williams, W.A., *The Tragedy of American Diplomacy*, 2nd edn, New York: Dell Publishing, 1972.

Wilson, H., *The Labour Government 1964–1970: A Personal Account*, London: Weidenfeld & Nicolson, 1971.

Winand, P., *Eisenhower, Kennedy, and the United States of Europe*, London: Macmillan, 1997.

Wohlstetter, A. *et al.*, *Lessons from Bosnia*, Santa Monica CA: Rand, 1993.

Wurm, C. (ed.), *Western Europe and Germany: The Beginnings of European Integration 1945–1960*, Oxford: Berg, 1995.

Yergin, D., *Shattered Peace: The Origins of the Cold War and the National Security State*, Boston: Houghton Mifflin, 1977.

Yergin, D., *The Prize: The Epic Quest for Oil, Money, and Power*, New York: Simon & Schuster, 1991.

Young, C., *Politics in the Congo: Decolonisation and Independence*, Princeton: Princeton University Press, 1965.

Young, J., *Britain and European Unity 1945–1999*, Basingstoke: Macmillan, 2000.

Articles and papers

Ahrari, E., 'Iran, China and Russia: The Emerging Anti-US Nexus?', *Security Dialogue* 32:4, 2001, 453–66.

Albright, M., 'The Testing of American Foreign Policy', *Foreign Affairs* 77:6, 1998, 50–64.

Allison, R., 'Strategic Reassertion in Russia's Central Asian Policy', *International Affairs* 80:2, 2004, 277–93.

Baldwin, D., 'The Concept of Security', *Review of International Studies* 23:1, 1997, 5–26.

Bass, W., 'The Triage of Dayton', *Foreign Affairs* 77:5, 1998, 95–108.

Bhagwati, J., 'The US–Japan Car Dispute: A Monumental Mistake', *International Affairs* 72:2, 1996, 261–79.

Bundy, M., 'From Cold War to Trusting Peace', *Foreign Affairs* 69:1, 1990, 197–212.

Cha, V.D. and D.C. Chang, 'The Korea Crisis', *Foreign Policy* May/June 2003, 20–27.

Chang, G.H., 'To the Nuclear Brink: Eisenhower, Dulles and the Quemoy-Matsu Crisis', *International Security* 12:4, 1988, 96–123.

Christopher, W., 'Securing US Interests while Supporting Russian Reform', US State Department Dispatch, 29 March 1993.

Christopher, W. 'America's Leadership: America's Opportunity', *Foreign Policy* 98, spring 1995, 6–27.

Cohen, D.B., 'From START to START II: Dynamism and Pragmatism in the Bush Administration's Nuclear Weapon Policies', *Presidential Studies Quarterly* 27:3, 1997, 412–29.

Cohen, H.J., 'The United States and Africa: Nonvital Interests Also Require Attention,' *American Foreign Policy Interests* 25:1, 2003, 19–24.

Cooper, W.H., 'EU–US Economic Ties: Framework, Scope and Magnitude', CRS Report for Congress, 15 April 2005.

Diamond, L., 'Is the Third Wave Over?', *Journal of Democracy* 7:3, 1996, 20–37.

Dobson, A.P., 'The Dangers of US Interventionism', *Review of International Studies* 28:3, 2002, 577–97.

Dobson, A.P., 'The Reagan Administration, Economic Warfare, and Starting to Close Down the Cold War', *Diplomatic History* 29:3, 2005, 531–57.

Doyle, M.W., 'Kant, Liberal Legacies and Foreign Affairs' Parts 1 & 2, *Philosophy and Public Affairs* 12:3, 1983, 205–35; 12:4, 1983, 323–53.

Evans, G., 'Asia Pacific in the Twenty-first Century: Conflict or Cooperation?', *World Today* 52:2, 1996, 50–52.

Feldstein, M., 'EMU and International Conflict', *Foreign Affairs* 76:6, 1997, 60–73.

Freedman, R.O., 'US Foreign Policy Toward the Middle East in Clinton's Second Term', *Middle East Review of International Affairs* 3:1, 1999, n.p.

Friedman, L. 'International Security: Changing Targets', *Foreign Policy* 110, spring 1998, 48–63.

Fukushima, K., 'The Revival of "Big Politics" in Japan', *International Affairs* 72:1, 1996, 53–72.

Gaddis, J.L., 'The Emerging Post-revisionist Thesis on the Origins of the Cold War', *Diplomatic History* 7:3, 1983, 171–90.

Gaddis, J.L., 'International Relations Theory and the End of the Cold War', *International Security* 17:3, 1992/93, 5–58.

Galeotti, M., 'Narcotics Knot', *World Today* 59:12, 2003, 4–6.

Gannon, K., 'Afghanistan Unbound', *Foreign Affairs* 83:3, 2004, 35–46.

Heinzig, D., 'Stalin, Mao, Kim and Korean War Origins, 1950: A Documentary Discrepancy', *Cold War International History Project Bulletin*, Issues 8–9, 1996/97, 240–43.

Horelick, A.L., 'US–Soviet relations: Threshold of a New Era', *Foreign Affairs* 69:1, 1989/90, 51–69.

Huntington, S.P., 'The Clash of Civilizations', *Foreign Affairs* 72:3, 1993, 22–49.

Kagan, R., 'Power and Weakness', *Policy Review* 113, June 2002, 3–28.

Kaiser, W., 'The Bomb and Europe: Britain, France, and the EEC Negotiations 1961–63', *Journal of European Integration History* 1:1, 1995, 65–85.

Kang, D., 'The Avoidable Crisis in North Korea', *Orbis* 47:3, 2003, 495–510.

Kapila, S., 'Iran in the Strategic Matrix of Russia, China and India', South Asia Analysis Group, paper 1284, 9 March 2005.

Kelleher, C., 'US Foreign Policy and Europe, 1990–2000', *Brookings Review* 8:4, 1990, 4–10.

Kennan, G.F., 'The Sources of Soviet Conduct', *Foreign Affairs* 25, July 1947, 566–82.

Knowles, I., 'Millennium Challenge Account: Implementation of a New Foreign Aid Initiative', CRS Report for Congress, 25 May 2005.

Kosyrev, A., 'The Lagging Partnership', *Foreign Affairs* 73:3, 1994, 59–65.

Kratchowil, F., 'The Embarrassment of Changes: Neo-realism as the Science of Realpolitik without Politics', *Review of International Studies* 19:1, 1993, 63–80.

Krauthammer, C., 'America and the World', *Foreign Affairs* 70:1, 1990/91, 23–33.

Krauthammer, C., 'The Unipolar Moment Revisited', *National Interest* 70, winter 2002–03, 5–17.

Lake, A., 'Confronting Backlash States', *Foreign Affairs* 73:2, 1994, 45–55.

Laney, J. and J. Shaplen, 'How to Deal with North Korea', *Foreign Affairs* 82:2, 2003, 16–30.

Lansford, T., 'Security and Marketshare: Bridging the Transatlantic Divide in the Defence Industry', *European Security* 10:1, 2001, 1–20.

Lefebvre, J.A., 'The United States, Ethiopia and the 1963 Somali–Soviet Arms Deal: Containment and the Balance of Power Dilemma in the Horn of Africa', *Journal of Modern African Studies* 36:4, 1998, 611–43.

Leffler, M.P., 'The American Conception of National Security and the Beginnings of the Cold War, 1945–48', *American Historical Review* 89:2, 1984, 346–81.

Legvold, R., 'All the Way: Crafting a U.S.–Russian Alliance', *National Interest*, winter 2002, 21–31.

Luttwak, E., 'Perceptions of Military Force and US Defence Policy', *Survival* 19:1, January/February 1977, 2–8.

Mahle, M.B., 'A Political–Security Analysis of the Failed Oslo Process', *Middle East Policy* 12:1, 2005, 79–96.

Makovsky, D., 'Gaza: Moving Forward by Pulling Back', *Foreign Affairs* 84:3, 2005, 52–62.

Marcum, J., 'Africa: A Continent Adrift', *Foreign Affairs* 68:1, 1988–89, 159–79.

Marsh, S., 'The US, Iran and Operation Ajax: Inverting Interpretative Orthodoxy', *Middle Eastern Studies* 39:3, 2003, 1–38.

Mearsheimer, J., 'Back to the Future: Instability in Europe After the Cold War', *International Security* 15:3, 1990, 5–57.

Metz, S., 'American Attitudes Toward Decolonisation in Africa', *Political Science Quarterly* 99:3, 1984, 515–34.

Moens, A., in collaboration with R. Domisiewicz, 'European and North American Trends in Defence Industry: Problems and Prospects of a Cross-Atlantic Defence Market', Ottawa: International Security Research and Outreach Programme, April 2001.

Moltke, G. von, 'Building a Partnership for Peace', *NATO Review* 42:3, 1994, 3–7.

Newman, A., 'Arms Control, Proliferation, and Terrorism: The Bush Adminis- tration's Post-September 11 Security Strategy', *Journal of Strategic Studies* 27:1, 2004, 59–88.

Newmann, W., 'The Structures of National Security Decision Making', *Presidential Studies Quarterly* 34:2, 2004, 437–48.

Nwachuku, L., 'The United States and Nigeria, 1960 to 1987: Anatomy of a Pragmatic Relationship', *Journal of Black Studies* 28:5, 1988, 575–93.

Nye, J.S., 'Understating US Strength', *Foreign Policy* 72, autumn 1988, 105–29.

Pant, H., 'The Moscow–Beijing–Delhi "Strategic Triangle": An Idea Whose Time May Never Come', *Security Dialogue* 35:3, 2004, 311–28.

Perthes, V., 'America's "Greater Middle East" and Europe: Key Issues for Dialogue', *Middle East Policy* 11:3, 2004, 85–97.

Pipes, R., 'Misinterpreting the Cold War', *Foreign Affairs* 74:1, 1995, 154–60.

Powell, C., 'US Forces: Challenges Ahead: Enormous Power, Sobering Responsibil- ity', *Foreign Affairs* 71:5, 1992, 32–45.

Puchala, D., 'The Atlantic Community in the Age of International Terrorism', *Journal of Transatlantic Studies* 3:1, 2005, 89–105.

Rice, C., 'Promoting the National Interest', *Foreign Affairs* 79:1, 2000, 45–63.

Rosner, J., 'Clinton, Congress and Assistance to Russia', *SAIS Review*, winter/spring 1995, 15–35.

Ross, D., 'The Middle East Predicament', *Foreign Affairs* 84:1, 2005, 61–74.

Rykhtik, M., 'Why Did Russia Welcome a Republican Victory?', PONARS Policy Memo 330, November 2004.

Sestanovich, S., 'Dual Frustration: America, Russia and the Persian Gulf', *National Interest*, winter 2002, 153–62.

Shambaugh, D., 'China and the Korean Peninsular: Playing for the Long Term' *Washington Quarterly* 26:2, 2003, 43–56.

Shaw, T. and M. Grieve, 'The Political Economy of Resources: Africa's Future in the Global Environment', *Journal of Modern African Studies* 16:1, 1978, 1–32.

Shepherd, G. Jr, 'The Conflict of Interests in American Policy on Africa', *Western Political Quarterly* 12:4, 1959, 996–1004.

Shepley, J., 'How Dulles Averted War', *Life Magazine* 40, 16 January 1956.

Singh, A., 'The Year of Africa's Economic Turnaround?', *eAfrica*, 8 March 2005.

Staar, R.F., 'A Russian Rearmament Wish List', *Orbis* 43:4, 1999, 605–12.

Stein, A.A., 'The Hegemon's Dilemma: Great Britain, the United States, and the International Economic Order', *International Organization* 38:2, 1984, 355–86.

Steinhilber, J., 'Millennium Challenge Account', Briefing Papers, 2004, FES Berlin.

Steininger, R., 'Great Britain's First EEC Failure in January 1963', *Diplomacy and Statecraft* 7:2, 1996, 404–35.

Strange, S., 'The Persistent Myth of Lost Hegemony', *International Organization* 41:4, 1987, 551–74.

Volman, D., 'Africa's Rising Status in American Defence Policy', *Journal of Modern African Studies* 22:1, 1984, 143–51.

Wall, D., 'North Korea and China', *World Today* 58:12, 2002, 21–22.

Waltz, K., 'The Emerging Structure of International Politics', *International Security* 18:2, 1993, 44–79.

Young, C., 'United States Policy Toward Africa: Silver Anniversary Reflections', *African Studies Review* 27:3, 1984, 1–17.

Cited and regularly consulted websites

http://www.afp.com/english/home/
http://www.airpower.maxwell.af.mil/airchronicles/aureview
http://www.allheadlinenews.com
http://www.americanhistory.si.edu
http://www.atimes.com/
http://www.atlanticcomunity.org
http://www.bits.de
http://www.cbsnews.com
http://www.cfr.org
http://www.defenselink.mil
http://www.economist.com
http://www.english.people.com.cn
http://www.eurasianet.org/departments/insight/index.shtml
http://www.europa.eu.int
http://www.eurunion.org

http://www.fpri.org
http://www.globalpolicy.org
http://www.globalsecurity.org
http://www.guardian.co.uk
http://www.hrw.org
http://www.imf.org
http://www.janes.com
http://www.nato.int
http://www.news.bbc.co.uk
http://www.news.ft.com
http://www.nixoncenter.org
http://www.nytimes.com/
http://www.observer.guardian.co.uk/
http://www.policyalmanac.org
http://www.ppionline.org
http://www.prb.org
http://www.reuters.com
http://www.sais-jhu.edu
http://www.stat.wto.org
http://www.state.gov
http://www.theepc.net
http://www.themoscowtimes.com
http://www.trade-info.cec.eu.int
http://www.un.org
http://www.usaid.gov/
http://www.useu.be
http://www.usinfo.state.gov
http://www.ustr.gov
http://www.washingtonpost.com/
http://www.washtimes.com
http://www.whitehouse.gov
http://www.worldbank.org
http://www.wto.org
http://www.xinhuanet.comm

Index

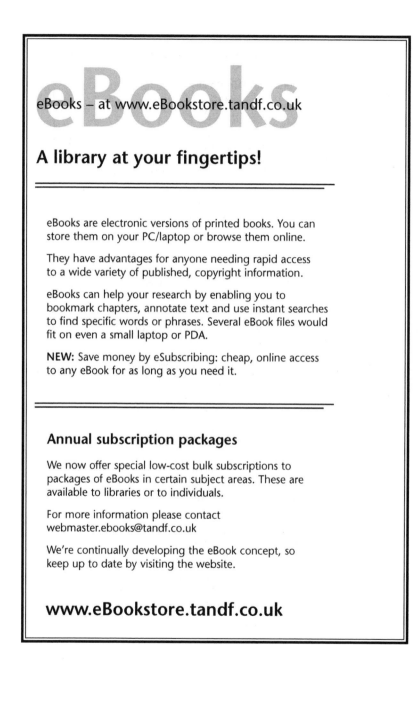

Routledge History

Conflicts in the Middle East since 1945
2nd Edition
Peter Hinchcliffe

Since the Second World War, conflicts such as the Iran-Iraq War and the Kuwait Crisis have made the Middle East the main focus of military attention. This book analyses the nature of conflict in the Middle East, with its racial, ethnic, political, cultural, religious and economic factors.

This second edition brings the book right up to date and includes an examination of the effects of 9/11 on the Middle East peace process and Bush's war on terrorism. Also included is an updated discussion of the superpower conflict in the Middle East and the Kurdish situation and a new chapter covering the recent war in Iraq.

ISBN10: 0–415–31786–X (hbk)   ISBN13: 978–0–415–31786–3 (hbk)
ISBN10: 0–415–31787–8 (pbk)   ISBN13: 978–0–415–31787–0 (pbk)

Islamic Fundamentalism since 1945
Beverley Milton-Edwards

Since the Second World War, Islam and politics have combined to form a potent force known as Islamic fundamentalism. This force has, in recent years, grabbed the headlines as a new and grave threat to the West. Milton-Edwards analyses the roots and emergence of the new Islamic movements and the main thinkers that inspired them.

Providing a much-needed historical overview, the main facets of Islamic fundamentalism are put in a global context, with a thematic debate of issues such as:
- the effects of colonialism on Islam
- secularism and the Islamic reaction
- Islam and violence
- globalisation and transnational Islamic movements
- Islam in the wake of 9/11.

ISBN10: 0–415–30172–6 (hbk)   ISBN13: 978–0–415–30172–5 (hbk)
ISBN10: 0–415–30173–4 (pbk)   ISBN13: 978–0–415–30173–2 (pbk)

Available at all good bookshops
For ordering and further information please visit:
www.routledge.com

Routledge History

Terrorists and Terrorism in the Contemporary World
David J. Whittaker

A concise and accessible survey of this topical and complex subject. This is the first book of its type to focus on the terrorists themselves, and on their psychology, in a historical context. Focusing on a variety of prominent terrorist groups together with a number of less notorious ones, the book encourages readers to think about the mindset, motivation and tactics of terrorists. David J. Whittaker analyses examples of terrorists working as individuals, such as Timothy McVeigh, and those working in groups, such as al-Qaida, over the last two or three decades. The author then goes on to discuss the problems of countering these terrorists. Also discussed are the possible forms terrorism could take in the future.

ISBN10: 0–415–32085–2 (hbk)   ISBN13: 978–0–415–32085–6 (hbk)
ISBN10: 0–415–32086–0 (pbk)   ISBN13: 978–0–415–32086–3 (pbk)

Available at all good bookshops
For ordering and further information please visit:
www.routledge.com

Routledge History

United Nations in the
Contemporary World
David J. Whittaker

Fifty years after the creation of the United Nations, there exists a vigorous debate as to its limitations and possibilities. In *United Nations in the Contemporary World*, David J. Whittaker examines how the UN works and assesses its position as a world organisation.

- The author explores the nature of the UN as a regime in contemporary international relations. He considers the changing terms of reference of the UN and includes discussion of:
- UN organisational procedures and principles
- recent historical case studies, including studies on peacekeeping
- the role of the UN in global urbanisation, arms control and in supplying aid for refugees
- past and future internal reform, goals, achievements.

With an annotated bibliography and a helpful glossary *United Nations in the Contemporary World* provides an interdisciplinary history of the UN and debates the key issues for its future.

ISBN10: 0–415–15317–4 (pbk)   ISBN13: 978–0–415–15317–1 (pbk)

Available at all good bookshops
For ordering and further information please visit:
www.routledge.com

Routledge History

Asylum Seekers and Refugees
in the Contemporary World
David J. Whittaker

Examining a number of case studies, including Palestinian, Afghan
and Iraqi refugees, David J. Whittaker's book provides a balanced
introduction to this controversial subject.

Fuelled by extensive coverage in the media, the issue of asylum seekers and
refugees is one of the most talked about subjects in contemporary politics.
Whittaker cuts through the emotive language to give an objective introduction to
the subject.

Asylum Seekers and Refugees in the Contemporary World discusses the international
as well as national implications of the issue, and the book looks in detail at the
issue as it has affected Britain and Europe in particular, as well as including
material on the UN and its response to the refugee 'problem'.

Including a final statement on the British government's 2005 proposals for dealing
with refugees, *Asylum Seekers and Refugees in the Contemporary World* is essential
reading for all students of the history of the modern world and is ideal for
newcomers to the subject.

ISBN10: 0–415–36090–0 (hbk)   ISBN13: 978–0–415–36090–6 (hbk)
ISBN10: 0–415–36091–9 (pbk)   ISBN13: 978–0–415–36091–3 (pbk)

Available at all good bookshops
For ordering and further information please visit:
www.routledge.com

Routledge History

Latin America
2nd Edition
John Ward

Latin America provides an introduction to the economic and political history of the region in the last half century. Beginning with a brief history of Latin America since 1492, John Ward discusses the interactions between economic, political and social issues, including:

- the long-term background to the 1980s debt crisis
- the effects of neo-liberal free market reforms
- relations with the United States and the wider world
- welfare provision in relation to wider economic issues
- social trends as reflected by changes in the status of women.

John Ward has updated the book throughout to take into account recent developments including Argentina's 2001 debt default and the 2002 presidential election in Brazil. Also included are biographies of the leading figures of the period and an expanded bibliography.

ISBN10: 0–415–31823–8 (hbk)   ISBN13: 978–0–415–31823–5 (hbk)

ISBN10: 0–415–31822–X (pbk)   ISBN13: 978–0–415–31822–8 (pbk)